Masterpieces of the National Museum of Cambodia

An Introduction to the Collection

Chefs-d'œuvre du Musée National du Cambodge

Introduction aux Collections

カンボジア国立博物館代表作品

所蔵品の紹介

វត្ថុពិចិត្រនៅសារមន្ទីរជាតិ

ឆ្ពោះទៅរកសមុច្ច័យទាំងមូល

HELEN IBBITSON JESSUP
Text　Texte　本文　អ្នកនិពន្ធ

Ang Choulean
Khmer translation　Traduction khmère　クメール語訳　ប្រែសម្រួលជាភាសាខ្មែរ

Mariko Ikehara
Japanese translation　Traduction japonaise　日本語訳　ប្រែសម្រួលជាភាសាជប៉ុន

Thierry Zéphir
French translation　Traduction française　仏語訳　ប្រែសម្រួលជាភាសាបារាំង

John Gollings
Photographs　Photographies　写真　រូបថត

This book is published by Friends of Khmer Culture, Inc., USA

ISBN-10: 99950-836-0-4
ISBN-13: 978-99950-836-0-1

All objects are in the collection of the National Museum of Cambodia, Phnom Penh.

All photographs are by John Gollings © with the exception of catalogue numbers 5, 12, 16, 62, 76 by Ocelus/Darren Campbell ©, 2 by National Museum of Cambodia and 14, 50, 63 by Stone Conservation Workshop, National Museum of Cambodia ©.

Notes to the reader:
Khmer and Sanskrit words have been rendered in English and French in phonetic transliteration.
Dimensions of objects refer to height unless otherwise specified, in which case height is followed by width followed by depth.

Front cover: No. 34; back cover: No. 80

Printed and bound by Orientations, Hong Kong.

Cet ouvrage est publié par Friends of Khmer Culture, Inc., USA

ISBN-10: 99950-836-0-4
ISBN-13: 978-99950-836-0-1

Tous les objets appartiennent aux collections du Musée National du Cambodge, Phnom-Penh.

Toutes les photographies sont de John Gollings © à l'exception des numéros 5, 12, 16, 62, 76 d'Ocelus/ Darren Campbell ©, 2 du Musée National du Cambodge, et 14, 50, 63 de l'atelier de restauration du Musée National du Cambodge ©.

Notes au lecteur:
Les mots khmers et sanskrits apparaissent en translittération phonétique dans les textes anglais et français.
Les dimensions des objets concernent la hauteur, sauf mention contraire; dans ce cas, la hauteur est suivie par la largeur puis la profondeur.

Ill. de couverture: n° 34; ill. de quatrième de couverture: n° 80.

Imprimé et relié par Orientations, Hong Kong.

ផ្សព្វផ្សាយដោយ Friends of Khmer Culture, Inc.
សហរដ្ឋអាមេរិក

ISBN-10: 99950-836-0-4

ISBN-13: 978-99950-836-0-1

វត្ថុទាំងអស់ដែលបង្ហាញនៅទីនេះសុទ្ធសឹងនៅក្នុងសមុច្ច័យសារមន្ទីរជាតិ, ភ្នំពេញ។

រូបទាំងអស់ថតដោយ John Gollings © លើកលែងតែរូបលេខ ៥, ១២, ១៦, ៦២, ៧៦ ដែលថតដោយ Ocelus/Darren Campbell © និងរូបលេខ២ ថតដោយសារមន្ទីរជាតិ។ រូបលេខ១៤,៥០, ៦៣ ថតដោយរោងជាងជួសជុលវត្ថុថ្ម, សារមន្ទីរជាតិ ©។

សេចក្តីបញ្ជាក់៖ ទំហំនៃរូបដែលផ្តល់ជូន គឺសំដៅទៅលើកម្ពស់, វៀលែងតែមានការបញ្ជាក់ ពិសេសទៀត ប្រាប់ទទឹងនិងជម្រៅ។

រូបក្របខាងមុខ៖ លេខ៣៤, ខាងក្រោយ៖ លេខ៨០
បោះពុម្ពនៅ Orientations, ហុងកុង។

本カタログはフレンズ・オブ・クメール・カルチャーが出版したものである。

ISBN-10: 99950-836-0-4
ISBN-13: 978-99950-836-0-1

作品は全て在プノンペン・カンボジア国立博物館所蔵物

写真は全てジョン・ゴリングス©。ただしカタログ番号 5, 12, 16, 62, 76©はオセラス/ダレン・キャンベル©、2, 14, 50, 63はカンボジア国立博物館©。

クメール語とサンスクリット語の英語・フランス語表記は発音をアルファベット化したものである。

表紙写真 No. 34、裏表紙写真 No. 80

印刷・製本：オリエンテーションズ　（香港）

Table of Contents | Table des matières | មាតិកា | 目次

Preface

by

His Majesty Preah Karuna Preah Bat Samdech Preah Borom Neath Norodom Sihamoni, King of Cambodia

We are very pleased with the happy initiative of FOKCI (Friends of Khmer Culture, Inc.) in promoting the important and unique collections of the National Museum of Phnom Penh by selecting and publishing the eighty masterpieces of Khmer art that are presented here.

The catalogue in Khmer, English, French and Japanese will be useful to a wide public that is not always apprised of the subtleties of Khmer art and the religious concepts that underlie it.

We wish to express our keen appreciation to Dr. Helen Ibbitson Jessup for elaborating an explanatory text that will foster comprehension by the general public, to Dr. Ang Choulean, Mr. Thierry Zéphir and Ms. Mariko Ikehara for their respective translations, as well as to the Director, Mr. Khun Samen, for his contribution on the history of the National Museum, and to Mr. John Gollings for the excellent photographs that he created and generously donated.

I wish that visitors to our National Museum may draw maximum benefit from the enhanced appreciation of these works of global heritage and may appreciate the true value of the genius and talents of Khmer artists of the past under the stimulus of our ancient Kings.

Préface

De Sa Majesté Preah Karuna Preah Bat Samdech Preah Borom Neath Norodom Sihamoni, Roi Du Cambodge.

Nous nous félicitons de l'heureuse initiative prise par FOKCI (Friends of Khmer Culture, Incorporated) de promouvoir les importantes et uniques collections du Musée National de Phnom-Penh, en sélectionnant et publiant quatre-vingt chefs- d'oeuvre de l'art khmer qui y sont exposés.

Le catalogue en Khmer, Anglais, Français et Japonais sera utile à un large public qui n'est pas toujours avisé des arcanes de l'art khmer et des concepts religieux qui le sous-tendent.

Nous tenons à exprimer notre vive appréciation à Madame Helen Ibbitson Jessup pour l'élaboration d'un texte d'explication qui aidera à la compréhension du grand public, à Messieurs Dr. Ang Choulean, Thierry Zéphir et Madame Mariko Ikehara pour la version en leur langue respective, ainsi qu'à M. le Conservateur Khun Samen pour sa contribution à l'historique du Musée National, et enfin à M. John Gollings pour les excellentes photographies dont il est l'auteur et généreux donateur.

Je souhaite que les visiteurs de notre Musée National puissent en tirer profit au maximum, de la mise en valeur de ces oeuvres du patrimoine mondial et apprécier à leur juste valeur le génie et les talents des artistes khmers du passé, sous l'impulsion de nos anciens Rois.

ព្រះរាជសារនៃព្រះករុណាព្រះបាទសម្ដេចព្រះបរមនាថ នរោត្ដម សីហមុនី

ខ្ញុំមានហឫទ័យរីករាយនឹងកិច្ចការដែលអង្គការ FOKCI (Friends of Khmer Culture) ធ្វើឡើងដើម្បីលើកតម្លៃសមុច្ច័យដ៏មានសារសំខាន់នៃសារមន្ទីរជាតិ ភ្នំពេញ ដោយជ្រើសរើសយកវត្ថុពិចិត្រចំនួន៨០មកបង្ហាញ។

សៀវភៅជាភាសាខ្មែរ, អង់គ្លេស, បារាំង និងជប៉ុននេះ មានប្រយោជន៍ណាស់ដល់សាធារណជនទូទៅ ដែលជួនកាលពុំជ្រួតជ្រាបច្បាស់លាស់អំពីសិល្បៈខ្មែរ ព្រមទាំងទស្សនៈសាសនាដែលនៅពីក្រោយនោះ។

ខ្ញុំសូមសម្ដែងការកោតសរសើរដល់អ្នកស្រី Helen Ibbitson Jessup ដែលបានរៀបចំអត្ថបទពន្យល់យ៉ាងក្បោះក្បាយសម្រាប់សាធារណជន, ដល់លោកអាំង ជូលាន, លោក Thierry Zéphir និងអ្នកស្រី Mariko Ikehara ដែលបានបកប្រែទៅជាភាសាជាតិរៀងៗខ្លួន។ម្យ៉ាងទៀត សូមកោតសរសើរដល់លោក យុន សាម៉េន ចំពោះការរៀបរាប់ប្រវត្តិសារមន្ទីរជាតិ ព្រមទាំងដល់លោក John Gollings ជាម្ចាស់នៃរូបថតយ៉ាងប្រណិត ហើយមានសន្ដានចិត្តល្អឱ្យយកមកប្រើនៅទីនេះ។

ខ្ញុំសង្ឃឹមថា អ្នកទស្សនាសារមន្ទីរជាតិរបស់យើងនឹងក្រេបជញ្ជក់នូវចំណេះដែលបានមកពីសៀវភៅនេះ ដែលជាការលើកតម្លៃវត្ថុជាបេតិកភណ្ឌពិភពលោក ព្រមទាំងយល់ច្បាស់នូវទេពកោសល្យនៃសិល្បករខ្មែរក្នុងអតីតកាល ក្រោមការដឹកនាំនៃព្រះរាជានានាសម័យនោះ។

メッセージ

カンボジア国王
ノロドム・シハモニ

プノンペン国立博物館所蔵の重要で比類のない、クメール芸術最高傑作８０点を紹介するフレンズ・オブ・クメール・カルチャーのイニシャティブに祝意を表したいと思います。

クメール語、英語、フランス語、日本語のカタログは、クメール芸術の巧みさ、およびそれが表現する宗教観に馴染みが薄い方に役立つことでしょう。

公衆の理解を深めるために役立つ説明を執筆されたヘレン・イビットソン・ジェサップ博士、またそれぞれの言語に翻訳されたアン・チュリアン博士、ティエリー・ゼフィール、池原麻里子各氏に感謝いたします。またクン・サメン国立博物館館長の貢献、ジョン・ゴリングス氏が撮影された素晴らしい写真を寄付してくださったことに感謝いたします。

国立博物館への来館者の皆様が世界遺産鑑賞で最大限の体験をされ、古代国王たちが奨励したクメール芸術家達の才能の真価を評価されることを望みます。

An Introduction to the National Museum

This museum was not conceived simply as a place to conserve and display collections. From the beginning it was integrally linked to the contiguous School of Cambodian Arts, whose mission was to train artisans in diverse skills. Such was the vision of its founder, George Groslier, who intended that objects from antiquity would provide a source of inspiration for a modern art that he considered somewhat sluggish after a long sleep, yet potentially powerful. That is why one finds 19th- and 20th- century objects of everyday life, not without artistic value, in the museum. Apprentices in jewelry, metal-casting, drawing, sculpting, weaving worked then in a most propitious atmosphere. It must also be said that antiquities had already begun to disappear from sites on their way to various foreign collections, legal controls for their protection doubtless still being uncertain. Ever since, the organization of a museum has clearly been even more indispensable.

In 1917 the first stone was solemnly laid, thus launching the project. Construction was completed in 1920, followed by the inauguration of the museum, then called "The Albert Sarraut Museum". Regardless of its first collections, the building itself was already perceived as a work of great distinction. The opinion was unanimous.

In 1951, responsibility for managing patrimony was transferred by the French Protectorate to Khmer authorities. It was then that the museum's name was changed to "The National Museum of Cambodia".

The museum was directed by a succession of French directors until 1966, when the first Cambodian was put in charge. It goes without saying that from the very beginning the archaeological and ethnographic collections (stone, wood, metal, ceramic) have been continuously enriched. A number of guides, as well as various catalogues and publications relevant to the collections, are already known to the public.

Here is a new and significant step in spreading knowledge of Khmer art through eighty of the museum's masterpieces, which are, one may say, representative of the ancient and middle periods of Cambodia. I would like to express my profound gratitude to Dr. Helen Ibbitson Jessup and Friends of Khmer Culture (FOKCI), of which she is the President, for producing this valuable work for the benefit of the National Museum.

Khun Samen
Director

Bref Historique du Musée National

Ce musée n'a pas seulement été conçu comme un simple lieu de conservation et d'exposition des collections. Il fut dès le départ organiquement lié à l'École des Arts Cambodgiens, attenante, dont la mission était de former des artisans dans diverses spécialités. Telle était la vision du fondateur George Groslier, dont le dessein était que les objets d'antiquité constituent la source d'inspiration d'un art moderne qu'il estimait quelque peu engourdi par un long sommeil, bien que potentiellement puissant. C'est ainsi qu'on trouve dans le musée des objets utilisés dans la vie quotidienne des 19ème et 20ème siècles, non sans quelque valeur artistique. Les apprentis joailliers, fondeurs, dessinateurs, sculpteurs, tisserands travaillaient alors dans une atmosphère artistique des plus propices. Il faut dire aussi que des antiquités commençaient déjà à disparaître des sites pour entreprendre des voyages vers diverses collections à l'étranger, le dispositif juridique pour leur protection étant sans doute encore vacillant. Dès lors l'organisation d'un musée apparut d'autant plus indispensable.

En 1917 la première pierre fut solennellement posée, lançant ainsi le chantier. Les travaux furent achevés en 1920, suivis de l'inauguration du musée, alors baptisé « Musée Albert Sarraut ». Abstraction faite de ses toutes premières collections, l'édifice en soi apparaît déjà comme une oeuvre d'un grand raffinement. L'avis est unanime.

En 1951 les compétences en matière de gestion du patrimoine furent transférées par le Protectorat français aux autorités khmères. C'est alors que le nom du musée changea en « Musée National du Cambodge ».

Le musée avait été successivement dirigé par des conservateurs français jusqu'en 1966, date à laquelle le tout premier responsable cambodgien fut nommé. Il va sans dire que, depuis sa création, les collections archéologiques et ethnographiques (pierre, bois, métal, céramique) n'ont cessé de s'enrichir. Un certain nombre de guides sont déjà connus du public, de même que divers catalogues et publications relatifs à ses collections.

Voici un pas nouveau, significatif, dans la diffusion de la connaissance de l'art khmer à travers 80 chefs-d'œuvre du musée, lesquels sont, on peut le dire, représentatifs des arts des époques ancienne et moyenne du Cambodge. Je voudrais exprimer ma profonde gratitude à Madame Helen Ibbitson Jessup et Friends of Khmer Culture (FOKCI) dont elle est la présidente d'avoir réalisé ce précieux travail au profit du Musée National.

Khun Samen
Directeur

ប្រវត្តិសង្ខេបនៃសារមន្ទីរជាតិក្រុងភ្នំពេញ

សារមន្ទីរនេះ កាលដើមឡើយគេពុំគ្រាន់តែកសាងឡើងក្នុងន័យថាជាទីរក្សានិងតាំងបង្ហាញវត្ថុបុរាណប៉ុណ្ណោះទេ ត្បិតការរៀបចំនិងគ្រប់គ្រងនោះភ្ជាប់ទៅសាលារចនា ដែលជាកន្លែងបណ្តុះបណ្តាលវិចិត្រករគ្រប់បែបយ៉ាងផង។ សូម្បីតែសព្វថ្ងៃនេះក៏អ្នក ខ្លះនៅតែហៅទីនេះថា "សាលារចនា" ដូច្នោះ។ ប្រការនេះបង្ហាញពីបំណងនៃលោក Georges Groslier ពោលគឺអ្នកបង្កើតមណ្ឌលទាំងមូលនេះ ដែលចង់ឱ្យបុរាណវត្ថុទាំងនោះទៅជាគំរូ ឬក៏ទៅជាប្រភពជំរុញឱ្យសិល្បៈជំនាន់ឥឡូវនេះមានសន្ទុះទៅមុខផង។ ដូច្នេះហើយ បានជានៅក្នុងសារមន្ទីរគេឃើញមានវត្ថុប្រើប្រាស់ដែលមានលក្ខណៈជាសិល្បៈស.វ.ទី១៩និង២០ដែរ។ មានន័យថាសិស្សសាលារចនាដែលរៀនការជាងនានា ដូចជាជាងទង, ជាងស្មិត, ជាងគំនូរ, អ្នករៀនឆ្លាក់ឬត្បាញ... ពេលនោះរស់នៅក្នុងបរិស្ថានសិល្បៈដ៏ប្រពៃមួយ។ ក្រៅអំពីនោះ វត្ថុបុរាណនៅតាមទីផ្សេងៗក៏ចាប់ផ្តើមបាត់បង់ខ្លះៗ ដោយសារការលក់ដូរទៅអឺរ៉ុប ដោយជំនាន់នោះពុំទាន់មានច្បាប់ទម្លាប់តឹងតែងក្នុងការការពារផង។ ដូច្នេះការរៀបចំសារមន្ទីរដើម្បីថែរក្សា និងលើកតម្កើងគឺជាការចាំបាច់ដែរ។

នៅឆ្នាំ១៩១៧គេបញ្ចុះបឋមសិលាដើម្បីបើកការដ្ឋាននោះ។ លុះដល់ឆ្នាំ១៩២០ ការសាងសង់ចប់ជាស្ថាពរ ហើយគេក៏សម្ពោធន៍សារមន្ទីរនេះជាមួយនឹងសមុច្ច័យរបស់ខ្លួនជាដំបូងដោយឱ្យឈ្មោះថា អាល់ប៊ែរសារ៉ូ។ យើងពុំចាំបាច់បង្ហាញអំពីសមុច្ច័យពេលនោះទេ គ្រាន់តែមើលទៅស្ថាបត្យកម្មនៃអាគារដ៏ស្កឹមស្កៃនេះ នរណាក៏ទទួលស្គាល់ដែរថា សំបកខ្លួនទទេនៃសារមន្ទីរក៏អាចចាត់ទុកថាជាវត្ថុសិល្បៈទៅហើយដែរ។

អាណាព្យាបាលបារាំងប្រគល់សមត្ថកិច្ចគ្រប់គ្រងបេតិកភណ្ឌមកខ្មែរនៅឆ្នាំ១៩៥១។ ពេលនោះហើយដែលសារមន្ទីរដូរឈ្មោះមកជា "សារមន្ទីរជាតិនៃកម្ពុជា"។

សារមន្ទីរជាតិដឹកនាំដោយអភិរក្សជាតិបារាំងបន្តបន្ទាប់គ្នាជាច្រើនរូប លុះមកដល់ឆ្នាំ១៩៦៦ទើបមានអភិរក្សខ្មែរជាលើកដំបូង។ ឯបុរាណវត្ថុ (ថ្ម. លោហៈ. ឈើ. កុលាលភាជន៍) និងវត្ថុប្រើប្រាស់នាបច្ចុប្បន្នដែលតែងធ្វើឱ្យជាតិពន្ធុវិទូចាប់អារម្មណ៍ ក៏តែងតែចូលមកក្នុងសារមន្ទីរពុំដែលដាច់។ សៀវភៅមគ្គុទ្ទេសក៍ផ្ទាល់ស្តីពីសមុច្ច័យនៃសារមន្ទីរ ឬសៀវភៅនិយាយពីសមុច្ច័យនេះជាប្រយោលក៏មានមួយចំនួនហើយដែរ។

នេះជាជំហានថ្មីមួយទៀតក្នុងការផ្សព្វផ្សាយសិល្បៈខ្មែរតាមរយៈសារមន្ទីរក្រុងភ្នំពេញ ត្បិតវត្ថុពិចិត្រទាំង៨០ដែលអ្នកនិពន្ធយកមកបង្ហាញនិងធ្វើអត្ថាធិប្បាយសឹងអាចពោលថាតំណាងឱ្យវត្ថុសម័យបុរាណ និងសម័យកណ្តាលទាំងមូលដែលមាននៅទីនេះ។ ខ្ញុំសូមអរគុណជាអនេកដល់អ្នកស្រី Helen Ibbitson Jessup និងអង្គការ Friends of Khmer Culture ដែលបានធ្វើឱ្យការងារដ៏ប្រពៃនេះសម្រេចឡើង។

ឃុន សាម៉េន. ប្រធានសារមន្ទីរជាតិ

国立博物館紹介

この博物館は単にコレクションを保存し、展示する場所として建立されたわけではありません。設立当初から、アルチザンにさまざまな技術を教えるため隣りに創設されたカンボジア美術学校と密に関係していました。これは設立者ジョルジュ・グロリエのビジョンによるものです。グロリエは古代の作品が近代美術のインスピレーションの源になると考えたのです。ですから博物館には19世紀から20世紀の美術的価値を供えた日常品を観ることができます。宝飾、鋳造、デッサン、彫刻、織物の実習生は恵まれた環境で訓練できたのです。アンティークはすでにさまざまな海外収集家の手に渡り始めていました。その法的保護は現在でも確保されていません。したがって博物館は今まで以上に不可欠な存在なのです。

礎石が1917年に置かれ、博物館は1920年に完成し、「アルベール・サロー博物館」として開館しました。当初のコレクションはともかく、建物は偉大な作品として賞賛を浴びました。

1951年、博物館運営はフランス保護領からカンボジアに委譲され、名前も「カンボジア国立博物館」と改名されました。

その後も博物館はフランス人館長の指揮下にありましたが1966年、初代のカンボジア人館長が就任しました。石、木、金属、陶器製の考古学的、民族学的コレクションも増えました。コレクションのカタログや出版物も出ています。

このカタログにある国立博物館の80の古代、中世のカンボジアの代表作を通じて、クメール芸術の知識が更に大幅に深まることでしょう。国立博物館のためにこのカタログを作成してくださったヘレン・イビットソン・ジェサップ博士と博士が代表と務められているフレンズ・オブ・クメール・カルチャー（FOKCI）に深い感謝の意を表したく思います。

国立博物館館長
クン・サメン

Preface

As the numbers of visitors to the National Museum of Cambodia increase, the need has arisen for a multilingual publication to introduce some of the masterpieces of this great collection. Friends of Khmer Culture, dedicated to preserving and promoting Cambodia's cultural heritage, has responded by producing this book. It describes eighty of the museum's greatest treasures in the languages spoken by the four largest national groups attending the institution. Profits from the sale of the book will be dedicated to projects helping the Museum.

Many visitors to the National Museum come from countries with cultures very different from Cambodia's, so for each work of art we have provided a detailed caption explaining its style and iconography. We hope a brief chronology, historical introduction, glossary, and bibliography will place the objects in context and help viewers enjoy the works more fully.

Friends of Khmer Culture is deeply honored to have endorsement from Cambodia's gracious Monarch. We are indebted to the National Museum staff, especially the Director, Mr. Khun Samen, and the Deputy Director, Mr. Hab Touch, for their constant support. In addition, we warmly thank the distinguished scholars who contributed their expertise and time to translate the texts and advise us: Dr. Ang Choulean, Ms. Mariko Ikehara, and M. Thierry Zéphir. Profound thanks are due to Mr. John Gollings for permitting the *pro bono* use of his magnificent photographs, kindly endorsed by the National Gallery of Art, Washington, and the Réunion des Musées Nationaux, Paris, for the exhibition *Sculpture of Angkor and Ancient Cambodia, Millennium of Glory*, which commissioned them. We also thank the Stone Conservation Workshop, National Museum of Cambodia, and Mr. Darren Campbell for additional fine photographs. Finally, we are most grateful to Ms. Betti Deutsch for her generous grant towards publication. We salute these friends' devotion to the glorious culture of the Khmer people.

Helen Ibbitson Jessup
President, Friends of Khmer Culture

Préface

Avec l'augmentation constante du nombre de visiteurs au Musée National du Cambodge, le besoin d'une publication multilingue présentant quelques-uns des grands chefs-d'œuvre du musée se faisait ressentir. Friends of Khmer Culture, organisation vouée à la préservation et à la promotion de l'héritage culturel du Cambodge, a donc entrepris la publication du présent ouvrage. Quatre-vingts des plus belles œuvres du musée sont présentées dans les langues respectives des quatre principaux groupes de visiteurs de cette institution. Tous les bénéfices générés par la vente du livre seront reversés à des projets concernant le musée.

Les visiteurs du Musée National sont pour beaucoup originaires de pays culturellement très différents du Cambodge; ainsi, chaque œuvre est-elle présentée dans une notice détaillée expliquant son style et son iconographie. Une chronologie sommaire, une introduction historique et un glossaire permettent de remettre les œuvres dans leur contexte afin d'aider le visiteur à les apprécier pleinement. Une bibliographie propose à ceux qui souhaiteraient en savoir plus une liste d'ouvrages essentiels sur le sujet.

Friends of Khmer Culture est profondément honoré de la caution que Sa Majesté Preah Karuna Preah Bat Samdech Preah Borom Neath Norodom Sihamoni a bien voulu apporté à cette publication.

Nous tenons par ailleurs à exprimer notre reconnaissance à l'ensemble du personnel du Musée National, tout particulièrement son directeur, M. Khun Samen, et son vice-directeur, M. Hab Touch, pour leur généreux soutien. Nos vifs remerciements s'adressent aussi à nos collègues Dr. Ang Choulean, Mme Mariko Ikehara et M. Thierry Zéphir, pour leurs conseils et le soin qu'ils ont apporté à la traduction des textes. Notre gratitude va également à M. John Gollings qui nous a gracieusement autorisé à reproduire les magnifiques photographies réalisées en 1996 pour la National Gallery of Art, Washington, et la Réunion des Musées Nationaux, Paris, à l'occasion de l'exposition *Sculpture of Angkor and Ancient Cambodia - Millennium of Glory*. Nous remercions également l'atelier de restauration du Musée National du Cambodge et M. Darren Campbell pour les belles photographies complémentaires qu'ils nous ont fournies. Enfin, nous souhaitons rendre hommage à la générosité de Mme Betti Deutsch à l'égard de cette publication. Que soient ici chaleureusement remerciés ces amis de la glorieuse culture du peuple khmer.

Helen Ibbitson Jessup
Présidente, Friends of Khmer Culture

អារម្ភកថា

ចំនួនអ្នកមកទស្សនាសារមន្ទីរជាតិកាន់តែកើនច្រើនឡើង។ ជាហេតុតម្រូវឱ្យមានសៀវភៅមួយផ្សព្វផ្សាយជាច្រើនភាសា ហើយដែលណែនាំអ្នកទាំងនោះឱ្យស្គាល់សមុច្ច័យទាំងមូលតាមរយៈវត្ថុពិចិត្រមួយចំនួន។ Friends of Khmer Culture សម្រេចថានឹងធ្វើសៀវភៅនោះឱ្យចេញជារូបរាង ត្បិតគោលបំណងរបស់ខ្លួន គឺរួមចំណែកក្នុងការរក្សា និងលើកតម្លៃមរតកវប្បធម៌នៃកម្ពុជា។ នៅទីនេះយើងបង្ហាញជូននូវស្នាដៃដ៏ថ្នើមចំនួន៨០ ដោយប្រើភាសាបួន ពោលគឺភាសានៃសមាជិកនៅក្នុងស្ថាប័នរបស់យើង។ ប្រាក់កាសដែលបានមកពីការលក់ យើងនឹងយកទៅប្រើទាំងស្រុងក្នុងគម្រោងនានា ដើម្បីជួយសារមន្ទីរជាតិ។

អ្នកទស្សនាមួយចំនួនធំសុទ្ធសឹងមកពីប្រទេសដែលមានអារ្យធម៌ផ្សេងពីខ្មែរ។ ដូច្នេះហើយបានជាយើងព្យាយាមផ្ដល់ទិន្នន័យលម្អិតអំពីរចនាបថ និងបដិមាសាស្ត្រដែលទាក់ទងនឹងវត្ថុនីមួយៗ។ យើងមានបង្ហាញពីកាលប្រវត្តិ និងប្រវត្តិសាស្ត្រសង្ខេប ហើយម្យ៉ាងទៀតមានផ្ដល់សទ្ទានុក្រមនិងឯកសារយោងផងដើម្បីបើកផ្លូវឱ្យអ្នកទាំងនោះជ្រួតជ្រាបកាន់តែច្បាស់អំពីវត្ថុដែលខ្លួនទស្សនា។

Friends of Khmer Culture សូមសម្ដែងអំណរគុណដ៏ជ្រាលជ្រៅចំពោះបុគ្គលិកទាំងអស់នៃសារមន្ទីរជាតិ ពិសេសលោក ឃុន សាម៉េន, ប្រធាន និងលោក ហាប់ ទូច, អនុប្រធាន ដែលបានគាំទ្រយើងខ្ញុំដោយសុទ្ធចិត្ត។ ក្រៅអំពីនេះយើងសូមអរគុណដល់អ្នកស្រាវជ្រាវដែលបានប្រើវិជ្ជានិងពេលវេលារបស់ខ្លួនដើម្បីបកប្រែសៀវភៅនេះឱ្យទៅជាភាសាខ្មែរ, ជប៉ុន និង បារាំង ពោលគឺលោក អាំង ជូលាន, អ្នកស្រី Mariko Ikehara និងលោក Thierry Zéphir។ ម្យ៉ាងទៀតយើងក៏សូមលោក John Gollings ទទួលអំណរគុណនេះដែរ ដោយលោកអនុញ្ញាតឱ្យយើងប្រើរូបថតដ៏ល្អត្រចង់ ដែលជាស្នាដៃរបស់លោក។ យើងសូមសម្ដែងគារវកិច្ចចំពោះមិត្តទាំងអម្បាលម៉ាននេះ ដែលស្មោះស្ម័គ្របម្រើវប្បធម៌ដ៏រុងរឿងនៃប្រជាជាតិខ្មែរ។

Helen Ibbitson Jessup
ប្រធាន, Friends of Khmer Culture

ごあいさつ

カンボジア国立博物館への来館者が増え、同博物館の偉大な所蔵品の逸品の一部を紹介するカタログの必要性が高まりました。フレンズ・オブ・クメール・カルチャーはカンボジアの文化と伝統を維持し、推進することを目的とした団体として、そのニーズに応えるべくこのカタログを出版しました。この博物館の訪問者が最も利用している４言語で、博物館の作品80点を説明しています。このカタログの売り上げは全て、博物館を支援するプロジェクトに利用されます。

国立博物館はカンボジアとは全く異なった文化を持つ国からの来館者が多いので、それぞれの作品についてその様式と図像を説明しました。さらにカタログにある簡単な年表と歴史の紹介、用語説明、参考文献によって、作品の全体像を把握することができます。

カンボジア国王のご支持を光栄に思います。国立博物館職員のみなさま、特にクン・サメン館長、およびハブ・トゥーシュ副館長の多大な支援に感謝します。また時間をかけてカタログを翻訳してくださった識者の方々―アン・チュリアン博士、池原麻里子氏、ティエリー・ゼフィール氏に感謝します。また素晴らしい写真を無償で提供してくださったジョン・ゴリングス氏と写真をコミッションしたワシントンの国立美術館にも心から感謝します。カンボジア国立博物館及びダレン・キャンベル氏の写真にも感謝します。最後にこのカタログを助成してくださったベティー・ドイチ氏にも深く感謝します。カンボジア国民の栄光ある文化に対するこの友人たちの貢献に敬意を表したいと思います。

ヘレン・イビットソン・ジェサップ
フレンズ・オブ・クメール・カルチャー代表

Brief Chronology

Dates in Common Era

1st century	probable beginnings of recorded foreign contacts with Khmer region
3rd century	Oc Eo as maritime center of Funan
6th century	Chinese report dominance of Zhenla over Funan
7th century	temples at Angkor Borei, Phnom Da style
c. 616-635	Ishanavarman I reigns in Ishanapura (Sambor Prei Kuk)
7th century	Sambor Prei Kuk style (1st half)
7th century	Prei Kmeng style (2nd half)
7th century	Prasat Andet style (late)
8th century	Prasat Ak Yum, first temple mountain
c. 790	return to Cambodia of Jayavarman II
9th century	beginning of Angkor period
802	consecration of Jayavarman II on Mt. Kulen
802-after 830	Jayavarman II
1st 3/4 9th c.	Kulen style
877-889	Indravarman ruling at Hariharalaya (Roluos)
late 9th c.	Preah Ko style
879	Preah Ko temple
881	Bakong temple, first huge temple mountain
889-early 10th c.	Yashovarman I
893	Lolei temple, on island in Indratataka baray (now Roluos)
early 10th c.	Bakheng style Yashovarman establishes Yashodharapura (Angkor) construction of Bakheng temple mountain
921/928-942	Jayavarman IV, possible usurper, reigns at Koh Ker
944-968	Rajendravarman II returns capital to Angkor
952	East Mebon temple
961	Pre Rup temple
967	Banteay Srei temple (by Brahman Yajñavaraha)
968-1000/1001	Jayavarman V
early 11th c.	Ta Keo temple, completion date uncertain
1002/1010-49	Suryavarman I
1st half 11th c.	Preah Vihear temple, Phnom Chisor temple
1050-1066	Udayadityavarman II, construction of western baray
1010-c.1080	Baphuon style
c. 1060	Baphuon temple
1113	Suryavarman II (till at least 1045)
1st half 12th c.	Angkor Wat, Beng Mealea, Banteay Samre temples
1st three quarters	Angkor Wat style
1177	Cham invasion of Angkor, death of Khmer king in battle
1181-1218 (?)	Jayavarman VII; Mahayana Buddhism state religion
1186	Ta Prohm temple dedicated to king's mother
1191	Preah Khan temple dedicated to king's father
last quarter 12th c.	Bayon style, construction of Angkor Thom
1243-1298	Jayavarman VIII; Brahmanism returns
1296-7	visit of Chinese envoy Zhou Daguan to Angkor
14th c.	Theravada Buddhism widespread
1431	abandonment of Angkor after Thai raids
1516-1566	Ang Chan I, temporary return to Angkor
17th c. - on	Khmer kings rule from Phnom Penh region
1863	establishment of the French Protectorate
1953	Cambodian independence

Chronologie sommaire

Les dates sont exprimées en ère chrétienne

1er s.	début probable des relations du pays khmer avec l'étranger.
3ème s.	Oc Eo, centre de commerce maritime du Funan
6ème s.	conquête du Funan par le Zhenla d'après les sources chinoises.
7ème s.	temples à Angkor Borei, style du Phnom Da.
c. 616-635	règne d'Ishanavarman à Ishanapura (Sambor Prei Kuk).
7ème s.	(première moitié du) style de Sambor Prei Kuk.
7ème s.	(deuxième moitié du) style de Prei Kmeng.
7ème s.	(fin du) style de Prasat Andet.
8ème s.	style de Kompong Preah ; Prasat Ak Yum, le premier temple-montagne.
c. 790	début de la carrière de Jayavarman II au Cambodge.
9ème s.	début de l'époque angkorienne.
802	consécration de Jayavarman II sur le Phnom Kulen.
802-après 830	Jayavarman II.
9ème s.	(trois premiers quarts du) style du Kulen.
877-889	Indravarman règne à Hariharalaya (Roluos).
9ème s.	(fin du) style de Preah Ko.
879	temple de Preah Ko.
881	temple de Bakong, premier temple-montagne important.
889-début 10ème s.	Yashovarman I.
893	temple de Lolei, sur une île dans le baray de Roluos (l'antique Indratataka).
10ème s.	(début du) style du Bakheng, fondation de Yashodharapura par Yashovarman, construction du temple-montagne du Bakheng.
921/928-c. 940	Jayavarman IV règne à Koh Ker.
944-968	Rajendravarman II ramène la capitale à Angkor.
953	temple du Mebon oriental.
961	temple de Pre Rup.
967	temple de Banteay Srei (fondé par le brahmane Yajñavaraha).
968-1000/1001	Jayavarman V.
10ème s.	(fin du) temple-montagne de Ta Keo.
1002/1010-1049	Suryavarman I
c. 1010-c. 1080	style du Baphuon.
11ème s.	(première moitié du) temples de Preah Vihear et du Phnom Chisor.
1050-1066	Udayadityavarman II, achèvement (?) du baray occidental.
c. 1060	temple-montagne du Baphuon.
1113-au moins 1145	Suryavarman II.
12ème s.	(première moitié du) temples d'Angkor Vat, Beng Mealea, Banteay Samre…
12ème s.	(trois premiers quarts du) style d'Angkor Vat.
1177	invasion d'Angkor par les Cham, mort du roi khmer au combat.
1181-1218 (?)	Jayavarman VII, bouddhisme Mahayana religion d'État.
1186	temple de Ta Prohm pour la mère du roi.
1191	temple de Preah Khan pour le père du roi.
12ème s.	(dernier quart du) style du Bayon, construction de l'enceinte d'Angkor Thom.
1243-1298	Jayavarman VIII, retour au brahmanisme.
1296-1297	séjour du chinois Zhou Daguan à Angkor.
14ème s.	diffusion du bouddhisme Theravada.
1431	date traditionnelle de l'abandon d'Angkor devant la pression militaire thaï.
1516-1566	Ang Chan I, retour temporaire à Angkor.
17ème s. et suiv.	les rois khmers règnent depuis la région de Phnom-Penh.
1863	établissement du Protectorat français.
1953	indépendance du Cambodge.

កាលប្បវត្តិសង្ខេប

(កាលបរិច្ឆេទជាគ្រិស្តសករាជ)

ស.វ.ទី១ រវាងជំនាន់នោះ ប្រហែលចាប់ផ្ដើមមានទំនាក់ទំនងរវាងបរទេសនិងតំបន់ដែលខ្មែររស់នៅ។

ស.វ.ទី៣ Oc Eo ក្លាយជាមណ្ឌលពាណិជ្ជកម្មផ្លូវសមុទ្រនៃនគរហ្វូណាន់។

ស.វ.ទី៦ ឯកសារចិននិយាយថា ចេនឡាគ្រប់គណ្ដប់លើហ្វូណាន់។

ស.វ.ទី៧ គេកសាងប្រាសាទនៅអង្គរបុរី, រចនាបថភ្នំដា។

៦១៦_៦៣៥ ព្រះបាទឦសានវរ្ម័នទី១សោយរាជ្យនៅឦសានបុរ (សម្បូណ៌ព្រៃគុក)។

ស.វ.ទី៧ រចនាបថសម្បូណ៌ព្រៃគុក (ផ្នែកទី១នៃស.វ.នោះ)។

ស.វ.ទី៧ រចនាបថព្រៃក្មេង (ផ្នែកទី២នៃស.វ.នោះ)។

ស.វ.ទី៧ រចនាបថប្រាសាទអណ្ដែត (ចុងស.វ.នោះ)។

ស.វ.ទី៨ ប្រាសាទភ្នំទី១៖ អកយំ។

៧៩០ ព្រះបាទជ័យវរ្ម័នទី២ត្រឡប់មកកម្ពុជាវិញ។

ស.វ.ទី៩ ដើមសម័យអង្គរ។

៨០២ ព្រះបាទជ័យវរ្ម័នទី២ប្រកាសរាជ្យនៅលើភ្នំគូលែន។

៨០២_ក្រោយ ៨៣០ រាជ្យរបស់ព្រះបាទជ័យវរ្ម័នទី២។

៣/៤នៃស.វ.ទី៩ រចនាបថគូលែន។

៨៧៧_៨៨៩ ព្រះបាទឥន្ទ្រវរ្ម័នសោយរាជ្យនៅហរិហរាល័យ (រលួស)។

ចុងស.វ.ទី៩ រចនាបថព្រះគោ។

៨៧៩ សាងប្រាសាទព្រះគោ។

៨៨១ សាងប្រាសាទបាគង (ប្រាសាទភ្នំទ្រង់ទ្រាយធំលើកដំបូង)។

៨៨៩_ដើមស.វ.ទី១០ រចនាបថបាខែង។

ព្រះបាទយសោវរ្ម័នរៀបចំបុរីយសោធរ (អង្គរ)។

ប្រាសាទបាខែង (ដែលជាប្រាសាទភ្នំ)។

៩២១/៩២៨_៩៤២ ព្រះបាទជ័យវរ្ម័នទី៤ជ្រែករាជ្យ ហើយតាំងទីនៅកោះកេរ្តិ៍។

៩៤៤_៩៦៨ ព្រះបាទរាជេន្ទ្រវរ្ម័នទី២នាំរាជធានីមកអង្គរវិញ។

៩៥២ ប្រាសាទមេបុណ្យ (ខាងកើត)។

៩៦១ ប្រាសាទប្រែរូប។

៩៦៧ បន្ទាយស្រី (សាងដោយព្រាហ្មណ៍ឈ្មោះ យជ្ញវរាហ)។

៩៦៨_១០០០/១ រាជ្យព្រះបាទជ័យវរ្ម័នទី៥។

ដើមស.វ.ទី១០ ប្រាសាទកែវ (សាងចប់នៅពេលណា ដឹងមិនច្បាស់)។

១០០២/១០១០_៤៩ រាជ្យព្រះបាទសូរ្យវរ្ម័នទី១។

ផ្នែកទី១នៃស.វ.ទី១១ ប្រាសាទព្រះវិហារ, ប្រាសាទភ្នំជីសូរ្យ។

១០៥០_១០៦៦ រាជ្យព្រះបាទឧទ័យាទិត្យវរ្ម័នទី២។ សាងបារាយទឹកថ្លា។

១០១០_១០៨០ រចនាបថបាភួន។

១០៦០ ប្រាសាទបាភួន។

១១១៣ ព្រះបាទសូរ្យវរ្ម័នទី២សោយរាជ្យ (យ៉ាងហោចណាស់រហូតដល់ ១០៤៥)។

ផ្នែកទី១នៃស.វ.ទី១២ អង្គរវត្ត, បេងមាលា, បន្ទាយសំរែ។

៣ភាគ៤នៃស.វ.ទី១២ រចនាបថអង្គរវត្ត។

១១៧៧ ចាមលុកលុយអង្គរ។ ព្រះរាជាខ្មែរសុគតក្នុងសង្គ្រាម។

១១៨១_១២១៨(?) រាជ្យព្រះបាទជ័យវរ្ម័នទី៧។ ពុទ្ធសាសនាមហាយានកាន់ជាផ្លូវការ។

១១៨៦ ប្រាសាទតាព្រហ្មសាងឡើងដើម្បីឧទ្ទិសដល់ព្រះមាតានៃព្រះរាជា។

១១៩១ ប្រាសាទព្រះខ័នសាងឡើងដើម្បីឧទ្ទិសដល់ព្រះបិតានៃព្រះរាជា។

១/៤ក្រោយបង្អស់នៃស.វ.ទី១២ រចនាបថបាយ័ន្ត។ សាងអង្គរធំ។

១២៤៣_១២៩៨ រាជ្យព្រះបាទជ័យវរ្ម័នទី៨។ ព្រហ្មញ្ញសាសនាត្រឡប់មកវិញ។

១២៩៦_៩៧ អ្នកការទូតចិនឈ្មោះ ជីវតាក្វាន់ មកអង្គរ។

ស.វ.ទី១៤ ព្រះពុទ្ធសាសនាថេរវាទរីកសាយឡើង។

១៤៣១ អង្គរត្រូវបោះបង់ចោល ក្រោយពីសៀមលុកលុយច្រើនដង។

១៥១៦_១៥៦៦ ព្រះបាទអង្គចន្ទទី១ (ព្រះចន្ទរាជា) មកគង់នៅអង្គរមួយរយៈ។

ចាប់ពីស.វ.ទី១៧ទៅ ព្រះរាជាខ្មែរតាំងទីនៅតំបន់ជុំវិញភ្នំពេញ។

១៨៦៣ សន្ធិសញ្ញាអាណាព្យាបាលបារាំងលើកម្ពុជា។

១៩៥៣ កម្ពុជាបានឯករាជ្យពេញលេញ។

年表

1世紀	クメール地域と外部の接触が始まる
3世紀	オケオが扶南王国の海洋商業中心地となる
6世紀	中国史書によると真蝋が扶南を統治
7世紀	プノン・ダ様式のアンコール・ボレイ建立
616〜635年頃	イーシャーナヴァルマン１世がイーシャーナプラを統治（サンボール・プレイ・クック）
7世紀	サンボール・プレイ・クック様式（7世紀前半）
7世紀	プレイ・クメン様式（7世紀後半）
7世紀	プラサート・アンデート様式（7世紀末）
8世紀	プラサート・アクヨム聖山
790年頃	ジャヴァヤルマン2世がカンボジアに戻る
9世紀	アンコール時代の始まり
802年	ジャヴァヤルマン2世がプノン・クレーンで即位
802〜830年頃	ジャヴァヤルマン2世
9世紀最初の75年	クレーン様式
887〜889年	インドラヴァルマン１世がハリハラーラヤ（ロルオス）を統治
9世紀末	プレア・コー様式
879年	プレア・コー建立
881年	バコン寺院（初の大規模聖山）
889年〜10世紀初め	ヤショーヴァルマン1世
893年	貯水池インドラタターカの中央にロレイを建立
10世紀初め	バケーン様式
	ヤショーヴァルマン１世がヤショーダラプラ（アンコール）を造営
	バケーン山頂に寺院建立
921/928〜942年	ジャヴァヤルマン４世がコ・ケーを統治
944〜968年	ラージェーンドラヴァルマン2世がアンコールに還都
952年	東メボン様式
961年	プレ・ループ様式
967年	バンテアイ・スレイ建立（バラモン僧ヤジャニャヴァラーハ）
968〜1000/1年	ジャヤヴァルマン５世
11世紀初め	タ・ケオ建立（完成時期不明）
1002/1010〜1049年	スーリヤヴァルマン１世
11世紀前半	プレア・ヴィヒア、プノン・チソル建立
1050〜1066年	ウダヤーディティアヴァルマン2世、西バライ建立
1010〜1080年頃	バプーオン様式
1060年頃	バプーオン建立
1113年	スーリヤヴァルマン2世（少なくとも1045年まで）
12世紀前半	アンコール・ワット、ベン・メアレア、バンテアイ・サムレ建立
12世紀最初の75年	アンコール・ワット様式
1177年	チャンパによるアンコール侵攻、クメール王殺害
1181〜1218年(?)	ジャヤヴァルマン７世、大乗仏教が国家宗教
1186年	タ・プロームを母の菩提寺として建立
1191年	プレア・カンを父の菩提寺として建立
12世紀最後の25年	バイヨン様式。アンコール・トム建立
1243〜1298年	ジャヤヴァルマン８世。バラモン教の復活
1296〜7年	元の使節、周達観がアンコール訪問
14世紀	小乗仏教が普及
1431年	アユタヤのアンコール攻略によるアンコール王都放棄
1516〜1566年	アン・チャン１世がアンコールに逗留
17世紀以後	クメール王たちはプノンペン地域から統治
1863年	フランス保護領カンボジア王国
1953年	カンボジア王国独立

Brief overview of Cambodian history

1. The earliest polities

The earliest historical evidence of Cambodia occurs in Chinese records of the 3rd century. What its inhabitants, the Khmers, called their country is unknown, but the Chinese referred to it as Funan. They reported that its inhabitants worshipped many-armed gods, indicating the presence of Brahmanism or Buddhism and showing that influences from India were already established in the region. Archaeological evidence, including Roman coins, shows that Funan's port, Oc Eo, was a prosperous entrepôt for trade between the West and China. The capital was probably to the south of present-day Phnom Penh near Angkor Borei, a region where Buddhism and Brahmanism existed simultaneously, judging from the evidence of statuary. Masterly sculpture in the style known as Phnom Da (from the name of a hill near Angkor Borei) is mostly Vishnuite, created there in the 7th century (#2, 3, 4). Only ruins remain of the temples of this area, with the exception of Ashram Maha Rosei.

By the early 7th century the centre of power had moved north to a polity the Chinese called Zhenla. As with the southern centre, we do not know what the Khmers themselves called it. Its centre was in a city called Ishanapura (now Sambor Prei Kuk), founded by Ishanavarman I, who had family connections with Funan although he came from a northern clan near the Dangrek ranges. More than two hundred Brahmanistic temples, many in good condition, built in three groups at three periods, define a prototype for later Khmer temple construction. Single-towered prasats resembling the Indian shikhara, they are built of brick with sandstone doorframes, colonettes, and lintels, all carved with consummate skill. Most are square or rectangular in plan, but some are octagonal, their external walls decorated with relief carvings depicting pavilions occupied by court personages. Several inscriptions inform us about the king, and the sanctuaries have yielded important freestanding statues (#11, 12). Descendants of the northern chieftains continued to rule the expanding polity, and by the early 8th century Queen Jayadevi may have settled near what was later to become Angkor near the Tonle Sap lake.

During the 8th century there was also a flourishing state further east, on the Mekong river at Shambhupura (now Sambor on the Mekong). Three of its rulers were queens, and it yielded memorable sculptures of goddesses (#13). The settlements of Funan, the cities of Ishanavarman's royal line and of the Mekong kingdom all developed near major rivers, the lifeline of lands in monsoonal regions where rain falls only in one season. Water is important in both social development and symbolism in Khmer history, and the Cambodians were skilled in hydraulic techniques from the earliest days.

The expansion of Khmer authority beyond the Dangrek range (in what is now Northeast Thailand) seems to have begun in the 8th century, the first stage in an evolution from small trading centre to far-flung empire. Some of the most renowned Khmer bronze images, primarily of bodhisattvas, were found in what is now Buriram province in Thailand (#25). The late 8th century yielded few inscriptions, so the sequence of events is unclear. An inscription of 770, however, refers to a Jayavarman, who later as Jayavarman II was to launch the age of Angkor.

2. The 9th century and the beginnings of Angkor

According to the inscription of Sdok Kak Thom, Jayavarman II (802-c.830 CE) was consecrated as universal monarch, or chakravartin, in 802. The ceremony took place on Phnom Kulen, which was referred to as Mahendraparvata (the mountain of the god Indra) and involved the installation of a devaraja (literally, god-king, though its exact identity is uncertain). There is no evidence that it implied the divinity of the monarch, and the term is probably the Sanskrit translation of an Old Khmer term for an indigenous ruler, but it certainly seems to have been identified with divinely sanctioned kingly authority and legitimacy. Many 9th-century temples remain on Phnom Kulen, most comprising a single-towered brick sanctuary, but some having towers in groups of three, with false storeys and corbelled roofs (bricks in a cantilevered stack). Doorframes, false doors, lintels and colonettes were of sandstone. Several statues of Vishnu were found in the Kulen temples (#27). These project an increased formality and rigidity compared with the humanistic spirituality of the statuary of Phnom Da and Sambor Prei Kuk.

Jayavarman II moved his capital several times, twice locating it in Hariharalaya (present-day Roluos), which was probably also the capital of his successor, Jayavarman III. The site had possibly been settled earlier and might have been the capital of Queen Jayadevi (680/81-c.713), as inscriptions on the nearby small pyramid temple of Ak Yum are dated in her reign. Hariharalaya was also chosen as capital by Indravarman I (877-889), the nephew of Jayavarman II. He constructed the ancestor temple of Preah Ko with six brick towers on a common platform. The importance attached to forebears by the Khmer - an importance still attested by the continuing role of Neak Ta, or ancestor spirits, in Cambodian life - can be seen in this temple's inscriptions invoking male and female ancestors in association with deities.

Indravarman's state temple was the temple mountain of Bakong, rising more than 30m on five levels and surrounded by many subsidiary temples and gateways. Although not the first example of a temple in pyramid form (8th-century Ak Yum, mentioned above, preceded it, as did Krus Preah Aram Rong Chen on Phnom Kulen), Bakong was the first monumental version. Like others that followed, it was a microcosm representing Mount Meru, the mythological home of the Brahmanic gods. Sculpture found in the sanctuaries of Bakong and Preah Ko (#28, 29) has an iconic monumentality, perhaps reflecting the growing size and central organization of the Khmer state and the intention of the monarch to express power. Indravarman was also responsible for Indratataka, the first of the huge reservoirs, or barays (now mostly dry), that are among the remarkable hydraulic constructions created by the Khmer.

Yashovarman I (889-early 10th century) succeeded his father, Indravarman. Towards the end of the 9th century he built the four-towered temple of Lolei, probably an ancestor temple like Preah Ko, on an artificial island in the middle of Indratataka. In about 900 he moved his capital, which he called Yashodharapura, to the area that would become Angkor, hewing his temple mountain from the solid rock of Phnom Bakheng, the hill that gave its name to both the temple and the sculptural style of the first quarter of the 10th century.

3. The 10th century and the growing complexity of the Khmer state

By the end of his reign, in addition to the Phnom Bakheng state temple, Yashovarman I had built three-towered temples on the summit of Phnom Bok and Phnom Krom and had created the now dry eastern baray (7 x 2 km). Inscriptions asserting his authority were placed as far away as present-day NE Thailand and Wat Phu in Laos. Increasingly hieratic style with refined precision characterized both relief and free-standing sculpture in this period (#30).

Yashovarman's son, Harshavarman I, probably succeeded to the throne in 912. Although he built no state temple, he began the small temple of Baksei Chamkrong (completed by his cousin Rajendravarman in 948). An inscription reveals that it was dedicated to his parents. During his reign the five-towered temple of Prasat Kravan (921) was dedicated to Vishnu. Another inscription indicates that his brother, Ishanavarman II, had become king by 925. His brief reign ended in 928.

While Harshavarman I and Ishanavarman II were ruling from Angkor, their authority was challenged by their uncle, husband of Yashovarman's sister. In 921 he proclaimed himself Jayavarman IV and ruled from his huge estate, Chok Gargyar, situated about 100 km. northeast of Angkor. Now called Koh Ker, this site comprised several hundred temples on a grandiose scale that reached its apogee in Jayavarman IV's temple mountain, Prasat Thom. With the now missing upper structures in perishable materials that stood on its five-tiered pyramidal base, this monument would have reached 60 metres in height. Massive scale and dynamic perfection of carving typify Koh Ker sculpture (#31-34). When Ishanavarman II died in 928, Jayavarman IV was undisputed monarch until his death in 942. His son, Harshavarman II, also ruled briefly from Koh Ker, but in 944 was succeeded by his cousin Rajendravarman, the fourth member of his generation to become king of the Khmer realm.

Rajendravarman (944-968) made Angkor the capital again, retaining its former name of Yashodharapura. He dedicated the East Mebon, possibly an ancestor temple, on an artificial island in the eastern baray in 953, and his state temple of Pre Rup in 961. Both are temple mountains where refined carving of lintels and colonettes, among the finest in Khmer architecture, is echoed in the sculptural style known as Pre Rup (#35, 36).

During Rajendravarman's reign there were serious threats from the Chams, whose kingdom (in today's central Vietnam) attacked the Khmers for centuries. The Buddhist temple of Bat Chum (960) and the Shivite temple of Banteay Srei (967-8) signaled the first sacred constructions to be instigated by high dignitaries rather than the monarch. The latter, regarded as one of the gems of Khmer architecture, was built at the behest of the guru of the king's son and dedicated at the end of Rajendravarman's reign. Its relief carving and freestanding sculptures show intricate perfection (#37-39).

Jayavarman V succeeded his father in 968. His long reign (till 1000 or 1001 CE) was a period of relative stability with fewer threats from the Chams. Although he constructed no temple mountain, it is thought that he established the Royal Palace in its current location and possibly initiated the royal chapel of Phimeanakas.

4. The 11th century and the expansion of the Khmer empire

The details of succession from Jayavarman V to Udayadityavarman I (1001-02) and then to Jayaviravarman (1002-10) are unclear, as is the identity of the constructor of the temple mountain of Ta Keo. This 22-metre-high monument with five upper towers in quincunx arrangement (a tower at each corner and one in the centre) is in Khleang style (#40), as is the temple mountain Phimeanakas in the Royal Palace compound. The appellation 'Khleang' ('emporium') is derived from two buildings (function unknown) east of the Royal Palace. In Ta Keo and Phimeanakas we see the first appearance of the surrounding galleries that were important for circumambulation and the presentation of narrative reliefs in Angkor Wat and Bayon.

Records are scant from what seems to have been a turbulent decade. Just as Jayaviravarman assumed power, a prince from the eastern regions, Suryavarman I, also claimed the throne. The overlapping reigns ran from 1002 to 1010, but in a 1011 inscription on the gateway of the palace's five-metre walls, Suryavarman I affirmed 1002 as his accession date. The walls, new to the palace, perhaps indi cate an increased need for security. Suryavarman's lineage was not direct but derived from the maternal line of Indravarman I, which may account for the inscription's requirement for the signatories to affirm their loyalty to the king and thus legitimize his power.

During his long and relatively peaceful reign (until 1049) Suryavarman I built no state temple mountain, opting instead for huge temples, housing state lingas of gold, to establish the furthest limits of his territory. To the west he founded Wat Ek and Wat Baset; to the north, on the Dangrek escarpment, he built Preah Vihear; Bakan, (formerly Preah Khan of Kompong Svay), the largest of all Khmer temple precincts, was created to the northeast, and Phnom Chisor to the south. Towards the end of Suryavarman's reign and during the next, hundreds of lingas and images of Vishnu in Cosmic Sleep were carved into the bed of the Stung Rusei, a tributary of the Siem Reap river, at Kbal Spean.

The huge western baray (8 x 2 km) was constructed by Suryavarman I or his successor, Udayadityavarman II (1050-166). In about 1060, this king, a descendant of Suryavarman's queen, built Baphuon, one of the most imposing of Cambodia's temple mountains. This monument's name has been lent to the graceful and naturalistic sculptural style of most of the 11th century (#41, 43-48). In addition Suryavarman constructed West Mebon temple on an artificial island in the western baray; in its ruins the great reclining Vishnu (#45) was discovered. Udayadityavarman II's reign was marked by many upheavals and he was succeeded by his brother, Harshavarman III (1066-80), about whom little is known but who might have been overthrown by his successor.

In 1080 a new infusion entered the Khmer royal line through a prince from the Dangrek region's Mahidharapura family, which probably ruled the area in vassalage to Angkor. He assumed the title Jayavarman VI and ruled until 1107. His connection with the northwest, now Northeast Thailand, probably explains the increasing Khmer influence in that region during the twelfth century.

5. The 12th century and the age of Angkor Wat

According to the 1186 inscription of Ta Prohm, Jayavarman VI reigned from Mahidharapura (in today's Nakhon Ratchasima province in Thailand). At that time two temples that presaged Angkor Wat, Prasat Phimai and Prasat Phnom Rung, were built on existing sacred structures in that region. Both have tapering sanctuary towers, where a smooth profile is suggested through multiple false storeys set with sculpted antefixes, that are predictive of the five towers of Angkor's most famous monument.

In 1107 or 1108 Jayavarman VI was succeeded by his older brother, Dharanindravarman I, who ruled until 1112. Dharanindravarman's successor was Suryavarman II, his great-nephew. The 12th-century inscription of Ban That says that when the fifteen-year-old Suryavarman had completed his studies he was "in the dependency of two masters", suggesting that Harshavarman III's followers might still have been claiming sovereignty in Angkor while Dharanindravarman was ruling from Mahidharapura. Though the facts are uncertain, it seems that Suryavarman came to the throne in 1113 by overcoming the king in a one-day battle.

Temples constructed during Suryavarman II's reign include Thommanon, Chau Say Tevoda, Banteay Samre, and the enormous complex of Beng Mealea, 80 km northeast of Angkor. There were also additions to Preah Vihear and Wat Phu. Magnificent though these temples are, none surpasses Suryavarman's creation of Angkor Wat itself. Constructed during the first half of the century, it is 200 hectares in area and surrounded by a 190-metre-wide moat. It is a five-level temple mountain, a microcosm of the home of the gods on Mount Meru. With five towers on the upper level, it is in quincunx form, the central tower rising to a height of 42 m. Unlike most Khmer temples, Angkor Wat faces west, the direction of sunset and death, which suggests to some scholars that it was a funerary temple for Suryavarman. However, its orientation could possibly be explained by its dedication to Vishnu, who is associated with that direction.

The awe-inspiring architecture of Angkor Wat is enhanced by its relief carvings. These comprise not only almost 2000 celestial nymphs, or apsaras but also lively scenes on lintels and pediments. The crowning glory is the almost 1 km-long series of narrative reliefs encircling the third enclosure in a columned gallery with corbelled roof. Divided into eight panels, the reliefs include dynamic scenes from the

Mahabharata, the *Ramayana*, Yama's judgment of who should go to heaven or hell, the Churning of the Ocean of Milk, as well as historical scenes from Suryavarman's reign. Refinement of carving is a hallmark of the Angkor Wat style, which dominated sculpture for three-quarters of the 12th century. Perfection in the depiction of garments and jewels is visible in somewhat iconic stone statuary as well (#49, 50, 52, 54, 55), but it is bronze figures that epitomize Angkor Wat style at its best (#51, 53, 56-60).

Suryavarman II extended the boundaries of the Khmer empire, though six wars he waged (against the Dai Viet and the Chams) were largely unsuccessful. The last inscription mentioning him is dated 1145, but he may have ruled until 1150, when his successor, his Buddhist cousin Dharanindravarman II, seems to have occupied the throne for some time. Only one inscription is known between 1145 and 1180, so the facts are uncertain, but Dharanindravarman (father of the future Jayavarman VII) was succeeded by Yashovarman II, possibly a distant relative. In 1165 Yashovarman was overthrown by a usurper, Tribhuvanadityavarman, who was killed in a Cham invasion of Angkor in 1177.

6. Jayavarman VII, Angkor Thom and Bayon

For four years after the 1177 Cham invasion of Angkor, the Khmer prince who was to become Jayavarman VII gathered forces to expel the invaders and succeeded in regaining the capital. Buddhist like his father, Dharanindravarman II, he was more than fifty years old when he succeeded to the throne in 1181. During his reign, when Mahayana Buddhism became the state religion, Jayavarman extended the boundaries of the Khmer empire to their widest extent, reaching the borders of present-day Myanmar in the west, the area of Vientiane in Laos to the north, Champa – which he subdued after three attempts in 1199 – to the east, and the sea to the south.

The royal capital of Angkor Thom was constructed during Jayavarman's reign, its 3-km boundaries, with 8-metre-high walls and 120-metre-wide moat, enclosing 900 hectares. Its five monumental gates, crowned with towering heads, are preceded across the moats by causeways flanked by rows of giant figures pulling a naga. Such causeways are also found at the entrances of several temples of the era, including Ta Prohm and Preah Khan. At Angkor Thom's centre stands the state temple of Bayon, famous for its towers, originally 49 in number, each with four heads that gaze mysteriously in the four cardinal directions. It also offers rich narrative reliefs from which much can be learned about mythology, history, and daily life in Angkor. Bayon was Buddhist in dedication, but Jayavarman VII seems to have been ecumenical in his outlook, and in the ancestor temples of Ta Prohm and Preah Khan there are shrines for Brahmanistic deities as well as the Buddha.

Inscriptions abound from Jayavarman's reign, notably those on the stele of Ta Prohm (1186) and Preah Khan (1191). They inform us that 12,640 people lived in the former, and that the latter was served by 97,840. These figures bolster recent claims that Greater Angkor was the largest of all pre-industrial age cities. It was an age of huge architectural projects, including the large temples of Banteay Kdei, Banteay Chmar and extensions to Bakan, and numerous arched bridges, hospitals and rest houses along the roads of Jayavarman's kingdom. The most famous of these was the Royal Way along which Buddhist pilgrims passed from the temple of Phimai, beyond the Dangrek mountains, to Bayon.

Sculpted images of the king and his queen, Jayarajadevi, who died young, were placed throughout the kingdom by his second queen, her older sister. These embody spiritual serenity and humanism (#61-63, 73) and constitute the grace of the Bayon style, which offers numerous statues of the bodhisattva of compassion, Lokeshvara, the goddess of transcendental wisdom, Prajnaparamita, and the Buddha himself, often seated on the naga. The period also saw masterly bronze-casting (#64-72, 74).

Several uprisings and rebellions marked Jayavarman's reign. The economic burden of these, along with the cost of the astonishing numbers of architectural projects of the period, possibly contributed to a weakening of the kingdom. From late in the 12th century and into the 13th the rising power of the Thai state began to threaten the security and integrity of the Khmer empire, which was not to maintain the pre-eminence it had enjoyed since the 10th century. The date of Jayavarman VII's death is uncertain, but it was probably around 1218, when he would have been more than eighty years old.

7. Cambodia after Angkor

Indravarman II (1218-43), who was a Mahayana Buddhist, succeeded Jayavarman VII. The only inscription known from his reign concerns his death, and little is known about the period. It is probable that Preah Palilay and some of the temples of the Preah Pithou group date from this time. Indravarman's successor, Jayavarman VIII (1243-95), reinstituted Brahmanism as the state religion and his reign saw iconoclasm of Buddhist temples such as Preah Khan as well as the construction of the last Khmer monument in stone, Mangalartha, and possibly the famous kneeling statue of Yama (#76) though current thinking assigns a considerably earlier date to it.

During the reign of Indravarman III (1295-1307) there were frequent incursions from the Thai kingdom of Ayutthaya. Despite this, the detailed description of Zhou Daguan, a Chinese delegate who visited Angkor in 1296-97, reveals that the Khmer court still exhibited grandeur and opulence. Although a Thai attack of 1431 provoked the abandonment of Angkor, it is possible that the court's move south to the Phnom Penh region reflected not so much a flight as a desire for greater access to the trading opportunities afforded by the southern location with its links, via the Tonle Sap and the Mekong, to maritime connections. There were twelve missions to China between 1371 and 1419, for example, suggesting increased commerce with China during the Ming dynasty.

The growing dominance of Theravada Buddhism and a return to the roots of Khmer culture from the 13th century onwards is revealed in statuary, increasingly made from wood (#80) and showing stylistic influences possibly stemming from Theravadin Sri Lanka by way of Thailand (#77). Monumental statues of the Buddha created for Angkor Wat (#79), which became a place of Buddhist pilgrimage, date from the reign of Ang Chan (1516-1566) and his successor, who moved the Khmer capital back to Angkor for a few decades.

The royal line of Cambodia continued through the next four centuries until today, albeit without control of the Thai-dominated northern regions until the French-negotiated return of the territory in 1907. The French Protectorate, and later colonial control, saw the stimulation of European interest in Cambodia, beginning with the journeys of Henri Mouhot in 1858-61 and the drawings and descriptions of Louis Delaporte from 1866-68. The creation of l'École française d'Extrême-Orient in 1898 led to a period of intense exploration, restoration and scholarship by French, and later other foreign researchers.

Many of the fruits of the efforts to conserve Khmer culture may be enjoyed in the collections of the National Museum of Cambodia, which houses not only the extraordinary sculpture in stone, bronze and wood that this book presents, but also a rich collection of ceramics, paintings, and ceremonial objects that could not be included. The ceramics, mostly dating from the 11th and 12th centuries, offer characteristic brown glazes and classical shapes as well as whimsical representations of zoomorphic vessels. The paintings, predominantly 19th- and 20th-century creations, usually depict Buddhist scenes. Ritual objects and artifacts connected with rites of passage demonstrate the ongoing skills of Khmer craftspeople in wood, bronze and precious metals.

L'histoire du Cambodge: un bref survol.

1. Les royaumes anciens

Les plus anciens témoignages historiques sur le Cambodge apparaissent dans des sources chinoises du 3ème siècle. Si le nom que les habitants donnait à leur pays est inconnu, les Chinois le nomment Funan. Ces sources précisent que les habitants vénèrent des divinités à bras multiples, indiquant ainsi la présence du brahmanisme et du bouddhisme et montrant que les influences de l'Inde avait déjà fait leur chemin en Asie du Sud-Est à cette époque. Divers témoignages archéologiques, dont des monnaies romaines, attestent que le grand port du Funan, Oc Eo, était un centre de commerce prospère entre la Chine et l'Occident. La capitale se trouvait probablement au sud de Phnom-Penh, près d'Angkor Borei, dans une région où coexistaient le bouddhisme et l'hindouisme, si l'on en juge par la statuaire qui y a été retrouvée. Une magistrale école de sculpture s'était développée dans cette région autour du 7ème siècle (#2, 3, 4). Les œuvres qui en sont caractéristiques sont plus particulièrement vishnuites et se classent dans le style dit du Phnom Da, du nom d'une colline près d'Angkor Borei. Les temples anciens ne subsistent plus qu'à l'état de ruines, à l'exception de l'Ashram Maha Rosei.

Au début du 7ème siècle, le centre du pouvoir s'était déplacé vers le Nord, autour d'un royaume que les Chinois nomment Zhenla. De même que pour le Funan, nous ignorons comment les Khmers eux-mêmes appelaient ce royaume. Son centre se trouvait dans la cité d'Ishanapura (actuel site de Sambor Prei Kuk), fondée (?) par le roi Ishanavarman I que des liens de parenté unissait aux rois du Funan mais qui venait lui-même d'un clan septentrional près de la chaîne des Dangrek. Plus d'une centaine de temples brahmaniques, dont beaucoup sont encore bien conservés, ont été édifiés en trois ensembles principaux à des époques différentes, constituant les prototypes de l'architecture khmère à venir. P rasat isolés assez proches des tours-sanctuaires des temples de l'Inde du Sud, ces monuments sont construits en brique avec des encadrements de porte, colonnettes et linteau, en grès, tous sculptés avec une science consommée. La plupart sont de plan carré ou rectangulaire, mais certains présentent un plan octogonal original. Les murs sont ornés de bas-reliefs représentant des architectures peuplées de multiples personnages. Certaines inscriptions se rapportent au roi fondateur et quelques sanctuaires ont livré de remarquables statues en ronde bosse (#11, 12). Au cours du 7ème siècle, les descendants d'Ishanavarman ont continué à régner sur un royaume en constante expansion. Au début du 8ème siècle, la reine Jayadevi, a dû s'établir dans la région de la future Angkor, non loin des berges du Tonle Sap.

Au 8ème siècle, un autre royaume florissant prospérait plus à l'Est, autour de Shambhupura (près de l'actuelle Sambor du Mékong). Trois des dirigeants de ce royaume ont été des reines et l'on doit remarquer l'extraordinaire qualité des sculptures féminines retrouvées dans la région (#13). Les établissements du Funan, les villes où ont œuvré les membres de la lignée royale d'Ishanavarman et le royaume du Mékong se sont tous développés près de cours d'eau majeurs, une situation vitale dans les zones soumises au régime de la mousson où la pluie ne tombe que le temps d'une courte saison. L'eau est un élément aussi important au plan social qu'au plan symbolique dans l'histoire khmère; et les Cambodgiens se sont révélés maîtres dans les techniques hydrauliques dès les époques les plus anciennes.

Le développement de l'autorité khmère au-delà de la chaîne des Dangrek (dans le nord-est de l'actuelle Thaïlande) semble avoir débuté au 8ème siècle. Il s'agit là d'une première étape dans le passage du statut de chefferie à celui d'état constitué. Quelques-uns des plus beaux bronzes khmers, principalement des représentations de bodhisattva, ont été retrouvés dans ce qui est l'actuelle province de Buriram en Thaïlande (#25). Peu d'inscriptions se rapportent à la fin du 8ème siècle et le déroulement des événements historiques est peu clair pour cette époque. Vers 770, toutefois, l'épigraphie mentionne celui qui allait devenir le fondateur de la royauté angkorienne: le futur Jayavarman II.

2. Le 9ème siècle: les débuts de l'époque angkorienne

D'après l'inscription de Sdok Kak Thom, Jayavarman II (r. 802-c. 830) fut sacré souverain universel (chakravartin) en l'an 802. La cérémonie se déroula sur le Phnom Kulen, dénommé jadis Mahendraparvata: la montagne du grand Indra. À cette occasion on consacra aussi le devaraja (littéralement le dieu-roi), dont l'identité exacte demeure incertaine. Il n'existe aucune preuve permettant de dire que ce devaraja était le souverain divinisé; le terme est probablement la traduction sanskrite d'un vocable vieux khmer désignant un dieu particulièrement important. Quoi qu'il en soit, son association avec l'autorité royale et la légitimité des monarques ne semble pas faire de doute. Divers monuments du 9ème siècle, tours-sanctuaires isolées ou groupées par trois, subsistent sur le Phnom Kulen; ces édifices en brique possèdent une toiture en encorbellement constituée de faux étages décroissants dérivant des modèles antérieurs. Comme à l'époque préangkorienne, les éléments décoratifs des encadrements de porte – linteaux et colonnettes – sont en grès. Plusieurs images de Vishnu ont été retrouvées dans les temples du Kulen (#27). Ces œuvres sont plus hiératiques et formelles que les sculptures des styles du Phnom Da ou de Sambor Prei Kuk, empreintes de spiritualité humanisée.

Jayavarman II déplaça la capitale à plusieurs reprises; il résida deux fois à Hariharalaya (l'actuel site de Roluos) qui demeura aussi la capitale de son successeur, Jayavarman III. La région d'Angkor n'en était pas à sa première occupation, comme le montrent de nombreux vestiges architecturaux parmi lesquels on peut citer le modeste temple-montagne d'Ak Yum, sur la berge méridionale du baray occidental. Hariharalaya fut aussi retenue comme capitale par Indravarman I (877-889), un petit-neveu de Jayavarman II. Il édifia le temple aux ancêtres de Preah Ko, un ensemble composé de six tours-sanctuaires en brique disposées en deux rangées sur une terrasse commune. L'importance attachée aux ancêtres dans la société khmère – encore bien vivace de nos jours, ainsi que le souligne l'attention portée aux Neak Ta, ces génies ancestraux – transparaît dans les inscriptions du temple invoquant les prédécesseurs du roi, en association avec les divinités auxquelles les sanctuaires sont consacrés.

Le temple d'État d'Indravarman, Bakong, s'élève à plus de 30 m. sur une pyramide à cinq gradins; il est entouré de nombreux bâtiments annexes, portes, etc. Bien qu'il ne s'agisse pas du premier exemple connu (Ak Yum, au 8ème siècle, et Krus Preah Aram Rong Chen, sur le Phnom Kulen, sont antérieurs), Bakong est le plus ancien temple-montagne à nous être parvenu en bon état de conservation. Comme certains de ceux qui l'ont suivi, il s'agit d'un microcosme représentant le mont Meru, séjour mythique des dieux brahmaniques. Les œuvres provenant de Preah Ko et Bakong (#28, 29) possèdent une majestueuse grandeur, reflétant sans doute la puissance et le centralisme accrus de l'empire khmer; elles sont également un manifeste de l'importance du pouvoir royal. Indravarman est, par ailleurs, associé avec la réalisation ou l'achèvement de l'Indratataka (à sec aujourd'hui), le premier de ces grands réservoirs ou baray figurant au nombre des plus remarquables aménagements hydrauliques du Cambodge ancien.

Yashovarman I (889-début du 10ème s.), fils et successeur d'Indravarman, édifia vers la fin du 9ème siècle (893) les quatre tours-sanctuaires de Lolei - un temple aux ancêtres, tout comme Preah Ko - sur l'île artificielle située dans l'Indratataka. Vers 900, il procéda au déplacement de la capitale, désormais nommée Yashodharapura, vers la zone qui allait devenir Angkor, faisant aménager son temple-montagne au sommet du Phnom Bakheng, la colline qui donne son nom au monument lui-même et au style statuaire du premier quart du 10ème siècle. La pyramide du Phnom Bakheng est taillée à même la roche de la colline, à la différence des autres temples-montagnes dont les pyramides sont artificielles. Outre le Phnom Bakheng, Yashovarman fit édifier deux temples composés de trois tours-sanctuaires au sommet du Phnom Bok et du Phnom Krom et aménagea le baray oriental (7 x 2 km), aujourd'hui à sec. Les inscriptions qui attestent son autorité se retrouvent dans des régions aussi éloignées d'Angkor que le nord-est de l'actuelle Thaïlande ou Vat Phu, au Laos. La sculpture en ronde bosse et les bas-reliefs sont caractérisés par un hiératisme toujours plus marqué.

3. Le 10ème siècle: la complexité croissante de l'État khmer

Harshavarman I, le fils de Yashovarman, accéda au trône peu avant 912. On lui doit la fondation du petit temple-montagne de Baksei Chamkrong qui devait plus tard, en 948, être restauré et achevé par son cousin Rajendravarman. Une inscription révèle que ce temple était consacré aux parents de Harshavarman. Sous son règne, en 921, une famille de dignitaires fit élever les cinq tours-sanctuaires en brique du Prasat Kravan, un monument original consacré à Vishnu. Le frère de Harshavarman, Ishanavarman II, devint roi en 925; son règne bref s'acheva en 928.

L'autorité royale de Harshavarman I et Ishanavarman II à Angkor semble avoir été assez vite contestée par leur oncle par alliance, le futur Jayavarman IV. Dès 921, ce dernier régnait de manière indépendante sur son domaine de Chok Gargyar, à une centaine de km au nor d-est d'Angkor. Ce n'est qu'à la disparition d'Ishanavarman II, en 928, que Jayavarman IV devint roi de tout le Cambodge, jusqu'à sa mort vers 940. Connu aujourd'hui sous le nom de Koh Ker, ce site comportait autrefois un très grand nombre de temples dont certains présentaient d'imposantes dimensions, comme le temple-montagne du Prasat Thom. La pyramide à sept gradins, au sommet de laquelle aurait pu se trouver un sanctuaire en matériaux périssables, culmine à quelque 60 m. de hauteur. Des proportions monumentales et un certain sens du mouvement caractérisent les œuvres du style de Koh Ker (#31-34). Le fils de Jayavarman IV, Harshavarman II, eut un règne bref à Koh Ker; il fut remplacé en 944 par son cousin, Rajendravarman, qui devint donc, après Harshavarman I, Ishanavarman II et Harshavarman II, le quatrième membre de sa génération à accéder au trône.

Rajendravarman (944-968) réinstalla la capitale à Angkor/Yashodharapura. En 953, il édifia le Mebon oriental, un temple aux ancêtres, sur l'île artificielle du baray oriental et, en 961, consacra le magnifique temple-montagne de Pre Rup. Ces deux monuments se distinguent par la finesse particulière des linteaux et des colonnettes qui sont parmi les plus beaux de tout l'art khmer. Cette délicatesse du décor architectural trouve un vibrant écho dans la statuaire (#35, 36).

Sous Rajendravarman, de sérieux heurts semblent avoir eu lieu entre le Cambodge et le Champa (un royaume indianisé situé dans le centre de l'actuel Vietnam); les Cham vont d'ailleurs se révéler par la suite les ennemis les plus constants de l'empire khmer. Le temple bouddhique de Bat Chum (960) et le temple shivaïte de Banteay Srei (967-8) figurent parmi les plus importantes fondations non royales de l'époque angkorienne. Banteay Srei, considéré comme l'un des joyaux de l'architecture khmère, fut édifié par le guru du fils de Rajendravarman et consacré à l'extrême fin du règne de ce grand monarque. Les bas-reliefs et la statuaire de ce monument présentent une rare perfection (#37-39).

Jayavarman V succéda à son père en 968. Son long règne, jusqu'en 1000 ou 1001, fut une période de relative stabilité au cours de laquelle les Cham ne semblent plus avoir été une menace. Il paraît possible d'associer à son règne l'établissement de l'enceinte du palais royal et, peut-être, le premier état de la chapelle royale du Phimeanakas.

4. Le 11ème siècle: l'expansion de l'empire khmer

Les détails de la succession de Jayavarman V restent mal connus; deux souverains se succèdent sur le trône dans les premières années du 11ème siècle: Udayadityavarman I (1001) et Jayaviravarman (1002-10). On ignore auquel de ces monarques il convient d'attribuer la construction du temple-montagne inachevé de Ta Keo. Ce monument couronné de cinq tours-sanctuaires disposées en quinconce au sommet des cinq gradins de la pyramide appartient au style des Khleang (#40). Le nom de Khleang (magasin) a été attribué à deux bâtiments de fonction énigmatique situés à l'est du palais royal. À Ta Keo, tout comme au Phimeanakas, où le dispositif semble légèrement plus tardif, on relève l'apparition de galeries dites pourtournantes, importantes pour la circumambulation et utilisées ultérieurement, à Angkor Vat et au Bayon, comme emplacement privilégié pour les bas-reliefs narratifs.

Les témoignages sur ce qui apparaît être une décennie troublée sont rares. Alors que Jayaviravarman montait sur le trône, un prince des régions du Nord-Est, le futur Suryavarman I, cherchait à prendre le pouvoir. La confrontation semble avoir duré de 1002 à 1010. Dans une inscription de 1011, gravée sur les murs de la porte d'accès au palais royal, Suryavarman - qui descendait de la famille maternelle d'Indravarman I - affirme toutefois qu'il est monté sur le trône en 1002, gommant du même coup le règne éphémère de son rival. Son besoin de légitimité est trahi par la nature de l'inscription en question dans laquelle il fait prêter serment de loyauté aux fonctionnaires.

Pendant un règne long et relativement paisible, Suryavarman ne fit pas construire de temple-montagne mais un ensemble de grands sanctuaires consacrés à Shiva aux quatre coins de son empire. À l'Ouest, ce sont les temples de Vat Ek et Vat Baset; au Nord, sur un escarpement des Dangrek, le majestueux temple de Preah Vihear; à l'Est, le temple qui allait devenir par la suite l'une des plus vastes fondations provinciales, Bakan (autrefois Preah Khan de Kompong Svay); au Sud, enfin, le spectaculaire temple du Phnom Chisor. Vers la fin du règne de Suryavarman I, et par la suite également, des centaines de linga et des représentations de Vishnu étendu sur le serpent d'éternité ont été sculptés à Kbal Spean et sur les rochers affleurant le long du lit du stung Rusei, un affluent de la rivière de Siemreap.

C'est à Suryavarman I, ou à son successeur, Udayadityavarman II (1050-1066), que l'on attribue l'aménagement de l'immense baray occidental (8 x 2 km). Aux environs de 1060, ce dernier édifia le Baphuon, l'un des plus imposants temples-montagnes d'Angkor. Le nom de ce monument a été donné au style gracieux et naturaliste qui couvre la majeure partie du 11ème siècle (#41, 43-48). C'est dans les vestiges du Mebon occidental, dans l'île du grand baray, que les fragments d'un grand Vishnu couché en bronze (#45) ont été retrouvés. Le règne d'Udayadityavarman II fut marqué par une série de soulèvements. Son frère, Harshavarman III (1066-1080) lui succéda mais on sait peu de chose sur lui, si ce n'est qu'il pourrait avoir été détrôné par son successeur.

En 1080, une nouvelle lignée royale, probablement vassale des rois d'Angkor à l'origine, accède au trône en la personne d'un prince venu de Mahidharapura, ville située dans la région des Dangrek. Ce prince prit le nom de règne de Jayavarman VI et se maintint sur le trône jusqu'en 1107. Son origine explique probablement l'interaction de l'architecture angkorienne et de l'art des régions du nord-est de l'actuelle Thaïlande au cours du 12ème siècle. Dès cette époque, deux temples majeurs édifiés à l'emplacement de fondations plus anciennes, préfigurent le célèbre temple d'Angkor Vat. La ligne douce des toitures de ces deux sanctuaires, avec leurs nombreux antéfixes disposés sur les corniches de chacun des faux-étages, annonce, en effet, celle des cinq tours-sanctuaires du plus célèbre de tous les monuments d'Angkor.

5. Le 12ème siècle: l'âge d'Angkor Vat

En 1107 ou 1108, Jayavarman VI est remplacé sur le trône par son frère aîné, Dharanindravarman I, qui règne jusqu'en 1112 et auquel succèdera son petit-neveu, le fameux Suryavarman II. L'inscription de Ban That explique qu'à l'issue de ses études, le jeune Suryavarman se saisit par la force de la royauté qui était alors dans la dépendance de deux maîtres. Cette information laisse à penser que les fidèles de Harshavarman III, ce roi qui avait été dépossédé de son trône par Jayavarman VI, contestaient le pouvoir suprême à Dharanindravarman lequel régnait vraisemblablement, comme son prédécesseur Jayavarman VI, depuis son fief de Mahidharapura. Bien que les faits demeurent incertains, c'est à l'issue d'un combat d'une journée que Suryavarman II monta sur le trône en 1113.

Les temples construits sous le règne de Suryavarman II sont nombreux: Thommanon, Chau Say Tevoda, Banteay Samre et l'immense complexe de Beng Mealea, à une quarantaine de km au nord-est d'Angkor. Diverses adjonctions furent également faites à Preah Vihear et à Vat Phu. Aussi beaux que soient ces temples, aucun, pourtant, ne surpasse Angkor Vat. Edifié au cours de la première moitié du 12ème siècle, Angkor Vat est entouré de douves de 190 mètres de large et couvre une superficie de 200 hectares. Les cinq sanctuaires principaux disposés en quinconce se dressent sur une pyramide à cinq degrés symbolisant le mont Meru, demeure de tous les dieux du panthéon brahmanique. La tour centrale atteint 42 m. de hauteur. À l'inverse de la plupart des temples khmers, Angkor Vat ouvre vers l'Ouest, la direction du soleil couchant et de la mort; cette particularité a conduit certains spécialistes à accorder un caractère funéraire au monument. Cette orientation, toutefois, pourrait aussi correspondre au fait que le temple est consacré à Vishnu, un dieu traditionnellement associé à cette direction cardinale.

L'extraordinaire architecture d'Angkor Vat est magnifiée par les bas-reliefs décorant le monument. Sans compter les quelque 2000 nymphes célestes ou apsaras ciselées sur les murs et les nombreuses scènes sculptées sur les frontons et les linteaux, la gloire d'Angkor Vat réside dans les bas-reliefs narratifs de la galerie-enceinte du premier gradin de la pyramide. Sous une voûte en encorbellement soutenue par un mur, vers l'intérieur, et des piliers, vers l'extérieur, se déploient huit grands panneaux présentant les batailles finales des épopées du *Mahabharata* (bataille du Kurukshetra) et du *Ramayana* (bataille de Lanka), le jugement des morts par Yama qui indique aux défunts le chemin à suivre selon les mérites de chacun, vers les cieux ou vers les enfers, le barattage de l'Océan de lait, mais aussi une scène historique dans laquelle les troupes de Suryavarman II défilent devant le roi. La finesse est le maître mot du style d'Angkor Vat qui couvre les trois premiers quarts du 12ème siècle. La perfection de traitement des bas-reliefs marque naturellement la statuaire en pierre (#49, 50, 52, 54, 55) et, plus encore, les images en bronze, lesquelles présentent le style dans ce qu'il a de meilleur (#51, 53, 56-60).

Même si certaines d'entre elles ne furent pas victorieuses, notamment contre le Dai Viet et le Champa, Suryavarman II mena diverses campagnes militaires qui lui permirent d'agrandir son empire. La dernière inscription mentionnant le monarque date de 1145, mais il est possible que son règne ait duré jusqu'en 1150 lorsque son successeur, son cousin Dharanindravarman II, dont la religion personnelle était le bouddhisme, occupe le trône pour une brève période. Les données épigraphiques incertaines pour la période allant de 1145 à 1180 indiquent que Dharanindravarman II, le père du futur Jayavarman VII, fut remplacé à la tête de l'empire par Yashovarman II, un de ses parents éloignés. En 1165, ce souverain est déposé par un usurpateur, Tribhuvanadityavarman, qui allait lui-même être tué lors de l'invasion d'Angkor par les Cham en 1177.

6. Jayavarman VII, Angkor Thom et le Bayon

Durant les quatre années qui suivirent l'invasion d'Angkor par les Cham, un prince khmer, le futur Jayavarman VII, allait rassembler les forces vives du pays pour redresser une situation particulièrement difficile, chasser l'envahisseur et reconquérir la capitale. Bouddhiste comme son père Dharanindravarman II, Jayavarman avait plus de cinquante ans lorsqu'il accéda au trône en 1181. Sous son règne, alors que le bouddhisme Mahayana devenait religion d'État, les frontières de l'empire furent portées plus loin que jamais auparavant, atteignant la frontière de l'actuel Myanmar, à l'Ouest, la région de Vientiane au Laos, au Nord, le Champa – qui fut l'objet de conquêtes à partir de 1190 – à l'Est, et la mer, au Sud.

Jayavarman VII dota sa capitale, Angkor Thom, d'une enceinte carrée de 3 km de côté, couvrant une superficie de 900 hectares. Les murs, ceints de douves de 120 m de large, atteignent 8 m de haut; cinq portes monumentales couronnées de visages colossaux et précédées de chaussées bordées de géants soutenant le corps d'un naga polycéphale donnent accès à la ville. Des chaussées comparables existent aussi aux entrées du temple de Preah Khan. Au centre d'Angkor Thom se dresse le Bayon, célèbre pour ses 49 tours ornées de visages scrutant intensément l'espace dans les quatre directions cardinales. Ce temple possède aussi de magnifiques bas-reliefs narratifs riches en informations sur la mythologie, l'histoire et la vie quotidienne à Angkor. Le Bayon est un grand sanctuaire bouddhique, mais, à l'instar des temples aux ancêtres de Ta Prohm et Preah Khan, certains sanctuaires étaient consacrés à des divinités relevant d'autres religions, particulièrement l'hindouisme.

Les inscriptions du règne de Jayavarman VII sont nombreuses et riches d'informations, notamment celles de Ta Prohm (1186) et Preah Khan (1191). On sait ainsi que 12 640 personnes étaient attachées au premier de ces deux complexes, cependant que 97 840 autres travaillaient pour le second. Ces chiffres viennent étayer l'opinion selon laquelle Angkor aurait été la plus grande de toutes les villes de l'ère préindustrielle. L'époque de Jayavarman VII fut caractérisée par une véritable frénésie architecturale avec l'édification de grands temples comme Banteay Kdei ou Banteay Chmar, les adjonctions importantes faites au Preah Khan de Kompong Svay (actuel Bakan), mais aussi les nombreux ponts, hôpitaux et gîtes d'étape aménagés partout dans l'empire, particulièrement le long des routes dont la plus importante reliait Phimai, au-delà des Dangrek, à Angkor.

Des portraits sculptés du roi et de sa première épouse, la reine Jayarajadevi, furent commandités par la seconde épouse du monarque, la propre sœur aînée de Jayarajadevi, pour être placés dans les plus grands sanctuaires de l'empire. Ces œuvres incarnent l'idéal de sérénité et l'humanisme du style du Bayon qui nous a laissé, par ailleurs, nombre de représentations du bodhisattva de la compassion, Lokeshvara, de la déesse de la connaissance suprême, Prajñaparamita, et du Buddha lui-même, souvent figuré assis sur un naga censé le protéger (#61-63, 73). De magnifiques bronzes ont également été réalisés à cette époque (#64-72, 74).

Le règne fut marqué par diverses révoltes. Les difficultés économiques qu'elles ont engendré, de même que le coût du nombre exorbitant de grands projets architecturaux, ont peut-être contribué à un certain affaiblissement de l'empire. Dès la fin du 13ème siècle et au cours du 14ème, la puissance naissante du Siam commença à menacer la sécurité et l'intégrité du Cambodge qui n'allait plus pouvoir maintenir la prééminence dont il jouissait depuis le 10ème siècle. La date de la mort de Jayavarman VII est inconnue. Elle pourrait se situer vers 1218, alors qu'il était âgé de plus de quatre-vingts ans.

7. Le Cambodge après Angkor

On sait peu de chose sur le roi bouddhiste Indravarman II (1218?-43), le successeur de Jayavarman VII: la seule donnée sûre se rapporte à son décès, survenu en 1243. Sous Jayavarman VIII (1243?-95), le brahmanisme retrouva son rang prééminent et le règne fut témoin d'une période d'iconoclasme au cours de laquelle d'innombrables images du Buddha furent bûchées dans les monuments de Jayavarman VII. On rattache à cette période mal connue divers temples comme Preah Palilay, les Preah Pithu, Mangalartha et peut-être aussi la célèbre statue assise dans l'attitude du délassement royal dite du roi lépreux (#76), en fait une représentation de Yama, le juge des morts.

Sous Indravarman III (1295-1307), le royaume thaï de Sukhothaï se livra à de nombreuses incursions militaires en territoire khmer. Malgré cela, la description détaillée du voyageur chinois Zhou Daguan, qui visita Angkor en 1296-97, révèle un royaume encore puissant et opulent. S'il semble que l'attaque d'Angkor par les Thaï du royaume d'Ayutthaya en 1431 ait poussé la cour à abandonner la capitale et à s'établir dans la région de Phnom-Penh, des raisons économiques ont aussi pu jouer leur rôle dans ce changement important. Le désir d'augmenter les possibilités offertes par un accès plus simple et plus rapide à la mer par le delta du Mékong a pu participer de ce déplacement, autant que le désir de se protéger d'un voisin trop ambitieux. Douze missions furent envoyées en Chine entre 1371 et 1419, témoignage éloquent d'un certain développement des liens commerciaux qui unissaient le Cambodge à l'Empire du milieu à cette époque.

À partir du 14ème siècle, l'impact grandissant du bouddhisme Theravada et l'abandon de la pierre pour le bois dans la statuaire (#80) accompagnent l'influence cinghalaise qui marque à cette époque l'ensemble des arts du sud-est asiatique. Des statues monumentales du Buddha retrouvées à Angkor Vat (#79), qui avait été transformé en temple bouddhique, pourraient remonter aux règnes d'Ang Chan (1516-66) et de ses successeurs, qui revinrent s'établir temporairement à Angkor.

Avec des fortunes diverses, la royauté khmère s'est maintenue au Cambodge jusqu'à nos jours. La région d'Angkor, qui était passée sous domination thaï, ne revint au Cambodge qu'en 1907, au terme d'un accord négocié par les Français. La période du protectorat ouvre donc les Occidentaux aux merveilles du Cambodge et d'Angkor avec les récits de voyage d'Henri Mouhot (1858-61) ou les dessins de Louis Delaporte (1866-68). En 1898, la création de l'École française d'Extrême-Orient allait inaugurer une période intense de recherche, de restauration et d'étude principalement menées par les Français, relayés aujourd'hui par les chercheurs de nombreux pays.

Les fruits du désir de protection et de mise en valeur du riche patrimoine khmer peuvent aujourd'hui être pleinement appréciés dans les collections du Musée National du Cambodge qui, outre les extraordinaires œuvres en pierre, bronze et bois présentées dans cet ouvrage, abrite aussi de belles collections de céramiques, peintures et objets cérémoniels que nous n'avons pas souhaité inclure dans le présent volume. Les céramiques, dont beaucoup remontent aux 11ème et 12ème siècles, présentent des couvertes brunes caractéristiques; leurs formes sont classiques ou parfois fantasques, notamment dans les pièces zoomorphes. Les peintures, essentiellement datables des 19ème et 20ème siècles, traitent de sujets bouddhiques. Les objets rituels associés aux rites de passage démontrent, quant à eux, la constance dans l'excellence des traditions artisanales khmères, qu'il s'agisse du travail du bois, du bronze ou des métaux précieux.

សង្ខេបប្រវត្តិសាស្ត្រកម្ពុជា

១. ពពួករដ្ឋខ្មែរដែលចាស់ជាងគេ

ឯកសារចាស់បំផុតទាក់ទងនឹងកម្ពុជាដែលយើងស្គាល់ គឺជាសំណេរកត់ត្រារបស់ចិននៅគ.ស.ទី៣។ យើងពុំដឹងថា ខ្មែរហៅប្រទេសខ្លួនថាដូចម្ដេចទេ ប៉ុន្តែចិនហៅថា "ហ្វូណាន់ "។ ចិនពោលថា ពេលនោះគេស្គាល់និងនិយមព្រហ្មញ្ញសាសនា ឬព្រះពុទ្ធសាសនាដែលមានប្រភពមកពីឥណ្ឌាហើយ។ គេប្រទះឃើញបុរាណវត្ថុ ដែលក្នុងនោះមានកាក់ជាលោហធាតុ បញ្ជាក់ថាកំពង់ផែហ្វូណាន់ ពោលគឺ Oc-Eo ជាចំណតដ៏សំខាន់មួយសម្រាប់ពាណិជ្ជកម្មរវាងបស្ចិមប្រទេសនិងចិន។ រាជធានីពេលនោះប្រហែលជានៅប៉ែកខាងត្បូងភ្នំពេញសព្វថ្ងៃ ត្រង់ម្ដុំអង្គរបុរី។ ទីនោះគេប្រទះឃើញបដិមាច្រើន ដែលជាព្រះពុទ្ធរូបផង ជារូបទេពសាសនាព្រាហ្មណ៍ផង។ ភាគច្រើនបំផុតជាបដិមាដែលនៅក្នុងនិកាយព្រះនារាយណ៍ ស្ថាបនានៅស.វ.ទី៧ (រូបលេខ២, ៣, ៤) ហើយដែលគេរាប់ថានៅក្នុងរចនាបថភ្នំដា (យកតាមឈ្មោះភ្នំមួយនៅអង្គរបុរី)។ អ្វីៗនៅតំបន់នេះខូចខាតស្ទើរតែទាំងអស់ លើកលែងតែកូនប្រាសាទមួយឈ្មោះអាស្រម មហាឫសី។ .

នៅរវាងដើមស.វ.ទី៧ រាជ្យអំណាចប្ដូរទៅខាងជើង ហើយចិនហៅនគរនោះថា "ចេនឡា "។ នៅឯណេះក៏ដូចគ្នា ដែរ យើងពុំដឹងថាខ្មែរហៅប្រទេសខ្លួនឯងថាដូចម្ដេចទេ។ មណ្ឌលធំនៅទីនោះមានឈ្មោះថា "ឦសានបុរ" (គឺសម្បូណ៌ព្រៃគុកនាបច្ចុប្បន្ននេះ) ដែលរៀបចំឡើងដោយព្រះបាទឦសានវរ្ម័នទី១។ ព្រះរាជានេះជាប់ខ្សែស្រឡាយនឹងហ្វូណាន់ក៏ពិតមែន ប៉ុន្តែព្រះអង្គយាងមកពីតំបន់ភ្នំដងរែកទៅវិញទេ។ ក្រុងនោះមានប្រាសាទព្រាហ្មណ៍ជាងមួយរយ ក្នុងនោះមួយចំនួននៅល្អនៅឡើយ។ ប្រាសាទទាំងនោះមានបីក្រុមសាងក្នុងរយៈពេលបីខុសគ្នា ហើយសុទ្ធសឹងជាគម្រូនៃប្រាសាទខ្មែរជំនាន់ក្រោយៗមកទៀតផង។ ប្រាសាទទោលនានាមានរូបរាងប្រហែលគ្នានឹងប្រាសាទដែលនៅឥណ្ឌាគេហៅថា "សិខរ " គឺសាងពីឥដ្ឋ ហើយប្រើថ្មភក់សម្រាប់ក្របទ្វារ, សសរ, ផ្ដែរ ដែលសុទ្ធសឹងតែមានចម្លាក់រចនា។ ប្លង់ប្រាសាទភាគច្រើនរាងបួនជ្រុងស្មើ ឬបួនជ្រុងទ្រវែង ប៉ុន្តែមានខ្លះរាងប្រាំបីជ្រុង រីឯជញ្ជាំងក្រៅមានឆ្លាក់រូបមន្ទីរផ្សេងៗ ដែលនៅក្នុងវាំង ព្រមទាំងអ្នករស់នៅជាមួយនោះផង។ មានសិលាចារឹកច្រើនដែលធ្វើឱ្យយើងមានពត៌មានខ្លះពីព្រះរាជា ហើយប្រាសាទតែងមានតម្កល់បដិមា (លេខ១១, ១២)។ ព្រះរាជាដែលចុះពូជពង្សពីភូមិភាគខាងជើង ស្នងរាជ្យតៗគ្នាជាលំដាប់មក ហើយពង្រីករាជ្យអំណាចធំឡើងៗ។ នៅរវាងដើមស.វ.ទី៨ព្រះនាងជ័យទេវីប្រហែលជាមកតាំងទីនៅទីកដីមួយ ដែលក្រោយមកក្លាយទៅជារាជធានី អង្គរ ពុំឆ្ងាយប៉ុន្មានពីទន្លេសាប។

នៅស.វ.ទី៨នោះ មានរាជ្យអំណាចមួយទៀតនៅភូមិភាគខាងកើត កៀកនឹងទន្លេមេគុង ហៅថា "សម្ភុបុរ " (គឺម្ដុំ "សម្បូណ៌ " ក្នុងខេត្តក្រចេះសព្វថ្ងៃ)។ ក្នុងប្រវត្តិទីនេះ មានស្ដេចបីអង្គដែលជារាជនី ឯតំបន់នោះក៏សម្បូណ៌ទៅដោយបដិមាទេពស្រី (លេខ១៣, ១៤)។ បុរីនៃហ្វូណាន់, បុរីនានាដែលសាងឡើងដោយខ្មែរ ស្រឡាយព្រះបាទឦសានវរ្ម័នព្រមទាំងសម្ភុបុរ សុទ្ធសឹងតែរៀបចំឡើងនៅជិតផ្លូវទឹក ពោលគឺអាយុជីវិតនៃតំបន់មូសុងដែលភ្លៀងមានតែមួយរដូវក្នុងមួយឆ្នាំ។ ក្នុងប្រវត្តិសាស្ត្រខ្មែរ ទឹកមានសារសំខាន់ក្នុងការរៀបចំដែនដីផង និងក្នុងតួនាទីជានិមិត្តរូបផង។ តាំងពីដើមមក ខ្មែរបុរាណប៉ិនប្រសប់ខ្លាំងណាស់ក្នុងបច្ចេកទេសប្រើប្រាស់ទឹក។

រាជ្យអំណាចខ្មែរប្រហែលជារាតទីទៅផ្នែកខាងជើងភ្នំដងរែក (សព្វថ្ងៃនេះជាភាគឦសាននៃប្រទេសថៃឡង់ដ៏) តាំងពីស.វ.ទី៨មកម្ល៉េះ។ នេះគឺជាលទ្ធផលនៃការរុករកធ្វើជំនួញខ្លះៗជាមួយប្រទេសដែលនៅឆ្ងាយៗ។ វត្ថុបុរាណខ្មែរធ្វើអំពីសម្រិតដែលល្បីៗមួយចំនួន (សម្បូណ៌ជាងគេគឺរូបព្រះពោធិសត្វ) គឺប្រទះឃើញនៅខេត្តបុរីរម្យ នាប្រទេសថៃឡង់ដ៏ (លេខ២៥)។ មានសិលាចារឹកតិចតួចណាស់ដែលចារនៅចុងស.វ.ទី៨ ជាហេតុឱ្យប្រវត្តិសាស្ត្រនៅសតវត្សនោះមានភាពស្រពិចស្រពិល។ តែគេប្រទះឃើញសិលាចារឹកមួយ ដែលឱ្យកាលបរិច្ឆេទត្រូវនឹងគ.ស.៧៧០ ហើយដែលទាក់ទងនឹងព្រះបាទជ័យវរ្ម័នទី២ ពោលគឺអ្នកដែលនឹងទៅបើកឆាកសម័យអង្គរ។

២. សតវត្សទី៩និងការចេញដំណើរនៃសម័យអង្គរ

យោងតាមសិលាចារឹកស្ដុកកក់ធំ ព្រះបាទជ័យវរ្ម័នទី២ (រវាង៨០២_៨៣០) ទទួលអភិសេកជាស្ដេចចក្រពត្តិនៅគ.ស.៨០២។ ពិធីនោះធ្វើឡើងនៅលើភ្នំគូលែន (ហៅថាមហេន្ទ្របព៌ត ពោលគឺភ្នំជាលំនៅនៃព្រះឥន្ទ្រ) ដោយភ្ជាប់ទៅការបូជា "កម្រតេងជគតតរាជ " (ជាសំស្ក្រឹតហៅថា "ទេវរាជ") ផង។ គេពុំច្បាស់ថាពិធីនេះធ្វើឡើងសំដៅថាព្រះរាជាមានលក្ខណៈជាទេពឬយ៉ាងណាទេ គ្រាន់តែយល់ថាជាការទទួលស្គាល់ដល់រាជ្យអំណាចដែលទុកជាទីសក្ការៈ។ ប្រាសាទដែលសាងនៅស.វ.ទី៩ មួយចំនួនស្ថិតនៅលើភ្នំគូលែន។ ភាគច្រើនជាប្រាសាទទោល, ធ្វើពីឥដ្ឋ ប៉ុន្តែខ្លះជាក្រុមប្រាសាទបី, ទាំងអស់នោះសុទ្ធតែមានជាន់បញ្ឈាត ព្រមទាំងដំបូលស្តួចទៅលើ ដោយគេញែកឥដ្ឋឱ្យផុតពីគ្នាបន្តិចម្ដងៗ។ ក្របទ្វារ, ទ្វារបញ្ឆោត, ផ្ដែរ និងសសរ តែងធ្វើអំពីថ្មភក់។ នៅភ្នំគូលែននេះគេប្រទះឃើញបដិមាព្រះនារាយណ៍ជាច្រើន (លេខ២៧)។ រូបទាំងនោះប្ដូរផ្លាស់ឥរិយាបថទៅរកភាពទ្រឹង, ត្រង់ខ្លួនពីលើដល់ក្រោម ពុំដូចនៅភ្នំដា ឬសម្បូណ៌ព្រៃគុក ដែលបដិមាមានភាពស្រឡូន បត់បែនដូចមនុស្សទៀតឡើយ។

ព្រះបាទជ័យវរ្ម័នទី២ប្ដូររាជធានីញឹកញាប់, មានការតាំងទីពីរលើកនៅហរិហរាល័យ (សព្វថ្ងៃគឺតំបន់រលួស) ដែលប្រហែលជារាជធានីនៃព្រះបាទជ័យវរ្ម័នទី៣បន្ទាប់ពីនោះមកដែរ។ តំបន់នោះអាចនឹងមានមកមុននោះទៅទៀត ហើយប្រហែលជាព្រះនាងជ័យទេវី (៦៨០/៨១_ ៧១៣) គង់នៅទីនោះផងក៏ពុំដឹង ព្រោះគេប្រទះឃើញសិលាចារឹកមួយពីជំនាន់នោះនៅប្រាសាទអកយំ។ ព្រះបាទឥន្ទ្រវរ្ម័ន (៨៧៧_៨៨៩) ដែលត្រូវជាក្មួយនៃព្រះបាទជ័យវរ្ម័នទី៣ ក៏គង់នៅទីនោះដែរ។ ព្រះអង្គសាងប្រាសាទព្រះគោ ប្រកបដោយតួប៉មខនៅលើខឿនជាមួយគ្នា ដើម្បីឧទ្ទិសទៅដល់បុព្វការីជននៃព្រះអង្គទាំងស្រីទាំងប្រុស ហើយដែលភ្ជាប់ខ្លួនទៅនឹងទេពផង។ នេះឆ្លុះបញ្ចាំងឱ្យឃើញពីសារៈសំខាន់នៃការគោរពបូជាដូនតា ដែលខ្មែរតែងតែមានមកដូចជាសព្វថ្ងៃគេនៅតែគោរពអ្នកតាដែរ។

បាគងជាប្រាសាទដែលព្រះបាទឥន្ទ្រវរ្ម័នសាងសម្រាប់ការបូជាទូទៅ។ ប្រាសាទនេះកម្ពស់លើស៣០ម. មាន៥ថ្នាក់ ព្រមទាំងប្រាសាទជាបរិវារនិងក្លោងទ្វារនៅជុំវិញនោះផង។ ប្រាសាទដែលមានរាងពីរ៉ាមីត ពីមុនមកនោះមានអកយំ (ស.វ.ទី៨) និងគ្រឹះអារាមរោងចិន នៅលើភ្នំគូលែន ប៉ុន្តែដែលធំស្កប់ស្កែងដំបូង គឺបាគងនេះឯងហើយ មិនតែប៉ុណ្ណោះផ្ដល់ជាគំរូដល់ប្រាសាទក្រោយៗមកទៀត។ ប្រាសាទភ្នំរបៀបនេះគឺជាលោកទាំងមូលដែលបង្រួមមកនៅខ្នាតតូច (ហៅថាសុខុមលោកក៏បាន) ហើយតំណាងដោយភ្នំព្រះសុមេរុ ដែលជាលំនៅនៃទេពក្នុងសាសនាព្រាហ្មណ៍។ បដិមាដែលប្រទះឃើញនៅព្រះគោ និងនៅបាគង (លេខ២៨, ២៩) មានរាងត្រង់, បញ្ចេញអនុភាព, ហាក់ដូចជាឆ្លុះបញ្ចាំងពីរាជ្យ អំណាចដែលកាន់តែរីកធំទៅៗ។ ក្រៅពីនេះព្រះបាទឥន្ទ្រវរ្ម័នកសាងឥន្ទ្រតដាក ពោលគឺបារាយ ដែលមានទ្រង់ទ្រាយធំ ទីមួយ (សព្វថ្ងៃកកស្ទះអស់ ហើយ) ក្នុងចំណោមបារាយផ្សេងៗទៀតដែលខ្មែរសាងដោយប៉ិនប្រសប់ក្រៃលែង។

ព្រះបាទយសោវរ្ម័នទី១ (៨៨៩_ដើមស.វ.ទី១០) សោយរាជ្យបន្តពីព្រះបាទឥន្ទ្រវរ្ម័នដែលជាព្រះបិតា។ នៅចុងស.វ.ទី៩ ព្រះអង្គសាងប្រាសាទលលៃដែលមានប៉មបួន នៅកណ្ដាលឥន្ទ្រតដាកនោះ ហើយដែលឧទ្ទិសទៅបុព្វការីជន ដូចប្រាសាទព្រះគោដែរ។ នៅវាំងគ.ស.៩០០ ព្រះរាជាដូររាជធានីមកកន្លែងមួយទៀត ហើយឱ្យឈ្មោះថា "យសោធរ" (គឺរាជធានីអង្គរ)។ ព្រះអង្គសាងប្រាសាទមួយដោយចាំងថ្មលើភ្នំបាខែងជាពីរ៉ាមីត។ រីឯរចនាបថសិល្បៈនៅ១/៤ខាងដើមស.វ.ទី ១០នោះ ក៏ឈ្មោះថាបាខែងដូច្នោះ។

៣. សតវត្សទី១០ និងរចនាសម្ព័ន្ធរដ្ឋបាលខ្មែរដែលកាន់តែដុះដាលទៅ

មិនត្រឹមតែសាងភ្នំបាខែងប៉ុណ្ណោះទេ, នៅចុងរាជ្យព្រះអង្គ, ព្រះបាទយសោវរ្ម័នទី១សាងជូរប្រាសាទបីនៅពីរកន្លែងទៀត គឺនៅភ្នំបូកនិងភ្នំក្រោម ព្រមទាំងសាងបារាយមួយដែលមានទំហំ ៧គ.ម. × ២គ.ម. (សព្វថ្ងៃរីងស្ងួតអស់ហើយ, ហៅថាថ្នល់បារាយ)។

ទីតាំងនៃសិលាចារឹកជំនាន់នោះឱ្យយើងដឹងថា រាជ្យអំណាចព្រះអង្គវាតទីទៅដល់ភាគឥសាននៃប្រទេសថៃឡង់ដ៏សព្វថ្ងៃ ព្រមទាំងតំបន់វត្តភូនៃប្រទេសលាវបច្ចុប្បន្នផង។ ចម្លាក់លើផ្ទាំងថ្ម ឬជាបិមាក្ដី កាន់តែបង្ហាញភាពទ្រឹងត្រង់ស្អក តែប្រកបដោយក្បូរក្បាច់រចនាលម្អិត (រូបលេខ៣០)។

ព្រះរាជបុត្រនៃព្រះរាជានេះ ពោលគឺព្រះបាទហសិវរ្ម័នទី១ ប្រហែលជាសោយរាជ្យបន្តនៅឆ្នាំ៩១២។ ថ្វីត្បិតតែព្រះអង្គពុំបានសាងប្រាសាទអ្វីមួយធំធេង តែព្រះអង្គបានផ្ដើមសាងប្រាសាទបក្សីចាំក្រុង (ដែលក្រោយមកព្រះបាទរាជេន្ទ្រវរ្ម័នសាងបញ្ចប់នៅឆ្នាំ៩៤៨)។ សិលាចារឹកមួយឱ្យដឹងថាប្រាសាទនេះឧទ្ទិសទៅដល់ព្រះមាតាបិតាព្រះអង្គ។ ក្រោមរាជ្យនេះ គេសាងប្រាសាទក្រវ៉ាន់ដែលមានតួប៉ម៥ (ឆ្នាំ៩២១) ដើម្បីឧទ្ទិសទៅព្រះនារាយណ៍។ សិលាចារឹកមួយទៀតឱ្យដឹងថា ព្រះអនុជព្រះអង្គ ព្រះនាមឦសានវរ្ម័នទី២ ឡើងសោយរាជ្យនៅឆ្នាំ៩២៥។ តែរាជ្យនេះខ្លីទេ គឺចប់នៅវាំងឆ្នាំ៩២៨។

ក្នុងរយៈពេលដែលព្រះបាទហសិវរ្ម័នទី១និងឦសានវរ្ម័នទី២សោយរាជ្យនៅអង្គរនោះ ក្សត្រជាឪពុកមាមួយអង្គ ពោលគឺបងថ្លៃនៃព្រះបាទយសោវរ្ម័ន មិនទទួលស្គាល់រាជ្យនោះឡើយ។ នៅឆ្នាំ៩២១ ក្សត្រនោះប្រកាសខ្លួនជាស្ដេចព្រះនាម ជ័យវរ្ម័នទី៤ ហើយតាំងទីនៅ "ចោកគគ្យ៉រ" ចម្ងាយប្រមាណ១០០គ.ម. ខាងឦសានអង្គរ។ ឈ្មោះទីនោះក្លាយមកជា "កោះកេរ្ដិ៍" ហើយប្រកបទៅដោយប្រាសាទរាប់រយ ក្នុងនោះមានមួយជាប្រាសាទភ្នំស្ពឹមស្ពៃ ហៅថាប្រាសាទធំ។ តួប៉មនិងសំណង់លើពីរ៉ាមីតដែលមាន៥ថ្នាក់ ហើយដែលមានកម្ពស់ប្រមាណ៦០ម.នោះ មិនគង់វង្សទៀតទេ ដោយសារសាងពីវត្ថុធាតុពុំមែនជាថ្ម។ នៅកោះកេរ្ដិ៍ អ្វីៗក៏សុទ្ធតែធ្វើឡើងមានទំហំធំជាងសព្វដង (រូបលេខ៣១_៣៤)។ ពេលដែលព្រះបាទឦសានវរ្ម័នទី២សុគតនៅឆ្នាំ៩២៨ ព្រះបាទជ័យវរ្ម័នទី៤សោយរាជ្យតែមួយអង្គឯងរហូតដល់ពេលសុគតនៅឆ្នាំ៩៤២។ ព្រះបាទហសិវរ្ម័នទី២ ដែលជាព្រះរាជបុត្រ សោយរាជ្យបានតែមួយភ្លែត ពោលគឺដល់ឆ្នាំ៩៤៤។ ពេលនោះព្រះបាទរាជេន្ទ្រវរ្ម័ន ដែលត្រូវជាជីដូនមួយ ឡើងគ្រងរាជ្យលើអាណាចក្រខ្មែរទាំងមូល។

ព្រះបាទរាជេន្ទ្រវរ្ម័ន (៩៤៤_៩៦៨) នាំរាជធានីមកអង្គរវិញ ហើយទុកឈ្មោះដដែលថា យសោធរ។ ព្រះអង្គឧទ្ទិសប្រាសាទមេបុណ្យដែលសាងនៅឆ្នាំ៩៥៣ ចំកណ្ដាលបារាយខាងកើត ទៅដល់បុព្វការីជន ហើយសាងប្រាសាទប្រែរូបនៅឆ្នាំ៩៦១សម្រាប់ការបូជាទូទៅ។ ទាំងពីរនោះសុទ្ធសឹងជាប្រាសាទភ្នំ ដែលប្រកបទៅដោយចម្លាក់រចនាវិចិត្រនៅលើផ្ដែរនិងសសរ។ រចនាបថហៅថាប្រែរូបនោះ (លេខ៣៥,៣៦) ស្ថិតនៅក្នុងចំណោមសំណង់ដែលត្រចះត្រចង់បំផុតនៃសិល្បៈ ខ្មែរ។

រាជ្យព្រះបាទរាជេន្ទ្រវរ្ម័ននោះ មានទទួលការគំរាមកំហែងជាច្រើនដងពីចាម្ប (នគរនោះសព្វថ្ងៃជាវៀតណាមភាគកណ្ដាល) ដែលធ្លាប់ប្រទូស្ដរាយនឹងខ្មែររាប់សតវត្ស។ បាតជុំ (៩៦០) ដែលជាប្រាសាទពុទ្ធសាសនា និងបន្ទាយស្រី (៩៦៧_៦៨) ដែលជាប្រាសាទព្រហ្មញ្ញសាសនា គួរឱ្យកត់សម្គាល់ ដោយសារជាសំណង់សាសនារបស់មន្ត្រីធំៗ ពោលគឺពុំមែនជារបស់ព្រះរាជា។ បន្ទាយស្រី គេចាត់ទុកថាជារ័ត្នមួយនៃស្ថាបត្យកម្មខ្មែរ។ អ្នកសាងជាព្រះគ្រូនៃព្រះរាជបុត្រព្រះរាជា ដែលចាប់ផ្ដើមសាងនៅចុងរាជ្យព្រះបាទរាជេន្ទ្រវរ្ម័ន។ បដិមានិងចម្លាក់លើផ្ទាំងថ្មទាំងអម្បាលម៉ានបង្ហាញថាជាវិចិត្រកម្មដ៏ឥតខ្ចោះ (លេខ៣៧_៣៩)។

ព្រះបាទជ័យវរ្ម័នទី៥គ្រងរាជ្យតពីបិតានៅឆ្នាំ៩៦៨។ រាជ្យនោះវែង ត្បិតបន្តមកដល់ឆ្នាំ១០០០ ឬ១០០១ ហើយគ្មានវិជើបវិជួលអ្វីឡើយ ក្រៅពីជម្លោះខ្លះៗជាមួយចាម្ប។ ព្រះអង្គឥតមានសាងប្រាសាទភ្នំ ឬអ្វីធំដុំឡើយ ប៉ុន្តែគេយល់ថាប្រហែលជាព្រះអង្គជាអ្នកផ្ដើមសាងព្រះរាជវាំង ព្រមទាំងប្រាសាទភិមានអាកាសដែលនៅក្នុងនោះ។

៤_ ការរីកសាយនៃអាណាចក្រខ្មែរនៅស.វ.ទី១១

គេដឹងដោយស្រពិចស្រពិលខ្លាំងណាស់អំពីការផ្លាស់ប្ដូររាជ្យពីព្រះបាទជ័យវរ្ម័នទី៥ទៅព្រះបាទឧទ័យាទិត្យវរ្ម័នទី១ (ឆ្នាំ១០០១_០២) ហើយបន្ទាប់មកព្រះបាទជ័យវីរវរ្ម័ន (ឆ្នាំ១០០២_១០១០)។ រីឯនរណាជាអ្នកសាងប្រាសាទកែវ ក៏មិនច្បាស់ដែរ។ ប្រាសាទដែលមានកម្ពស់២២ម.នេះ មាន៥ថ្នាក់ ខាងលើបង្អស់មានប៉ម៥ ហើយនៅក្នុងរចនាបថឃ្លាំង (លេខ៤៤)។ ឯភិមានអាកាសក៏នៅក្នុងរចនាបថនោះដែរ។ "ឃ្លាំង" ជាឈ្មោះនៃសំណង់ពីរដែលគេពុំដឹងថាមានតួនាទីជាអ្វី ហើយដែលស្ថិតនៅខាងកើតព្រះរាជវាំង។ នៅប្រាសាទកែវនិងភិមានអាកាស យើងចាប់ផ្ដើមឃើញមានថែវតាមថ្នាក់ផ្សេងៗ។ នេះជាគំរូដែលក្រោយមកគេធ្វើតាមនៅអង្គរវត្តនិងនៅបាយ័ន្ត សម្រាប់មនុស្សដើរជុំវិញមើលថែវចម្លាក់។

ក្នុងទសវត្សដំបូងនៃស.វ.ទី១១នោះ យើងមានពត៌មានស្ដួចស្ដើងណាស់។ ពេលដែលព្រះបាទជ័យវីរវរ្ម័ននៅគ្រងរាជ្យ ក្សត្រមួយអង្គនៅតំបន់ខាងកើត, ពោលគឺអនាគតព្រះបាទសូរ្យវរ្ម័នទី១, ទាមទារយករាជ្យអំណាចនោះពីឆ្នាំ១០០២ដល់១០១០។ ឃើញថាមានរាជ្យអំណាចពីរ ប៉ុន្តែនៅឆ្នាំ១០១១មានសិលាចារឹកកម្ពស់៥ម. ចារនៅលើកោងទ្វារព្រះរាជវាំង ដែលអះអាងថាព្រះបាទសូរ្យវរ្ម័នទី១សោយរាជ្យនៅឆ្នាំ១០០២។ ទ្វារនិងកំពែងព្រះរាជវាំងសុទ្ធសឹងសាងនៅជំនាន់នោះ ប្រហែលក្នុងគោលបំណងពង្រឹងសន្តិសុខ។ ព្រះបាទសូរ្យវរ្ម័នមិនចុះពូជពង្សត្រង់ពីរាជ្យមុនទេ តែជាប់ខ្សែស្រឡាយខាងព្រះមាតានៃព្រះបាទឥន្ទ្រវរ្ម័នទី១។

នៅក្នុងរាជ្យដ៏វែងសុខសាន្តនេះ (រហូតដល់ឆ្នាំ១០៤៩) ព្រះបាទសូរ្យវរ្ម័នទី១ពុំមានសាងប្រាសាទភ្នំទេ ប៉ុន្តែបានសាងប្រាសាទធំៗច្រើន ដើម្បីតម្កល់លិង្គមាស ហើយប្រាសាទទាំងនេះជាទីបញ្ជាក់សីមាខ័ណ្ឌនៃអាណាចក្រផង។ នៅខាងលិច ព្រះអង្គសាងវត្តឯក និងវត្តបាសែត។ នៅខាងជើង, នៅលើជួរភ្នំដងរែក ព្រះអង្គសាងប្រាសាទព្រះវិហារ។ បាកាណ (អ្នកស្រាវជ្រាវធ្លាប់ហៅថាព្រះខ័ននៃកំពង់ស្វាយ) ជាប្រាសាទដែលមានកំពែងធំបង្អស់មកទល់ពេលនេះ ហើយសាងឡើងនៅខាងឦសាន។ រីឯភ្នំជីសូរ្យសាងនៅខាងត្បូង។ នៅខាងចុងរាជ្យនោះ ព្រមទាំងក្នុងរាជ្យបន្ទាប់មក មានចម្លាក់រូបលិង្គ ព្រមទាំងរូបព្រះនារាយណ៍ផ្ទំ

រាប់ពុំអស់ដែលសាងឡើងតាមបាតស្ទឹងនិងតាមគែមស្ទឹងឫស្សី ពោលគឺដៃមួយនៃស្ទឹងសៀមរាប, ត្រង់កន្លែង "ក្បាលស្ពាន"។

នៅខាងលិចមានបារាយយ៉ាងធំមួយ (៨គ.ម.×២គ.ម.) ដែលពុំច្បាស់ថាសាងដោយព្រះបាទសូរ្យវរ្ម័នទី១ ឬអ្នកស្នងរាជ្យព្រះអង្គ ពោលគឺព្រះបាទឧទ័យាទិត្យវរ្ម័នទី២ (១០៥០_១០៦៦)ឡើយ។ រវាងឆ្នាំ១០៦០ ព្រះរាជាខាងក្រោយនេះ ដែលជាប់ខ្សែស្រឡាយខាងព្រះជាយារបស់ព្រះបាទសូរ្យវរ្ម័នទី១ សាងបាភួនដែលជាប្រាសាទភ្នំមួយធំធេងណាស់នៅកម្ពុជា។ ឈ្មោះប្រាសាទនេះក្លាយទៅជាឈ្មោះរចនាបថមួយនៅស.វ.ទី១១ ដែលចម្លាក់ផ្សេងៗចម្លងតាមធម្មជាតិ (លេខ៤០_៤៣, ៤៥_៤៨)។ ពុំតែប៉ុណ្ណោះ ព្រះបាទសូរ្យវរ្ម័នសាងមេបុណ្យនៅលើកោះមួយដែលលើកឡើងចំកណ្តាលបារាយនោះ។ នៅទីនោះហើយដែលគេប្រទះឃើញរូបព្រះនារាយណ៍ផ្ទំ ដែលមានភាពខូចខាតច្រើន (លេខ៤៥)។ ក្នុងរាជ្យព្រះបាទឧទ័យាទិត្យវរ្ម័នទី២នោះ មានការរំជើបរំជួលជាច្រើន ហើយទីបំផុតទៅ ព្រះបាទហសិវរ្ម័នទី៣ (១០៦៦_៨០) ស្នងរាជ្យបន្ត។ គេពុំដឹងអ្វីច្បាស់ទេពីរាជ្យខាងក្រោយនេះ គ្រាន់តែស្មានថាប្រហែលក្សត្រខាងក្រោយមកបានទម្លាក់ឱ្យចេញពីរាជ្យ។

នៅឆ្នាំ១០៨០មានខ្សែស្រឡាយថ្មីមកលាយចូលក្នុងព្រះញាតិវង្ស ពោលគឺតាមរយៈត្រកូលមួយមកពីតំបន់ភ្នំដងរែក ហៅថា មហីធរបុរ ដែលពីមុនមកប្រហែលជាត្រកូលស្តេចត្រាញ់គ្រប់គ្រងតំបន់ជាយអាណាចក្រអង្គរ។ ព្រះរាជាថ្មីនោះមាននាមថាព្រះបាទជ័យវរ្ម័នទី៦ ហើយគ្រប់គ្រងស្រុកដល់ឆ្នាំ១១០៧។ ព្រះអង្គមានទំនាក់ទំនងខ្លាំងនឹងតំបន់ពាយព្យ (សព្វថ្ងៃនេះគឺតំបន់ឦសាននៃប្រទេសថៃឡង់ដ៍) ប្រហែលដូច្នេះហើយបានជាឥទ្ធិពលខ្មែររីកសាយខ្លាំងឡើងនៅម្តុំនោះ នាស.វ.ទី១២។

៥_ ស.វ.ទី១២ និងអនុភាពអង្គរវត្ត

បើយោងតាមសិលាចារឹកតាព្រហ្ម ចារឡើងនៅឆ្នាំ១១៨៦ ព្រះបាទជ័យវរ្ម័នទី៦តាំងទីនៅមហីធរបុរ (សព្វថ្ងៃនៅក្នុងខេត្តនគររាជនៃប្រទេសថៃឡង់ដ៍)។ ជំនាន់នោះគេសាងប្រាសាទពីរ ដែលហាក់ដូចជាគំរូសម្រាប់ប្រាសាទអង្គរវត្តទៅថ្ងៃមុខ, គឺប្រាសាទភិមាយ, និងប្រាសាទភ្នំរុង សាងឡើងលើទីតាំងដែលមានសំណង់ជាទីសក្ការៈស្រាប់។ ប្រាសាទភ្នំទាំងពីរនេះ សុទ្ធសឹងមានគូប៉មរាងស្រឡូន ដែលដំបូលប្រកបដោយជាន់ថ្នាក់ មានកញ្ចាំងនៅតាមជ្រុង។ ទាំងនេះហើយដែលក្រោយមកយើងឃើញមាននៅតួប៉មទាំង៥នៃអង្គរវត្ត។

នៅឆ្នាំ១១០៧ ឬ១១០៨ ព្រះបាទជ័យវរ្ម័នទី៦ មានបងមកសោយរាជ្យបន្ត, គឺព្រះបាទធរណីន្ទ្រវរ្ម័នទី១ ដែលកាន់អំណាចរហូតដល់ឆ្នាំ១១១២។ ក្សត្រដែលសោយរាជ្យបន្តមកទៀត គឺព្រះបាទសូរ្យវរ្ម័នទី២ ដែលត្រូវជាចៅក្មួយ។ សិលាចារឹកពីស.វ.ទី១២ ដែលរកឃើញនៅ Ban That ពោលថាកាលព្រះអង្គព្រះជន្ម១៥ព្រះវស្សា ហើយកំពុងសិក្សារៀនសូត្រ ព្រះបាទសូរ្យវរ្ម័នទី១ "ស្ថិតនៅក្រោមការគ្រប់គ្រងរបស់គ្រូពីរនាក់" ជាហេតុធ្វើឱ្យយើងគិតថាមានអ្នកគាំទ្រព្រះបាទហសិវរ្ម័នទី៣ ដែលនៅតែទាមទាររាជ្យអំណាចនៅអង្គរក្នុងពេលដែលព្រះបាទធរណីន្ទ្រវរ្ម័នសោយរាជ្យអំពីទីតាំងមហីធរបុរ។ ថ្វីត្បិតតែគ្មានអ្វីជាទីសំអាងពិតប្រាកដ ព្រះបាទសូរ្យវរ្ម័នប្រហែលឡើងសោយរាជ្យនៅឆ្នាំ១១១៣ ដោយទម្លាក់ព្រះរាជាមុនពីរាជ្យ ក្នុងចម្បាំងមួយយ៉ាងខ្លី។

ក្នុងចំណោមប្រាសាទដែលសាងនៅក្រោមរាជ្យព្រះបាទសូរ្យវរ្ម័នទី២ គេឃើញមានប្រាសាទធម្មនន្ទ, ចៅសាយ, បន្ទាយសម្រែ និងបេងមាលា ដែលជាប្រាសាទដ៏ធំធេង ស្ថិតនៅចម្ងាយ៨០គ.ម.ពីអង្គរ។ ក្រៅពីនោះក៏មានសាងបន្ថែមនៅប្រាសាទព្រះវិហារនិងវត្តភូដែរ។ ក្នុងចំណោមអស់ទាំងនោះ ឥតមានប្រាសាទណាមួយដែងប្រាសាទអង្គរវត្តបានឡើយ។ អង្គរវត្តសាងនៅភាគទី១នៃស.វ.ទី១២ លើផ្ទៃដីមួយទំហំ២០០ហិចតា, ព័ទ្ធជុំវិញទៅដោយកសិន្ធុដែលមានទទឹង១៩០ម.។ អង្គរវត្តចែកជា៥រូត, គឺជាសុខុមលោកបង្ហាញពីលំនៅស្ថាននៃទេពផ្សេងៗនៅភ្នំព្រះសុមេរុ។ រូតលើបង្អស់មានប៉ម៥ គឺបួននៅតាមមុំ និងមួយទៀតនៅកណ្តាល ដែលមានកម្ពស់៤២ម.។ អង្គរវត្តពុំដូចប្រាសាទខ្មែរភាគច្រើនទេ ដោយសារបែរមុខទៅខាងលិច ពោលគឺទិសដែលព្រះអាទិត្យអស្តង្គត និងជាទិសនៃសេចក្តីស្លាប់។ ដូច្នេះហើយបានជាអ្នកស្រាវជ្រាវខ្លះ យល់ថា មានទាក់ទងនឹងផ្នូរនៃព្រះបាទសូរ្យវរ្ម័នទី២។ ប៉ុន្តែទិសនេះក៏ជាទិសនៃព្រះនារាយណ៍ដែរ។

ចំណុចមួយដែលធ្វើឱ្យអង្គរវត្តមានភាពអស្ចារ្យនោះ គឺចម្លាក់នៅពាសពេញប្រាសាទ។ នេះគឺមិនត្រឹមតែទេពអប្សរ ចំនួនជិត២០០០នោះទេ គឺនិយាយតាំងតែពីចម្លាក់នៅលើផ្តែរនិងហោជាងផង ដែលសុទ្ធសឹងតែមានភាពរស់រវើក។ រីឯចម្លាក់ដែលល្បីល្បាញបំផុតនោះ គឺផ្ទាំងនិទានរឿងប្រវែងរាប់រយម៉ែត្រ នៅក្នុងរបៀងរូតទី៣។ ជញ្ជាំងរបៀងទាំងមូលនោះចែកចេញជា៨ផ្ទាំង៖ សម្រង់រឿងមហាភារត, រឿងរាមកេរ្តិ៍, ព្រះយមរាជបញ្ជូនអ្នកស្លាប់ឱ្យទៅនរកឬសួគ៌, កូរសមុទ្រទឹកដោះ ព្រមទាំងព្រឹត្តិការណ៍ប្រវត្តិសាស្ត្រក្នុងរាជ្យព្រះបាទសូរ្យវរ្ម័នទី២។ ចម្លាក់នៅអង្គរវត្តមានភាពផ្ចិតផ្ចង់លម្អិតខ្លាំងណាស់ សោភ័ណភាពនេះគ្របដណ្តប់ទៅលើរយៈពេល៣/៤នៃស.វ.ទី១២។ ការសម្អិតសមាងទៅលើសម្លៀកបំពាក់និងអលង្ការគួរជាទីកត់សម្គាល់ (លេខ៤៩, ៥០, ៥២, ៥៤, ៥៥) ប៉ុន្តែគឺសិល្បៈសិរិតដែលមានលក្ខណៈប្រសើរបំផុតក្នុងរចនាបថអង្គរវត្ត (លេខ៥១, ៥៣, ៥៦_៦០)។

ព្រះបាទសូរ្យវរ្ម័នទី២លាតសន្ធឹងខ័ណ្ឌសីមាព្រះនគរទៅឆ្ងាយទៅទៀត ថ្វីត្បិតតែចម្បាំង៦គ្រាដែលព្រះអង្គធ្វើឡើងជាមួយប្រទេសដាយវៀតនិងចម្ប៉ាពុំបានជោគជ័យក៏ដោយ។ សិលាចារឹកចុងក្រោយបង្អស់ដែលពោលពីព្រះអង្គ គឺចារនៅឆ្នាំ១១៤៥ ប៉ុន្តែគេយល់ថាព្រះអង្គប្រហែលសោយរាជ្យរហូតដល់ឆ្នាំ១១៥០។ បន្ទាប់មកព្រះបាទធរណីន្ទ្រវរ្ម័នទី២ ដែលជាជីដូនមួយ សោយរាជ្យបន្តក្នុងមួយរយៈពេល។ នៅចន្លោះឆ្នាំ១១៤៥ និង១១៨០ គេប្រទះឃើញសិលាចារឹកតែមួយគត់ ជាហេតុធ្វើឱ្យប្រវត្តិសាស្ត្រពេលនោះមានភាពស្រពិចស្រពិល ប៉ុន្តែគេដឹងថាព្រះបាទធរណីន្ទ្រវរ្ម័នទី២ (ដែលជាព្រះបិតានៃអនាគតព្រះបាទជ័យវរ្ម័នទី៧) បានបន្តរាជ្យទៅឱ្យព្រះបាទយសោវរ្ម័នទី២ ដែលប្រហែលជាជាប់សាច់ញាតិឆ្ងាយ។ នៅឆ្នាំ១១៦៥ ព្រះបាទយសោវរ្ម័នត្រូវអ្នកដណ្តើមរាជ្យម្នាក់ឈ្មោះត្រីភូវនាទិត្យវរ្ម័ន ធ្វើឃាត។

៦_ ព្រះបាទជ័យវរ្ម័នទី៧, អង្គរធំ និងបាយ័ន្ត

ក្នុងរយៈពេល៤ឆ្នាំ ក្រោយពីចាម្បវាយលុកអង្គរនៅឆ្នាំ១១៧៧ក្លាមមក ក្សត្រមួយអង្គដែលក្រោយមកក្លាយជាព្រះបាទជ័យវរ្ម័នទី៧ បានកែណកម្លាំងនានាដើម្បីដេញខ្មាំងចេញ ហើយយុទ្ធនាការនេះបានជោគជ័យពេញលេញ។ ព្រះអង្គកាន់ព្រះពុទ្ធសាសនាដូចជាព្រះបិតារបស់ព្រះអង្គដែរ (ព្រះបាទធរណីន្ទ្រវរ្ម័នទី២) ហើយមានព្រះជន្មាយុជាង៥០ព្រះវស្សា ពេលដែលព្រះអង្គឡើងសោយរាជ្យនៅឆ្នាំ១១៨១។ ក្នុងរាជ្យនោះព្រះពុទ្ធសាសនាមហាយានក្លាយទៅជាសាសនាធំ។ ជាងពេលណាទាំងអស់ ទឹកដីនៃអាណាចក្ររីកធំខ្លាំង៖ ខាងលិចទៅទល់នឹងប្រទេសភូមាបច្ចុប្បន្ន, ខាងជើងទៅដល់តំបន់វៀងច័ន្ទ, ខាងកើតទៅទល់នឹងចម្ប៉ា (ដែលព្រះរាជាកៀបសង្កត់បាន ក្រោយពីវាយប្រហារ៣លើកនៅឆ្នាំ១១៩៩), ខាងត្បូងទៅទល់នឹងសមុទ្រ។

ព្រះបាទជ័យវរ្ម័នទី៧សាងរាជធានីអង្គរធំនៅពេលនោះ ដែលមានទំហំ៩០០ហិចតា ក្នុងកំពែង៤ជ្រុង ដែលមួយជ្រុងៗមានប្រវែង៣គ.ម. ហ៊ុំពាត់ទៅដោយកសិន្ធុដែលមានទទឹង១២០ម.។ កំពែងនោះមានកម្ពស់៨ម. មានក្លោងទ្វារ៥ ប្រកបដោយកំពូលច្លាក់រូបមុខទេពបែរទៅទិសធំៗទាំង៤។ ក្លោងទ្វារនីមួយៗភ្ជាប់ទៅស្ពានដែលឆ្លងកាត់កសិន្ធុនោះ ហើយដែលមានភ្នាក់ដៃសងខាងជារូបយក្សនិងទេពទាញនាគ។ ស្ពានឆ្លងរបៀបនេះ ឃើញមាននៅផ្លូវចូលប្រាសាទខ្លះ ដូចជាប្រាសាទតាព្រហ្មនិងប្រាសាទព្រះខ័នជាដើម។ នៅចំកណ្ដាលអង្គរធំ គឺប្រាសាទបាយ័ន្តយ៉ាងល្បីល្បាញ ដោយសារតួប៉មនីមួយៗ (ដើមឡើយទាំងអស់មាន៥៩) សុទ្ធសឹងមានមុខ៤ សម្លឹងទៅទិសធំៗទាំង៤។ លក្ខណៈសម្បត្តិមួយទៀត គឺផ្ទាំងចម្លាក់និទានទេវកថា, ប្រវត្តិសាស្ត្រ ឬក៏បង្ហាញពីជីវិតធម្មតារាល់ថ្ងៃរបស់ប្រជាជននៅអង្គរ។ បាយ័ន្តជាប្រាសាទព្រះពុទ្ធសាសនា ប៉ុន្តែព្រះបាទជ័យវរ្ម័នទី៧ហាក់ដូចជារាប់រកសាសនាទាំងអស់ ត្បិតបើយើងមើលទៅប្រាសាទតាព្រហ្មនិងព្រះខ័នដែលឧទ្ទិសទៅបុព្វការីជនរបស់អង្គនោះ ឃើញថាទេពដែលតម្កល់នៅទីនោះជាទេពក្នុងសាសនាព្រាហ្មណ៍ផង ក្នុងព្រះពុទ្ធសាសនាផង។

ក្នុងរាជ្យនេះគេប្រទះឃើញសិលាចារឹកច្រើន ជាអាទិ៍គឺសិលាចារឹកតាព្រហ្ម (១១៨៦) និងសិលាចារឹកព្រះខ័ន (១១៩១)។ សិលាចារឹកទាំងនោះនិយាយថា មានមនុស្ស១២៦៤០នាក់រស់នៅក្នុងបរិវេណប្រាសាទតាព្រហ្ម និង៩៧៨៤០នាក់ក្នុងបរិវេណប្រាសាទព្រះខ័ន។ តួលេខទាំងនេះធ្វើឱ្យយើងជឿកាន់តែខ្លាំងឡើងថា រាជធានីអង្គរជាបុរីមួយធំបំផុតក្នុងចំណោមក្រុងជំនាន់បុរាណ ដែលពុំទាន់ស្គាល់ឧស្សាហកម្ម។ ជំនាន់នោះមានការសាងសង់ធំៗជាច្រើន ដូចជាប្រាសាទបន្ទាយក្ដី, បន្ទាយឆ្មារ, ការពង្រីកប្រាសាទបាកាណ, ស្ពាន, មន្ទីរពេទ្យ, សាលាសំណាក់ដែលនៅតាមមាត់ផ្លូវធំៗនៃអាណាចក្រ។ ផ្លូវដែលសំខាន់ជាងគេគឺផ្លូវដែលពុទ្ធសាសនិកធ្វើដំណើរពីប្រាសាទភិមាយឆ្លងកាត់តាមភ្នំដងរែក ដើម្បីមកដល់បាយ័ន្ត។

មានបដិមាជាច្រើនជារូបព្រះរាជា និងព្រះជាយា ពោលគឺព្រះនាងជ័យរាជទេវីដែលសោយទិវង្គតនៅក្នុងព្រះជនក្មេងនៅឡើយ ហើយដែលសុទ្ធសឹងតែសាងឡើងដោយព្រះរៀមព្រះអង្គដែលក្លាយជាព្រះអគ្គមហេសីបន្ទាប់មក។ ព្រះរូបទាំងនោះ មើលទៅឃើញថាបញ្ចេញភាពស្ងប់ស្ងាត់និងស្រទន់ក្រៃលែង (លេខ ៦១_៦៣, ៧៣) ហើយជាលក្ខណៈពិសេសនៃរចនាបថបាយ័ន្តដែលគ្របដណ្ដប់ទៅលើបដិមាច្រើនបែបយ៉ាង ដូចជាព្រះលោកេស្វរ ជាពោធិសត្វនៃករុណា, ព្រះប្រជ្ញាបារមី ជាទេវីនៃការចេះដឹង និងព្រះពុទ្ធអង្គឯងផង ដែលច្រើនតែគង់នៅលើនាគ។ ជំនាន់នោះ សិល្បៈសំរិតក៏ខ្ពស់ណាស់ដែរ (លេខ៦៤_៧២, ៧៤)។

ក្នុងរាជ្យព្រះបាទជ័យវរ្ម័ននោះ មានការរំដើបរំជួលបះបោរច្រើនលើកច្រើនសា។ សេដ្ឋកិច្ចក៏រងគ្រោះដោយសារអសន្តិសុខនេះ ហើយលុះយកទៅបូកបញ្ចូលនឹងសំណង់ធំៗរាប់មិនអស់ដែលតម្រូវឱ្យចំណាយធនធានច្រើនផងនោះ ប្រហែលជាហេតុដែលធ្វើឱ្យអាណាចក្រមានការចុះស្រុត។ ចាប់ពីចុងស.វ. ទី១២ ឆ្លងមកក្នុងរហូតស.វ.ទី១៣ រដ្ឋថៃលេចអំណាចផ្លោឡើង ហើយបញ្ចេញការគំរាមគំហែងមកលើអាណាចក្រខ្មែរម្ដងបន្តិចៗ ដែលធ្លាប់តែខ្លាំងក្លាតាំងពីស.វ.ទី ១០មក។ យើងមិនដឹងថាព្រះបាទជ័យវរ្ម័នទី៧សុគតនៅឆ្នាំណាច្បាស់ទេ គ្រាន់តែស្មានថាប្រហែលនៅឆ្នាំ១២១៨ ក្នុង ព្រះជន្មាយុលើស៨០ព្រះវស្សា។

៧. ប្រទេសកម្ពុជាក្រោយសម័យអង្គរ

ព្រះបាទឥន្ទ្រវរ្ម័នទី២ (១២១៨_៤៣) ដែលកាន់ព្រះពុទ្ធសាសនាមហាយាននោះ ស្នងរាជ្យតពីព្រះបាទជ័យវរ្ម័នទី៧។ យើងមានពត៌មានស្ដួចស្ដើងណាស់ ហើយសិលាចារឹកតែមួយគត់ដែលពាក់ព័ន្ធនឹងរាជ្យនោះ ពោលតែត្រង់កន្លែងដែលព្រះអង្គសោយទិវង្គត។ តាមស្មានមើលទៅប្រាសាទបាលិល័យ និងប្រាសាទខ្លះទៀតនៅក្រុមព្រះពិធូរ ប្រហែលជាសាងនៅជំនាន់នោះ។ អ្នកសោយរាជ្យបន្ទាប់មកគឺព្រះបាទជ័យវរ្ម័នទី៨ (១២៤៣_៩៥)។ ព្រះអង្គលើកតម្កើងព្រហ្មញ្ញសាសនាឡើងវិញ ហើយមានការលុបឬដាប់ព្រះពុទ្ធរូបចោល ដូចជានៅប្រាសាទព្រះខ័នជាដើម។ ប្រាសាទធ្វើអំពីថ្មចុងក្រោយបង្អស់ ពោលគឺប្រាសាទមង្គលអាថ៌ សាងឡើងនៅជំនាន់នោះឯង រីឯរូបយមរាជលុតជង្គង់ (លេខ៧៦) ក៏ប្រហែលដូច្នោះដែរ។

នៅក្រោមរាជ្យព្រះបាទឥន្ទ្រវរ្ម័នទី៣ (១២៩៥_១៣០៧) មានការលុកលុយពីអយុធ្យាជាញឹកញយ។ ទោះជាយ៉ាងនោះក៏ដោយ កំណត់ហេតុអ្នកការទូតចិនឈ្មោះជីវតាក្វាន់ ដែលមកអង្គរនៅឆ្នាំ១២៩៦_៩៧ បង្ហាញថារាំងខ្មែរពេលនោះនៅមានភាពរុងរឿងនៅឡើយ។ សៀមវាយលុកអង្គរក្រោយបំផុតនៅឆ្នាំ១៤៣១ បណ្ដាលឱ្យខ្មែរបោះបង់រាជធានីនេះចោល។ ប៉ុន្តែការដែលជ្រើសរើសរាជធានីនៅតំបន់ភ្នំពេញ ប្រហែលជាមកពីសម្លឹងឃើញថាទីនោះមានអំណោយផលសម្រាប់ជំនួញតាមទន្លេសាបក្ដី ឬតាមទន្លេមេកុងទៅរកសមុទ្រក្ដី។ នៅចន្លោះឆ្នាំ១៣៧១និង១៤១៩ គេដឹងថាមានដំណើរពីខ្មែរទៅស្រុកចិន១២ដងដែលបង្ហាញថាពាណិជ្ជកម្មពេលនោះកើនឡើងជាមួយប្រទេសចិនជំនាន់សន្តិវង្ស Ming។ ការរីកដុះដាលនៃព្រះពុទ្ធសាសនាថេរវាទចាប់ពីស.វ.ទី១៣មក និងការត្រឡប់ទៅរកឫសគល់ដើមរបស់ខ្មែរវិញនោះ លេចធ្លោឡើងតាមរយៈបដិមាដែលច្រើនតែធ្វើអំពីឈើ (លេខ៨០) ហើយដែលហាក់ដូចជាទទួលឥទ្ធិពលពីស្រីលង្កាមក ដោយឆ្លងតាមប្រទេសសៀម (លេខ៧៧)។ ពុទ្ធបដិមាធំៗដែលតម្កល់នៅអង្គរវត្ត (លេខ៧៩) សាងឡើងជំនាន់ព្រះបាទអង្គច័ន្ទ (១៥១៦_១៥៦៦)។ ព្រះរាជាអង្គនេះព្រមទាំងស្ដេចដែលសោយរាជ្យបន្ទាប់មក យករាជធានីមកនៅអង្គរវិញបានពីរ_បីទសវត្ស។

សន្តតិវង្សខ្មែរនៅគ្រងរាជ្យបន្តមកដល់សព្វថ្ងៃនេះ ថ្វីត្បិតតែនៅក្រោមការត្រួតត្រារបស់សៀមនៅតំបន់ខាងជើង រហូតទាល់តែអាណាព្យាបាលបារាំងចចារបានមកវិញនៅឆ្នាំ១៩០៧។ ការដែលបារាំងត្រួតនោះ បង្ហាញថាអឺរុបចាប់អារម្មណ៍លើទឹកដីនេះ ដោយរាប់តាំងពីដំណើររបស់លោក Henri Mouhot រហូតមកដល់ Louis Delaporte នៅឆ្នាំ១៨៦៦_៦៨ ដែលបានគូររូបនិងធ្វើការរៀបរាប់ពីប្រាសាទជាច្រើន។ ការបង្កើត "សាលាបារាំងចុងបូព៌ា" នៅឆ្នាំ១៨៩៨ ជំរុញឱ្យមានការរុករកស្រាវជ្រាវ, ជួសជុលបុរាណដ្ឋានយ៉ាងសកម្មពីសំណាក់បារាំង ហើយក្រោយមកពីសំណាក់អ្នកស្រាវជ្រាវបរទេសផ្សេងៗទៀត។

លទ្ធផលនៃការប្រឹងប្រែងទាំងអម្បាលម៉ានដើម្បីវប្បធម៌ខ្មែរនេះ គឺមានសមុច្ច័យសារមន្ទីរជាតិដ៏ល្អបញ្ចាំងស្រាប់។ នៅទីនេះ គេមិនត្រឹមឃើញតែចម្លាក់ពិចិត្រអំពីថ្ម, សំរិត និងឈើ ដូចឃើញមានក្នុងសៀវភៅនេះប៉ុណ្ណោះទេ គឺគេឃើញមានកុលាលភាជន៍, ផ្ទាំងគំនូរ និងវត្ថុប្រើប្រាស់ក្នុងពិធីទៀតផង។ បើពោលពីកុលាលភាជន៍ ដែលច្រើនតែមកពីស.វ.ទី១១និង១២នោះ គឺច្រើនមានស្រទាប់រលោងពណ៌ត្នោត និងទ្រង់ទ្រាយច្រើនបែបយ៉ាង រាប់បញ្ចូលទាំងចានក្បានមានរូបរាងជាសត្វទៀតផង។ ឯរូបគំនូរវិញ គឺច្រើនតែនៅស.វ.ទី១៩និង២០ ហើយបង្ហាញពីរឿងរ៉ាវនានាក្នុងពុទ្ធសាសនា។ ចំពោះវត្ថុប្រើប្រាស់ក្នុងពិធីវិញ គឺសុទ្ធសឹងជ្លះបញ្ចាំងពីទឹកដៃសិល្បៈឈើ, សំរិត ឬក៏មាសផង។

カンボジア史概観

1. 初期の統治形態

カンボジア初期の歴史は中国の３世紀の記録に残っている。当時のカンボジアの住民クメール人による自国名は不明だが、中国人は扶南と呼んでいた。中国人によると、クメール人は腕が多数ある神を崇拝していたと記しており、ヒンドゥー教または仏教、およびインドの影響があったことが伺える。ローマ金貨などの考古学的証拠から、扶南の港オケオが西欧と中国間の貿易港として栄えていたことが明らかだ。首都は現在のプノンペンの南、アンコール・ボレイ近辺だったと思われる。ここはヒンドゥー教と仏教が同時に栄えた地域だったことが彫刻からわかる。プノン・ダ（アンコール・ボレイ近くの山の名前）様式の彫刻の大半はビシュヌ派で、７世紀に作られたものである（No. 2、3、4）。アスラム・マハ・ルセイ以外、この地域の寺院は残骸しか残っていない。

７世紀初めには、権力の中心地は中国人が真臘と呼ぶ北方の国に移動していた。扶南同様、クメール人自身による自国名は不明である。イーシャナヴァルマン１世が造営したイーシャナプラ（今日のソンボール・プレイ・クック）が真臘の首都だった。イーシャナヴァルマン１世はダンレック山脈近くの北部の一族の出身だが、扶南と血族関係があった。現在でもよい状態で残っているが、３期間にわたって建立された３群、100以上のバラモン寺院は、後のクメール寺院の原型となっている。レンガ造りの塔堂は、インドのシカラ（塔）に類似しており、完璧な技巧で彫刻された砂岩の戸枠、脇支柱、リンテルがついている。塔堂の大半は正方形か長方形だが、一部は八角形である。外壁には宮廷の有力者たちの姿を描いたレリーフで飾られている。また王に関する情報が碑文に記されており、重要な像も発見された（No.11、12）。北部の支配者の子孫は勢力範囲を拡張し続け、８世紀初めにはジャヤデーヴィー王女が後にアンコールとなるトンレサープ湖付近を拠点とした。

8世紀、東部にはメコン川ほとりサンブプラ（メニンのサンポール）に繁栄する国家が存在した。その支配者の３人は王女で、印象的な女神像を残した（No.13）。扶南の植民地、イーシャーナハヴァルマン一族の都市、メコン川の王国など、全て年一回雨季を迎えるモンスーン気候にとっての生命線である川の周辺で発展した。クメール史上、水は社会発展、および象徴として重要であり、カンボジア人は初期から水力学に秀でていた。

クメールの権力がダンレック山脈（現在、タイ北東部）まで拡張し、小規模の貿易中心地から、大帝国に変身するのは、８世紀以後のことである。主として仏像を中心とする有名なクメールのブロンズ像は、現在のタイのブリラム県から発見された。８世紀末の銘文はあまり存在しないため、前後関係は不明だが、770年の碑文には、アンコール期をスタートしたジャヤヴァルマン２世への言及がある。

2. 9世紀：アンコール期の始まり

スドック・カック・トム碑文によると、ジャヤヴァルマン２世（802~830年頃）は802年にチャクラヴァルティン（転輪聖王、正義をもって国を治める理想の王）に即位した。即位式ではマヘンドラパルヴァタ（大インドラの山）であるプノン・クレーン高丘でデーヴァラージャ（宇宙の主即王）の祭儀が執り行われた。王が神格視されたという証拠は残っておらず、統治者という言葉の古代クメール語のサンスクリット訳だと思われるが、神から授けられた王の権威と正当性を意味するものである。プノン・クレーンには９世紀の寺院が数多く残っており、その大半はレンガ造りの塔堂１基からできているが、一部は塔堂が３基あり、持送り式天蓋がついている。戸枠、偽扉、リンテル、小円柱は砂岩製である。プノン・クレーン高丘の寺院から幾つかのヴィシュヌ像が発見されている（No.27）。これらの像はプノン・ダーやサンボール・プレイ・クックの人間的でスピリチュアリティーが感じられる像より、フォーマルで硬い印象を与えるものである。

ジャヤヴァルマン２世は何度か遷都しており、二度ほどハリハラーラヤ（現在のロルオス）に王都を移し、後継者ジャヤヴァルマン３世もここを王都とした。ここはそれ以前から住民がおり、ジャヤデーヴィー王妃（680または681～713年）の王都であったようだ。近辺にあるアク・ヨムの小ピラミッド型寺院の碑文は王妃の統治時期に彫られたものである。ジャヤヴァルマン２世の甥インドラヴァルマン１世（877～889年）もハリハラーラヤを王都とした。祖先たちのために祠堂６基から成る祖寺プレア・コーを建立した。クメール人の祖先支配は、現在でもネアク・ター（祖先の霊）を重要視していることにもうかがえるが、プレア・コーの碑文は神とともに男女の祖先にも言及している。

インドラヴァルマン１世の国家鎮護寺院バコンは５段の基壇を積み上げた上に30メートル以上の高さでそびえ、周囲には数多くの小祠堂と参道が存在する。山岳型寺院には8世紀のアク・ヨム、プノン・クレーンのクルス・プレア・アラム・ロン・チェンなどがあり、バコンが最初ではないが、大規模なものはこれが初めてである。その後の寺院と同様、バコンはヒンズー教神々の住処であるメル山を象徴している。バコンとプレア・コーの中央祠堂で発見された彫刻は精巧で、クメール国家の繁栄と中央権力、国王の権力顕示の意図を反映している。インドラヴァルマン１世は初の巨大な貯水池、インドラタターカを建設した。現在では大半が乾いているが、クメールの貯水池の中でも大きい。

インドラヴァルマン１世の息子、ヤショヴァルマン１世（889～10世紀初め）が後継者となった。9世紀終わり、ヤショヴァルマン１世はインドラタターカの人工島にロレイ寺院を建てた。プレア・コー同様、先祖を祭ったロレイ寺院は４祠堂から成る。900年頃、ヤショヴァルマン１世は都城ヤショダラプーラを後にアンコールとなる地域に遷都した。都城はプノン・バケン小丘を中心に整備された。プノン・バケンは寺院と10世紀第一四半期の彫刻の名称となる。

３．10世紀：クメール国家の発展

ヤショヴァルマン１世はプノン・バケン寺院のほか、プノン・ボックとプノン・クロム両小山の頂上にも３祠堂の寺院、そして現在は枯渇している東バライ（7 x 2km）を建設した。現在のタイ東北部およびラオスのワットプーに、支配領域を示した碑文が配置された。この時代のレリーフや像は、より聖美術的で質の高い彫刻である（No.30）。

ヤショヴァルマン１世の跡を912年に継いだのは、息子のハルシャヴァルマン１世である。ハルシャヴァルマン１世は国家鎮護寺院ではなく、バクセイ・チャムクロン小祠堂を建立した。小祠堂は948年、いとこラージェンドラヴァルマン王が完成した。ハルシャヴァルマン１世が建立した５祠堂のプラサート・クラヴァン寺院（921年）はヴィシュヌ神に捧げられたことが碑文で判る。弟イーシャーナヴァルマ２世が925年に王位を継承したが、928年に亡くなった。

ハルシャヴァルマン１世やイーシャーナヴァルマン２世がアンコールを統治していたが、彼らのおじにあたる、ヤショヴァルマン１世の妹の夫に挑戦された。おじは921年、ジャヤヴァルマン４世と名乗り、アンコールから北東100kmに位置するチョク・ガルヤルを統治していた。チョク・ガルヤルは現在のコ・ケー地方であり、数百の大寺院が存在している。その頂点はジャヴヤヴァルマン４世のプラサート・トム大寺院である。山岳型のこの寺院は上部が崩れ落ちているが、高さ60mあったと思われる。大きなスケールとダイナミックな完璧さがコ・ケー形式の彫刻の特徴である（No.31～34）。イーシャーナヴァルマン2世が928年に死亡した後、ジャヤヴァルマン４世が942年まで統治した。死後はその息子ハルシャヴァルマン２世がコ・ケーから短期間、統治したが、944年にはいとこのラージェンドラヴァルマン王がクメール王国統治者となった。

ラージェンドラヴァルマン王（944～968年）はアンコールに再遷都し、ヤショダラプラという以前の名前を維持した。東バライの人工の小島に東メボンの名前で知られる先祖を祭る寺院を953年に、国家鎮護寺院プレ・ループを961年に建立した。両院とも山岳型で、まぐさ石や小円柱の精巧な彫刻は、クメール建築の中でも最も素晴らしいプレ・ループ形式である（No.35、36）。

ラージェンドラヴァルマン王は何世紀もクメールを襲撃したチャンパー（現在のベトナム中部）からの脅威に晒された。仏教寺院バッ・チュム（960年）とシヴァ派のバンテアイ・スレイ寺院（967～8年）は初めて王ではなく、高官によって建立された寺院である。バンテアイ・スレイ寺院はクメール建築の至宝であり、国王の息子の王師がラージェンドラヴァルマン王の治世の末期に完成した。そのレリーフと彫刻には繊細な完成度がうかがえる（No.37～39）。

ラージェンドラヴァルマン王の息子、ジャヤヴァルマン５世が968年、即位し、1000年か1001年まで長年、統治した。チャンパーからの脅威も少ない、比較的平和な時代となった。山岳型寺院は建立しなかったが、王宮を建立し、ピミヤナカス寺院を建立し始めた。

４．11世紀：クメール帝国の拡張

ジャヤヴァルマン５世からウダヤディティヤヴァルマン１世（1001～2年）、そしてジャヤヴィーラヴァルマン王（1002～10年）への継承の詳細も、タ・ケオ山岳型寺院の建立者も明らかではない。５祠堂あるタ・ケオは高さ22mで、王宮敷地内にあるピミヤナカス寺院同様、クレアン様式（No.40）である。クレアンという呼び名は王宮東の一対の建築物に由来している。タ・ケオ寺院とピミヤナカス寺院で初めて回廊が誕生し、後にアンコール・ワットやバイヨン寺院で重要なレリーフが刻まれることになる。

波乱の時代らしく、碑文は数少ない。ジャヤヴィーラヴァルマン王が権力の座につくと、東部の王子スールヤヴァルマン１世も名乗りを上げた。1002年から1010年まで両王が並立していたが、王宮の5mの防御壁の門にある1011年の碑文には、スールヤヴァルマン１世が1002年に即位したと記してある。王宮の防御壁は新しく、敵を意識したものである。スールヤヴァルマン１世はインドラヴァルマン１世の母方の家計の出身だったため、官僚達から誓約をとりつけ、碑文に刻ませて、権力を正当化した。

スールヤヴァルマン１世は1049年まで比較的平和な時代を統治したが、国家鎮護寺院ではなく、巨大な山岳型寺院を建立し、金のリンガを設置し、自国の領域を示した。西にはワット・エクとワット・バセット、北にはダンレック山脈突出部にプレア・ヴィヘア寺院、東北部にはクメール寺院最大のバカーン（コンポン・スヴァイの大プレア・カーン寺院）、南にはプノン・チソール寺院を建立した。スールヤヴァルマン１世時代の終わりから後継者の時代にかけて、シェムリアップ川の支流クバル・スピアンの川床に数百のリンガや眠るヴィシュヌ神像が彫られた。

スールヤヴァルマン１世、または後継者ウダヤディティヤヴァルマン２世（1050～66年）が巨大な西バライを建設した。1060年頃、スールヤヴァルマンの王妃の親戚関係にあったウダヤディティヤヴァルマン２世は、カンボジア山岳型寺院の中でも最も大きいバプーオン寺院を建立した。バプーオン様式とは11世紀の壮麗で自然な彫刻スタイルを意味する（No.41、43～48）。スールヤヴァルマン１世は西バライの人口島に西メボン寺院を建設した。ここからヴィシュヌ神の横臥像が発見された（No 45）。ウダヤディティヤヴァルマン２世の治世は波乱万丈で、後継者の弟ハルシャヴァルマン３世（1066～80年）についてはあまり知られていないが、その後継者によって追放されたと思われる。

1080年、アンコール朝の属国のダンレック山脈地方のマヒーダラプラ一族の王子が登場した。ジャヤヴァルマン６世を名乗り、1107年まで統治した。北西部（現在のタイ東北部）との関係があったため、12世紀、この地域へのクメールの影響が増した。

5．１２世紀：アンコール朝最盛期

タ・プローム寺院の1186年の碑文によると、ジャヤヴァルマン６世はマヒーダラプラ（現在のタイのナコン・ラチャシマ）から統治した。アンコール・ワット建立以前、ここにはピマイ寺院とパノン・ルン寺院が建立されていた。両寺院とも砲弾形状の塔堂があり、そのスムーズな外形はアンコール・ワットの５尖塔を思い起こさせる。

ジャヤヴァルマン６世の没後（1107年か1108年）、兄ダラニンドラヴァルマン１世が1112年まで王位を引き継いだ。その後、甥スールヤヴァルマン２世が即位した。バン・タットの12世紀の碑文によると、スールヤヴァルマン２世が15歳で勉学を終えたとき、2人の師に依存したとのことだ。つまりダラニンドラヴァルマン１世がマヒーダラプラから統治している間、ハルシャヴァルマン３世の支持者がアンコールで主権を主張していたようである。事実は明らかでないが、スールヤヴァルマン２世は1日の戦いで王位を獲得したようだ。

スールヤヴァルマン２世の治世中、トマノン、チャウ・サイ・デヴォダ、バンテアイ・サムレ、アンコールから北東80kmにあるベン・メリアと多くの寺院が建設された。プレア・ヴィヘア、ワット・プー寺院も改修された。これらの寺院は素晴らしいが、アンコール・ワットには及ばない。12世紀前半に建立されたアンコール・ワットは200ヘクタールあり、190mの環濠に囲まれている。５段式山岳型寺院で、神々が住むメル山を象徴している。５尖塔がある中央祠堂は42mある。大半のクメール寺院と異なって、アンコール・ワットは日没と死を意味する西向きであることから、一部の学者はこれがスールヤヴァルマン２世を弔う寺院であると主張している。しかし、西向きなのは西の神であるヴィシュヌ神を祭っているためと思われる。

アンコール・ワット建築はレリーフでさらに素晴らしいものになっている。2,000のデヴァター（女神）のほか、まぐさ石や破風に生き生きとした風景が彫られている。最も素晴らしいのは第一回廊の１kmあまりのレリーフである。８つのパネルにはインドの大叙事詩「マハーバーラタ」「ラーマーヤナ」、閻魔大王が天国と地獄行きの審判を下す場面、乳海攪拌の場面、スールヤヴァルマン２世の統治の歴史などが描かれている。洗練された彫り方は、12世紀の３四半期の彫刻に見られるアンコール・ワット様式の特徴である。その完璧さは石像の衣服や宝石の彫り方にも見られるが（No.49、50、52、54、55）、それを一番よくあらわしているのはブロンズ像である（No.51、53、56～60）。

スールヤヴァルマン２世はクメール帝国を拡張したが、大越（ベトナム）とチャンパーとの６回にわたる戦争は不成功に終わった。存命中最後の碑文は1145年に記されたが、1150年まで統治したようだ。スールヤヴァルマン２世の没後、いとこで仏教徒のダラニンドラヴァルマン２世が登位したと思われる。

1145年から1180年にかけて碑文が１つしか存在しないため、事実関係は定かでないが、ダラニンドラヴァルマン２世（後のジャヤヴァルマン７世の父）の後継者は遠戚と思われるヤショヴァルマン2世だった。1165年、ヤショヴァルマン2世は王位簒奪者トリブヴァナーディティヤヴァルマンの反乱で落命し、トリブヴァナーディティヤヴァルマン自身もチャンパーによるアンコール侵攻によって1177年に落命した。

6. ジャヤヴァルマン７世：アンコール・トムとバイヨン

1177年のチャンパーによるアンコール侵攻から4年後、後日ジャヤヴァルマン7世となるクメールの王子は見方を集結し、侵略者を追放し、王都を奪回した。ジャヤヴァルマン7世は父ダラニンドラヴァルマン２世同様仏教徒で、1181年に即位したときには50歳以上だった。大乗仏教を国家宗教としたジャヤヴァルマン7世は、クメール帝国を最大限に拡張し、その範囲は西は現在のミャンマー、北はラオスのビエンチャン、東は3回目1199年に制圧したチャンパー、南は海に至った。

ジャヤヴァルマン7世は都城アンコール・トムを建立した。アンコール・トムは一辺３キロ、900ヘクタールの広さで、高さ8メートルの周壁と幅120メートルの濠に囲まれている。巨大な５つの塔門には、四面仏尊顔がそびえている。５塔門へ向かう濠を横切る陸橋には蛇の胴体で綱引きする巨人が向かい合っている。同様の陸橋はタ・プロームやプレア・カーンなど、同時代の他の寺院の入り口にも見られる。アンコール・トムの中心部には国家鎮護寺院バイヨンが存在する。バイヨンは仏塔で有名である。そもそも49あった仏塔の仏尊顔は神秘的に四方向を見つめている。表現豊かな壁面浮彫りから神話や歴史、アンコールの日常生活について学ぶことができる。バイヨンは仏教寺院だが、ジャヤヴァルマン7世は仏教にこだわらず、タ・プロームやプレア・カーンなど先祖を祀った寺院の祠堂には、仏陀以外にブラマン教の神々を安置した。

ジャヤヴァルマン7世時代の数多くの碑石が残っているが、特に注目すべきなのはタ・プロームの1186年とプリヤ・カーンの1191年の碑文である。これらの碑文はタ・プロームでは12,640人が生活し、プレア・カーンには97,840人が仕えていたと記している。以上の数字からアンコールが産業時代以前、最大の都市であったことが判る。バンテアイ・クデイ寺院、バンテアイ・チュマール寺院、バカンの拡張など、巨大な建物が建立され、王国の道には無数の陸橋、施療院、宿駅が設置された。ピーマイ寺院からダンレック山脈を越え、バイヨンまで仏教徒巡礼者が通った王道は有名である。

ジャヤヴァルマン7世と若くして逝去したジャヤラージャドゥヴィー王妃の彫像が、同王妃の死後第一王妃となった王妃の姉によって王国中に設置された。これらの彫刻は精神的な安らかさとヒューマニズムをあらわし、バイヨン様式の優雅さを示している（No.61～63、73）。慈悲の菩薩ボディサットヴァ・ロケシュヴァラ（観世音菩薩）、真理を悟った菩薩プラージュニャパーラミター（般若波羅密多）、ナーガに座った仏陀など数多くのバイヨン様式の彫像が存在する。ブロンズ鋳造技術も進歩した（No.64～72、74）。

ジャヤヴァルマン7世時代、幾度か反乱が起きた。反乱の抑圧や多数の建築プロジェクトの経済的負担によって、王国は弱体化したと思われる。12世紀末から13世紀にかけて、タイの台頭にクメール帝国は脅かされ、10世紀以後の勢力は維持できなくなった。ジャヤヴァルマン7世の逝去時期は不明だが、80歳を越えた1218年頃と思われる。

7．アンコール朝後のカンボジア

ジャヤヴァルマン７世の後継者インドラヴァルマン2世（1218～43年）も大乗仏教信者だった。当時の碑文にあるのは没年だけで、それ以外は不明である。プレア・パリライやプレア・ピトゥの幾つかの寺院はこの時代に建立されたようだ。インドラヴァルマン2世の後継者ジャヤヴァルマン8世（1243～95年）は再びヒンドゥー教を国家宗教とした。プレア・カーン寺院の仏陀や、アンコール期最後の建築物マンガラータ寺院、そして有名なひざまずいたヤマ神像（No.76）が作られた。

インドラヴァルマン3世（1295～1307年）時代、アユタヤ王国がアンコールを幾度も攻略した。しかし、1296~1297年にアンコール都城を訪れた中国人周達観によると、アンコールの宮廷は絢爛豪華だった。アユタヤの1431年の攻撃で、アンコール王都は放棄され、プノンペン南部に遷都したが、アユタヤからの逃避というより、トンレサップ湖とメコン河を通じた海路へのアクセスを目的としたものであったかも知れない。例えば1371年から1419年にかけて中国に12回、使節団を派遣しており、明朝との交易が増したことがわかる。

13世紀以後、上座部仏教が栄え、クメール文化のルーツに戻ったことは、木製の彫像が増え、タイ経由で入ってきたスリランカの上座部仏教の様式の影響が観られることから明らかだ。アンコール・ワット向けに巨大な仏陀像（No.79）が作られ、アン・チャン１世（1516～1566年）と王都を数十年、アンコールに戻したその後継者の時代から、同寺院は仏教徒の巡礼地となった。

カンボジア王族はその後4世紀続き、今日に至る。フランスの交渉で1907年に返還されるまで、北部はタイが統治していた。アンリ・ムオの1858～61年にかけての旅、そしてルイ・ドゥラポルトの1866～68年の訪問時のスケッチと報告によって、フランスの保護領、そして植民地だったカンボジアに対する欧州の関心は高まった。1898年にはフランス極東学院が設立され、フランス人、後にその他の研究者による探検、修復、研究が始まった。

クメール文化保存努力の結果はカンボジア国立博物館のコレクションに観ることができる。同博物館は本書にある類稀な石、ブロンズ、木製の彫像以外にも、本書に掲載できなかった陶器や絵画、儀式用具を多数、所蔵している。11～12世紀の陶器は茶色のうわ薬が特徴で、伝統的な形のほか、動物をかたどったものがある。絵画の大半は19~20世紀のもので、仏教のシーンを描いた作品が多い。儀式用具や通過儀礼用具は、クメール職人の木、ブロンズ、貴金属技術を示している。

1. Ritual Urn. Khum Chak Angre, Kandal, Bronze Age. Bronze, 0.56 m. Ga 2083.

This masterpiece of early bronze casting probably dates from the period spanning about 300 BCE to about 300 CE. Many ritual objects of this type, as well as bells, axes and drums, were found in the village of Dongson in Vietnam that has given its name to the ancient civilisation and its dispersed artifacts. Similar vessels, which might have contained substances for religious or agricultural ceremonies, with motifs of spirals, circles, elongated triangles, stars, and boats, have been found all over Southeast Asia, including Yunnan, but their fabrication place is not certain. Their wide distribution may indicate trading patterns, or a pervasive culture that was the ancestor of diverse civilisations that emerged later.

1. Urne rituelle. Kandal, âge du bronze. Bronze, 0,56 m. Ga 2083.

Ce chef-d'œuvre de l'art du bronze ancien remonte probablement à la période s'étendant des environs de 300 av. J.-C. à 300 ap. J.-C. De nombreux objets rituels de ce type, ainsi que des cloches, des haches et des tambours, ont été découverts sur le site de Dong Son dans le nord du Vietnam; ils sont caractéristiques de l'une des plus brillantes périodes de la protohistoire du sud-est asiatique. Des récipients semblables à cette urne ont été retrouvés un peu partout en Asie du Sud-Est, de même qu'au Yunnan, en Chine du Sud, mais leur lieu de fabrication demeure sujet à controverse. Destinés à des cérémonies rituelles, sans doute dans le cadre de cultes agraires, ces objets sont ornés de spirales, de cercles, de triangles, d'étoiles et de bateaux. Leur diffusion sur une vaste aire géographique témoigne de l'importance des relations commerciales entre les différentes régions de l'Asie du Sud-Est, mais aussi d'une culture largement répandue, ancêtre des grandes civilisations qui se sont épanouies par la suite.

១_ កោដ្ឋ ចាក់អង្រែ, កណ្តាល, យុគសំរិត, សំរិត, ០,៥៦ម, គ ២០៨៣

វត្ថុដ៏វិចិត្រពីយុគសំរិតនេះ ប្រហែលស្ថិតនៅចន្លោះប្រមាន៣០០ឆ្នាំមុនគ.ស. ទៅដល់៣០០ឆ្នាំក្រោយគ.ស.។ វត្ថុសម្រាប់ប្រើប្រាស់ក្នុងពិធីប្រភេទនេះ តួយ៉ាងដូចជាជួង, ផ្លែដឹង និងស្គរ គេធ្លាប់ប្រទះឃើញនៅភូមិ Dong Son នៃប្រទេសវៀតណាម។ គឺឈ្មោះនេះហើយដែលឲ្យឈ្មោះទៅដល់អារ្យធម៌មួយទាំងមូល ព្រមទាំងវត្ថុផ្សេងៗដែលមានក្នុងនោះ។ ភាជន៍ផ្សេងៗស្រដៀងនឹងវត្ថុនេះ ខ្លះប្រហែលជាប្រើប្រាស់នៅក្នុងពិធីសាសនាឬទាក់ទងនឹងកសិកម្ម សុទ្ធសឹងមានក្បូរក្បាច់ខ្យងហៀន, រង្វង់មូល, ត្រីកោណទ្រវែង, ផ្កា និងនាវា គេតែងរកឃើញនៅពាសពេញអាស៊ីអាគ្នេយ៍ គិតទាំងតំបន់យូណាន់ផង។ ប៉ុន្តែមណ្ឌលផលិតពុំច្បាស់ថានៅទីណាឡើយ។ ទីតាំងឆ្ងាយពីគ្នានៃវត្ថុទាំងនេះអាចឱ្យគំនិតពីផ្លូវពាណិជ្ជកម្ម ព្រមទាំងចំណុចនៃមណ្ឌលអារ្យធម៌ផ្សេងៗ ដែលផុសចេញអំពីនោះផង។

1. 儀式用壺. カンダール州、クンチャク・アングレ、青銅器時代、青銅、0.56m、Ga 2083

この青銅器は紀元前300年から紀元300年の間に鋳造されたと思われる。この様式の儀式用品や鈴、斧、鼓などが、ヴェトナムのドンソン村から発見されたため、古代ドンソン文化と呼ばれるようになった。渦巻きや環、三角形、星、船などを描いた、信仰または農耕儀式用と思われる同様の壺が、雲南はじめ東南アジア一帯から発見されているが、その製造場所は定かでない。広範囲に流布していることから、交易があったか、後日誕生する様々な文明の基盤となった共通の文化の存在を示していると思われる。

2. Vishnu. Phnom Da, Angkor Borei, Takeo, late ?6th - early 7th C. Sandstone, 2.87 m. Ka 1639.

This eight-armed Vishnu with its commanding mitre represents the god's cosmic manifestation as universal ruler, or chakravartin. One of the earliest and most magnificent of Khmer sculptures, it shows the practice of retaining an arch of the original stone block to support the head, arms and the attributes held in the hands. Some of these (flame, deer skin, flask) are not usually carried by Vishnu and may invoke the broader divine powers of the eight guardians of the cardinal and subcardinal directions. The Phnom Da style, the earliest Brahmanic style in Khmer art, is characterised by hieratic deities with an oval face, aquiline nose, sensitively modelled mouth and elegant continuous arch of the brow. Also typical are the naturalistic modelling of the torso and delicate rendition of the draped cloth.

2. Vishnu. Phnom Da, Angkor Borei, Takeo, fin 6ème (?) - début 7ème s. Grès, 2,87 m. Ka 1639.

Cette statue de Vishnu, coiffé d'une mitre cylindrique et doté de huit bras, représente la manifestation cosmique du dieu en tant que souverain universel ou chakravartin. C'est l'une des plus anciennes et des plus belles sculptures khmères; l'arc de soutien en forme de fer à cheval entourant l'image était destiné à en renforcer la solidité. Certains des attributs (flamme, dépouille de cervidé, vase) ne sont pas traditionnellement associés à ce dieu. Ils pourraient se rapporter aux divinités gardiennes des points cardinaux et inter cardinaux dont Vishnu assumerait ainsi les pouvoirs. Le style du Phnom Da, sans doute le plus ancien de la statuaire brahmanique khmère, se caractérise par des images hiératiques au visage ovale, au nez aquilin et à la bouche délicatement modelée. On notera aussi la ligne continue et élégante des sourcils, le rendu naturel du torse et la finesse d'exécution des plis du costume.

២_ ព្រះនារាយណ៍ ភ្នំដា, អង្គរបុរី, តាកែវ, ចុងស.វ.ទី៦_ដើមស.វ.ទី៧, ថ្មភក់, ២,៨៧ម, ក ១៦៣៩

ព្រះនារាយណ៍ដៃ៨ដែលមានមកុដរាងបំពង់នេះ គឺជាទេពចក្រពត្តិនៃលោកទាំងមូល។ បដិមាដ៏វិចិត្រដែលមានចំណាស់នេះ នៅមានប្រើវង្វង់រាងក្រចកសេះ ដែលជាប់ចេញពីថ្មជាមួយគ្នា ដើម្បីទប់ពង្រឹងព្រះកេស, ដៃ ព្រមទាំងវត្ថុនានាដែលនៅក្នុងដៃនោះ។ គេតនភណ្ឌខ្លះ ពោលគឺអណ្តាតភ្លើង, ស្បែកម្រឹគ, ថូ ជាធម្មតាពុំដែលឃើញព្រះនារាយណ៍កាន់ទេ។ នេះប្រហែលជាគេចង់បញ្ហាញពីអនុភាពនៃទេពនារាយណ៍ ដែលសាយភាយទៅទិសទាំង៨។ រចនាបថភ្នំដា ដែលជារចនាបថចាស់ជាងគេក្នុងសិល្បៈខ្មែរ តែងបង្ហាញពីទេពដែលឈរត្រង់ភ្លឹង មុខរាងទ្រវែង, ច្រមុះមានក្តោង, បបូរមាត់លេចចេញច្បាស់, ចិញ្ចើមជាប់គ្នាយ៉ាងស្រស់។ លក្ខណៈមួយទៀត គឺដងខ្លួនមានសណ្ឋានដូចធម្មជាតិ រីឯសំពត់ក៏រមូតជាប់នឹងខ្លួនដែរ។

2. ヴィシュヌ. タケオ州、アンコール・ボレイ、プノン・ダ、6世紀末？~7世紀初め、砂岩、2.87m、Ka 1639

このヴィシュヌは８臂で、威厳ある宝冠は宇宙の支配者、転輪聖王（チャクラヴァルティン）の象徴である。初期アンコール彫像の中でも最も素晴らしいこの像は、頭部、腕、手の持物を支えるために原石のアーチを残す手法が使われている。持物の一部（炎、鹿皮、杯）は、通常ヴィシュヌの持物ではないので、四方四維の守護神の力を表すものと思われる。アンコール美術の初期ヒンドゥー教様式であるプノン・ダ様式は、わし鼻、繊細な形の口、優雅な眉をした卵形の顔が特徴である。胴体の自然な形や、ドレープがかかった衣の繊細な描き方も同様式の特徴だ。

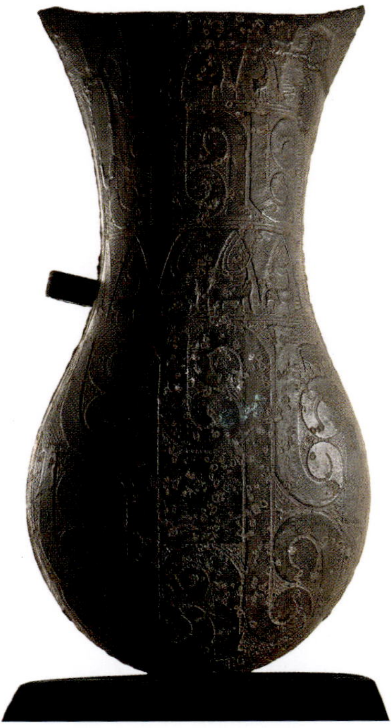

1

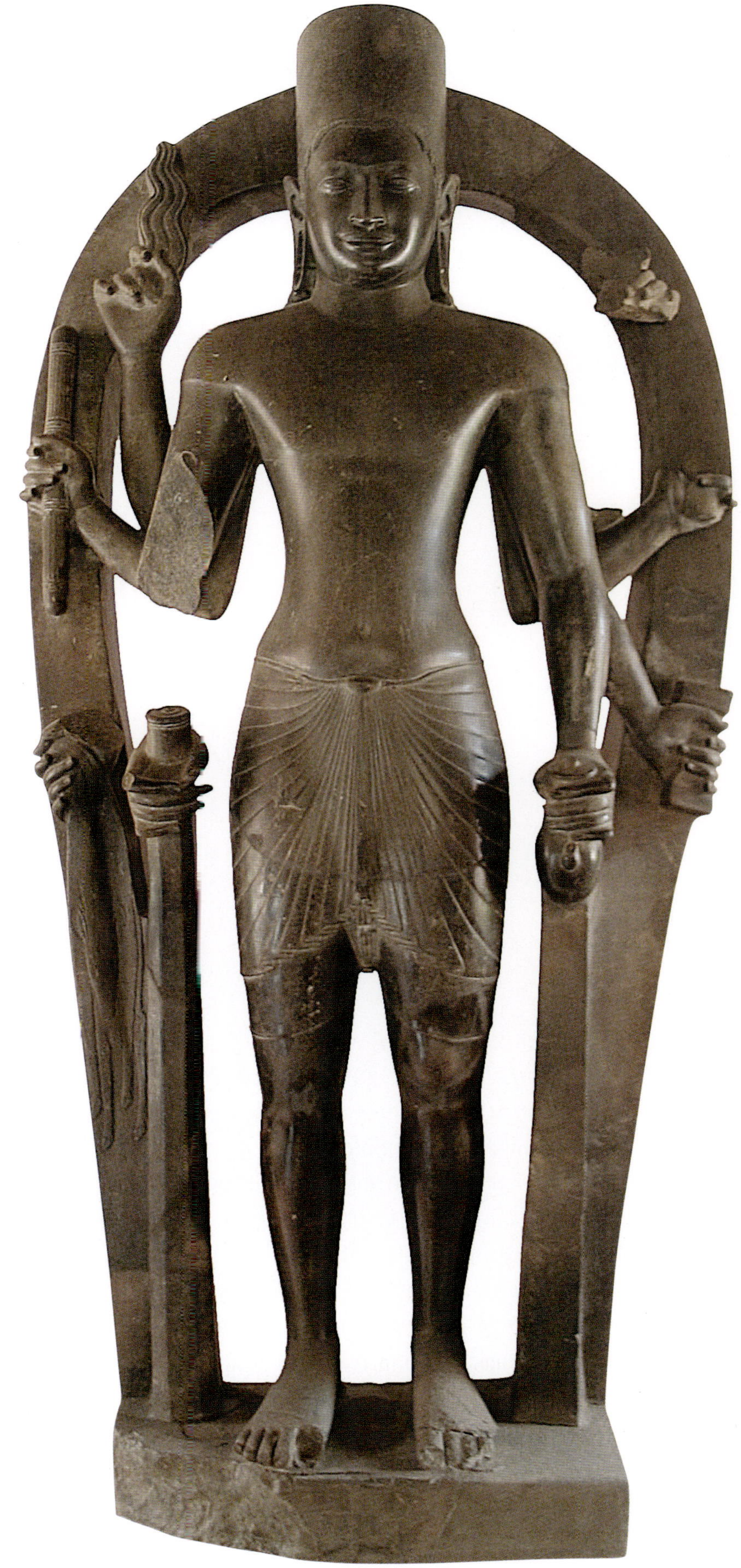

2

3. **Krishna Govardhana.** Vat Koh, Angkor Borei, Takeo, late ?6th-7th C. Sandstone, 1.60 m. Ka 1625.

This high-relief image shows the youthful god Krishna, one of the twenty-four manifestations, or avatars, of Vishnu, holding up Mount Govardhana to protect shepherds from torrential rains inflicted on them as punishment by Indra, god of storms. The tightly curled locks with triple peaks are characteristic of young gods. The naturalistic rendering of musculature and of the oval face are typical of Phnom Da style, which, like Krishna's hip-flexed posture (tribhanga), shows the influence of the Gupta style of India.

3. **Krishna Govardhana.** Vat Koh, Angkor Borei, Takeo, fin 6ème (?) - 7ème s. Grès, 1.60 m. Ka 1625.

Cette sculpture en haut-relief représente le jeune dieu Krishna - l'une des vingt-quatre manifestations du dieu Vishnu - soulevant le mont Govardhana afin de protéger hommes et troupeaux des pluies torrentielles déchaînées par Indra, le dieu de l'orage. La coiffure à trois mèches que porte Krishna est caractéristique des divinités juvéniles. Le traitement naturel de la muscula-ture et le visage ovale sont typiques du style du Phnom Da qui, avec la posture déhanchée du dieu (tribhanga), illustre l'influence de l'art indien d'époque Gupta (4ème -6ème siècles) sur la statuaire khmère ancienne.

៣_ ព្រះក្រឹស្នាទ្រភ្នំគោវធ៌ន វត្តកោះ, អង្គរបុរី, តាកែវ, ចុងស.វ.ទី៦_ដើមស.វ.ទី៧, ថ្មភក់, ១,៦០ម, ក១៦២៥

ផ្ទាំងក្បាច់ក្រឡោតខ្ពស់នេះ បង្ហាញពីព្រះក្រឹស្នាក្នុងយុវវ័យ ដែលជាអវតារមួយក្នុងចំណោម អវតារទាំង២៤នៃព្រះនារាយណ៍ ហើយដែលកំពុងលើកស្ទួយភ្នំគោវធ៌នឡើង ដើម្បីការពារពួកគង្វាលគោឲ្យផុតពីព្យុះភ្លៀង ដែលព្រះឥន្ទ្របង្អុរឡើងក្នុងបំណងដាក់ទណ្ឌកម្មពួកគេ។ សក់មានរាងគូថខ្យង ព្រមទាំងមានកំពោយ៣ដែលជាលក្ខណៈសម្គាល់ទេពក្នុងវ័យក្មេង។ ចម្លាក់ដងខ្លួនធ្វើឡើងដូចធម្មជាតិ រីឯមុខមានរាងទ្រវែង ដែលសុទ្ធសឹងជាចំណុចសំខាន់ៗនៃរចនាបថភ្នំដា ហើយម្យ៉ាងទៀតជំហរខ្លួនទាំងមូលដែលកាច់ជា៣ (ត្រីភង្គ) បង្ហាញថាមានឥទ្ធិពលពីរចនាបថគុប្តនៃប្រទេសឥណ្ឌា។

3. **ゴーヴァルダナ山を持ち上げるクリシュナ.** タケオ州、アンコール・ボレイ、ワット・コー、6世紀末？~7世紀、砂岩、1.60m、Ka 1625

このレリーフはヴィシュヌの24の化身の１つであるクリシュナの若々しい姿を表している。クリシュナはゴーヴァルダナ山を持ち上げて、嵐の神インドラが罰として降らせた大雨から牛飼いたちを守っている。３重の螺髪は若い神の特徴である。自然で逞しい体つきや卵形の顔はプノン・ダ様式の特徴であり、腰をくねらせた姿勢とともにインドのグプタ様式の影響を示している。

4. **Vajimukha.** Kuk Trap, Kandal, 7th C. Sandstone, 1.35 m. Ka 1642.

Vajimukha is Sanskrit for 'horse face'. The image represents one of the two equine forms of Vishnu, Kalkin, the avatar who is yet to come, Vishnu's incarnation at the end of time, and Hayashiras (Hayagriva), the avatar who rescued the sacred Veda texts from demons. In the absence of attributes it cannot be determined which version this sculpture represents. The graceful blend of human and horse features has been rendered with sensitivity and dignity, while the naturalistic treatment of the torso with its hip-swayed posture typifies the Phnom Da style.

4. **Vajimukha.** Kuk Trap, Kandal, 7ème s. Grès, 1,35 m. Ka 1642.

Vajimukha est un terme sanskrit signifiant "face de cheval". Cette sculpture représente l'une des deux formes équines de Vishnu: Kalkin, sa manifesta-tion à venir lors de la fin des temps, ou Hayasiras (Hayagriva), l'aspect sous lequel le dieu a sauvé les textes sacrés du Veda de l'emprise des démons. En l'absence d'attributs, il est impossible de préciser à quelle forme on a affaire ici. L'association du corps humain et de la tête de cheval est rendue avec une dignité et une sensibilité toutes particulières; le traitement du torse et le léger déhanchement sont typiques du style du Phnom Da.

៤_ ពាជីមុខ គុកត្រប់, កណ្ដាល, ស.វ.ទី៧, ថ្មភក់, ១,៣៥ម, ក១៦៤២

ពាជីមុខ មានន័យថា "មុខសេះ"។ បដិមានេះហាក់ដូចជាបង្ហាញពីទិដ្ឋភាពណាមួយនៃអវតារពីររបស់ព្រះនារាយណ៍។ មួយនោះជាសេះ ហៅថា "កល្កិ" ហើយពុំទាន់បានមកបង្ហាញខ្លួននៅលោកយើងនេះនៅឡើយ ទាល់តែដល់ចុងកល្បទើបចុះមក។ ឯមួយទៀតជាសេះដែរ ឈ្មោះថា "ហយសីរស" (ឬ ហយគ្រិវ) ពោលគឺជាសេះដែលបានស្រោចស្រង់គម្ពីរវេទទាំង៤ឲ្យផុតពីដៃយក្ស។ ដោយសារគេគនភណ្ឌផ្សេងៗបាត់បង់អស់ហើយនោះ យើងពុំប្រាកដថាជាអវតារណាមួយឡើយ។ ក្បាលសេះដែលជាប់នឹងដងខ្លួនមនុស្ស ព្រមទាំងត្រគាកដែលកាច់បន្តិចនោះ គេឆ្លាក់ឡើងមើលទៅសមរម្យក្រៃលែង ដែលជាលក្ខណៈរចនាបថភ្នំដា។

4. **ヴァージムカ.** カンダール州、クック・トラップ、7世紀、砂岩、1.35m、Ka 1642

ヴァージムカとはサンスクリット語で馬の顔を意味する。未来に現れるヴィシュヌの最後の化身である馬頭人身のカルキン、または聖典ヴェーダを魔神から取り戻した化身ハヤシラ（ハヤグリヴァ）を表している。持物が不明なので、この石像がどちらの化身なのかは確定できない。人間と馬の特徴が優雅に調和しており、繊細で尊厳がある。胴体の自然さと腰のひねりはプノン・ダ様式の特徴である。

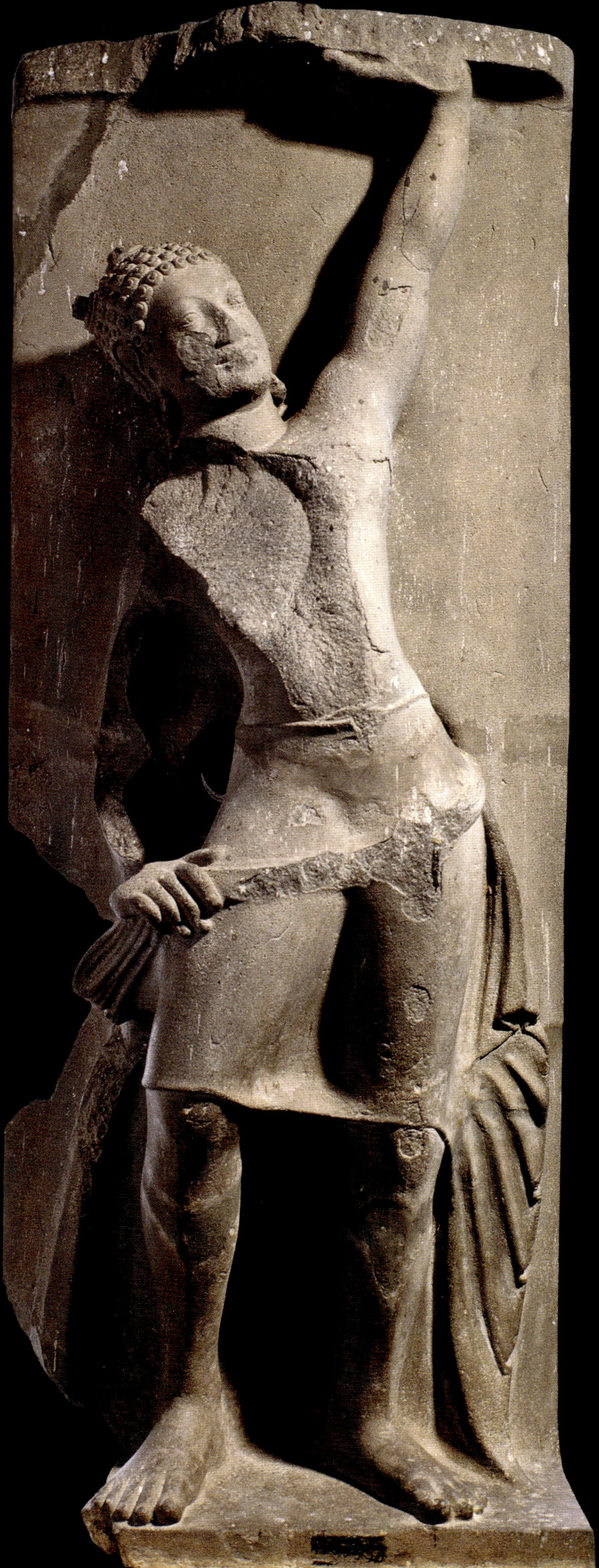

3

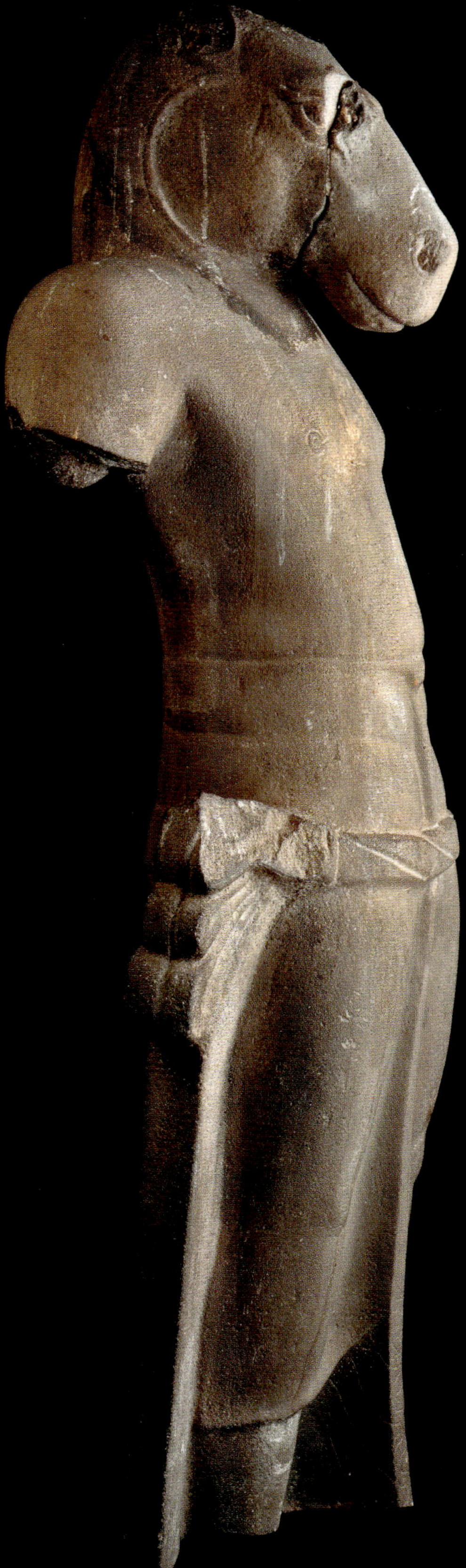

4

5. Vishnu. Tuol Dai Buon, Prei Veng, 7th C. Sandstone, 1.83 m. Ka 1597.

This majestic yet benign image of Vishnu shows the four-armed (chaturbhuja) form of the god, whose hands usually carry a globe, a disk, a conch and a mace as distinguishing attributes. Here only the disk, or chakra, remains, supported by the surviving half of an arch. Though not from Phnom Da, this figure shares the tribhanga posture, naturalistic representation of musculature, delicately carved fingers and refined facial features of that style. The sampot, the Cambodian garment in which a length of cloth is wound round the hips, pulled between the legs and tucked in at the waist, shows the beginnings of a pleated treatment of its ends that would become increasingly elaborate in Khmer morphology.

5. Vishnu. Tuol Dai Buon, Prei Veng, 7ème s. Grès, 1,83 m. Ka 1597.

Cette majestueuse et bienveillante image de Vishnu présente le dieu sous son aspect le plus courant, doté de quatre bras (chaturbhuja). Il porte ses attributs distinctifs: une sphère (la terre), un disque, une conque marine et une massue. Ici, seul le disque (chakra) a subsisté, raccordé à la tête par une réserve de pierre. Bien que ne provenant pas du Phnom Da, cette statue en offre toutes les caractéristiques stylistiques: léger déhanchement, traitement naturel de la musculature, doigts souples et déliés, visage aux traits fins et délicats. Le sampot - ce vêtement khmer traditionnel composé d'une pièce d'étoffe drapée autour des hanches, passée entre les jambes et serrée à la taille - présente des extrémités plissées, à l'avant et à l'arrière, appelées à devenir toujours plus élaborées par la suite.

៥_ ព្រះនារាយណ៍ ទួលដៃបួន, ព្រៃវែង, ស.វ.ទី៧, ថ្មភក់, ១,៨៣ម, ក ១៥៩៧

ថ្វីត្បិតតែមានទំហំធម្មតា បដិមាដែលបង្ហាញពីព្រះនារាយណ៍ដៃ៤នេះ មានភាពស្ងប់ស្ងែងណាស់។ ជាធម្មតាដៃទាំងនេះកាន់ផែនដី, ចក្រ, ស័ង្ខ និងដំបង ជាកេតនភណ្ឌ។ រីឯបដិមានេះ មានតែចក្រប៉ុណ្ណោះដែលនៅគង់វង្ស ដោយសារជាប់នឹងផ្នែកមួយនៃរង្វង់ទល់ទ្រវាងក្រចកសេះ។ រូបនេះពុំមកពីតំបន់ភ្នំដាមែនពិត ប៉ុន្តែអាចបញ្ចូលទៅក្នុងរចនាបថនោះបាន ដោយសារមានជំហរខ្លួនកាច់ជា៣, សាច់ដុំដងខ្លួនដូចធម្មជាតិ, ម្រាមដៃឆ្លាក់ឡើងដោយផ្ចិតផ្ចង់ ព្រមទាំងទម្រង់មុខមានភាពរស់រវើក។ សំពត់ដែលពាសជុំវិញត្រគាកនោះ មានកន្ទុយក្បិនវាត់មកក្រោយ ហើយញាត់នៅចង្កេះ។ តំណក្រោយមក សំពត់ក្បិននេះកាន់តែបង្ហាញពីថ្នក់និងផ្នត់ដែលគេរៀបចំឲ្យកាន់តែស្អេកស្កះ។

5. ヴィシュヌ. プレイヴェン州、トゥオル・ダイ・ブオン、7世紀、砂岩、1.83m、Ka 1597

威厳と慈悲深さを備えたヴィシュヌ像である。ヴィシュヌの４臂は通常、法螺貝・円輪・棍棒・蓮華を持物としている。この像では円輪（チャクラ）だけが補強のためのつなぎと共に残っている。プノン・ダからのものではないが、腰をひねった姿、自然で逞しい体つき、繊細な指や洗練された顔などプノン・ダ様式である。サンポットと呼ばれる裙の折り返しには、後に凝った形になる兆がみられる。

6. Shiva. Kompong Cham Kau, Stung Treng, 7th C. Sandstone, 1.65 m. Ka 1636.

This slender and somewhat rigid figure with its unusually short sampot probably represents Shiva as an ascetic, or rishi, an identification based on the attribute in his right hand, a flask in gourd form. Anthropomorphic forms of Shiva like this are rare in early Khmer art, where the god is usually represented by a linga. Support structures include thin struts attaching the forearms to the torso and a residual web of stone between the ankles. The somewhat schematic treatment of limbs lacks the refinement of the Phnom Da style but the statue nevertheless has a commanding presence accentuated by the highly stylised treatment of the twisted and braided locks (jatamukuta) that flare from the head; (compare Shiva's coiffure in the scene on the lintel, #10, and the mukhalinga, #7).

6. Shiva. Kompong Cham Kau, Stung Treng, 7ème s. Grès, 1,65 m. Ka 1636.

Cette sculpture élancée mais quelque peu rigide, avec son sampot court plutôt inhabituel, représente probablement Shiva sous les traits d'un ascète, identification rendue possible grâce à l'attribut tenu dans la main droite: un vase en forme de gourde et doté d'un petit bec. Les images anthropomorphes de Shiva sont rares dans l'art khmer ancien où le dieu est plus souvent représenté sous la forme symbolique du linga. On notera ici la présence d'éléments de renfort peu courants comme les réserves de pierre raccordant les bras au torse ou unissant les chevilles entre elles. Si le traitement schématique des traits ne possède pas le raffinement du style du Phnom Da, l'œuvre présente néanmoins une certaine grandeur. Le chignon d'ascète (jatamukuta) stylisé qui se dresse au sommet du crâne est la coiffure caractéristique de Shiva.

៦_ ព្រះឥសូរ កំពង់ចាមកៅ, ស្ទឹងត្រែង, ស.វ.ទី៧, ថ្មភក់, ១,៦៥ម, ក ១៦៣៦

រូបដែលមានដងខ្លួនរាងស្រឡូន តែត្រង់ថ្កឹង ព្រមទាំងស្លៀកសំពត់ខ្លីខុសធម្មតានេះ ប្រហែលជារូបព្រះឥសូរក្នុងទិដ្ឋភាពជាឥសី ដោយយោងទៅតាមថូដែលកាន់នៅនឹងដៃ ហើយដែលស្រដៀងនឹងផ្លែឃ្លោក។ ព្រះឥសូរដែលមានរូបរាងជាមនុស្សរបៀបនេះ ពុំសូវសម្បូណ៌ឡើយនៅក្នុងសិល្បៈខ្មែរដំបូង ព្រោះគេច្រើនតែឆ្លាក់ជារូបលិង្គ។ ក្នុងចំណោមជន្ទល់ពង្រឹងទាំងអម្បាលម៉ាន ឃើញមាន នៅសល់ផ្នែកដែលភ្ជាប់ដៃមកដងខ្លួន ព្រមទាំងផ្នែកដែលភ្ជាប់កជើងទាំងពីរ។ អវៈយវៈឆ្លាក់ពុំបានស្អាតប្រសើរដូចក្នុងរចនាបថភ្នំដាឡើយ។ ប៉ុន្តែជាទូទៅ បដិមាទាំងមូលហាក់ដូចជាមានអនុភាពដែរ ដោយសារមានផ្នួងសក់បួងវេញឡើងលើរាងដូចជាម្កុដ (ចូរប្រៀបជាមួយរូបនៅលើផ្តែរលេខ១១ និងរូបមុខលិង្គលេខ៨)។

6. シヴァ. ストゥントレン州、コンポン・チャム・カウ、7世紀、砂岩、1.65m、Ka 1636

非常に短い裙をまとい、ほっそりしているが、やや硬直い印象を与えるこの石像は、右手にひょうたん形の細口びんを持っていることから、リシとしてのシヴァを表していると思われる。初期のクメール美術では通常、シヴァはリンガによって象徴され、このような人間姿のシヴァ像は稀である。前腕と胴は細い支柱でつながっており、両足首の間にも支柱が残っている。手足は形式化されており、プノン・ダ様式の洗練性はないが、髪束を花弁のように重ねた髪髻冠（ジャタムクタ）によって威厳のある姿になっている。（No.10リンテル、およびNo.7 ムカリンガのシヴァの髪を参照。）

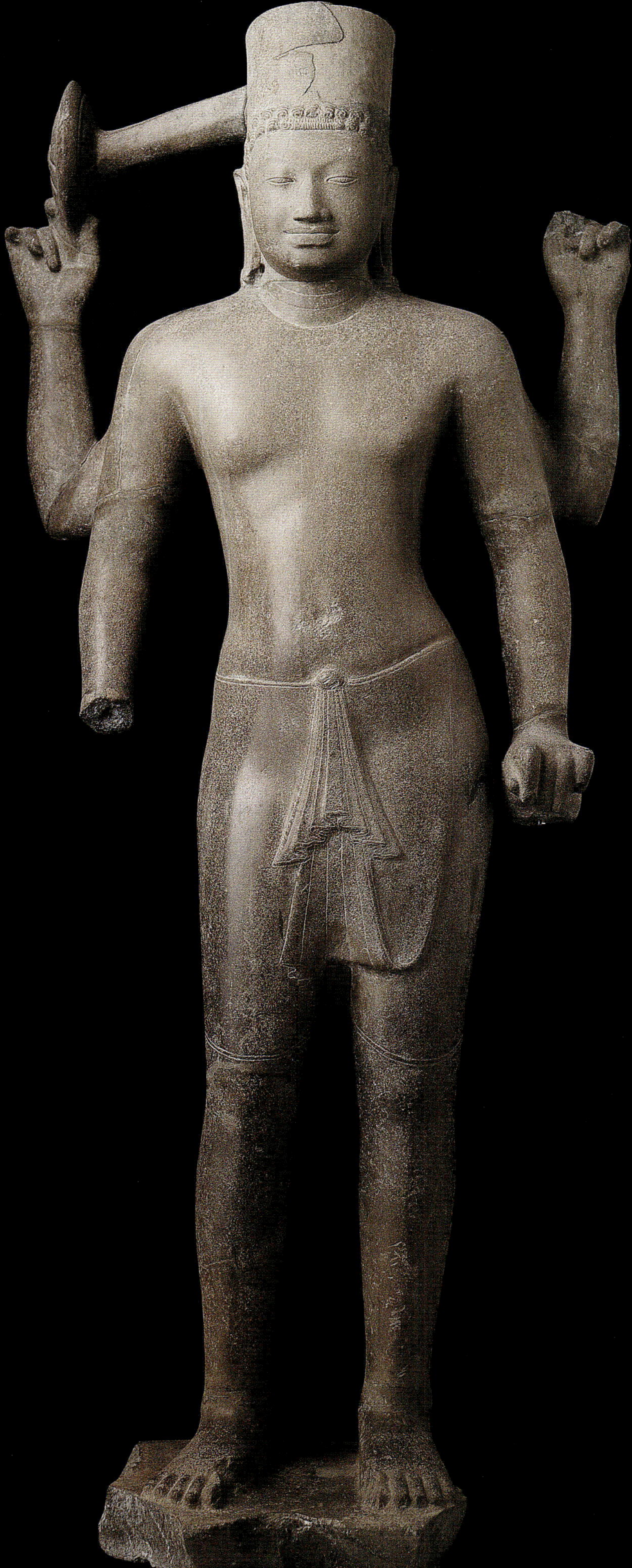

5

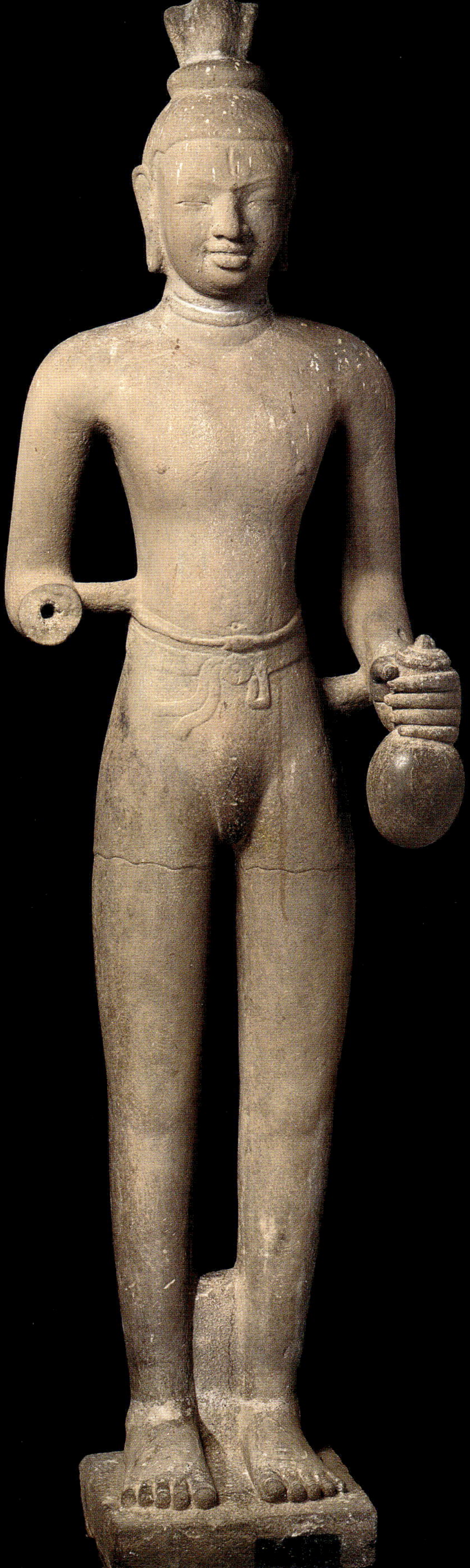

6

7. Mukhalinga. Wat Bodhi Metrei, Takeo, 7th-8th C. Sandstone, 0.83 m. Ka 1622.

Early Khmer representations of Shiva were usually non-manifest, that is, presented in the abstract form of the linga, phallic symbol of fertility. Some, like this example, had faces (mukha is Sanskrit for face), and most were carved in three sections representing the trimurti, or Hinduistic triad. Brahma, commanding the four cardinal directions, is symbolised in the square base. Vishnu, as in his chakravartin cosmic form, controls the eight cardinal and subcardinal directions in the middle octagonal section. Shiva, symbol of cosmic infinity, is represented in the cylindrical top third.

7. Mukhalinga. Vat Po Metrey, Takeo, 7ème - 8ème s. Grès, 0,83 m. Ka 1622.

Les représentations les plus anciennes de Shiva sont souvent non manifestes. Le dieu est figuré de manière abstraite par un symbole phallique associé à la fertilité: le linga. Certains linga, comme ici, possèdent des visages (mukha est le mot sanskrit pour visage). La plupart sont composés de trois sections représentant la trimurti ou triade hindoue. Brahma, le créateur (également gardien des points cardinaux), est symbolisé par la base de section carrée. Vishnu, le préservateur (régent des points cardinaux et inter cardinaux dans sa forme cosmique - voir le Vishnu à huit bras du Phnom Da, #2), se manifeste dans la partie médiane de section octogonale. Shiva, le destructeur (symbole de l'infini), est représenté par la partie supérieure de section circulaire.

៧_ មុខលិង្គ វត្តពោធិមេត្រីយ៍, តាកែវ, ស.វ.ទី៧_៨, ថ្មភក់, ០,៨៣ម, ក១៦២២

នៅដើមសិល្បៈខ្មែរ គេពុំសូវឆ្លាក់ព្រះឥសូរដែលមានរូបរាងដូចមនុស្សទេ គឺច្រើនតែឆ្លាក់ជាលិង្គ ដែលជានិមិត្តរូបនៃភោគផល។ ជួនកាលលិង្គនោះមានមុខ ដែលរូបនៅទីនេះជាឧទាហរណ៍ស្រាប់។ លិង្គគេឆ្លាក់ឲ្យមាន៣ភាគខុសៗគ្នា ដើម្បីបង្ហាញពីនិមិត្តរូបទាំង៣នៃសាសនាព្រាហ្ម។ ព្រះព្រហ្មដែលត្រួតត្រាលើទិសទាំង៤ មានរាង៤ជ្រុងនៅបាត។ ផ្នែកកណ្តាលមាន៨ជ្រុង គឺព្រះនារាយណ៍ក្នុងឋានៈជាទេពចក្រពត្តិ ដែលបញ្ជាទៅទិសនិងអនុទិសទាំង៨។ ព្រះឥសូរដែលជានិមិត្តរូបនៃចក្រវាឡ ហើយដែលគ្មានទីបញ្ចប់ មានរាងមូលនៅលើបង្អស់។

7. ムカリンガ. タケオ州、ワット・ボーディ・メトレイ、7~8世紀、砂岩、0.83m、Ka 1622

初期クメール美術において、シヴァは通常、人間姿ではなく、リンガという生殖を象徴する男根形として表される。リンガの一部には顔（ムカはサンスクリット語で「顔」）があり、その多くはヒンドゥー教の三神一体、トリムルティを象徴して三方向に彫られている。四方を支配するブラフマーは下の四角形に象徴されている。ヴィシュヌはチャクラヴァルティン（世界の支配者）の形態で、中央の八角形で四方四維を支配している。宇宙の無限の象徴シヴァは上部の円柱で表されている。

8. Nandin. Bassac, Rumduol, Svay Rieng, 7th C. Sandstone, 0.33 x 0.55 m. Ka 1584.

This highly naturalistic representation of the sacred bull Nandin, the mount, or vahana, of Shiva, is shown with the third eye that is borne in the forehead of Shiva himself. This suggests that he also invokes the animal manifestation of the god. Such sculptures were always placed in front of shrines of Shiva. Nandin is associated in Khmer myth with the story of Preah Ko, the sacred bull, and has acquired a national significance in Cambodia beyond the symbolism deriving from Indic iconography. The value attached to Nandin may account for the affectionate realism that typifies Khmer images of the sacred vehicle of Shiva.

8. Nandin. Bassac, Rumduol, Svay Rieng, 7ème s. Grès, 0,33 x 0,55 m. Ka 1584.

Cette représentation du taureau sacré Nandin, monture (ou vahana) de Shiva, possède un troisième œil figuré traditionnellement sur le front du dieu lui-même: ce détail indique qu'il s'agit aussi de sa forme animale. De telles images prenaient place à l'avant des sanctuaires dédiés à Shiva. À une époque indéterminée, sans doute après la période angkorienne, Nandin s'est trouvé associé à l'histoire de Preah Ko-Preah Keo dans la mythologie khmère. Au-delà de sa signification dans l'iconographie hindoue, il a acquis une importance fondamentale dans la culture religieuse cambodgienne moderne, entre autres en tant que symbole de fertilité. On notera la facture naturaliste attachante qui caractérise les représentations de Nandin tout au long de l'évolution de l'art khmer.

៨_ ព្រះគោ បាសាក់, រំដួល, ស្វាយរៀង, ស.វ.៧, ថ្មភក់, ០,៣៣ម × ០,៥៥ម, ក១៥៨៤

ព្រះគោនន្ទីដែលជាជំនិះនៃព្រះឥសូរនេះ គេឆ្លាក់ឱ្យឃើញដូចជាក្នុងធម្មជាតិពិត ហើយមានភ្នែកទី៣នៅកណ្តាលថ្ងាសដូចព្រះឥសូរដែរ។ នេះបង្ហាញថាលើសពីជំនិះទៅទៀត ព្រះគោជានិមិត្តម្យ៉ាងនៃព្រះឥសូរតែម្តង។ គេតែងតម្កល់រូបព្រះគោនៅតាមច្រកចូលទៅគុហាដែលតម្កល់បដិមាព្រះឥសូរ។ គោនន្ទីនៅប្រទេសកម្ពុជា ជាតួអង្គសំខាន់នៅក្នុងរឿងព្រះគោព្រះកែវ។ ចាប់តាំងពីសម័យកណ្តាលមក ក៏ក្លាយទៅជានិមិត្តរូបជាតិ ដែលមានន័យវែងឆ្ងាយជាងនៅក្នុងបដិមាសាស្ត្រឥណ្ឌាទៅទៀត។ ដោយសារតួនាទីពិសេសនៃជំនិះព្រះឥសូរនេះហើយ ទើបគេតែងស្ថាបនាព្រះគោដោយផ្ចិតផ្ចង់ក្រៃលែង មើលទៅដូចគោក្នុងធម្មជាតិដូច្នោះ។

8. ナンディン. スヴァイリエン州、ロムドゥオル、バサック、7世紀、砂岩、高0.33m、長0.55m、Ka 1584

この写実的な聖牛ナンディンはシヴァの乗り物であり、シヴァの額の第３眼と同じく第３眼が描かれ、神の化身の動物であることを示している。このような石像は通常、シヴァ寺院に安置される。ナンディンはプレア・コーというクメール神話の聖牛にも関係しており、カンボジアではインド以上、意味を持つようになった。クメールのシヴァの乗り物の描き方に愛情がこもり、写実的なのは、ナンディンを重視していたためと思われる。

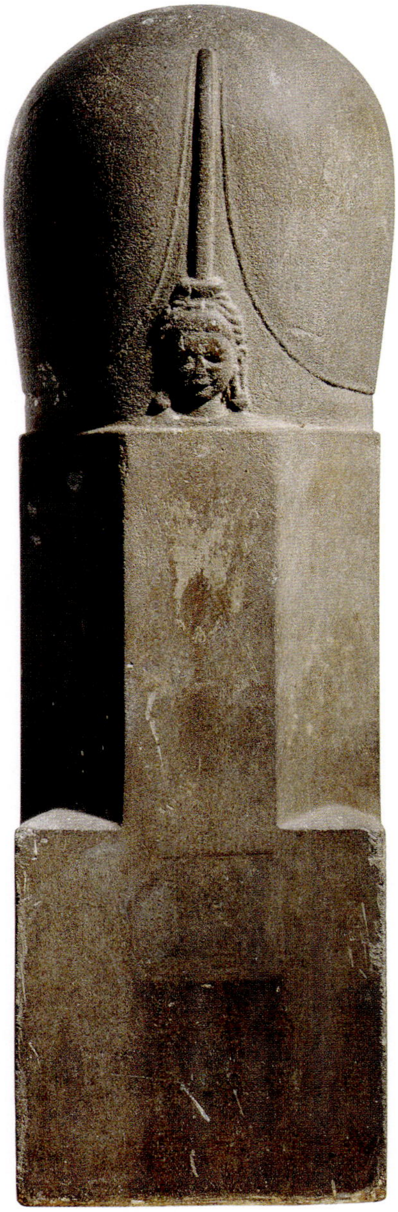

7

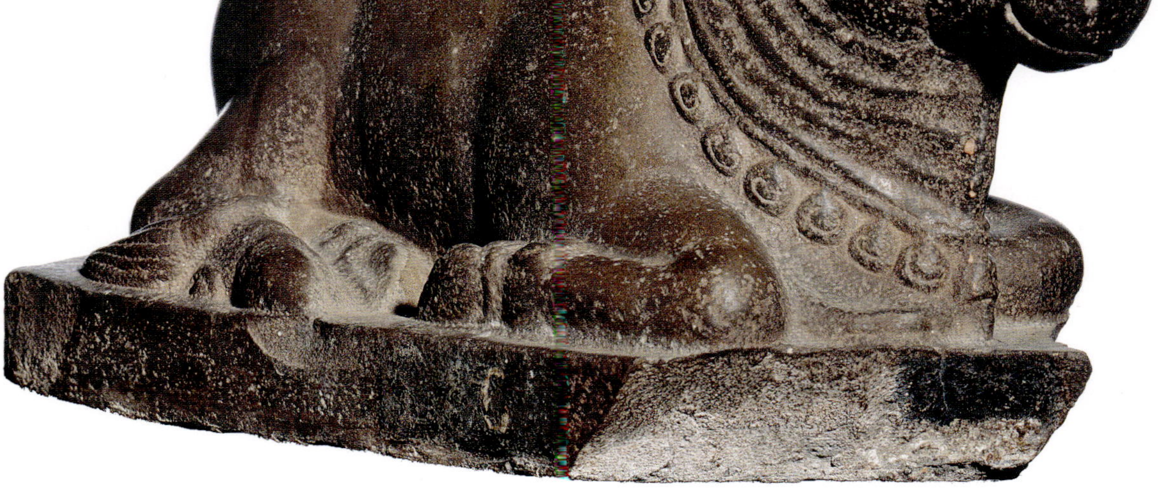

8

9. Ganesha. Tuol Pheakines, Kuk Trap, Kandal, 7th-8th C. Sandstone, 0.74 x 0.63 m. Ka 1588.

Ganesha is one of the most popular gods in the Brahmanic pantheon. The elephant-headed deity is the son of Shiva and Parvati whose human head was struck off by an enraged Shiva, according to one legend, when Ganesha tried to prevent his entry to Parvati's quarters. Shiva assuaged Parvati's grief by replacing the head with that of the first living creature to appear, an elephant. Ganesha is lord of categories and new enterprises, leading supplicants to caress his ample stomach. He is also lord of obstacles, which he may overcome but also instigate.

9. Ganesha. Tuol Pheakines, Kandal, 7ème - 8ème s. Grès, 0,74 x 0,63 m. Ka 1588.

Ganesha est l'une des divinités les plus populaires du panthéon brahmanique. Le dieu à tête d'éléphant est le fils de Shiva et Parvati. Selon l'une des légendes le concernant, Ganesha aurait été décapité par Shiva alors qu'il tentait de lui interdire l'accès aux appartements de la déesse. Pour apaiser la peine de son épouse, Shiva aurait alors commandé à ses serviteurs d'aller quérir la tête du premier être vivant qu'ils rencontreraient pour remplacer celle qu'il venait de trancher: ce fut un éléphant. Ganesha, Maître des "catégories" (d'êtres) et des nouvelles entreprises est aussi le Seigneur des obstacles qu'il peut aider à surmonter mais qu'il sait aussi susciter.

៩_ ព្រះគណេស ទួលភគណេស, គុកត្រប់, កណ្ដាល, ស.វ.ទី៧_៨, ថ្មភក់, ០,៧៤ម × ០,៦៣ម, ក ១៥៨៨

ព្រះគណេសស្ថិតនៅក្នុងចំណោមទេពដែលគេគោរពជាងគេនៅក្នុងសាសនាព្រាហ្មណ៍។ ទេពដែលមានព្រះកេសដំរីនេះ ជាបុត្រនៃព្រះឥសូរនិងនាងបាពតី។ រឿងនិទានថា ព្រះគណេសបានឃាត់ព្រះឥសូរ ដែលខ្លួនពុំស្គាល់ថាជាឪពុកមិនឲ្យចូលទៅជួបនាងបាពតី។ ឯព្រះឥសូរខ្វាល់ខ្លាំងពេកក៏កាត់ក្បាលនោះដាច់ទៅ។ លុះឃើញនាងបាពតីកើតទុក្ខខ្លាំង ព្រះអង្គក៏សន្យាថា ជនទី១ដែលដើរកាត់ទីនោះ ព្រះអង្គនឹងកាត់ក្បាលទៅភ្ជាប់ឲ្យបុត្រវិញ។ ចៃដន្យអ្វី ជនទី១នោះជាដំរី។ ព្រះគណេសជាទេពដែលជំរុញជនទានាឲ្យពុះពារក្នុងការងារផ្សេងៗ។ ដូច្នោះហើយ បានជាគេចូលចិត្តមកស្ទាបអង្អែលក្បាលពោះរបស់ព្រះអង្គ។ ម្យ៉ាងទៀតព្រះគណេសជាទេពដែលបង្កើតឧបសគ្គផង និងជំនះឧបសគ្គផង។

9. ガネーシャ. カンダール州、クック・トラップ、トゥオル・ペアクン、7~8世紀、砂岩、高0.74m、幅0.63m、Ka 1588

シヴァとパールヴァティーの息子で象頭人身のガネーシャは、ヒンドゥー教の神々の中でも最も人気がある。伝説によると、シヴァがパールヴァティーの部屋に入ろうとし、ガネーシャに阻止されたことを怒り、その首を切り落とした。嘆き悲しむパールヴァティーをなだめるために、シヴァは最初に遭遇した生き物である象の頭をガネーシャにつけ、生き返らせた。ガネーシャは知恵と新起業の神であり、信者はその太鼓腹をなでる。また障害の神でもあり、障害を取り除いたり、生み出す。

10. Lintel. Vat Eng Khna, Kompong Svay, Kompong Thom, 2nd half 7th C. Sandstone, 0.55 x 1.85 m. Ka 1774.

The horizontal vegetal band flanked by consoles and studded with three cartouches on this lintel is typical of the Prei Kmeng style. The cartouche to the viewer's left shows Brahma, the central one depicts Shiva, his linga surrounded by flames, while Vishnu, a conch in one of his left hands, is on the right. The scene represents the origin of the linga and Shiva's pre-eminence: Brahma, as a goose, flew high, while Vishnu, as a boar, dug deep to encompass the dimensions of an immense pillar of fire that appeared before them, but both failed. When the flames revealed Shiva, the other gods were forced to acknowledge his supremacy. The lower scene may depict a king's consecration, possibly invoking divine power by associating the ruler with the gods.

10. Linteau. Vat Eng Khna, Kompong Thom, 2nde moitié du 7ème s. Grès, 0,55 x 1, 85 m. Ka 1774.

Le bandeau horizontal orné de motifs végétaux, frappé de trois fleurons et flanqué de consoles de ce linteau est caractéristique du style de Prei Kmeng. Le fleuron de gauche est occupé par Brahma, le fleuron central présente Shiva, apparaissant dans un linga bordé de petites flammes, le fleuron de droite contient Vishnu, tenant sa conque dans la main supérieure gauche. La scène représente le mythe de l'origine du linga et démontre la supériorité de Shiva sur les deux autres dieux. Afin de prendre la mesure d'une immense colonne de feu apparue devant eux, Brahma, sous les traits d'une oie sauvage, s'éleva haut dans le ciel, cependant que Vishnu, sous ceux d'un sanglier, s'enfonça profondément dans la terre. Aucun des deux ne put atteindre les extrémités de cette colonne de flammes dans laquelle apparut finalement Shiva, démontrant ainsi sa suprématie. La scène du registre inférieur pourrait représenter la consécration d'un souverain sous la caution des divinités figurées au-dessus.

១០_ ផ្ដែរ វត្តឥន្ទ្រកុមារ, កំពង់ស្វាយ, កំពង់ធំ, ផ្នែកទី២នៃគ.ស.ទី៧, ថ្មភក់, ០,៥៥ម×១,៨៥ម, ក ១៧៧៤

ដងធ្នូផ្ដែរនេះមានទម្រនៅចុងសងខាង ព្រមទាំងមានសន្លឹក៣នៅតាមបណ្ដោយ។ ខាងឆ្វេងបង្ហាញពីព្រះព្រហ្ម។ កណ្ដាលជារូបលិង្គដែលមានព្រះភក្ត្រព្រះឥសូរ រីឯខាងស្ដាំគឺព្រះនារាយណ៍ដែលកាន់ស័ង្ខនៅព្រះហស្ដស្ដាំ។ ទាំងនេះបង្ហាញអំពីរឿងលិង្គព្រះឥសូរដែលមានមហិទ្ធិឫទ្ធិខ្លាំងក្លា៖ ព្រះព្រហ្មកាឡាខ្លួនជាហង្សហើរទៅលើឆ្ងាយ ឯព្រះនារាយណ៍តាំណែងខ្លួនជាជ្រូកព្រៃ ហើយឈ្មុលទៅក្នុងដីយ៉ាងជ្រៅ ដើម្បីរកឲ្យឃើញដើមនិងចុងនៃសសរភ្លើងមួយដែលវែងហួសប្រមាណ។ ការរកដើមចុងនោះពុំបានលទ្ធផលឡើយ ទើបព្រះឥសូរនិមិត្តខ្លួនឡើងនៅសសរភ្លើងនោះ ដើម្បីឲ្យទេពទាំងពីរទទួលស្គាល់ថាព្រះអង្គមានអនុភាពលើសគេ។ ជួរក្រោមគឺពិធីរាជាភិសេកមួយដែលហាក់ដូចជាចង់ប្រៀបរាជ្យអំណាចស្ដេចទៅនឹងទេព។

10. リンテル. コンポントム州、コンポン・スヴァイ、ワット・エン・クナー、7世紀後半、砂岩、高0.55m、幅1.85m、Ka 1774

水平の植物の帯の両端の像にはさまれ、3つの花枠があるこのリンテルは典型的なプレイ・クメン様式である。向かって左側の像はブラフマー、中央の花枠は炎につつまれシヴァの顔をつけたリンガ、右側は左手に法螺貝を持ったヴィシュヌが浮き彫りにされている。リンガの由来とシヴァの優位性を表している。鵞鳥姿のブラフマーは空高く飛び、猪姿のヴィシュヌは地面を深く掘り、目前に現れた巨大な炎柱の大きさを測ろうとしたが、失敗した。炎からシヴァが現れたとき、他の神々はシヴァの優位を認めざるを得なかった。アーチ内部は王の即位を描いているようだ。神との関係を描くことで神授の権力を示していると思われる。

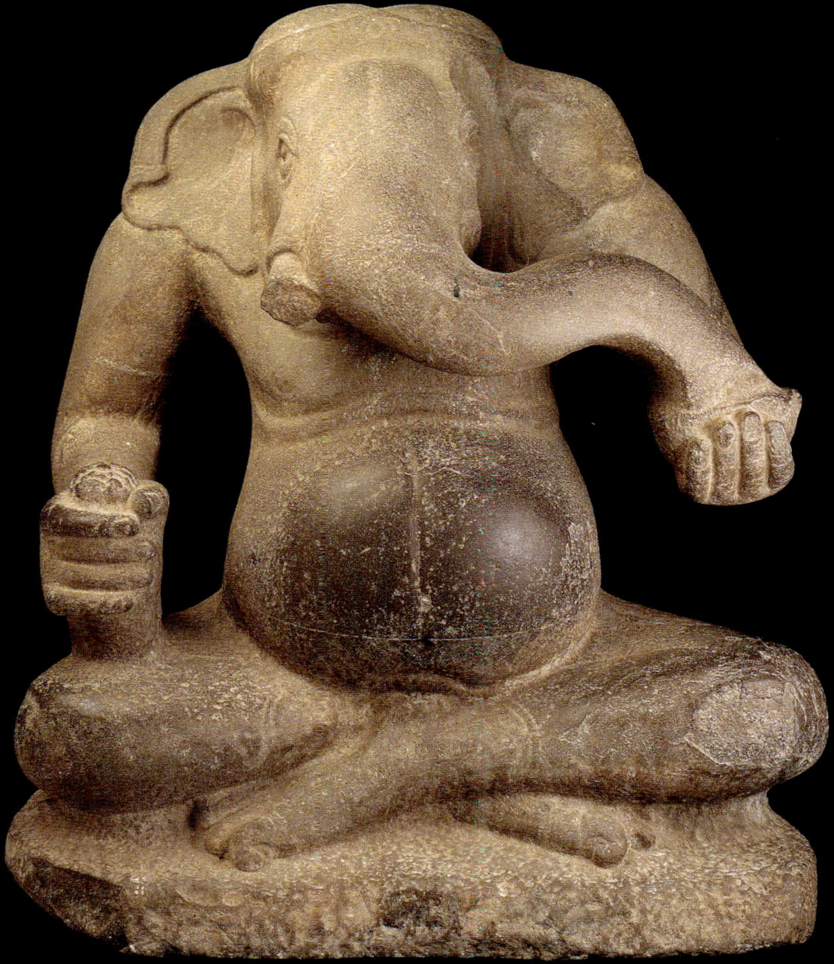

9

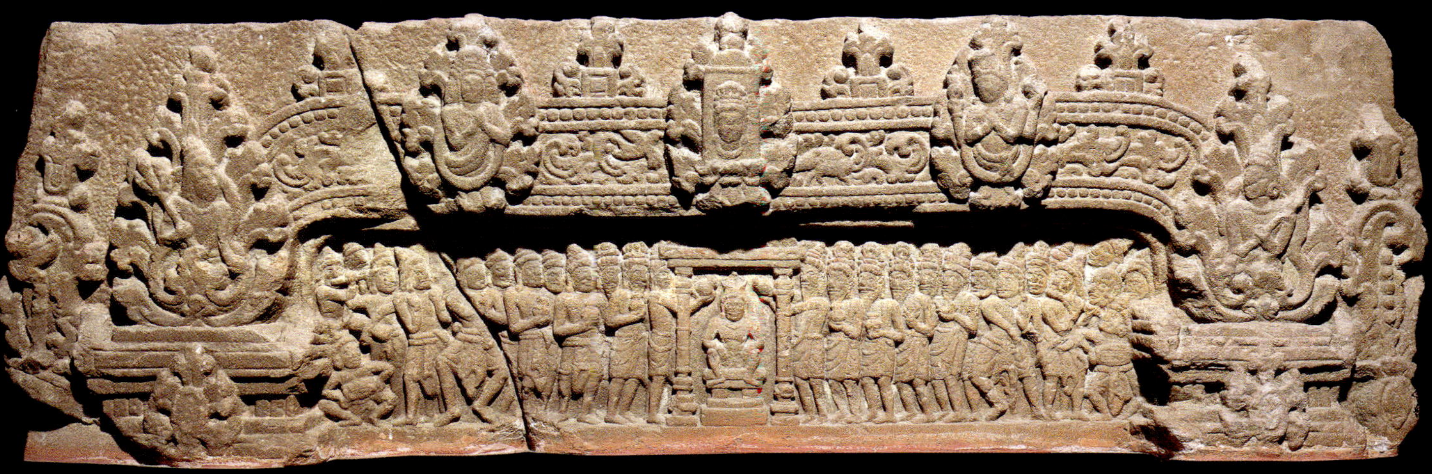

10

11. Durga Mahishasuramardini. Sambor Prei Kuk, N 9, Kompong Thom, 1st quarter 7th C. Sandstone, 1.65 m. Ka 1593.

Perhaps one of the most memorable of all Khmer sculptures, this represents the goddess Durga, who is related to both Shiva and Vishnu and was widely worshipped in Cambodia. Her double divinity endows Durga alone among the gods with the strength to slay the powerful buffalo demon, Mahishasura, who would originally have been represented beneath her feet. The dynamic image typifies the realism and grace of the northern Sambor Prei Kuk style (as distinct from the southern Phnom Da style), the sensuous torso in its triple-flexed posture embodying the beauty, vigour and power synonymous with the invincible goddess.

11. Durga Mahishasuramardini. Sambor Prei Kuk, N 9, Kompong Thom, 1er quart du 7ème s. Grès, 1,65 m. Ka 1593.

Cette sculpture, sans doute l'une des plus belles de tout l'art khmer, représente la déesse Durga - divinité associée à la fois à Shiva et à Vishnu -, particulièrement vénérée à l'époque préangkorienne. Incarnant la puissance de tous les dieux réunis, Durga seule était à même de détruire le puissant démon buffle, Mahishasura, dont l'image figurait à l'origine sous les pieds de la déesse. Cette œuvre dynamique est caractéristique du style "septentrional" de Sambor Prei Kuk, par opposition au style "méridional" du Phnom Da. La posture déhanchée, toute de vigueur et de puissance contenues, ainsi que la sensualité du modelé du torse s'accordent avec le caractère invincible de la déesse.

១១_ នាងទុគ៌ាសម្លាប់ក្របី សម្បូណ៌ព្រៃគុក, N9, កំពង់ធំ, ផ្នែកខាងដើមនៃស.វ.ទី៧, ថ្មភក់, ១,៦៥ម, ក ១៥៩៣

នេះគឺជាចម្លាក់ខ្មែរដ៏សំខាន់មួយ ដែលជារូបនាងទុគ៌ា ពោលគឺទេវីដែលទាក់ទងនឹងព្រះឥសូរផង ព្រះនារាយណ៍ផង ព្រមទាំងដែលគេគោរពជាទូទៅនៅកម្ពុជាសម័យបុរាណ។ កម្លាំងទេពទាំងពីរនោះ បញ្ចូលមកស្ថិតនៅក្នុងនាងទុគ៌ានេះ ដើម្បីទៅពិឃាតអសោរក្របី ដែលគេឆ្លាក់នៅក្រោមជើងនាង ប៉ុន្តែដែលថ្មនោះបាក់បែកទៅ។ ភាពរស់រវើកដូចក្នុងធម្មជាតិ ព្រមទាំងទ្រង់ទ្រាយដ៏បវរនៃបដិមានេះជាលក្ខណៈសម្គាល់រចនាបថសម្បូណ៌ព្រៃគុកខាងជើង ដែលតែងបង្ហាញពីដងខ្លួនដ៏ស្រឡូន កាច់អែនជាបី។ ទាំងនេះបង្ហាញពីសម្រស់លាយគ្នានឹងមហិទ្ធិឫទ្ធិផង ត្បិតជាទេវីដែលពុំមាននរណាផ្ចាញ់បាន។

11. ドゥルガー. コンポントム州、サンボール・プレイ・クック第9祠堂、7世紀第1四半期、砂岩、1.65m、Ka1593

クメール像の中でも最も印象深いこの石像は女神ドゥルガーで、シヴァとヴィシュヌと関係があり、カンボジアでは広範に亘って崇拝された。シヴァとヴィシュヌと関係があるドゥルガーだけが、水牛の魔神マヒシャを刺し殺す力を与えられた。この像も原型では足下にマヒシャが描かれていたはずである。ダイナミックな姿はリアリズムと優雅さが特徴の北サンボール・プレイ・クック様式の代表作であり、柔らかな胴体は無敵の女神の美、迫力と権力を象徴している。

12. Harihara. Sambor Prei Kuk, N 10, Kompong Thom, 1st quarter 7th C. Sandstone, 1.69 m. Ka 1607.

Harihara is a composite deity, often represented in pre-Angkorian Cambodia but seldom afterwards, with Shiva embodied on his proper right side and Vishnu on his left. In this example, where much of the supporting arch remains, the only attributes still existing are Vishnu's disk in the upper left hand and Shiva's rosary in the lower right. The right side of the head shows Shiva's headdress, the ascetic's jatamukuta, formed from twisted locks, and the left is crowned with Vishnu's cylindrical mitre. In addition, half of Shiva's third eye is visible on the forehead. The naturalistic depiction of the tense musculature of the torso and the refinement of the gentle face and delicate fingers typifies the Sambor Prei Kuk style.

12. Harihara. Sambor Prei Kuk, N 10, Kompong Thom, 1er quart du 7ème s. Grès, 1,69 m. Ka 1607.

Harihara est une divinité composite, fréquemment représentée à l'époque préangkorienne, plus rarement par la suite. Shiva constitue la moitié droite propre de l'image, Vishnu, la moitié gauche. Dans cette œuvre, où une partie importante de l'arc de soutien subsiste, le disque de Vishnu apparaît dans la main supérieure gauche, le rosaire de Shiva dans la main antérieure droite. La coiffure se compose d'une moitié de chignon d'ascète pour le côté Shiva et d'une moitié de mitre cylindrique pour le côté Vishnu. Sur le front, un demi-œil frontal caractérise le côté de Shiva. Le réalisme de la musculature de l'abdomen et le raffinement des doigts et du visage sont typiques du style de Sambor Prei Kuk.

១២_ ព្រះហរិហរ សម្បូណ៌ព្រៃគុក, N10, កំពង់ធំ, ផ្នែកខាងដើមនៃ ស.វ.ទី៧, ថ្មភក់, ១,៦៩ម, ក ១៦០៧

ហរិហរកើតឡើងដោយទេពពីរអង្គផ្សំគ្នា ពោលគឺផ្នែកខាងស្តាំជាព្រះឥសូរ និងផ្នែកខាងឆ្វេងជាព្រះនារាយណ៍។ បដិមាដែលប្រទះឃើញសុទ្ធតែសាងឡើងនៅមុនសម័យអង្គរ។ ផ្នែកច្រើននៃវង្វង់ទល់ទ្រវាងក្របកសេះនៅសល់នៅឡើយ តែកេតនភណ្ឌវិញនៅសល់តែចក្រ ដែលកាន់នៅដៃឆ្វេង។ ប៉ុន្តែគេដឹងថារូបនេះជាព្រះហរិហរដោយសារចំហៀងព្រះកេសខាងស្តាំជាព្រះកេសព្រះឥសូរ ពោលគឺមានផ្នួងសក់ដែលបួងវេញឡើងទៅលើ ហើយដែលចំហៀងខាងឆ្វេងពាក់មកុដជារាងបំពង់។ ពុំតែប៉ុណ្ណោះ មានភ្នែកទីពាមួយចំហៀងនៅលើថ្ងាសទៀតផង។ ដងខ្លួននិងសាច់ដុំឆ្លាក់តាមលំនាំធម្មជាតិពិត។ រីឯមុខញញឹមក្នុងភាពស្រទន់ ព្រមទាំងម្រាមដៃដ៏ស្រឡូននេះ សុទ្ធសឹងជាទីសម្គាល់នៃរចនាបថសម្បូណ៌ព្រៃគុក។

12. ハリハラ. コンポントム州、サンボール・プレイ・クック第10祠堂、7世紀第1四半期、砂岩、1.69m、Ka1607

ハリハラは前アンコール時代に見られる複合体の神で、その右半身はシヴァ、左半身はヴィシュヌである。この像の支柱はほぼ残っているが、持物ではヴィシュヌの上左腕の円輪、シヴァの下右腕の数珠だけが残っている。頭の右半分はシヴァの髪束を花弁のように重ねた髪髻冠ジャタムクタ、左半分はヴィシュヌの円柱形の宝冠である。また額にはシヴァの第3眼の半分が見られる。自然な胴体と優しい表情、繊細な指はサンボール・プレイ・クック様式の特徴である。

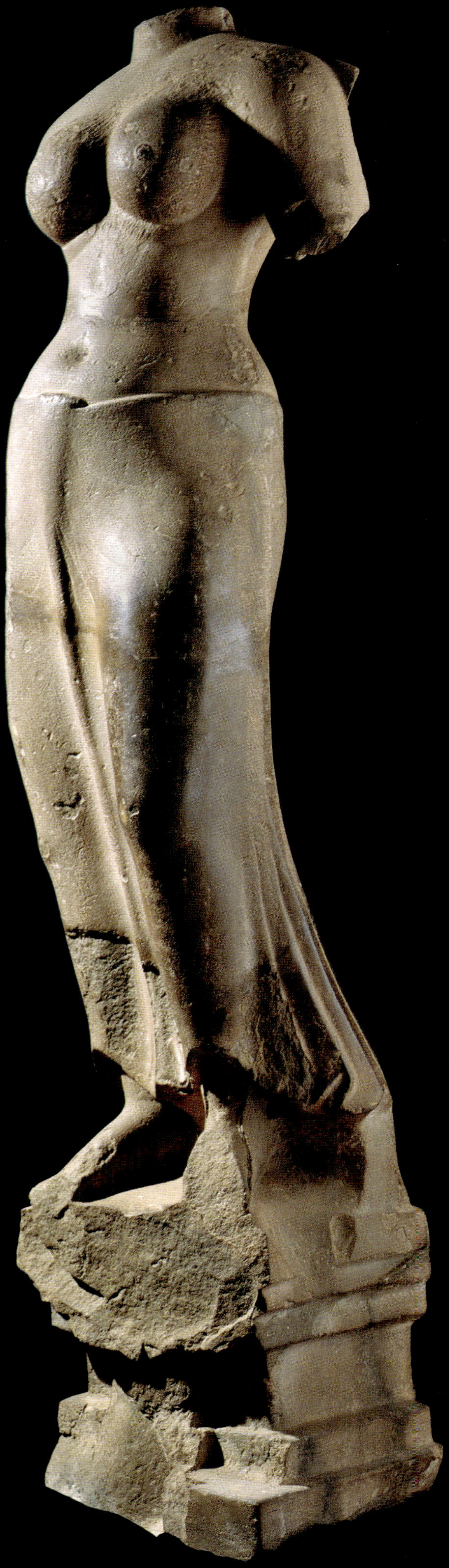
11

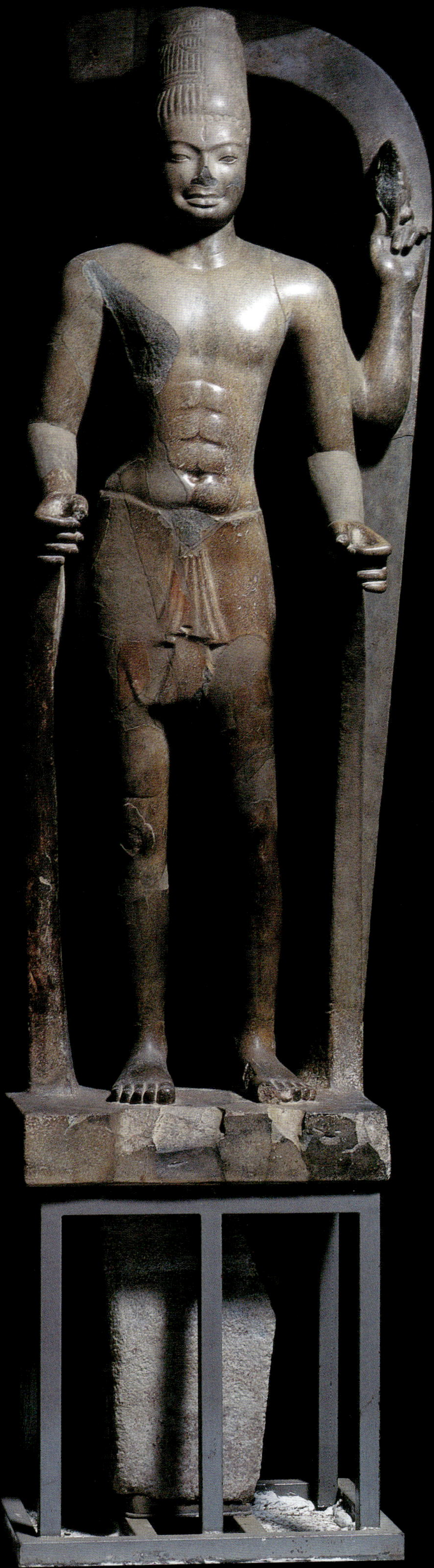
12

13. Devi. Koh Krieng, Sambor on the Mekong, Kratie, 1st half 7th C. Sandstone, 1.27 m. Ka 1621.

This image comes from the eastern part of Cambodia where several sovereign queens reigned in pre-Angkorian times. The highly particularised features, where the slightly indistinct chin line and the maternal breasts and rounded abdomen suggest maturity, have led to the supposition that it could be a portrait, perhaps of a queen in the guise of a goddess. The humane gaze and dignity of this figure, a type perpetuated in Khmer women to this day, make it one of the most appealing of Khmer sculptures. From the evidence of the braided and banded locks piled on her head, it probably represents Devi, shakti (female emanation or consort) of Shiva. The lines below the breasts are marks of beauty.

13. Devi. Koh Krieng, Sambor du Mékong, Kratie, 1ère moitié du 7ème s. Grès, 1,27 m. Ka 1621.

Cette statue provient de l'est du Cambodge où plusieurs souveraines sont attestées au cours de l'époque préangkorienne. Ses caractéristiques morphologiques très individualisées, comme le menton quelque peu empâté, la poitrine légèrement tombante et l'abdomen doucement arrondi ont conduit à supposer qu'il s'agissait d'une déesse figurée sous les traits d'un personnage réel. L'humanité et la dignité de l'expression, dont on retrouve l'écho chez de nombreuses Cambodgiennes aujourd'hui, rendent cette sculpture particulièrement attachante. La coiffure en chignon semble suggérer qu'on a ici affaire à une image de Devi, shakti (contrepartie féminine et énergie) de Shiva. On notera les plis de beauté sous la poitrine.

១៣_ទេវី កោះក្រៀង, សម្បូណ៌, ក្រចេះ, ផ្នែកទី១នៃស.វ.ទី៧, ថ្មភក់, ១,២៧ម, ក ១៦២១

រូបនេះមកពីតំបន់ខាងកើតប្រទេសកម្ពុជា ដែលនៅមុនសម័យអង្គរមានរាជនីច្រើនអង្គសោយរាជ្យបន្តបន្ទាប់គ្នា។ ចម្លាក់ទាំងមូលមានភាពសម្រិតសម្រាំងខ្លាំងណាស់។ ចង្កាលេចចេញពុំសូវច្បាស់ដោយសារផ្ទៃមុខទាំងមូលពេញ។ ដើមទ្រូងនិងពោះមានសាច់ធ្លាក់បន្តិច ធ្វើឲ្យយើងគិតថាប្រហែលជាឆ្លាក់ចម្លងតាមនរណាម្នាក់ពិត គឺអាចជារាជនីណាមួយ ដែលគេប្រៀបប្រដូចទៅនឹងទេវីអ្វីមួយ។ ផ្ទៃមុខនិងក្រសែភ្នែកមានភាពស្រគត់ស្រគំថ្លៃថ្នូរឱ្យចាប់អារម្មណ៍ក្រៃលែង ត្បិតគេអាចសង្កេតឃើញលើស្រីខ្មែរសព្វថ្ងៃ។ សក់ដែលក្រងហើយបួងជាន់ៗលើគ្នានេះ ធ្វើឱ្យយើងគិតថាទេវីនេះជាសក្តិ (ព្រះជាយាឬនិមិត្តសញ្ញាទេពស្រី) នៃព្រះឥសូរ។ ផ្នត់សាច់៣ខ្សែនៅក្រោមដោះនោះ គេយល់ថាជាចំណុចមួយនៃសោភ័ណភាពស្រ្តី។

13. デヴィ. クロチェ州、メコンのサンボール、コ・クリエン、7世紀前半、砂岩、1.27m、Ka 1621

この女神が発見されたカンボジア東部では前アンコール時代、数人の女王が君臨していた。ふくよかな顔、母親のような乳房、腹部のふくらみなど成熟した女性を描いており、女神の姿をした女王像ではないかとも言われている。慈悲深いまなざしと尊厳は現在のカンボジアの女性にもみられ、この像を魅了あるものにしている。梳き上げ、編まれた髪は、この像がシヴァの神妃としてのデヴィであることを示している。乳房の下の線は美のしるしである。

14. Durga Mahishasuramardini. Tuol Kamnap, Krasang Char, Kompong Trabek, Prei Veng, 7th C. Sandstone, 1.06 m. Ka 1631.

The full cheeks and firm rounded body of this image of Durga suggests a youthful model. As is often the case with Khmer representations of the buffalo demon slayer, the buffalo is not fully realised but merely indicated in low relief below her feet. Although many of the traits of pre-Angkorian sculpture derive from Indian precedents, even voluptuous feminine figures like this do not project the sensuality that characterises the Indic models, a feature distinguishing Khmer art from Indian. This Durga wears a mitre indicating her connections to Vishnu.

14. Durga Mahishasuramardini. Tuol Komnap, Krasang Char, Kompong Trabek, Prei Veng, 7ème s. Grès, 1,06 m. Ka 1631.

Les joues pleines et les formes rondes de cette représentation de Durga se réfèrent à un modèle plus jeune que celui dont le sculpteur s'est inspiré dans la cas de l'œuvre précédente. Comme il en est souvent des représentations khmères de la Destructrice du démon buffle, l'animal est simplement indiqué en bas-relief sous les pieds de la déesse. Bien que nombre d'aspects de la statuaire préangkorienne dérivent de l'art indien, les œuvres khmères ne se sont jamais parées de la sensualité exacerbée de leur modèle. La mitre cylindrique que porte cette Durga rappelle les liens qui l'unissent à Vishnu dont elle est la sœur selon certaine lègendes.

១៤_នាងទុគ៌ាសម្លាប់ក្របី ទួលកំណប់, ក្រសាំងចារ, កំពង់ត្របែក, ព្រៃវែង, ស.វ.ទី៧, ថ្មភក់, ១,០៦ម, ក ១៦៣១

ថ្ពាល់មូលពេញ ព្រមទាំងដើមទ្រូងណែនក្តន់នៃចម្លាក់នេះ បង្ហាញថាជានាងទុគ៌ាដែលនៅក្នុងយុវវ័យ។ អសោរក្របីនៅទីនេះពុំខុសពីឧទាហរណ៍ដទៃទៀតឡើយ ពោលគឺគេឆ្លាក់សើៗនៅពីក្រោមជើងទេវីនេះ។ ថ្វីត្បិតតែចម្លាក់មុនសម័យអង្គរច្រើនតែមិនទាន់បែកចេញស្រឡះពីសិល្បៈឥណ្ឌានៅឡើយក្តី ក៏ភាពជាស្រ្តីគួរឲ្យត្រេកាលនៃរូបរាងទាំងមូលនេះមានបុគ្គលិកលក្ខណៈជាខ្មែរទៅហើយ ពោលគឺពុំបែរទៅរកគំរូចម្លាក់ពីឥណ្ឌាទៀតឡើយ។ នៅទីនេះផ្នួងសក់នាងទុគ៌ាមានរាងជាបំពង់ ដែលបង្ហាញថាមានទំនាក់ទំនងទៅនឹងព្រះនារាយណ៍។

14. ドゥルガー. プレイヴェン州、コンポン・トラベク、クラサン・チャ、トゥオル・カムナップ、7世紀、砂岩、1.06m、Ka 1631

ふっくらした頬と引き締まった丸みある体は、このドゥルガーのモデルが若かったことを示している。カンボジアでは水牛の魔神を刺し殺したドゥルガー像の水牛がしっかり描かれることなく、足下のレリーフとして描かれている。前アンコール時代の石像の大半はインドの石像の特徴に基づいているが、この石像のような豊満な女性の姿でも、インドのような肉感的な印象は与えない。これがクメール美術とインド美術の違いである。このドゥルガーは宝冠をかぶっており、ヴィシュヌとの関係を象徴している。

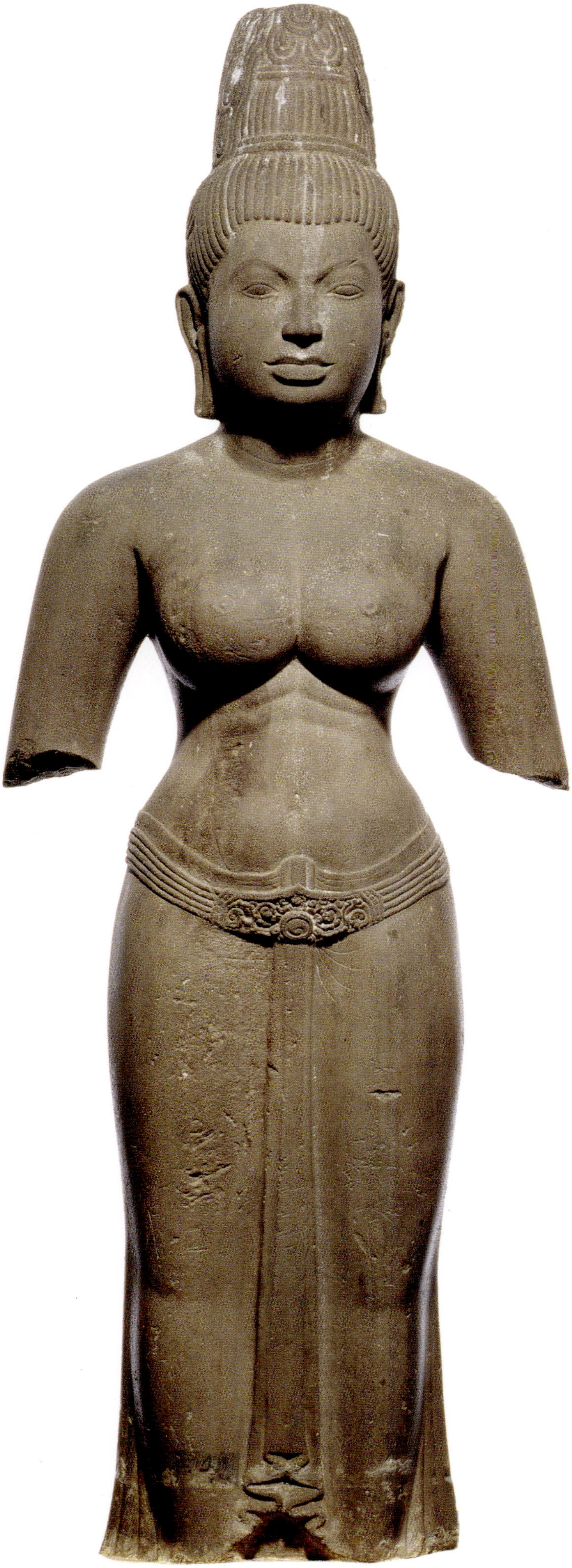

13

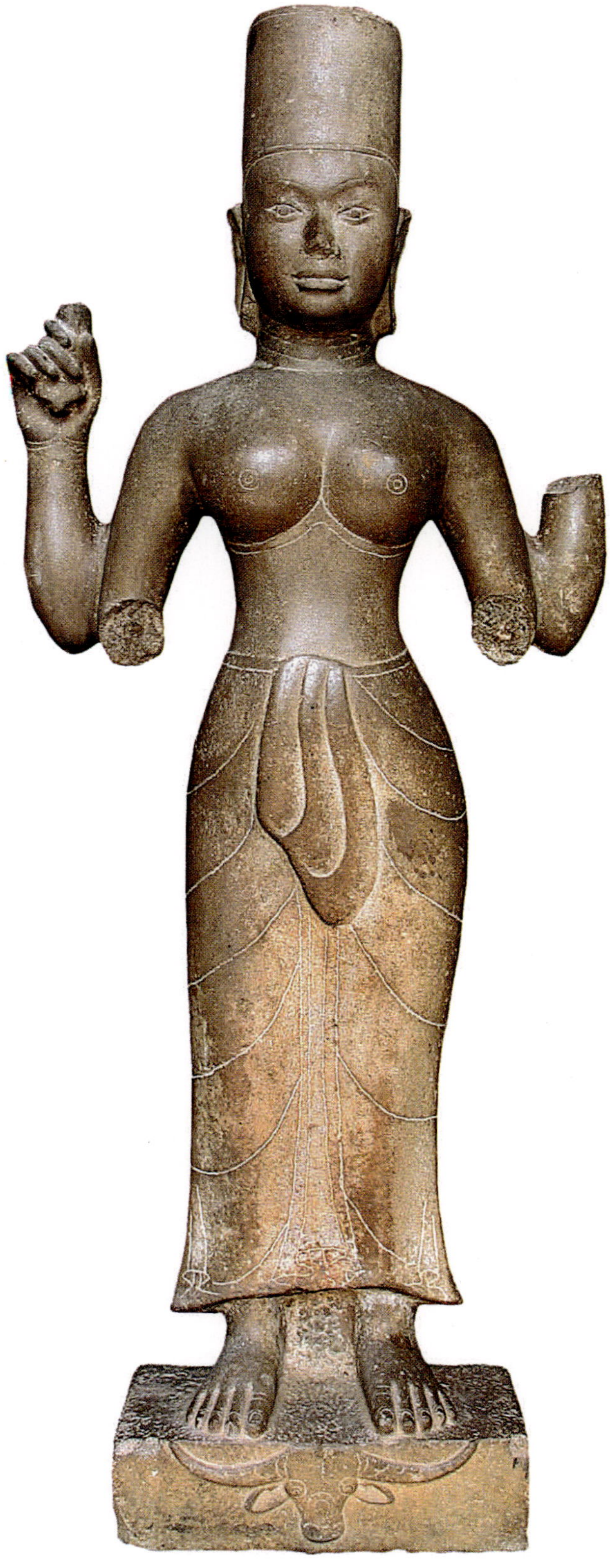

14

15. Stele with Nandin. Tuol Neak Ta Bak Ka, Dangkor, Kandal, 7th-8th C. Sandstone, 0.96 m. Ka 1760.

Inscriptions on stele supply us with most of the limited available written evidence of Cambodian history. The charming if somewhat naif image of Nandin recumbent in a lotus flower on this slab surmounts an eleven-line text in Khmer. The style of the inscription indicates its pre-Angkorian date though, unlike many other stele, it is not dated. The text deals with practical matters, as Khmer language inscriptions usually do. In this case a dignitary from a religious foundation issues instructions about the delivery of salt to a series of sanctuaries dedicated to the worship of Shiva. This explains the invocation of Nandin, not only the vehicle (vahana) but also a zoomorphic manifestation of that god.

15. Stèle orné de Nandin. Tuol Neak Ta Bak Ka, Dangkor, Kandal, 7ème - 8ème s. Grès, 0,96 m. Ka 1760.

Les inscriptions gravées sur stèles ou au piédroits des portes des temples ont fourni la majorité des données à partir desquelles l'histoire khmère ancienne a pu être restituée. L'image charmante, encore que naïve, de Nandin couché sur une fleur de lotus surmonte ici onze lignes de texte rédigé en vieux khmer. La forme des lettres est caractéristique de la graphie à l'époque préangkorienne. À l'inverse de nombreux autres documents, cette stèle ne comporte pas de date. L'inscription précise les dispositions pratiques d'une fondation, ainsi qu'il en est souvent des textes en vieux khmer, par opposition aux textes en sanskrit comportant des louanges à l'adresse des dieux ou des panégyriques royaux. Émanant d'un haut dignitaire, l'inscription se rapporte aux quantités de sel à livrer à divers sanctuaires shivaïtes. Sa teneur explique la présence du taureau Nandin au sommet, non seulement véhicule (vahana), mais aussi manifestation animale du dieu Shiva.

១៥_ ផ្ទាំងសិលាចារឹកមានរូបព្រះគោ ទួលអ្នកតាបាក់ក, ដង្កោ, កណ្ដាល, ស.វ.ទី៧_៨, ថ្មភក់, 0,៩៦ម, ក ១៧៦០

ក្នុងចំណោមអក្សរថ្មទាំងអស់ សិលាចារឹកដែលជាថ្មគោលឬផ្ទាំងដាច់តែឯងផ្ដល់ព័ត៌មានច្រើនជាងគេដែលពាក់ព័ន្ធនឹងប្រវត្តិសាស្ត្រប្រទេសកម្ពុជា។ ខាងលើផ្ទាំងនេះ យើងឃើញព្រះគោដែលគេឆ្លាក់ជាសាមញ្ញបំផុត តែមានរាងសមសួន អង្គុយនៅលើផ្កាឈូក។ នៅពីក្រោមនោះ មានអក្សរ១១បន្ទាត់ជាភាសាខ្មែរ។ ទម្រង់អក្សរបង្ហាញថាចារនៅមុនសម័យអង្គរ ប៉ុន្តែពុំមានកាលបរិច្ឆេទ។ ជាទូទៅសិលាចារឹកជាភាសាខ្មែរច្រើនតែរៀបរាប់អំពីរឿងរ៉ាវធម្មតាដែលទាក់ទងនឹងជីវិតជាក់ស្ដែង។ នៅទីនេះក៏ដូច្នោះដែរ គឺអ្នកមានបណ្ដាសក្ដិម្នាក់ចេញបញ្ញត្តិកម្រិតការប្រើប្រាស់អំបិលសម្រាប់ប្រាសាទមួយដែលឧទ្ទិសទៅព្រះឥសូរ។ ព្រះគោនៅទីនេះមិនត្រឹមតែជាយាននៃទេពនេះទេ ប៉ុន្តែជានិមិត្តរូបនៃទេពនោះតែម្ដង។

15. ナンディンが浮彫された石碑. カンダール州、ダンカーオ、トゥオル・ネアック・タ・バック・コー、、7~8世紀、砂岩、0.96m、Ka 1760

碑文はカンボジア史に関する数少ない史料である。碑頭には素朴ながら愛らしいナンディンが蓮華上に臥しており、その下には11行の古クメール語の碑文が記されている。他の石碑と異なり、日付は記されていないが、書体から前アンコール時代のものであることがわかる。他の古いクメール語の碑文同様、実務的な内容が記されており、宗教組織の高官がシヴァ寺院に塩を納めるように命じている。この碑文から碑頭のナンディンがシヴァの乗り物であると同時に、シヴァの姿も表していることがわかる。

16. Harihara. Prasat Andet, Kompong Thom, last quarter 7th C. Sandstone, 1.97 m. Ka 1635.

The slender elegance of this deity characterises the canon of Prasat Andet style, named for the temple sanctuary where this statue was installed. The distinction between its Shiva and Vishnu halves is minimal, indicated only on the head. Half of Shiva's third eye is engraved on the forehead, while the jatamukuta formed by Shiva's twisted locks is incised on the god's right side, but subsumed into the smooth profile of Vishnu's tall mitre. The grace of the torso and slim limbs is allied with the sculptor's skill in giving naturalistic expression to the challenge of representing the anatomy of double arms.

16. Harihara. Prasat Andet, Kompong Thom, dernier quart du 7ème s. Grès, 1,97 m. Ka 1635.

L'originalité de cette sculpture a conduit à définir un style dit de Prasat Andet, du nom du temple dans lequel se dressait cette image de Harihara. En l'absence des attributs, les seuls détails permettant de reconnaître le dieu résident dans le traitement différent des deux moitiés de la coiffure - chignon d'ascète pour Shiva, mitre cylindrique pour Vishnu - et dans l'indication d'un demi troisième œil frontal pour la partie Shiva. Le chignon d'ascète s'inscrit dans un volume identique à celui de la mitre dont il ne se distingue plus, n'était l'indication des mèches en anses qui le composent (pour une différenciation nette des deux parties de la coiffure, voir le Harihara de Sambor Prei Kuk, #12). L'œuvre, particulièrement expressive, est celle d'un artiste d'exception qui a su rendre naturel l'étrange anatomie d'une image anthropomorphe dotée de quatre bras.

១៦_ ព្រះហរិហរ ប្រាសាទអណ្ដែត, កំពង់ធំ, ផ្នែកខាងចុងស.វ. ទី៧, ថ្មភក់, ១,៩៧ម, ក ១៦៣៥

ភាពស្រឡូននៃបដិមាទាំងមូលជាលក្ខណៈនៃរចនាបថប្រាសាទអណ្ដែត ដែលជាឈ្មោះនៃប្រាសាទដែលគ្រប់ដណ្ដប់លើទេពនេះ។ ចំណុចសម្គាល់ឲ្យឃើញខុសគ្នានៃផ្នែកព្រះឥសូរនិងផ្នែកព្រះនារាយណ៍មានបន្តិចបន្តួច គឺមានតែនៅលើព្រះកេសប៉ុណ្ណោះ។ ភ្នែកទីពនៃព្រះឥសូរ គេឆ្លាក់ឲ្យឃើញមួយចំហៀងនៅលើថ្ងាសរីឯផ្នួងសក់ក្រងនៃព្រះឥសូរស្ថិតនៅខាងស្ដាំ ប៉ុន្តែកន្លែងភ្ជាប់ទៅនឹងផ្នួងមានរាងជាប៉ើពង់នៃព្រះនារាយណ៍នោះ គឺគេជ្រើឲ្យចូលគ្នាបានស្មើល្អ។ ដងខ្លួនដ៏ស្រឡូនសក្តិសមនឹងទម្រង់ជើងទាំងទ្វេ ព្រមទាំងទៅនឹងដៃទាំង៤ ដែលទាល់តែវិចិត្រករនោះមានទេពកោសល្យខ្លាំងណាស់ទើបឆ្លាក់ឡើងបាន។

16. ハリハラ. コンポントム州、プラサート・アンデート、7世紀第４四半期、砂岩、1.97m、Ka 1635

このほっそりした優雅な像は、この石像が発見された祠堂名に由来するプラサート・アンデート様式の代表作である。シヴァとヴィシュヌの区別は極僅かで、頭部に限定されている。シヴァの第３眼の半分が額に彫られているが、右側のシヴァの髪束を花弁のように重ねた髪髻冠ジャタムクタは、ヴィシュヌの宝冠のスムーズな形をとっている（サンボール・プレイ・クック様式ハリハラＮｏ．２との相違に注意）。胴体とほっそりした手足の優雅さ、および４臂の自然さは優れた彫刻技術を示している。

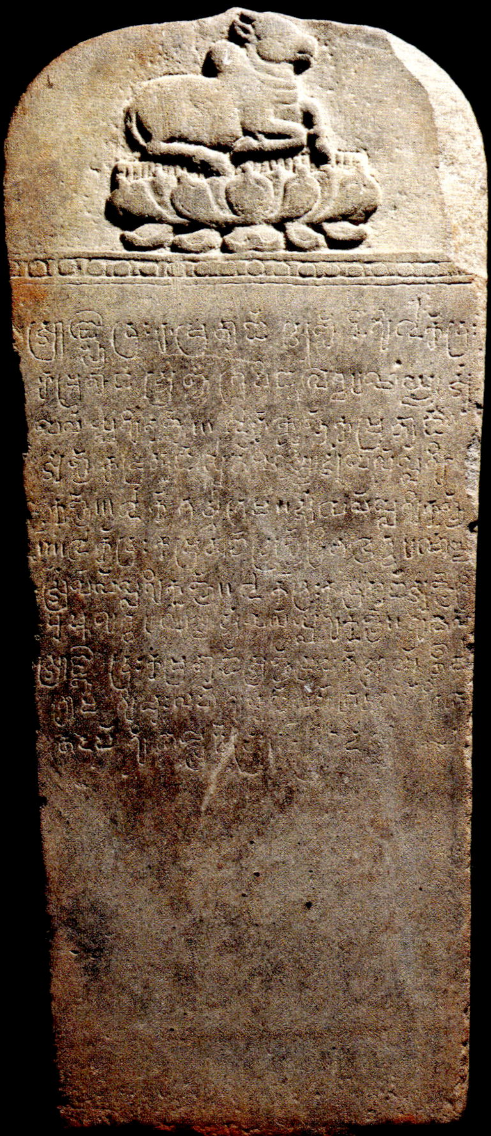

15

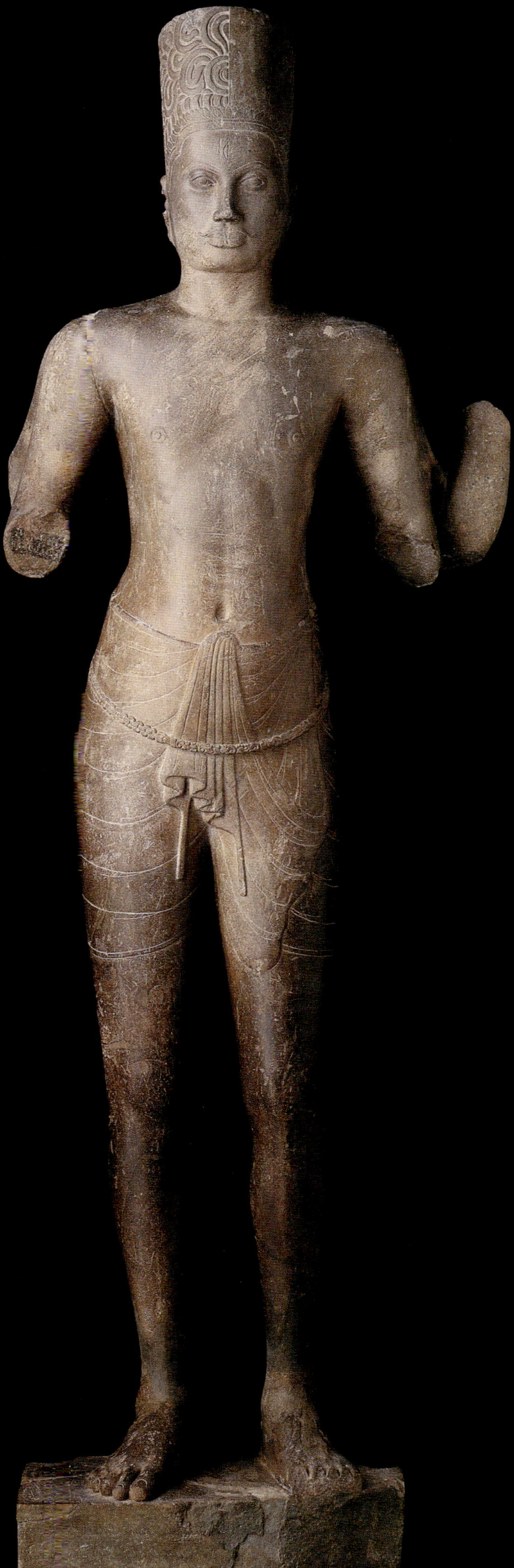

16

17. Head of Buddha. Vat Romlok, Angkor Borei, Takeo, 7th C. Sandstone, 0.25 m. Ka 1085.

The Angkor Borei site, at the centre of the ancient kingdom the Chinese called Funan, yielded many Buddhistic sculptures contemporary with the predominantly Vaishnavite statuary from the nearby site of Phnom Da. As with those Brahmanistic works, their morphology derives from India's Gupta style, with oval face, almond-shaped eyes under a continuous brow arch, and sensitively modelled mouth. This head illustrates some of the defining characteristics (lakshana) of the Buddha, including a cranial protuberance (ushnisha), empty earlobes indicating the rejection of the heavy jewellery that had stretched them in the sage's former princely existence, and short spiral curls that refer to the cutting of his princely hair when he renounced worldly existence.

17. Tête du Buddha. Vat Romlok, Angkor Borei, Takeo, 7ème s. Grès, 0,25 m. Ka 1085.

Le site d'Angkor Borei, au cœur de l'ancien royaume désigné sous le nom de Funan par les Chinois, a livré de nombreuses images bouddhiques, contemporaines des œuvres essentiellement vishnuites provenant du site voisin du Phnom Da (voir le grand Vishnu, #2). L'esthétique et le style des œuvres des environs d'Angkor Borei dérivent de modèles indiens d'époque Gupta, avec des visages à l'ovale régulier, des yeux en amande et une bouche aux contours délicats. Cette tête présente certains des signes caractéristiques (lakshana) du Buddha: protubérance crânienne (ushnisha) - siège des connaissances supérieures du Saint Homme -, lobes d'oreilles distendus - témoins du port de lourds bijoux alors qu'il était encore le prince Siddhartha - et coiffure en petites boucles - représentant la chevelure du Bienheureux après sa première tonsure, lors de son renoncement au monde.

១៧_ព្រះកេសព្រះពុទ្ធ វត្តរំលក, អង្គរបុរី, តាកែវ, ស.វ.ទី៧, ថ្មភក់, ០,២៥ម, ក១០៨៥

អង្គរបុរីដែលជាមណ្ឌលនៃអាណាចក្រមួយដែលចិនហៅថាហ្វូណាន់នោះ សម្បូណ៌ទៅដោយបដិមា ព្រមទាំងរូបទេពក្នុងនិកាយព្រះនារាយណ៍ជំនាន់គ្នានោះដែរ ហើយដែលមកពីភ្នំដា។ បដិមាទាំងអស់នេះសុទ្ធសឹងតពូជពង្សពីសិល្បៈគុប្តនៃឥណ្ឌាមក គឺតែងមានមុខរាងទ្រវែង រីឯភ្នែកគេច្លាក់ឲ្យឃើញផ្នត់ស្តើងមួយតាមបណ្តោយលើក្រោម ហើយចុងទាំងសងខាងបញ្ចប់ចុងបន្តិច។ បបូរមាត់វិញក៏ដូចគ្នាដែរ។ ព្រះកេសនេះមានបង្ហាញពីលក្ខណៈអរិយបុគ្គលខ្លះ ដូចជាមូលី, ស្លឹកត្រចៀកវែងដែលគ្មានអលង្ការអ្វី ប៉ុន្តែដែលបញ្ជាក់ថាព្រះពុទ្ធអង្គ ដើមឡើយជាពូជក្សត្រធ្លាប់ពាក់អលង្ការរហូតដល់យារត្រចៀក. និងងសក់ដែលមានរាងគួចខ្យង។

17. ブッダ頭部. タケオ州、アンコール・ボレイ、ワット・ロムローク、7世紀、砂岩、0.25m、Ka 1085

中国が扶南と呼んだ王国の都アンコール・ボレイから、多くの仏像が発見された。一方、近くのプノン・ダからは同時代のヒンドゥー教の諸像が発見されている。ヒンドゥー教の諸像同様、仏像の卵形の顔立ち、杏仁形の目、つながった弓なりの眉、注意深く彫られた口などにインドのグプタ彫刻の影響が見られる。頭部の肉髻、王子時代に重い宝石で伸びた飾りのない耳たぶ、出家時に断髪した螺髪などブッダの特徴を表している。

18. Buddha. Phum Thmei, Kong Pisei, Kompong Speu, 7th C. Sandstone, 0.90 m. Ka 1591.

This Buddha seated in meditation posture on a lotus base shares stylistic traits with the Gupta-influenced style of Angkor Borei and Phnom Da, particularly in the oval face, full chin, arched brows and almond-shaped eyes. Naturalism is apparent in the treatment of the torso, particularly in the slight bulge at the waist resulting from the pressure of the undergarment and in the prominent thighbones of the crossed legs. The thin outer garment that leaves the right shoulder bare falls gracefully from the left forearm, its thin and supple fabric revealing the form of the chest below. The downcast gaze reinforces the impression of serenity and spirituality.

18. Buddha. Phum Thmei, Kong Pisei, Kompong Speu, 7ème s. Grès, 0,90 m. Ka 1591.

Ce Buddha assis en méditation sur une fleur de lotus partage certains traits stylistiques avec les œuvres d'Angkor Borei et du Phnom Da où transparaissent de fortes influences Gupta: visage ovale, yeux en amande, etc. Un certain naturel caractérise le traitement du torse, particulièrement dans le léger renflement sensible au niveau de l'abdomen et résultant du serrage du long pagne inférieur (antaravasaka) à la taille. Le fin manteau monastique (uttarasangha) découvre l'épaule droite et tombe avec grâce sur le poignet gauche, laissant transparaître le délicat modelé du buste. L'expression du visage est celle d'une méditation sereine et heureuse.

១៨_ព្រះពុទ្ធរូប ភូមិថ្មី, គងពិសី, កំពង់ស្ពឺ, ស.វ.ទី៧, ថ្មភក់, ០,៩០ម, ក១៥៩១

នេះជាព្រះពុទ្ធរូបទ្រង់ភ្នែននៅលើផ្កាឈូកមួយ ដែលទទួលឥទ្ធិពលពីសិល្បៈគុប្តដូចបដិមានៅអង្គរបុរីនិងភ្នំដាដែរ ជាពិសេសបើពោលពីមុខដែលមានរាងទ្រវែង, ចង្កាពេញ, ចិញ្ចើមរាងកោង និងភ្នែកដែលចុងទាំងអស់សុទ្ធតែបញ្ចប់ចុងបន្តិច។ ដងខ្លួនធ្លាក់តាមលំនាំធម្មជាតិ ជាពិសេសក្បាលពោះដែលលេចឡើងដោយសារផ្នែកស្បង់ដែលនៅត្រង់ចង្កេះរឹតដោយក្រវាត់ ព្រមទាំងឆ្អឹងជើងដែលលេចឡើងច្បាស់ដោយសារភ្នែន។ ស្មាខាងស្តាំនៅទទេ ដោយសារចីពរពាក់ជៀងមកខាងឆ្វេង ហើយចុងចីពរធ្លាក់សំយុងនៅកដៃគួរឲ្យគាប់ភ្នែករំភើលែង។ ចីពរដ៏ស្តើងនេះធ្វើឲ្យលេចទ្រូងយ៉ាងច្បាស់។ ក្រសែភ្នែកដែលទម្លាក់មកក្រោម កាន់តែជួយឲ្យឃើញភាពស្រគត់ស្រគំស្ងប់ស្ងាត់នៃបដិមានេះ។

18. ブッダ. コンポン・スプー州、コン・ピセイ、プム・トゥメイ、7世紀、砂岩、0.90m、Ka 1591

この蓮座に座禅を組むブッダには特に顔立ち、丸いあご、弓なりの眉、杏仁形の目など、グプタ彫刻に影響されたアンコール・ボレイ、およびプノン・ダ様式の特徴が見られる。下着からはみ出た胴回りの肉や、組んだ足の大腿骨など自然に描かれている。右肩がむき出しになった薄い外衣は左の前腕から優雅に垂れ下がっており、その下の胸の形がうかがえる。伏し目は安らかさと崇高な印象を与えている。

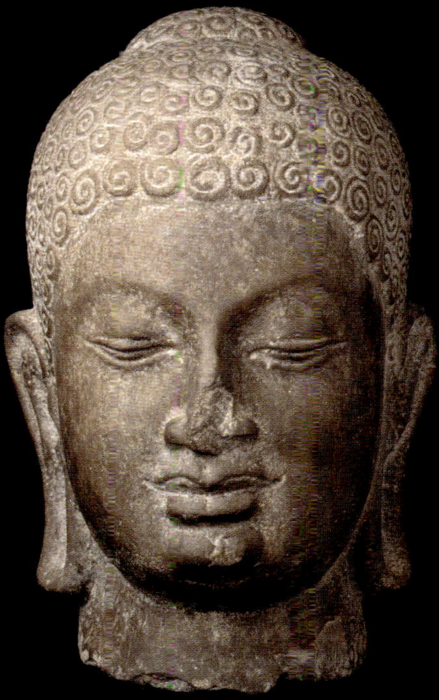

17

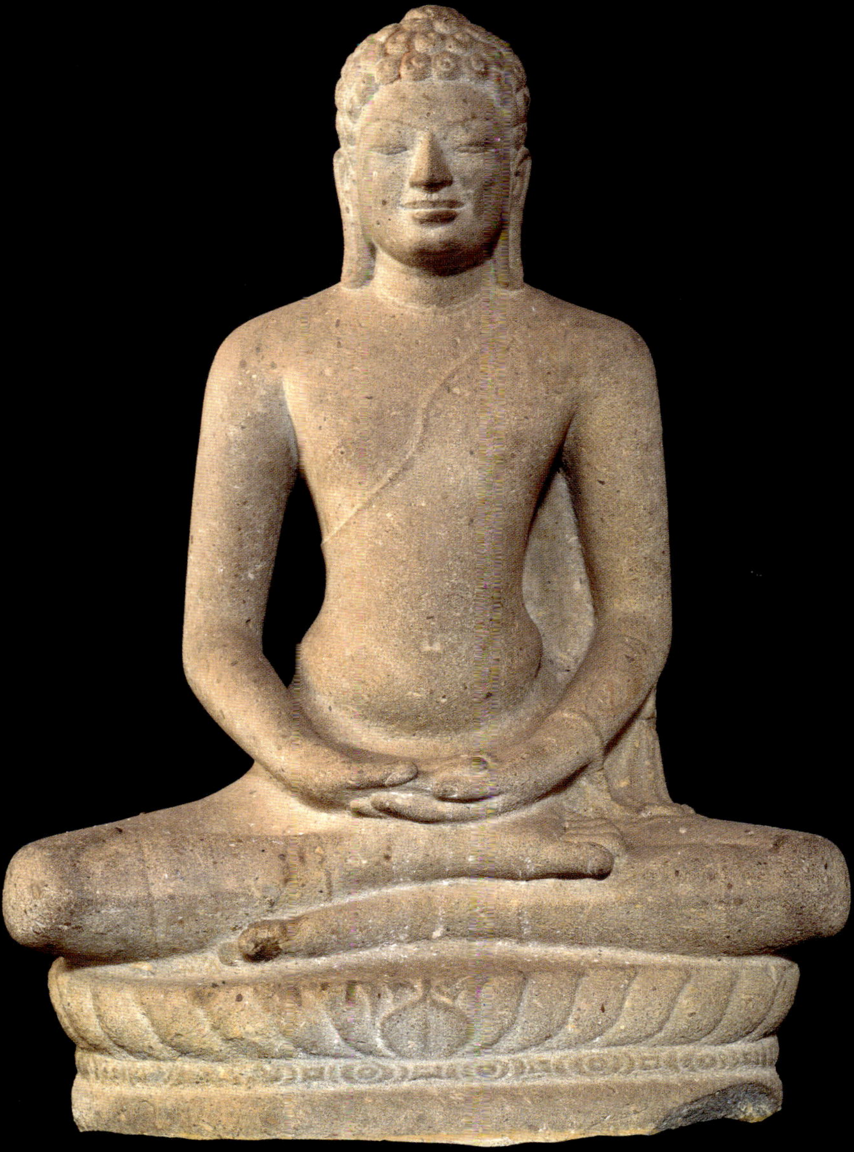

18

19. Buddha. Vat Romlok, Angkor Borei, Takeo, 7th C. Sandstone, 0.93 m. Ka 1595.

This Buddha, clad in an outer robe that covers both shoulders and clings to the body to reveal the sarong draped at the waist, as well as the contours of the body and limbs beneath, is one of the most spiritual images from Angkor Borei. The garments and the lakshana, or distinguishing marks of the Buddha such as the slight cranial protuberance, as well as the graceful hip-flexed posture (tribhanga) belong to the tradition stemming from Gupta precedents of about the 5th to 6th century in India. In Indian tradition the right hand might have made the gesture of the absence of fear (abhayamudra), with palm out and fingers pointing up, and the left might have made the gesture of gift-bestowing (varadamudra) with palm out and fingers pointing down. But it also possible that the missing hands made the same gesture, abhayamudra or vitarkamudra (gesture of discussion), a characteristic of the art of the Mon kingdom of Dvaravati in what is now central and northeast Thailand.

19. Buddha. Vat Romlok, Angkor Borei, Takeo, 7ème s. Grès, 0,93 m. Ka 1595.

Ce Buddha, vêtu d'un costume monastique épousant étroitement le corps et laissant transparaître les formes douces du torse et des jambes, est l'une des œuvres les plus délicates retrouvées à Angkor Borei. Le costume couvrant les deux épaules, la posture déhanchée et l'indication discrète de la protubérance crânienne renvoient à des œuvres indiennes d'époque Gupta, aux environs des 5ème - 6ème siècles. Selon toute vraisemblance, les mains étaient disposées de manière plus ou moins symétrique. En accord avec l'iconographie indienne, la main droite pourrait avoir effectué le geste de l'absence de crainte (abhayamudra), paume tournée vers le fidèle avec les doigts dirigés vers le haut, la main gauche, celui du don (varadamudra), paume tournée vers le fidèle avec les doigts dirigés vers le bas. Mais il est aussi possible que les deux mains aient esquissé la même mudra, auquel cas il aurait pu s'agir du geste de l'absence de crainte ou de celui de l'argumentation (vitarkamudra), paume tournée vers le fidèle, pouce et index joints, selon l'iconographie traditionnelle de l'art bouddhique de Dvaravati, un ancien royaume mon du centre et du nord-est de l'actuelle Thaïlande.

១៩_ ព្រះពុទ្ធរូប វត្តរំលក, អង្គរបុរី, តាកែវ, ស.វ.ទី៧, ថ្មភក់, ០,៩៣ម, ក១៥៩៥

ព្រះពុទ្ធរូបនេះបញ្ចេញភាពស្រគត់ស្រគំគួរជាទីសក្ការៈ ដូចព្រះពុទ្ធរូបមួយចំនួនទៀតដែលមកពីតំបន់អង្គរបុរីដែរ។ ចីពរឃ្លុំនោះស្តើង ហើយជាប់នឹងខ្លួនខ្លាំងណាស់ រហូតដល់បញ្ចេញឱ្យឃើញច្បាស់នូវដងខ្លួនទាំងមូល ព្រមទាំងស្បង់នៅក្នុង ដែលក្រវាត់ជាប់នៅចង្កេះផង។ ស្បង់ចីពរ, លក្ខណៈអរិយបុគ្គលដូចជាមូលីព្រមទាំងដងខ្លួនកាច់អែនជា៣ (ត្រីភង្គ) អាចភ្ជាប់ទៅសិល្បៈគុប្តនៃប្រទេសឥណ្ឌា (ស.វ.ទី៥_៦) ដែលព្រះហស្តស្តាំអាចធ្វើកាយវិការ "អភយ" រីឯព្រះហស្តឆ្វេងអាចធ្វើកាយវិការឱ្យទាន។ ព្រះហស្តដែលបាត់បង់នៅផ្នែកខាងចុងនោះប្រហែលជាបង្ហាញ "អភយមុទ្រា" ឬមួយក៏ "វិតក្កមុទ្រា" ដែលគេនិយមខ្លាំងនៅអាណាចក្រមនឈ្មោះ ទ្វារវតី (បច្ចុប្បន្ននេះនៅលើដីភូមាមួយភាគ និងថៃឡង់ដ៍មួយភាគ)។

19. ブッダ. タケオ州、アンコール・ボレイ、ワット・ロムローク、7世紀、砂岩、0.93m、Ka 1595

このブッダは大アンコール・ボレイ様式の最も崇高な像の１つである。衣が両肩を覆い、身体にまとわり、腰で折りたたみがつくられた下半身の裙と身体の外郭と足が見える。衣や肉髻、腰のひねりなど、インド５－６世紀のグプタ彫刻の影響が見られる。インドの伝統通りなら、右手は上に手を開いて指を伸ばし掌を見せる施無畏印、左手は下向きに手を開いて指を伸ばし掌を見せる与願印を表していたであろう。または現在のタイの中部と北東部にあったモン人王国ドヴァーラヴァティーの美術の特徴である両手とも施無畏印、または与願印を表していた可能性もある。

20. Buddha Dipankara. Tuol Ta Hoy, Vat Phnom Oudong, Kompong Speu, 7th C. Sandstone, 0.97 m. Ka 1589.

The transcendence of religion over political boundaries is often visible in statuary. This Buddha, while still showing influences of Gupta art, also embodies the youthful quality of Buddha images from Dvaravati. The left hand, a rare survival from the stresses of time, demonstrates the practice, which can still be observed in monks today, of holding up the outer robe on the left arm. The right hand makes a gesture (or mudra) of varadamudra, bestowing a gift. This rare iconography may indicate that this is a representation of the Dipankara Buddha, the first of the twenty-four predecessors of the historical Buddha

20. Le Buddha Dipankara. Tuol Ta Hoy, Vat Phnom Udong, Kompong Speu, 7ème s. Grès, 0,97 m. Ka 1589.

Tout en présentant une iconographie très proche, cette sculpture semble plus éloignée que la précédente des modèles indiens auxquels elle se rapporte: si le costume renvoie toujours à l'art Gupta, la posture et le traitement du visage se rapprochent plus précisément d'œuvres reflétant les tendances de l'art mon de Dvaravati. Compte tenu de l'ancienneté de cette pièce, la conservation des deux mains est exceptionnelle: la droite esquisse le geste du don (varadamudra) tandis que la gauche est dans une position de préhension destinée à évoquer le maintien d'une des extrémité du costume monastique. Cette iconographie rare semble caractériser les représentations du Buddha Dipankara, premier des vingt-quatre prédécesseurs du Buddha historique.

២០_ ព្រះពុទ្ធរូបទីបង្ករ ទួលតាហយ, វត្តភ្នំឧត្តុង្គ, កំពង់ស្ពឺ, ស.វ.ទី៧, ថ្មភក់, ០,៩៧ម, ក១៥៨៩

អនុភាពនៃសាសនាតែងសាយភាយផុតពីព្រំដែននគរនីមួយៗ ហើយប្រការនេះតែងលេចចេញផ្លោតាមបដិមាសាស្ត្រ។ បដិមានេះបង្ហាញថាមានឥទ្ធិពលសិល្បៈគុប្តខ្លះ ប៉ុន្តែក៏មានគួបផ្សំនឹងឥទ្ធិពលទ្វារវតីដែរ។ សំណាងល្អ ព្រះហស្តឆ្វេងពុំខូចខាតទេ ហើយបង្ហាញថាកាន់កន្ទុយចីពរ ពុំខុសអ្វីពីទម្លាប់ព្រះសង្ឃសព្វថ្ងៃឡើយ។ ព្រះហស្តស្តាំធ្វើកាយវិការឱ្យទាន (វរទមុទ្រា)។ បដិមាសាស្ត្ររបៀបនេះកម្រមានណាស់ ហើយប្រហែលជាបង្ហាញអំពីព្រះពុទ្ធរូបទីបង្ករ ដែលជាព្រះពុទ្ធមុនគេបង្អស់ក្នុងចំណោមព្រះពុទ្ធទាំង២៤អង្គ ដែលបានត្រាស់មុនក្រុមព្រះពុទ្ធទាំង៥។

20. ブッダ. コンポンスプー州、ワット・プノン・ウドン、トゥオル・ダ・ホイ、7世紀、砂岩、高0.97m、Ka 1589

国境を越えた宗教の影響は像に窺うことができる。このブッダ像にはグプタ美術の影響と同時に、ドヴァーラヴァーティー王国のブッダ像の若々しいイメージも見られる。左手は珍しく原型を留めており、今日の仏僧のように大衣を左腕に掛けている。右手は与願印を表している。この稀なイコノグラフィーから、この像はゴータマブッダ以前の24人の過去仏の１人目であるディーパンカラブッダであると思われる。

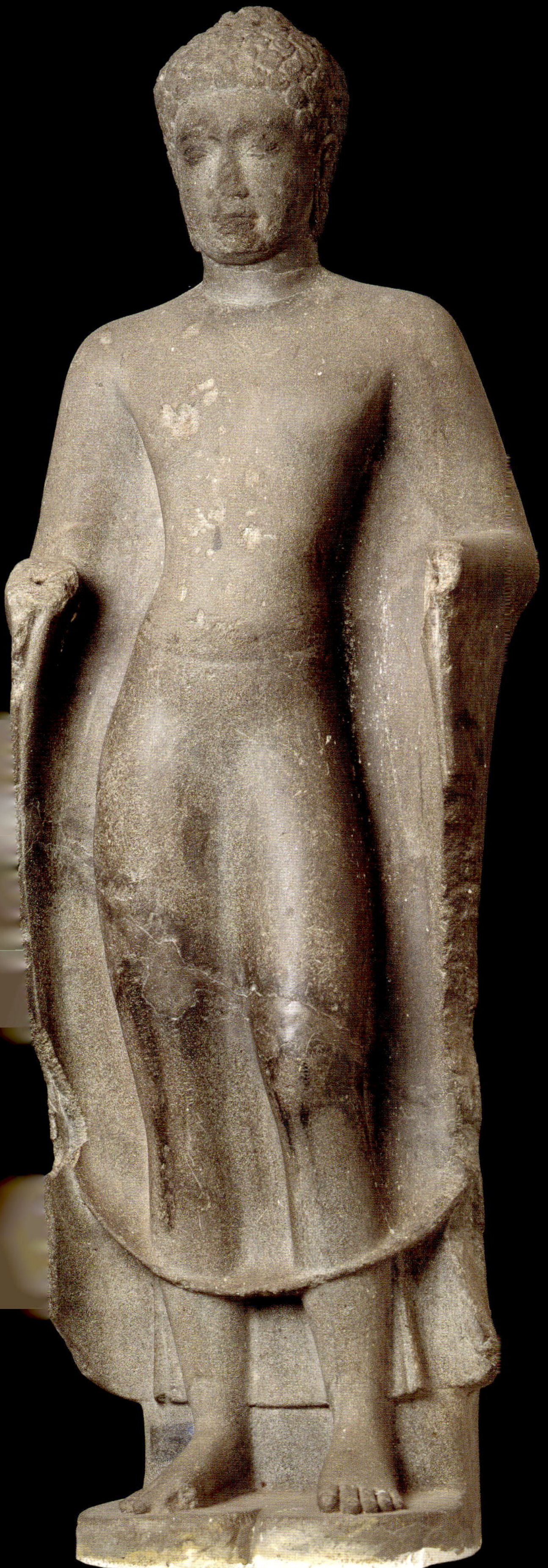
19

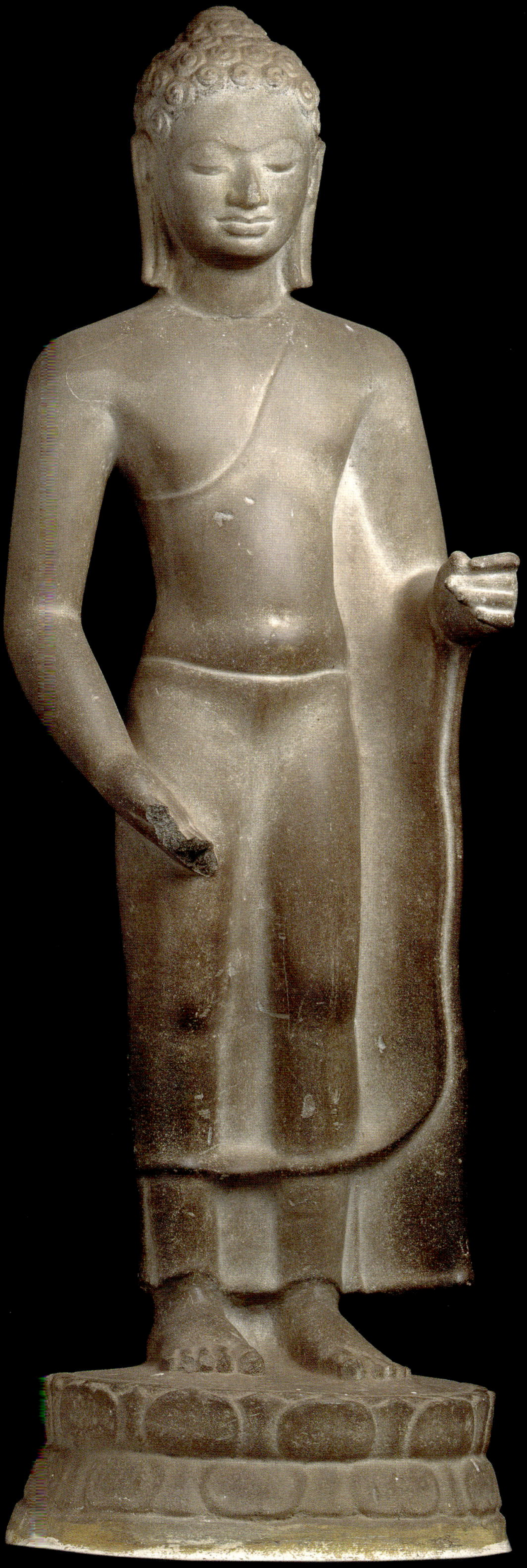
20

21. Buddha. Vat Banon, Battambang, 7th- 8th C. Bronze, 0.275 m. Ga 5412.

Bronze images like this were important conveyers of iconography, style and technique, being small and portable. The supple grace of this iconic figure, its right shoulder bare and its left arm supporting the outer garment, or uttarasangha, is consistent with the style of the stone images from Angkor Borei, but there is nothing to establish a connection between them. In the absence of any identifying features it is impossible to determine whether this Buddha represents the Theravada (Way of the Masters) or the Mahayana (Greater Vehicle, where bodhisattvas form part of the pantheon) school of Buddhism, though its simple spirituality would conform to the tenets of the former.

21. Buddha. Vat Banon, Battambang, 7ème - 8ème s. Bronze, 0,275 m. Ga 5412.

Les images en bronze, petites et aisément transportables, ont joué un rôle important dans la transmission des techniques, des styles et des iconographies. Bien que son lieu de découverte soit fort éloigné de la région d'Angkor Borei, cette souple et élégante statuette, drapée dans un fin manteau monastique laissant l'épaule droite découverte, se rapproche des œuvres en pierre provenant du sud du Cambodge. À défaut de contexte archéologique clair, il est généralement impossible de préciser à quelle école d'art bouddhique pouvait appartenir telle ou telle représentation du Buddha: Theravada (voie des Anciens, également petit Véhicule) ou Mahayana (grand Véhicule, dans lequel de nombreux bodhisattva forment un véritable panthéon).

២១_ ព្រះពុទ្ធរូប វត្តបាណន់, បាត់ដំបង, ស.វ.ទី៧_៨, សំរិត, ០,២៧៥ម, គ ៥៤១២

បដិមាតូចៗធ្វើអំពីសំរិតរបៀបនេះ ជាយានដែលចម្លងរចនាបថ និងបច្ចេកទេសពីកន្លែងមួយទៅកន្លែងមួយបានឆាប់រហ័ស ដោយសារមនុស្សស្រួលយកតាមខ្លួន។ ដងខ្លួនរាងស្តើងរៀវ, ស្មាខាងស្តាំនៅទទេដោយសារចីវរពាក់ចៀងទៅខាងឆ្វេង, ទាំងនេះប្រៀបប្រដូចបានទៅនឹងបដិមាថ្មនៅអង្គរបុរី។ ប៉ុន្តែគ្មានភស្តុតាងអ្វីក្រៅអំពីនេះដែលបង្ហាញថាមានទំនាក់ទំនងគ្នាឡើយ។ ដោយសារផ្នែកបាត់បង់មានច្រើនពេក យើងពុំដឹងថានេះជាពុទ្ធបដិមាថេរវាទ (ដែលដើរតាមគន្លងមហាថេរ) ឬមហាយាន (ដែលព្រះពោធិសត្វជាទេពមួយក្នុងចំណោមទេពច្រើន) ឡើយ។ តែភាពស្រគត់ស្រគំគួរជាទីសក្ការៈនៃរូបនេះ ហាក់ដូចជាបង្ហាញថានៅក្នុងបែបបទថេរវាទ។

21. ブッダ. バッタンバーン州、ワット・バノン、7~8世紀、ブロンズ、0.275m、Ga 5412

このようなブロンズ像は小さく、持ち運びやすいため、イコノグラフィー、様式、技術の伝達に重要な役割を果たした。この聖像の優雅さ、右肩を出し左肩だけ掛ける偏袒右肩の大衣の着方はアンコール・ボレイの石像のスタイルと類似しているが、両者に関連はない。確証となる特徴がないので、このブッダ像が上座仏教のものか、大乗仏教のものか不明だが、素朴なスピリチュアリティーは前者の信条に基づいているようだ。

22. Buddha. Western Baray, Angkor, Siem Reap, 7th-8th C. Bronze, 0.28 m. Ga 5405.

The outer robe of this Buddha covers both shoulders (compare #19) and the two forearms project at the same angle, suggesting that the missing hand might have been making the same gesture as the surviving right hand, with its thumb and index finger sketching the mudra of discussion, vitarkamudra. Like the gesture in #19, the duplicated mudra possibly indicates influences from the neighbouring Dvaravati kingdom, a Mon polity that occupied parts of present-day Myanmar and Thailand. The hollow in the ushnisha on top of the head was probably once filled with a gem.

22. Buddha. Baray occidental, Angkor, Siem Reap, 7ème - 8ème s. Bronze, 0,28 m. Ga 5405.

Le manteau monastique de ce Buddha couvre les deux épaules (comme il en est du Buddha de Vat Romlok, #19). Les bras sont symétriquement projetés vers l'avant et il est vraisemblable que la main gauche manquante effectuait le même geste que celle de droite: la vitarkamudra, le geste de l'argumentation, pouce et index joints. Si tel était le cas, le redoublement du même geste pour les deux mains tendrait à indiquer une influence du royaume voisin de Dvaravati, l'un des royaumes mon qui occupaient jadis une partie des actuelles Thaïlande et Myanmar. À l'origine, la cavité au sommet de l'ushnisha était sans doute sertie d'une pierre précieuse.

២២_ ព្រះពុទ្ធរូប បារាយទឹកថ្លា, អង្គរ, សៀមរាប, ស.វ.ទី៧_៨, សំរិត, ០,២៨ម, គ ៥៤០៥

នៅរូបនេះ ចីវរឃ្លុំខ្លួនជិត (ចូរប្រៀបទៅរូបលេខ១៩) ដៃទាំងពីរបត់ក្នុងទំហំមុមស្មើគ្នា ធ្វើឲ្យយើងគិតថាផ្នែកដៃខាងឆ្វេងដែលបាត់ទៅ ប្រហែលជាមានកាយវិការដូចដៃស្តាំដែរ ពោលគឺមេដៃនិងចង្អុលដែលបង្ហាញពីកាយវិការត្រិះរិះពិចារណា (វិតក្កមុទ្រា)។ មិនខុសអ្វីពីរូបលេខ១៩ទេ កាយវិការតែមួយនៅដៃទាំងសងខាងនេះ បញ្ជាក់ថាមានឥទ្ធិពលមកពីមន ដែលនៅអាណាចក្រទ្វារវតី (ភូមាមួយភាគ និងថៃឡង់ដ៍មួយភាគ)។ ប្រហោងដែលនៅលើមូលីនោះ ដើមឡើយប្រហែលជាបន្តុបដោយត្បូងអ្វីមួយដែលមានតម្លៃ។

22. ブッダ. シエムリエップ州、アンコール、西バライ、7~8世紀、ブロンズ、0.28m、Ga 5405

この像の大衣は両肩を被い（No.19を参照のこと）、２本の前腕は同じ角度で前方にかまえていることから、失われた左手は右手同様に第1・2指を相捻し、説法印を表していたと思われる。No.19の像同様、両手とも説法印の形をとっていたということは、ドヴァーラヴァーティー王国の影響を示している。空の肉髻の頂部には、貴石がはめこまれていたと思われる。

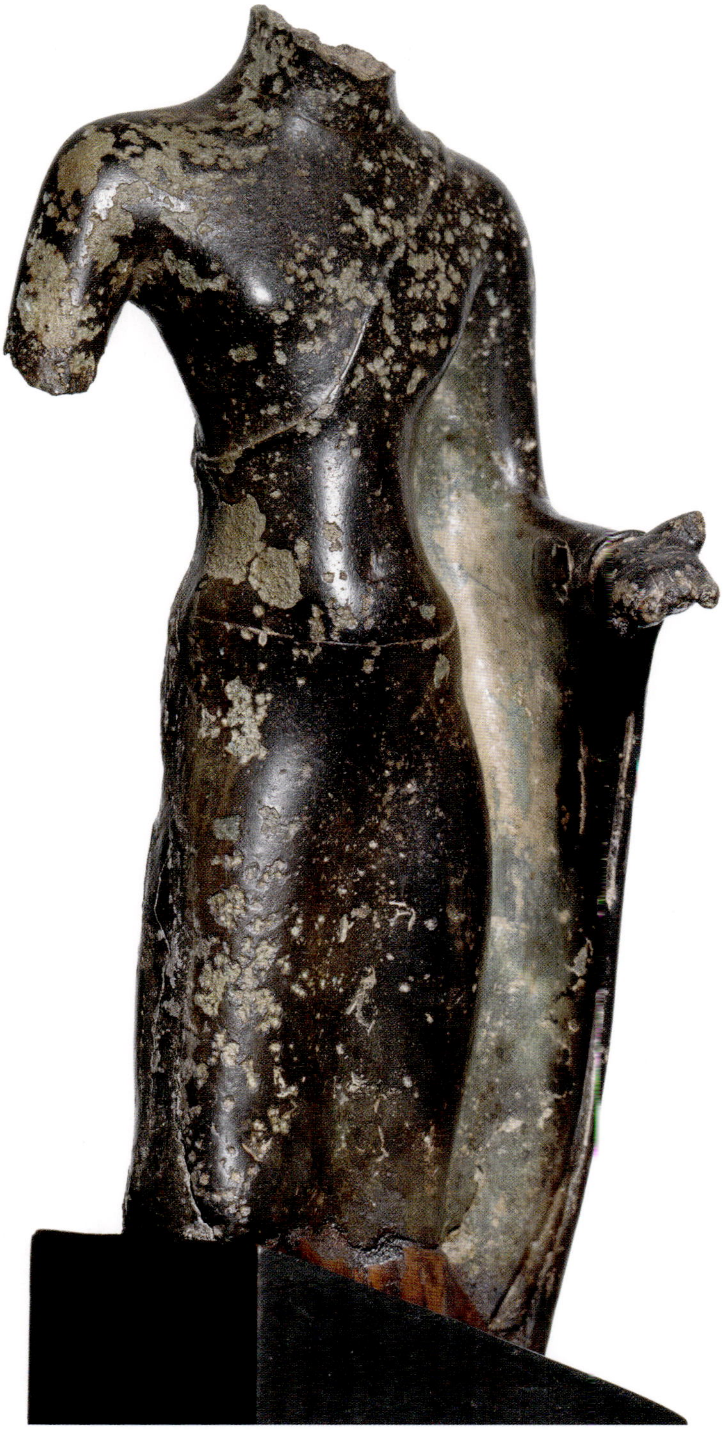

21

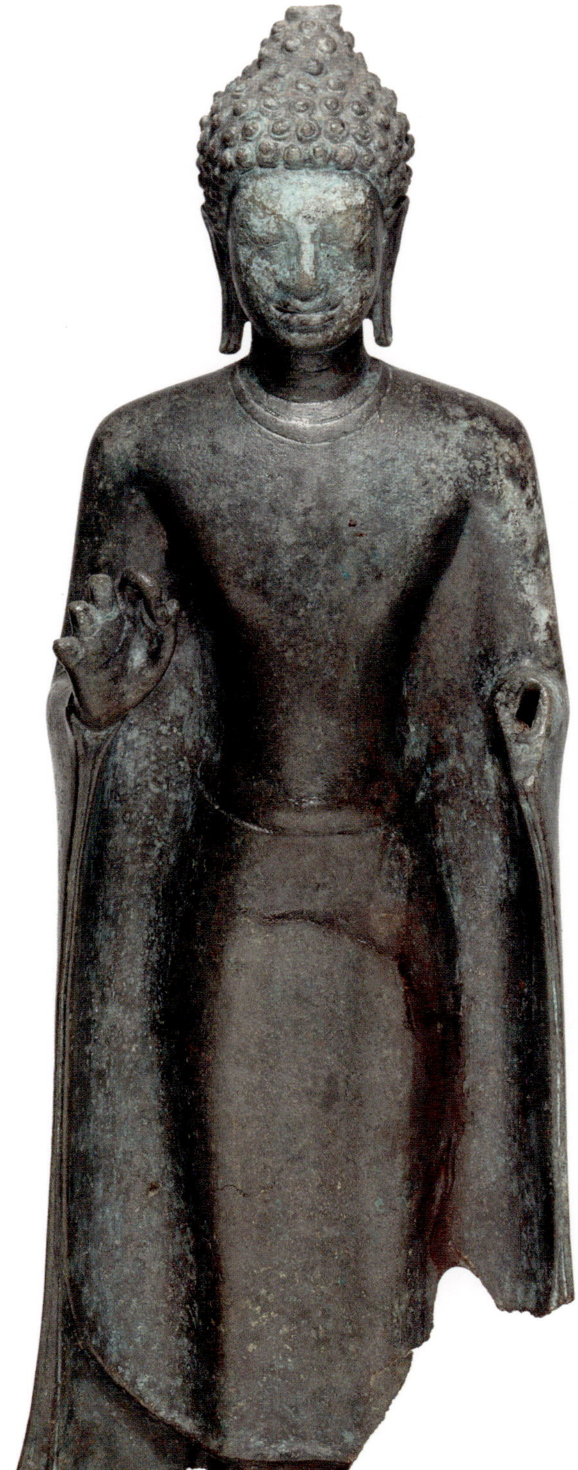

22

23. Avalokiteshvara. Vat Kompong Luong, Angkor Borei, Takeo, 7th C. Lead-tin alloy, 0.178 m. Ga 5330.

Avalokiteshvara is the bodhisattva of compassion. Bodhisattvas are beings who have gained enlightenment but postpone their accession to nirvana to help others achieve the blessed state. Avalokiteshvara is recognisable from the small figure of the meditating Buddha Amitabha in his headdress. This image establishes the presence of Mahayana Buddhism in seventh-century Cambodia, since only this school had a pantheon of bodhisattvas. Stylistically the headdress and short garment of the bodhisattva have traits in common with the art of neighbouring Champa (in central present-day Vietnam) as well as the figures represented in the lintel in #10. The left hand holds a lotus bud, or possibly a jewel (ratna).

23. Avalokiteshvara. Vat Kompong Luong, Angkor Borei, Takeo, 7ème s. Alliage d'étain et de plomb, 0,178 m. Ga 5330.

Avalokiteshvara est le bodhisattva de la compassion. Les bodhisattva sont des êtres qui ont toutes les qualités requises pour obtenir l'Éveil mais retardent le moment où ils deviendront Buddha afin d'aider tous les êtres dans leur progression spirituelle. Avalokiteshvara se reconnaît à la petite image du Buddha Amitabha placée dans sa coiffure. Cette statuette témoigne de la présence du bouddhisme du grand Véhicule, caractérisé par la présence des bodhisattva au sein de son panthéon, dans le Cambodge du 7ème siècle. La coiffure et le costume présentent certains traits communs avec l'art du royaume du Champa (centre de l'actuel Vietnam), comme il en est de certains personnages du linteau de Vat Eng Khna (#10). La main gauche tient une fleur de lotus ou, éventuellement, un joyau (ratna).

២៣_ ព្រះលោកេស្វរ វត្តកំពង់ហ្លួង, អង្គរបុរី, តាកែវ, ស.វ.ទី៧, សំលោហៈដែលភាគច្រើនជាសំណប៉ាហាំង, ០,១៧៨ម, គ ៥៣៣០

ព្រះលោកេស្វរ ជាពោធិសត្វដែលមានករុណាធម៌។ គឺជាអ្នកដែលបានត្រាស់ហើយ ប៉ុន្តែដែលសុខចិត្តពន្យាការចូលនិព្វាន ដើម្បីស្រោចស្រង់សត្វលោកដទៃ។ គេសម្គាល់ព្រះលោកេស្វរដោយមានរូបព្រះពុទ្ធព្រះនាម “អមិតភ” នៅលើផ្នួងសក់។ រូបនេះបង្ហាញថានៅស.វ.ទី៧មានពុទ្ធសាសនាមហាយានហើយនៅប្រទេសកម្ពុជា ត្បិតមានតែយាននេះទេដែលមានព្រះពោធិសត្វច្រើនបែបយ៉ាង។ បើពោលពីរចនាបថ ផ្នួងសក់និងសំពត់ខ្លីអាចប្រៀបធៀបទៅនឹងសិល្បៈនៃប្រទេសចាម្ប (បច្ចុប្បន្ននេះគឺវៀតណាមភាគកណ្ដាល) ហើយម្យ៉ាងទៀតក៏អាចប្រៀបទៅរូបនៅចម្លាក់ផ្ដែរលេខ១០។ ព្រះហស្តឆ្វេងទំនងជាកាន់ក្រពុំឈូក ឬក៏ជារ័ត្នអ្វីមួយ។

23. アヴァローキテーシュヴァラ(観音菩薩). タケオ州、アンコール・ボレイ、ワット・コンポン・ルオン、7世紀、鉛と錫の合金、0.178m、Ga 5330

観音菩薩は慈悲の菩薩である。菩薩は悟りを開いても涅槃に入らず、衆生が悟りを開くのを助けた。宝冠に阿弥陀仏の瞑想姿があるので、観音菩薩だとわかる。この像は7世紀のカンボジアに大乗仏教が伝来していたことを示している。宝冠と短い衣は隣国チャンパ（現在のベトナム中央部）の美術、およびNo.10のリンテルに描かれた姿と共通点が見られる。左手は蓮蕾か宝（ラトナ）を持っている。

24. Avalokiteshvara. Phnom Ta Kream, Battambang, 8th C. Bronze, 0.24 m. Ga 3548.

Many features of this bodhisattva suggest stylistic influence from the Buddhist Indonesian kingdom of Shrivijaya, which was flourishing in the 8th century with some hegemony in the Malay peninsula. These include the form of the double lotus base, the flaring headdress with the trailing curls falling to the shoulder, the full-cheeked oval face and heavy-lidded eyes, the presence of the aureole framing the head and attached to the back of the head and the shoulders, and the incised indication of the garment folds. The bodhisattva holds a water flask in his left hand, and would probably have held a rosary in the right.

24. Avalokiteshvara. Phnom Ta Kream, Battambang, 8ème s. Bronze, 0,24 m. Ga 3548.

Nombre de caractéristiques de ce bodhisattva évoquent une influence stylistique du royaume bouddhiste indonésien de Shrivijaya qui fut florissant dès le 8ème siècle sur la péninsule malaise. Parmi ces caractéristiques, on relèvera plus particulièrement la forme du lotus constituant la base, la coiffure avec ses mèches retombant sur les épaules, le visage aux joues pleines, la lourdeur des paupières, l'auréole entourant la tête et rattachée au niveau des épaules ainsi que le traitement du plissé au moyen d'incisions. Le bodhisattva porte un vase à eau dans la main gauche et devait tenir un rosaire dans la droite.

២៤_ ព្រះលោកេស្វរ ភ្នំតាគ្រៀម, បាត់ដំបង, ស.វ.ទី៨, សំរិត, ០,២៤ម, គ ៣៥៤៨

ចំណុចច្រើនបែបនៃដិមានេះបញ្ជាក់ថាមានឥទ្ធិពលសិល្បៈពីអាណាចក្រស្រីវិជ័យ (បច្ចុប្បន្ននេះនៅកោះសូម៉ាត្រា, ប្រទេសឥណ្ឌូនេស៊ី) ដែលព្រះពុទ្ធសាសនាថ្កុំថ្កើងខ្លាំងនៅស.វ.ទី៨ ហើយដែលជះឥទ្ធិពលទៅលើជ្រោយម៉ាឡាយូផង។ ចំណុចទាំងនោះ គឺទម្រដែលមានត្របកឈូកផ្ងារនិងផ្កាប់, សក់ក្រងធ្លាក់មកលើស្មាទាំងសងខាង, ថ្ពាល់ពេញ, មុខទ្រវែង, ត្របកភ្នែកធ្លាក់បន្តិច, កងពន្លឺនៅក្រោយព្រះកេសភ្ជាប់ទៅនឹងស្មា, ស្នាមផ្នត់នៅលើសំពត់ដែលបញ្ជាក់ថាជាផ្នត់។ ព្រះពោធិសត្វអង្គនេះកាន់ថូនៅព្រះហស្តឆ្វេង ហើយដើមឡើយព្រះហស្តស្ដាំប្រហែលជាកាន់ផ្គាំ។

24. アヴァローキテーシュヴァラ(観音菩薩). バッタンバーン州、プノン・タ・クリアム、8世紀、ブロンズ、0.24m、Ga 3548

この観音菩薩には8世紀、マレー半島まで覇権していたインドネシア仏教王国シュリーヴィジャヤの影響が多く見られる。つまり２重の蓮華座、肩まである蕨手状に巻く垂髪、張った頬、卵形の顔、重たいまぶた、後頭部と肩につながった頭光、くっきりに刻まれた衣文などである。この菩薩は左手に浄瓶を持っているが、右手には数珠があったと思われる。

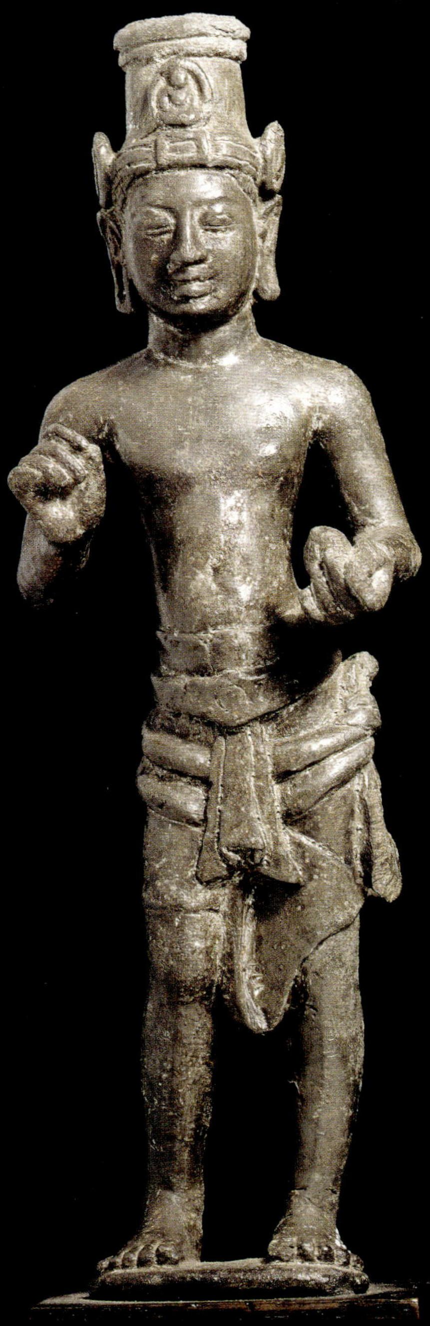

23

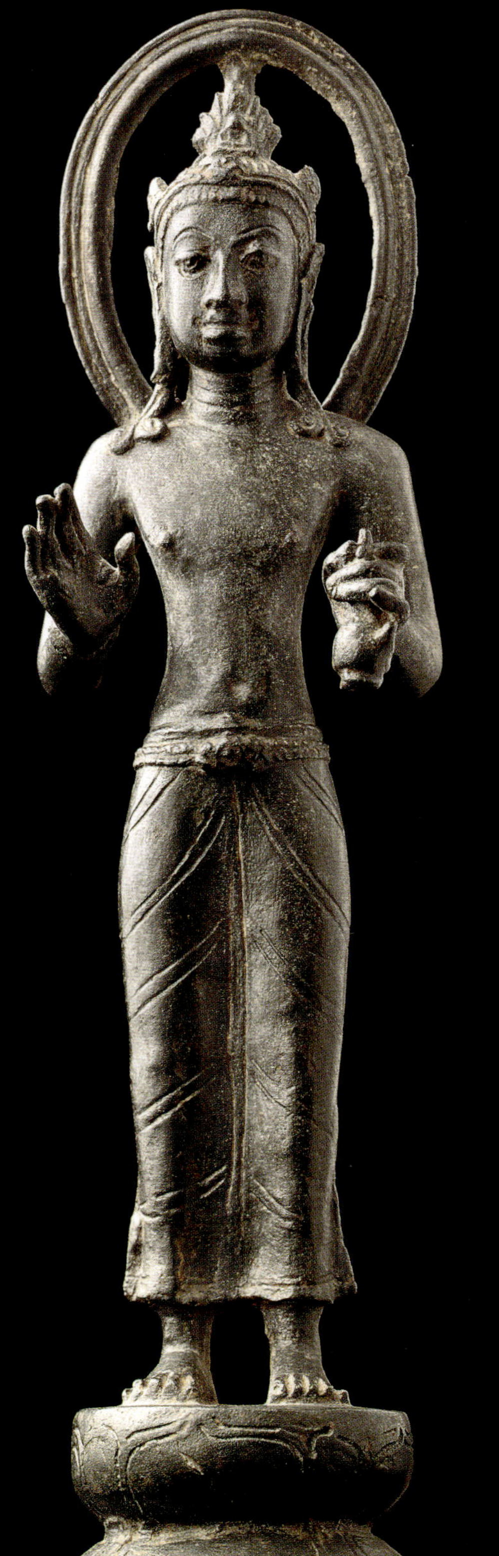

24

25. Maitreya. Unknown provenance, probably present-day Thailand, 7th-8th C. Bronze, 0.325 m. Ga 5428.

This highly naturalistic image of Maitreya with its delicately moulded limbs and digits and its elaborately coiled coiffure is reminiscent of the style of the bronzes found near Prakhon Chai, a village now in northeastern Thailand but under Khmer hegemony in the 8th century. Maitreya is not only a bodhisattva but also the Buddha of the Future, and is one of the few beings apart from the Buddha himself to be accepted in Theravada Buddhism. He is recognisable from the small stupa in his headdress.

25. Maitreya. Provenance inconnue, 7ème - 8ème s. Bronze, 0,325 m. Ga 5428.

Cette représentation très vivante de Maitreya, dont on notera la souplesse particulière des doigts et la coiffure très élaborée, se rapproche par sa facture des célèbres bronzes découverts près de Prakhon Chai, un village du nord-est de la Thaïlande, une région sous domination khmère au 8eme siècle. Maitreya n'est pas seulement un être de compassion: il est aussi le Buddha du futur et le seul bodhisattva - hormis le Buddha lui-même avant son Éveil - reconnu par le bouddhisme Theravada. Le petit stupa figuré dans sa coiffure permet de l'identifier malgré l'absence des attributs.

២៥_ព្រះស្រីអារ្យមេត្រីយ៍ មិនស្គាល់ប្រភពច្បាស់ (ប្រហែលជាថៃឡង់ដ៏បច្ចុប្បន្ន), ស.វ.ទី៧_៨, សំរិត, ០,៣២៥ម. គ ៥៤២៨

បដិមាព្រះស្រីអារ្យនេះសាងឡើងតាមលំនាំធម្មជាតិ។ អវៈយវៈព្រមទាំងម្រាមផ្សេងៗមានភាពផ្ចិតផ្ចង់ណាស់ ឯផ្នួងសក់ដែលមានរាងជារង្វេលក៏ដូច្នោះដែរ។ ចំណុចទាំងនេះគួរប្រៀបប្រដូចទៅនឹងសិល្បៈសំរិតដែលគេប្រទះឃើញនៅតំបន់ "ព្រះគោលជ័យ" ដែលស្ថិតនៅភូមិភាគឦសាននៃប្រទេសថៃឡង់ដ៏ ហើយដែលកាលពីស.វ.ទី៨នៅក្រោមការត្រួតត្រារបស់ខ្មែរ។ ព្រះស្រីអារ្យមេត្រីយ៍ពុំត្រឹមតែជាព្រះពោធិសត្វប៉ុណ្ណោះទេ ប៉ុន្តែគឺជាព្រះពុទ្ធអង្គដែលនឹងត្រាស់នៅពេលអនាគតផង។ ទេពប្រភេទនេះមានតិចតួចណាស់ ដែលព្រះពុទ្ធសាសនាថេរវាទទទួលស្គាល់។ ចំណុចសម្គាល់បដិមានោះ គឺមានចេតិយតូចមួយលើផ្នួងសក់។

25. マイトレーヤ(弥勒菩薩). 出土地不明、恐らく現在のタイ、7~8世紀、ブロンズ、0.325m、Ga 5428

この弥勒菩薩像は手足や指が繊細に鋳造されており、凝った髻は現在タイ北東部で8世紀にはクメール王国支配下にあったプラコン・チャイ周辺で出土したブロンズ像に類似している。弥勒菩薩は菩薩であるばかりか、未来のブッダであり、上座仏教でブッダ以外に受け入れられている数少ない存在である。髻に描かれた小さいストゥーパがその特徴である。

26. Harihara. Prasat Trapeang Phong, Roluos, Siem Reap, 8th C. Sandstone, 0.99 m. Ka 951.

Supported by an unusually well preserved arch, Vishnu's attributes (conch signifying the water of existence in the rear left hand, mace standing for the power of knowledge in the front left hand, and globe symbolising the earth in the front right hand) predominate in this version of the dual god, and only the trident represents Shiva's attributes. Vishnu's mitre dominates the head's profile, where the twisted locks forming Shiva's jatamukuta are reduced to stylised incisions. The somewhat rigid frontal stance indicates the growing hieratism of Khmer sculpture, while the oval face and slender torso of the Phnom Da style are replaced by a square jaw and sturdier body.

26. Harihara. Prasat Trapeang Phong, Roluos, Siem Reap, 8ème s. Grès, 0,99 m. Ka 951.

Supportés par un arc de soutien remarquablement bien conservé, les attributs de Vishnu (la conque - symbole de l'eau de la vie - dans la main postérieure gauche, la massue - symbole du pouvoir de connaissance - dans la main antérieure gauche et la sphère - symbole de la terre - dans la main antérieure droite) prédominent dans cette représentation du dieu hybride. Shiva, quant à lui, n'est évoqué que par son seul trident, dans la main postérieure droite. La mitre de Vishnu, par ailleurs, domine la composition de la coiffure où le chignon d'ascète de Shiva, simplement rehaussé d'incisions, affecte un volume identique. La posture frontale et quelque peu raide du dieu témoigne du caractère hiératique progressivement plus marqué de la statuaire khmère. Les visages souples et les torses déliés des œuvres préangkoriennes cèdent la place à des physionomies plus géométriques et à des corps plus lourds.

២៦_ព្រះហរិហរ ប្រាសាទត្រពាំងផុង, រលួស, សៀមរាប, ស.វ.ទី៨, ថ្មភក់, ០,៩៩ម, ក ៩៥១

ជាការកម្រណាស់ដែលរង្វង់ទល់ទ្ររាងក្រចកសេះមិនបាត់បង់ទៅណា ដូចនៅរូបនេះ។ គេតនភណ្ឌរបស់ព្រះនារាយណ៍មានច្រើនជាងគេ ពោលគឺកាន់ស័ង្ខជានិមិត្តរូបនៃជីវិត នៅដៃឆ្វេងក្រោយ, ដំបងជានិមិត្តរូបនៃចំណេះ នៅដៃឆ្វេងខាងមុខ, ដុំមូលជានិមិត្តរូបនៃផែនដី នៅដៃស្តាំខាងមុខ។ ឯគេតនភណ្ឌនៃព្រះឥសូរវិញមានតែត្រីសូល៍មួយមុខប៉ុណ្ណោះ។ សូម្បីតែសក់ក៏ផ្នួងរាងប៉ោងបន្តិច (ផ្នែកព្រះនារាយណ៍) ហាក់ដូចជាលេចធ្លោជាងផ្នួងជារង្វេល (ផ្នែកព្រះឥសូរ) ដែរ ត្បិតគេគ្រាន់តែចូតឱ្យមានស្នាម។ រូបប្រភេទនេះនឹងកាន់តែសម្បូណ៌ឡើងជាលំដាប់ រីឯទម្រង់មុខទ្រវែង, ដងខ្លួនស្រឡូន ដូចនៅក្នុងរចនាបថភ្នំដា ក៏ក្លាយទៅជាថ្គាមខ្លា និងខ្លួនរាងទ្រើងកាន់តែខ្លាំងឡើងៗ។

26. ハリハラ. シエムリエップ州、ロルオス、プラサート・トラペアン・ポン、8世紀、砂岩、0.99m、Ka 951

支柱がかなり完全な形で残っており、後ろの左手の生命の水を象徴する法螺貝、前の左手の知識力を象徴する棍棒、前の右手の地球を象徴する宝珠などヴィシュヌの持物が目立ち、シヴァの持物は三叉戟だけである。頭部はヴィシュヌの宝冠が大半を占め、シヴァのジャカムクタは編んだ髪が形式化して刻まれている。直立姿勢はクメール彫刻の聖美術化の傾向を示しており、プノン・ダ様式の卵形の顔とほっそりした胴体は、角張ったあごとしっかりした体躯に変化した。

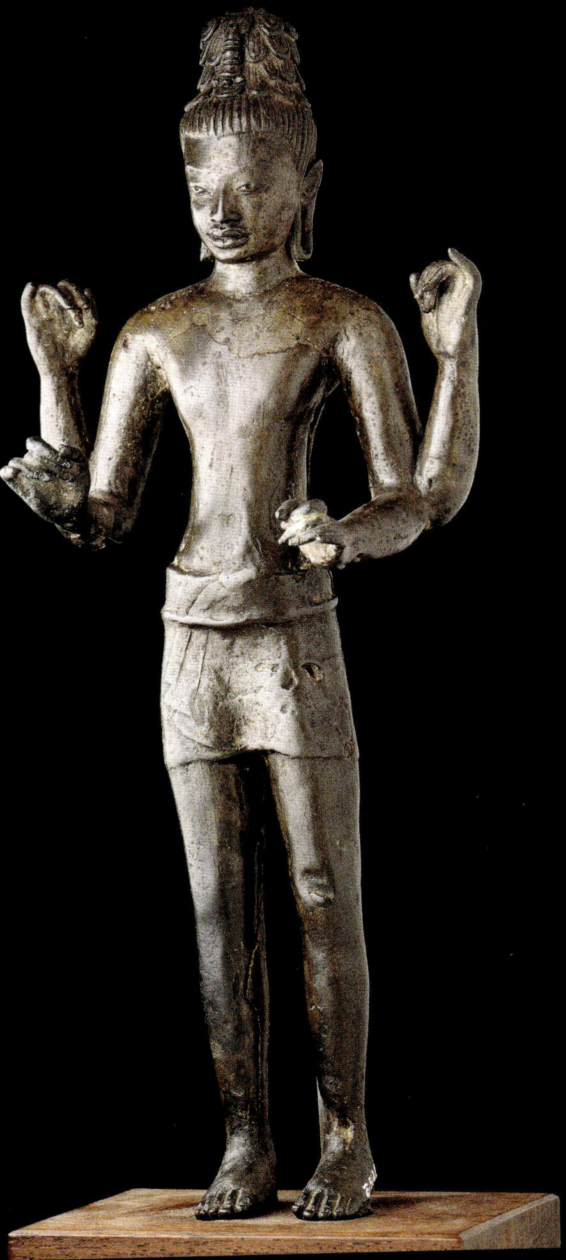

25

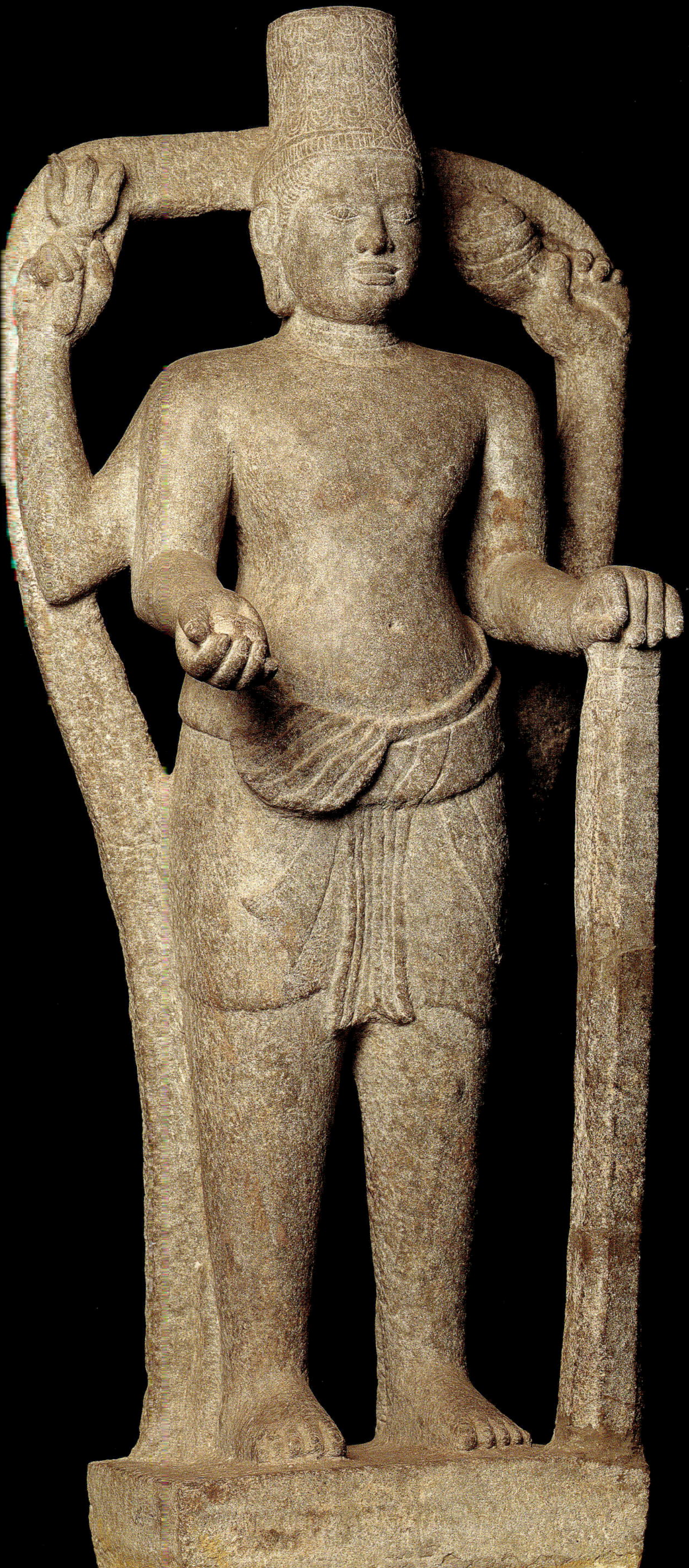

26

27. Vishnu. N. sanctuary, Prasat Krabei (formerly Damrei) Krap, Phnom Kulen, Siem Reap, 1st half 9th C. Sandstone, 1.79 m. Ka 882.

The four-armed Vishnu, Vishnu Chaturbuja (chatur is Sanskrit for 'four'), sculpted soon after Jayavarman II was proclaimed universal monarch in 802 CE on Mount Kulen, has retained all four attributes - clockwise from front right: globe, disk, conch and mace - a rare survival of vulnerable projections. It is an early example of sculpture where the supporting arch has been dispensed with. The iconic dignity of this figure suggests the growing emphasis on power in the Angkorian age. The face is sensitive but more detached than the spiritual expression characteristic of a pre-Angkorian Vishnu, #5. The torso is less naturalistic and the sampot more stylised, with schematic arrangement of folds and pleats.

27. Vishnu. Prasat Krabei (également Damrei) Krap, Phnom Kulen, Siem Reap, 1ère moitié du 9ème s. Grès, 1,79 m. Ka 882.

Ce Vishnu doté de quatre bras (chaturbhuja, chatur signifiant quatre en sanskrit) fut sans doute sculpté sous le règne de Jayavarman II, consacré souverain universel sur le Phnom Kulen en 802. De manière tout à fait exceptionnelle, le dieu a conservé ses quatre attributs - dans le sens des aiguilles d'une montre, depuis la main antérieure droite: la sphère, le disque, la conque et la massue. L'œuvre est l'une des plus anciennes dans lesquelles l'arc de soutien a disparu. La majesté de la sculpture semble un contrepoint à l'épanouissement du pouvoir monarchique à l'époque angkorienne. L'expression demeure sensible mais accuse moins de spiritualité que dans certains visages préangkoriens, par exemple celui du beau Vishnu du Tuol Dai Buon (#5). Le torse est moins naturel et le sampot plus stylisé avec son drapé et ses plis schématiques.

២៧_ព្រះនារាយណ៍ ប៉មខាងជើងនៃប្រាសាទក្របីក្រាប, ភ្នំគូលែន, សៀមរាប, ផ្នែកទី១នៃស.វ.ទី៩, ថ្មភក់, ១,៧៩ម, ក ៨៨២

ជាកុសលល្អ ព្រះនារាយណ៍ដៃ៤នេះឥតមានខូចខាតអ្វីឡើយ ហើយសាងឡើងបន្ទាប់ពីព្រះបាទជ័យវរ្ម័នទី២ប្រកាសខ្លួនជាស្តេចចក្រពត្តិនៅលើភ្នំគូលែន នាឆ្នាំ ៨០២។ ដៃស្តាំខាងមុខកាន់ផែនដី ខាងក្រោយកាន់ចក្រ រីឯដៃឆ្វេងខាងមុខកាន់ដំបង ខាងក្រោយកាន់ស័ង្ខ។ ចាប់ពីជំនាន់នោះមក គេពុំសូវប្រើរង្វង់រាងក្រចកសេះសម្រាប់ទល់ទ្រទៀតទេ។ អនុភាពដែលចេញពីបដិមាទនេះ ហាក់ដូចជាបង្ហាញរាជ្យអំណាចអាណាចក្រអង្គរ ដែលកាន់តែសាយភាយខ្លាំងទៅៗ។ ព្រះភ័ក្ត្រមានភាពរស់រវើកនៅឡើយ តែភាពស្រគត់ស្រគំជាទីសក្ការៈ ហាក់ដូចជាឃ្លាតឆ្ងាយពីសិល្បៈជំនាន់មុនអង្គរ ដូចមានព្រះនារាយណ៍លេខ៥ជាឧទាហរណ៍។ ដងខ្លួនមិនសូវធ្វើតាមធម្មជាតិដូចមុនទេ ឯផ្នត់និងថ្នក់សំពត់កាន់តែសង្ខេបជាងមុន។

27. ヴィシュヌ. シエムリエップ州、プノン・クレーン、プラサート・クラベイ・クラップ北祠堂、9世紀前半、砂岩、1.79m、Ka 882

この４臂ヴィシュヌ像はジャヤヴァルマン２世が802年、プノン・クーレン高丘でチャクラヴァルティン（転輪聖王）であることを宣言した直後に彫られたもので、右から宝珠・円輪・法螺貝・棍棒と４持物は全て残っている。支柱が消えた初期の作である。この威厳ある姿はアンコール王国で権力を強調するようになったことを示している。顔は繊細だが、No.5の前アンコール時代のヴィシュヌのようなスピリチュアルな表情より、超然としている。胴体は自然さを失い、裙の折り返しやプリーツなども形式化している。

28. Vishnu. Bakong, tower 7, Roluos, Siem Reap, last quarter 9th C. Sandstone, 1.59 m. Ka 1649.

This majestic Vishnu, from one of the subsidiary towers of the first monumental temple mountain, Bakong (881), in Indravarman I's capital of Hariharalaya (now Roluos), embodies authority, with its hieratic stance, iconic downcast gaze and the swelling volumes of the torso that suggest the prana, or inner breath, that signifies superhuman power. The mitre worn by pre-Angkorian Vishnu figures has evolved into a multi-tiered pagoda-shaped headdress bounded by an elaborate diadem comprising two registers, lozenges in the lower and alternating stems and petals in the upper. The finely chased line of the beard and the thin up-curving moustache are characteristic of the Preah Ko style, which this and Shiva, #29, typify.

28. Vishnu. Bakong, tour-sanctuaire 7, Roluos, Siem Reap, dernier quart du 9ème s. Grès, 1,59 m. Ka 1649.

Ce majestueux Vishnu provient de l'une des tours-sanctuaires secondaires du temple de Bakong, premier grand temple-montagne khmer, dont les divinités principales ont été consacrées sous le règne d'Indravarman I, en 881, dans sa capitale de Hariharalaya, l'actuel site de Roluos. Une impression d'autorité se dégage de ce corps hiératique où les volumes souples et amples du torse se rapportent à la notion de prana ou souffle intérieur, symbolisant la force et la possession de pouvoir surnaturels. La mitre cylindrique des Vishnu préangkoriens a évolué vers un couvre-chef en forme de pagodon octogonal, bordé sur le front par un diadème à deux registres de décor: losanges à la partie inférieure, fleurs de lotus et pétales à la partie supérieure. Le contour délicatement incisé de la barbe et la petite moustache se recourbant vers le haut sont caractéristiques du style de Preah Ko dont cette sculpture et le Shiva suivant (#29) sont très représentatifs.

២៨_ព្រះនារាយណ៍ ប្រាសាទបាគង, ប៉មទី៧, រលួស, សៀមរាប, ផ្នែកខាងក្រោយនៃស.វ.ទី៩, ថ្មភក់, ១,៥៩ម, ក ១៦៤៩

បដិមាព្រះនារាយណ៍នេះបានមកពីតួប៉មមួយនៃប្រាសាទបាគង (ឆ្នាំ៨៨១) ដែលជាប្រាសាទភ្នំទី១ សាងឡើងនៅហរិហរាល័យ (រលួស) ពោលគឺរាជធានីនៃព្រះបាទឥន្ទ្រវរ្ម័ន។ ជំហទាំងមូលត្រង់ភ្លឹងគួរឱ្យស្ញែង, ភ្នែកហាក់ដូចជាសម្លឹងមកដងខ្លួនប្រកបដោយទ្រូងពើង បញ្ជាក់ថាមានឥទ្ធិឫទ្ធិខ្លាំងក្លា។ ផ្នួងសក់រាងបំពង់ដែលធ្លាប់ឃើញពីមុនសម័យអង្គរ នៅទីនេះវិវឌ្ឍន៍ទៅជារាងជ្រុងថ្នាក់ៗបន្តុបលើគ្នា ដែលមានក្បាំងនៅពីមុខ។ ក្បាំងនោះមានក្បាច់លំអ២ជួរ, ខាងក្រោមជាក្បាច់ច័ក្កច័ន ឯខាងលើជាភ្ញី។ ពុកចង្ការត់តាមខ្សែស្មើល្អមួយ, ពុកមាត់ងចុងដូចជានៅលើរូបព្រះឥសូរលេខ២៩ដែរ ដែលជាលក្ខណៈសម្គាល់នៃរចនាបថព្រះគោ។

28. ヴィシュヌ. シエムリエップ州、ロルオス、バコン周壁外の第７祠堂、9世紀第４四半期、砂岩、1.59m、Ka 1649

この荘厳なヴィシュヌ像は、インドラヴァルマン１世の王都ハリハラーラヤ（現在のロルオス）の最初の大山岳型寺院であるバコン（881年建立）から発見された。聖美術的な姿勢、下向きの眼差し、超人的能力を象徴する内なる力（プラナ）を感じさせる胸の厚みなど権力を表している。前アンコール時代のヴィシュヌが纏っていた宝冠は、祠堂の屋根の形に変化した。そして豪華な冠帯は2段で、下部には菱形、上部には茎と花びらの模様がある。この像やNo.29のシヴァ像に見られる、あご髭の繊細な刻みと反り返った細い口ひげはプレア・コー様式の特徴である。

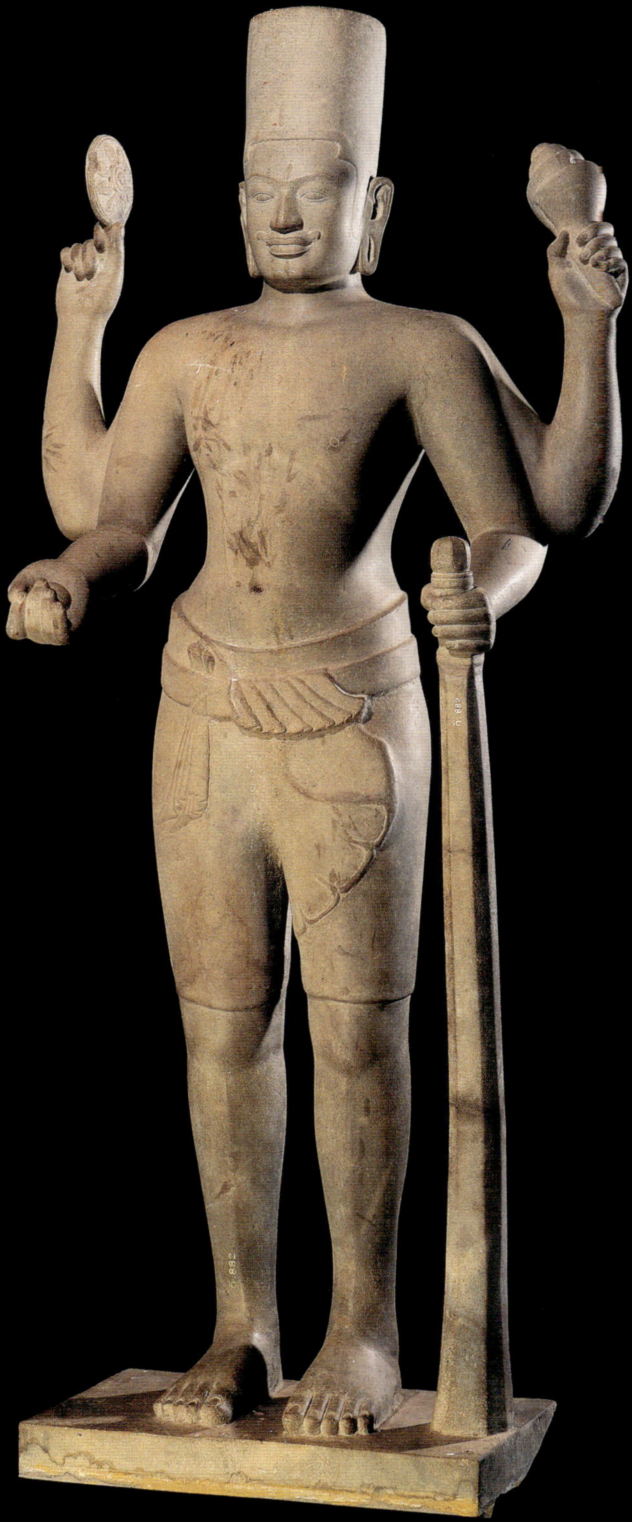

27

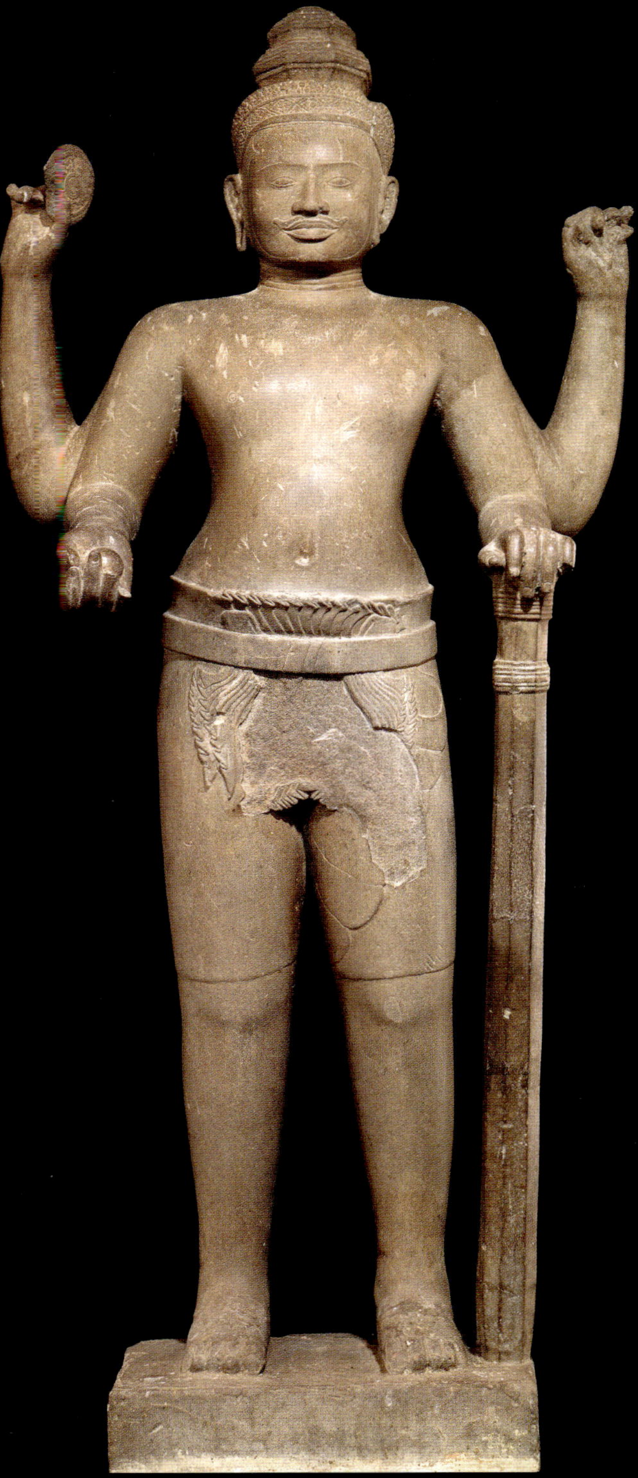

28

29. Shiva. Bakong, tower 9, Roluos, Siem Reap, last quarter 9th C. Sandstone, 1.86 m. Ka 1648.

The power emanating from this compelling Shiva image characterises Preah Ko style, contemporary with Bakong, the state temple of Indravarman I, where (like Vishnu, #28) this Shiva was found. The two gods wear the same kind of diadem. Shiva's headdress has evolved: the looped and braided locks of earlier jatamukutas have become highly stylised as horizontal bands towering in cylindrical form. The tense volume of the chest and abdomen suggest the inner breath, or prana, that indicates strength. The sampot's elaborate arrangement, with pleats and anchor-shaped front panel, presages a style that would dominate Khmer costume for three more centuries.

29. Shiva. Bakong, tour-sanctuaire 9, Roluos, Siem Reap, dernier quart du 9ème s. Grès, 1,86 m. Ka 1648.

La puissance émanant de cette remarquable représentation de Shiva est propre aux œuvres du style de Preah Ko, dont le temple de Bakong - temple d'État d'Indravarman I où cette sculpture et la précédente (#28) furent découvertes - est le plus bel exemple. Les deux dieux portent le même diadème. La coiffure de mèches en anses souples et larges des œuvres shivaïtes préangkoriennes a laissé la place à un cylindre de petites mèches en u superposées. La tension des volumes de la poitrine et de l'abdomen fait référence au prana, comme dans le cas du Vishnu précédent. Le sampot élaboré, avec son pan antérieur en forme d'ancre marine, préfigure l'aspect classique des costumes masculins pour les trois siècles à venir.

២៩_ព្រះឥសូរ ប្រាសាទបាគង, ប៉មលេខ៩, រលួស, សៀមរាប, ផ្នែកខាងក្រោយនៃស.វ.ទី៩, ថ្មភក់, ១,៨៦ម, ក ១៦៤៨

បដិមាព្រះឥសូរនេះយកមកពីប្រាសាទបាគង ដែលសាងឡើងដោយព្រះបាទឥន្ទ្រវរ្ម័ន ហើយដែលបញ្ចេញអនុភាពដូចរូបព្រះនារាយណ៍លេខ២៨ ក្នុងរចនាបថព្រះគោដូចគ្នាដែរ។ ក្បាំងមកុដនៃរូបទាំងពីរដូចគ្នា។ រីឯផ្នួងសក់ដែលពីមុនមកជាចង្វាយសក់ក្រង មកដល់ទីនេះវិវឌ្ឍន៍ជាររង្វេលសក់រាងបំពង់ ហើយដែលគេពុំធ្លាក់ឱ្យលម្អិតដូចធម្មជាតិឡើយ។ ដងខ្លួនដែលមានទ្រូងពើងដង្ហើមពេញ ក៏បញ្ជាក់ថាមានឥទ្ធិឫទ្ធិខ្លាំងក្លាដែរ។ សំពត់ជ្និតជ្ជង់ខ្លាំងណាស់ ហើយបង្ហាញពីផ្នត់ដែលគេរៀបចំឱ្យស្មើគ្នា បញ្ចប់ដោយជាយដែលមានរាងកន្ទុយត្រីនៅចំពីមុខ។ អំណើះតទៅ ការបង្ហាញសំពត់របៀបនេះកាន់តែមានភាពស្មុគស្មាញខ្លាំងទៅៗនៅក្នុងសិល្បៈខ្មែរបុរាណ។

29. シヴァ. シエムリエップ州、ロルオス、バコン周壁外の第9祠堂、9世紀第４四半期、砂岩、1.86m、Ka 1648

この力強いシヴァ像はNo.28のヴィシュヌ像同様、インドラヴァルマン１世の国家鎮護寺院バコンから発見されたプレア・コー様式の像である。ヴィシュヌ像とこのシヴァ像は同様の冠帯をつけている。シヴァの髻は輪状にの編んだ髪という初期の髪髻冠から、水平の帯が円柱状にそびえたつ形式化されたものに変化した。胸の厚みは内なる力、プラナを感じさせる。裙は装飾的で、前面には錨形のプリーツがあり、その後３世紀続くクメール衣装のスタイルの兆しがみられる。

30. Male torso. Phnom Bakheng, Angkor, Siem Reap, early 10th C. Sandstone, 1.52 m. Ka 1650.

Early in the 10th century, coinciding with Yashovarman's transfer of the capital from Hariharalaya to a city he called Yashodharapura in the region of Phnom Bakheng, the tendency to hieratism was intensified. The stance became more rigid, as in this male torso, the expression more detached, and the formalisation of costume more pronounced. Pleats, formerly visible in panels, became ubiquitous, their perfection of carving and elaborate symmetrical arrangement setting the standard of precision that characterises works in what is classified as Bakheng style. Relief carving on Bakheng temple-mountain conforms to the same canon.

30. Corps masculin. Phnom Bakheng, Angkor, Siem Reap, début du 10ème s. Grès, 1,52 m. Ka 1650.

Au début du 10ème siècle, au moment même où Yashovarman déplace la capitale de Hariharalaya vers Yashodharapura, autour du Phnom Bakheng, la statuaire s'oriente dans la voie d'un hiératisme toujours plus marqué. Les expressions sont plus détachées et impersonnelles, la stylisation des vêtements et des parures s'accentue et, ainsi qu'en témoigne ce corps masculin, les postures se font plus raides. Les plissés, jusque là réservés à certaines parties des costumes, deviennent omniprésents et affectent un traitement très régulier et géométrique dont la froide perfection est caractéristique du style du Bakheng. Le décor architectural du Phnom Bakheng, le temple-montagne fondé par Yashovarman au sommet de l'une des rares collines de la région d'Angkor, se conforme aux mêmes canons esthétiques.

៣០_ដងខ្លួនប្រុស ភ្នំបាខែង, អង្គរ, សៀមរាប, ដើមស.វ.ទី១០, ថ្មភក់, ១,៥២ម, ក ១៦៥០

នៅដើមស.វ.ទី១០ គឺសម័យដែលព្រះបាទយសោវរ្ម័នប្តូររាជធានីពីហរិហរាល័យមកយសោធរ ដោយយកភ្នំបាខែងជាមណ្ឌលនោះ បដិមាផ្សេងៗក៏បែរទៅរកជំហរត្រង់ក្ដឹងកាន់តែខ្លាំងទៅៗ ដោយគ្មានភាពអែនអនអ៊ីទាំងអស់។ រូបដែលនៅសល់តែដងខ្លួននេះក៏បង្ហាញពីជំហរាងផ្ទឹងដែរ រីឯសំពត់ក៏កាន់តែឃ្លាតចាកពីភាពបត់បែនតាមធម្មជាតិ ដោយបែរទៅរកទិដ្ឋភាពក្រៅ ដែលគ្រាន់តែជាការសន្មតប៉ុណ្ណោះ។ ផ្នត់សំពត់ដែលធ្លាប់មានតែដោយអន្លើ ឥឡូវនេះមាននៅគ្រប់កន្លែង។ ផ្នត់ទាំងនោះបង្ហាញដូចគ្នាទាំងសងខាង ព្រមទាំងធ្លាក់សម្អិតសម្អាងខ្លាំង ដែលជាលក្ខណៈសម្គាល់មួយនៃរចនាបថបាខែង។ ទាំងនេះពុំខុសពីចម្លាក់នៅប្រាសាទបាខែងផ្ទាល់ឡើយ។

30. 男性トルソ. シエムリエップ州、アンコール、プノン・バケン、10世紀初め、砂岩、1.52m、Ka 1650

10世紀初め、ヤショヴァルマン１世が王都をハリハラーラヤからヤショドハラプラに遷都した頃、聖美術の傾向が強まった。この男性トルソのように姿勢は硬直し、表情は超然とし、衣装は形式化した。プリーツは偏在化し、その完成した彫り方と対称な形は、精密なバケン様式の特徴である。バケン山岳型寺院のレリーフも同じ形式である。

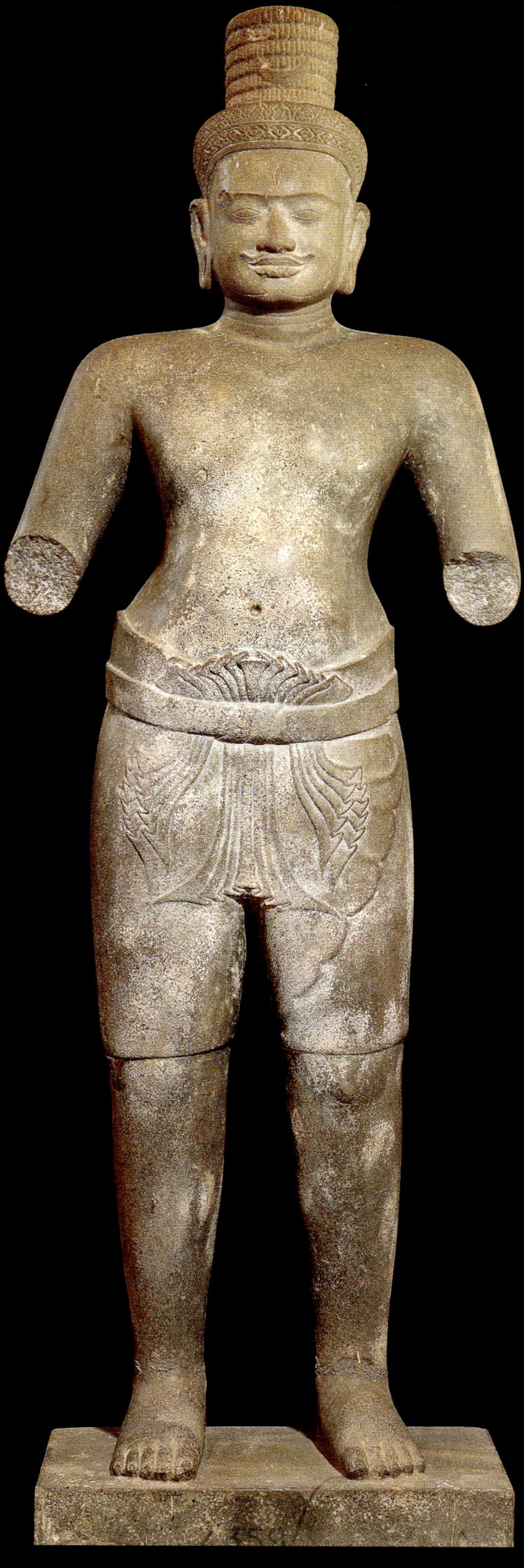

29

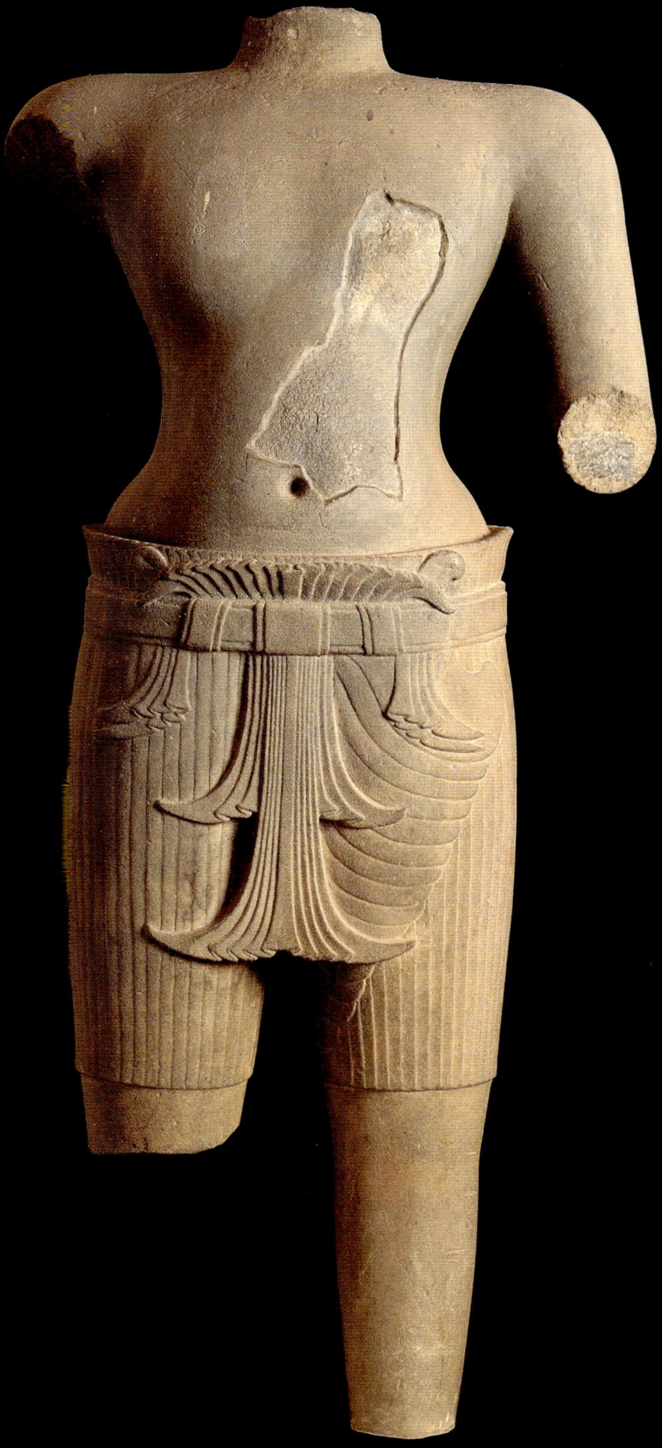

30

31. Wrestlers. **Prasat Thom, gopura II West, Koh Ker, Preah Vihear, 2nd quarter 10th C. Sandstone, 0.79 m. Ka 1657.**

Jayavarman IV proclaimed himself king in 921, though his nephews had been installed in succession to their father, Yashovarman, early in the century. He ruled from his estate at Chok Gargyar (Koh Ker), northeast of Angkor. In 928 he was finally consecrated as king of the state. Meanwhile he had constructed his capital on a vast scale, perhaps with a usurper's need to affirm power. Sculpture in Koh Ker style reflects the monarch's monumental ambition. Massive in proportion, yet finely carved, it is imbued with dynamism and naturalism, as seen in this pair of wrestlers who probably represent the *Mahabharata* episode of Arjuna and Shiva in disguise as a hunter, that set it apart from the hieratic styles that preceded it.

៣១_ អ្នកចំបាប់ **ប្រាសាទធំ, ក្លោងទ្វារទី២ខាងលិច, កោះកេរ្តិ៍, ព្រះវិហារ, មុនពាក់កណ្ដាលស.វ.ទី១០, ថ្មភក់, ០,៧៩ម, ក ១៦៥៧**

ព្រះបាទជ័យវរ្ម័នទី៤ប្រកាសព្រះអង្គថាជាស្ដេចនៅឆ្នាំ៩២១ ថ្វីត្បិតតែក្មួយផ្សេងៗនៃព្រះអង្គស្នងរាជ្យតគ្នាពីព្រះបាទយសោវរ្ម័ននៅដើមស.វ.ទី១០មក។ ពេលនោះរាជធានីផ្លាស់មកនៅ "ចោកគគ្យីរ" (កោះកេរ្តិ៍) ខាងឦសានតំបន់អង្គរ។ នៅឆ្នាំ៩២៨ព្រះអង្គទទួលអភិសេកជាស្ដេចពេញមុខ។ ការសាងសង់មានភាពធំធេងពាសពេញរាជធានី ហាក់ដូចជាព្រះរាជាចង់បង្ហាញពីអនុភាពព្រះអង្គ ដែលដើមឡើយគ្រាន់តែជាស្ដេចជ្រែករាជ្យគេប៉ុណ្ណោះ។ ចម្លាក់ទាំងឡាយនៅក្នុងរចនាបថកោះកេរ្តិ៍ច្បះបង្ហាញពីការចង់សម្ដែងអនុភាពនោះ។ រូបនេះមានទំហំធំហើយឆ្លាក់ដោយលម្អិតផ្ចិតផ្ចង់ ព្រមទាំងប្រកបដោយចលនារស់រវើកដូចក្នុងធម្មជាតិ។ រូបអ្នកចំបាប់នេះត្រូវចាត់ទុកដោយឡែកពីបដិមានានាដែលតែងតែមានជំហរទ្រឹង។

32. Hand from a Shiva statue. **Prasat Kraham, Prasat Thom, Koh Ker, Preah Vihear, 2nd quarter 10th C. Sandstone, 0.50 m. Ka 1868.**

The size of this hand indicates the colossal scale of the statue to which it belonged, an almost four-metre tall dancing Shiva with five heads and ten arms that stood in Prasat Kraham, the gopura (gate temple) of the third enclosure of Prasat Thom, Jayavarman IV's state temple at Koh Ker. Such figures represent the cosmic version of Shiva, though no other example in dance attitude is known. The god's hand rests on the finial of a club, not normally a Shaivite attribute. This and five other almost complete hands, as well as a foot fragment and two of the five heads are also stored in the National Museum, while parts of the torso are still in situ. They comprise all that remains of the figure, probably destroyed when overthrown by looters seeking treasure below its pedestal.

៣២_ ព្រះហស្តព្រះឥសូរ **ប្រាសាទក្រហម, ប្រាសាទធំ, កោះកេរ្តិ៍, ព្រះវិហារ, មុនពាក់កណ្ដាលស.វ.ទី១០, ថ្មភក់, ០,៥០ម, ក ១៨៧១**

ទំហំដៃនេះបញ្ជាក់ថាបដិមាទាំងមូលធំខ្លាំងណាស់។ រូបកម្ពស់ស្ទើរតែ៤មនោះជារូបព្រះឥសូររាំ មានក្បាល៥ និងដៃ១០ ហើយឈរនៅក្នុងប្រាសាទក្រហម ដែលជាក្លោងទ្វារនៃប្រាសាទធំ សាងឡើងក្នុងរាជ្យព្រះបាទជ័យវរ្ម័នទី៤។ នេះគឺព្រះឥសូរដែលគេបង្ហាញថាជាទេពនៃចក្រវាឡទាំងមូល ថ្វីត្បិតតែគេពុំដែលឃើញឧទាហរណ៍ដូចនេះនៅកន្លែងផ្សេងទៀត។ ដៃនេះមានកាន់ក្បាលដំបងមួយ ដែលធម្មតាពុំមែនជាកេតនភណ្ឌរបស់ព្រះឥសូរឡើយ។ មានដៃ៥ទៀតដែលស្ទើរតែនៅពេញលេញ ព្រមទាំងមានបំណែកដៃមួយទៀត និងបំណែកខាងក្រោមមួយនៃព្រះកេសដែលគេប្រទះឃើញ។ បដិមាទាំងមូលប្រហែលជាទទួលរងគ្រោះខូចខាតដោយការគាស់កកាយរកគ្រឿងបញ្ចុះនៅក្រោមបល្ល័ង្ក។

31. Lutteurs. **Prasat Thom, gopura II ouest, Koh Ker, Preah Vihear, 2nd quart du 10ème s. Grès, 0,79 m. Ka 1657.**

Dès 921, avant même la fin du règne des fils de Yashovarman à Angkor, au début du 10ème siècle, Jayavarman IV, leur oncle, se fait proclamer roi dans son domaine de Chok Gargyar (Koh Ker), au nord-est de la grande capitale. Il devient souverain de tout le Cambodge en 928. Sa capitale se développe sur une échelle monumentale, peut-être en liaison avec le besoin d'affirmer son pouvoir. Cette monumentalité s'exprime aussi dans la statuaire. Massive mais raffinée dans ses aspects décoratifs, la sculpture de Koh Ker se révèle dynamique et naturelle, ainsi que le montre ce groupe de lutteurs dans lesquels on peut reconnaître le fameux combat d'Arjuna et de Shiva, déguisé en chasseur kirata, dans le *Mahabharata*.

31. レスラー. **プレアヴィヒヤ州、コ・ケー、プラサート・トム第２周壁の西楼門、10世紀第４四半期、砂岩、0.79m、Ka 1657**

ジャヤヴァルマン4世は、自らの甥達であるヤショヴァルマン１世の息子達が10世紀初めに即位していたにもかかわらず、921年に王であると自称していた。アンコールの北東のコ・ケーから統治し始め、928年、正式に王位を掌中にした。その間、権力を正当化するためか、大規模な新都城造営の整備を始めていた。コ・ケー様式の石像は王の大きな野心を反映している。大規模だが、彫刻技術は優れており、ダイナミックで自然である。この像は狩人としてのシヴァとアスラを表していると思われ、それ以前の聖美術的傾向から乖離している。

32. Hand from a Shiva statue. **Prasat Kraham, Prasat Thom, Koh Ker, Preah Vihear, 2nd quart du 10ème s. Grès, 0,50 m. Ka 1868.**

Les dimensions de cette main montrent le caractère colossale de la statue à laquelle elle appartenait: une représentation de Shiva dansant, doté de cinq têtes et dix bras, de quelque quatre mètres de hauteur. Cette sculpture prenait place dans le Prasat Kraham, le gopura de troisième enceinte du Prasat Thom, temple d'État de Jayavarman IV à Koh Ker. La statue, unique en son genre, représentait l'aspect cosmique de Shiva. Cette main prend appui sur le pommeau d'une massue, attribut inhabituel pour ce dieu. D'autres éléments de cette sculpture sont conservés au musée national: diverses mains, un fragment de pied, deux des cinq têtes. Le buste et certains éléments du bassin sont encore dans le monument. L'œuvre fut probablement brisée il y a fort longtemps par des pillards à la recherche du dépôt de fondation sous le piédestal.

32. 棍棒を持つシヴァの手. **プレアヴィヒヤ州、コ・ケー、プラサート・トム、プラサート・クラハーム、10世紀第２四半期、砂岩、0.50m、Ka 1868**

この手の大きさから判断して、ジャヤヴァルマン４世のコ・ケーにある国家鎮護寺院プラサート・トムの楼門プラサート・クラハームに安置されていた５面10臂の踊るシヴァ像はほぼ高4メートルだったことがわかる。宇宙の主シヴァを表したものである。シヴァの手が持つのは棍棒の柄頭とみられるが、棍棒は通常シヴァの持物ではない。この手のほか、ほぼ完全な形の手５つと片足の断片、および５面のうち２面が国立美術館の保蔵されているが、胴の断片は現場に残っている。盗掘者が台座下の宝物を盗もうとした際、破壊されたと思われるこの像のその他の部分は残っていない。

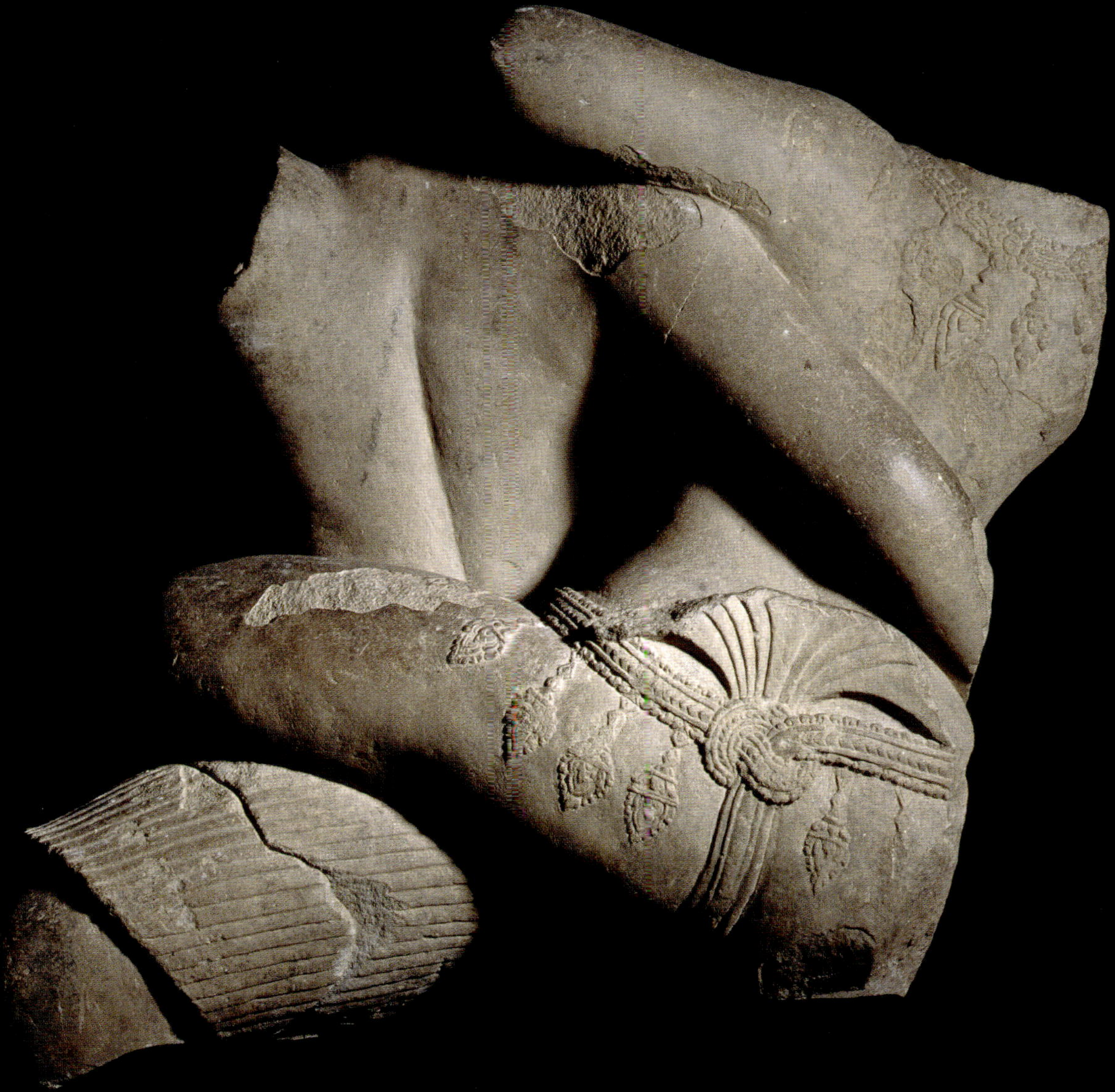

31

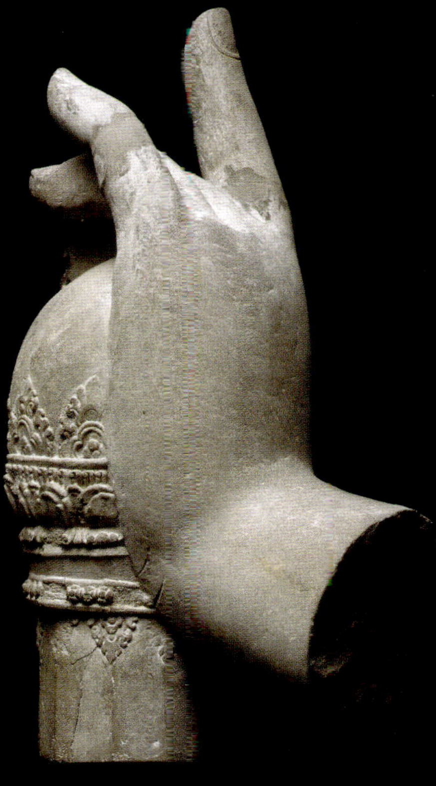

32

33. Wrestling Apes. Prasat Chen, Koh Ker, Preah Vihear, 2nd quarter 10th C. Sandstone, 2.87 m. Ka 1664.

These huge figures probably represent an episode from the *Ramayana*, the story of Valin and Sugriva, brothers and rival ape kings, in their struggle for supremacy. Sugriva, his throne usurped by Valin, enlisted the aid of Rama, one of the manifestations of Vishnu, in the fight, in return for helping Rama in the search for Rama's abducted wife, Sita. During the struggle, Valin was shot in the back by an arrow, probably at the hand of Rama. The size and dynamism of this sculpture, found in one of the many temples in the Koh Ker group, is typical of Koh Ker figures.

33. Combat des singes. Prasat Chen, Koh Ker, Preah Vihear, 2nd quart du 10ème s. Grès, 2,87 m. Ka 1664.

Ces deux énormes singes luttant représentent le célèbre combat des frères Sugriva et Valin dans le *Ramayana*. A la suite de l'usurpation du trône du royaume des singes par Valin, Sugriva obtint l'aide de Rama, l'un des aspects de Vishnu, pour recouvrer son pouvoir. En échange, Sugriva promit au héros de l'aider à retrouver son épouse, Sita, enlevée par le démon Ravana. Au cours du combat singulier des deux singes, Rama décocha une flèche dans le dos de Valin et Sugriva récupéra le trône. La taille colossale et le dynamisme de cette œuvre, découverte dans l'un des nombreux temples de Koh Ker, sont typiques de l'art du règne de Jayavarman IV.

៣៣_ ស្វាប្រយុទ្ធគ្នា ប្រាសាទចិន, កោះកេរ្តិ៍, ព្រះវិហារ, មុនពាក់កណ្តាល ស.វ. ទី១០, ថ្មភក់, ២,៨៧ម, ក ១៦៦៤

ចម្លាក់ដ៏ធំនេះ ប្រហែលជាស្រង់ពីរឿងរាមកេរ្តិ៍បុរាណត្រង់កន្លែងពាលីនិងសុគ្រីពប្រយុទ្ធគ្នា។ ស្វាជាបងប្អូនគ្នានេះប្រយុទ្ធគ្នាដោយចង់បានអំណាចជាធំរៀងខ្លួន។ ដោយសារពាលីជាបងដណ្តើមយករាជបល្ល័ង្កពីខ្លួន សុគ្រីពក៏ទៅពឹងពាក់អំណាចព្រះរាម ដែលជាអវតារនៃព្រះនារាយណ៍ ក្នុងការប្រយុទ្ធជាមួយបង។ រួចមកក៏សងគុណព្រះរាមវិញក្នុងការស្វែងរកព្រះមហេសីព្រះអង្គ គឺនាងសីតាដែលគេចាប់យកទៅបាត់។ ក្នុងការប្រយុទ្ធគ្នានេះ ពាលីត្រូវសរព្រះរាមដែលលួចបាញ់ពីក្រោយ។ ទំហំព្រមទាំងភាពរស់រវើកនៃចម្លាក់នេះ ជាលក្ខណៈដែលគួរកត់សម្គាល់ដូចជាចម្លាក់ដទៃទៀតដែលប្រទះឃើញនៅតួប៉មជាច្រើននៃក្រុមប្រាសាទកោះកេរ្តិ៍ដែរ។

33. 格闘する猿. プレアヴィヒヤ州、コ・ケー、プラサート・チェン、10世紀第２四半期、砂岩、2.87m、Ka 1664

この巨像は恐らく、ラマーヤナ物語の兄弟でライバル関係にある猿王、ヴァリンとスグリーヴァがどちらが覇権を握るか格闘している場面を描いたものであろう。ヴァリンに王座を奪われたスグリーヴァは、ヴィシュヌの化身ラーマ王子の略奪された王妃シータを探すのと引き換えに、王子の助けを借りる。格闘中、ヴァリンの背中にラーマが放ったと思われる矢が刺さる。この像の大きさとダイナミックさは典型的なコ・ケー様式で、コ・ケーの多くの寺院から発見されたものの１つである。

34. Garuda. Prasat Thom, Koh Ker, Preah Vihear, 2nd quarter 10th C. Sandstone, 2.13 m. Ka 1737.

The causeways connecting the many structures within the large complex of Prasat Thom, now extensively destroyed, were once flanked by huge balustrades formed by nagas (serpents) with upreared multiple heads. Behind them stood colossal figures of Garuda, the divine winged and raptor-headed vehicle of Vishnu, of which this sculpture is an example. The striding attitude of the figure suggests that he is in pursuit of the naga, of which Garuda is the traditional foe. The massiveness and energy constitute the essence of the Koh Ker style, which is also distinguished by the refinement of the details of feathers and the jewelled bands encircling chest and arms.

34. Garuda. Prasat Thom, Koh Ker, Preah Vihear, 2nd quart du 10ème s. Grès, 2,13 m. Ka 1737.

Les chaussées permettant d'accéder au cœur du complexe du Prasat Thom, aujourd'hui en grande partie détruites, étaient bordées de balustrades en forme de naga (serpents) dont les têtes multiples se relevaient dans une attitude menaçante aux extrémités. Derrière ces serpents, des garuda colossaux se dressaient dans une posture suggérant l'attaque: les garuda, en effet, sont les ennemis jurés des naga. L'aspect massif de cette oeuvre et l'énergie qui s'en dégage sont représentatifs de l'originalité du style de Koh Ker, également caractérisé par le raffinement du traitement des plumes et des bijoux.

៣៤_ គ្រុឌ ប្រាសាទធំ, កោះកេរ្តិ៍, ព្រះវិហារ, មុនពាក់កណ្តាលស.វ. ទី១០, ថ្មភក់, ២,១៣ម, ក ១៧៣៧

ផ្លូវចូលនានាដែលភ្ជាប់ប៉មផ្សេងៗពីមួយទៅមួយក្នុងបរិវេណប្រាសាទធំទាំងមូល ហើយដែលថ្មីៗនេះរងការបំផ្លាញខូចខាត ដើមឡើយសុទ្ធតែមានភ្នាក់ដៃជានាគដែលមានក្បាលច្រើន។ ក្រោយនាគនីមួយៗមានគ្រុឌ ពោលគឺបក្សីដែលជាជំនិះនៃព្រះនារាយណ៍ ដូចរូបនេះជាឧទាហរណ៍ស្រាប់។ ជើងទាំងពីរដែលឈាននេះបង្ហាញថាគ្រុឌកំពុងដេញចាប់នាគ ដែលតែងតែជាសត្រូវរបស់ខ្លួន។ នៅទីនេះរចនាបថកោះកេរ្តិ៍លេចធ្លោឡើងដោយសារទំហំធំ ព្រមទាំងមានចលនារស់រវើក ហើយម្យ៉ាងទៀតដោយចម្លាក់លម្អិតនៃស្លាប និងអលង្ការផ្សេងៗដែលពាក់ដងខ្លួន និងដៃ។

34. ガルーダ. プレアヴィヒヤ州、コ・ケー、プラサート・トム、10世紀第２四半期、砂岩、2.13m、Ka 1737

大きなプラサート・トム寺院の多くの建築物を連絡する参道の両側には、今では大半が破壊されてしまった多頭のナーガで形成された欄干があった。ナーガの背後にはヴィシュヌの乗り物で、鳥頭と聖なる翼を持つ巨大な聖鳥ガルーダが立っていた。これはガルーダが天敵ナーガを追う姿を描いたものである。大きさとエネルギー、同時に羽、胸と腕の宝石で飾られた帯の繊細な彫刻はコ・ケー様式の本質を示している。

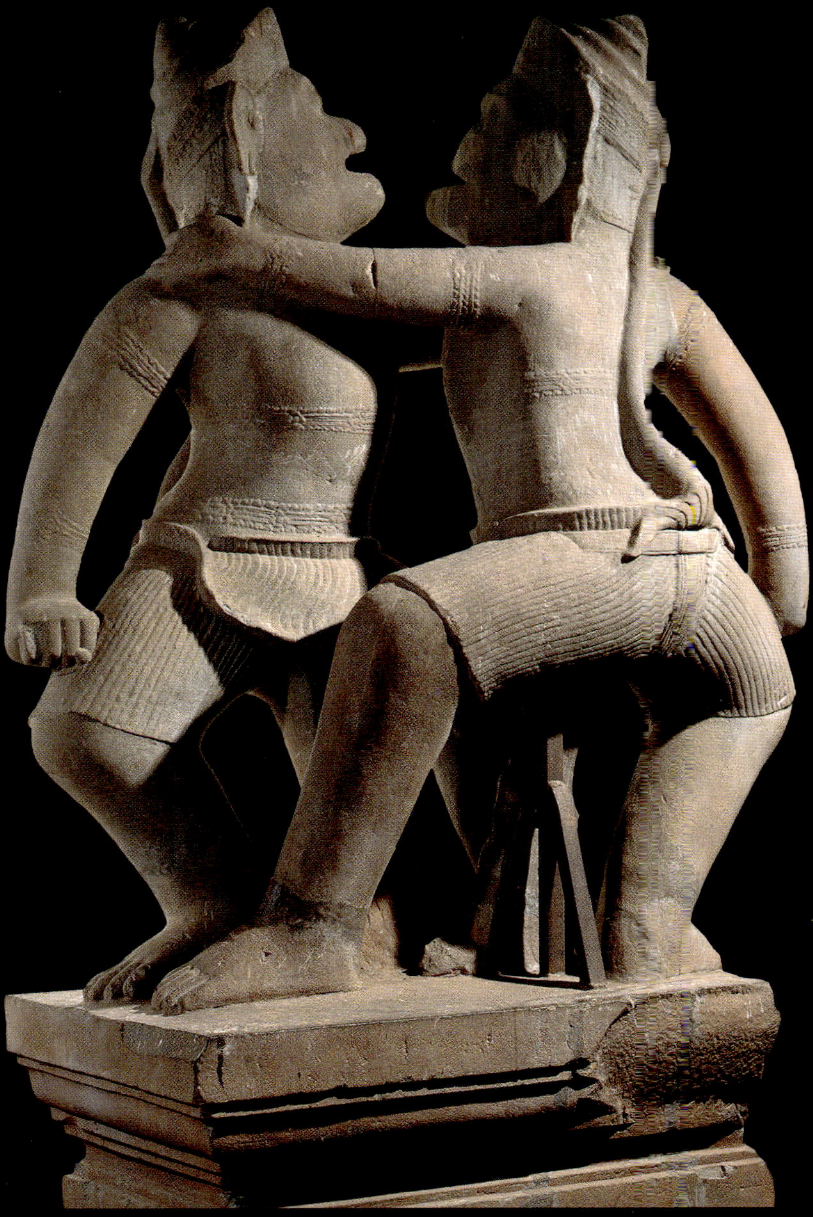

33

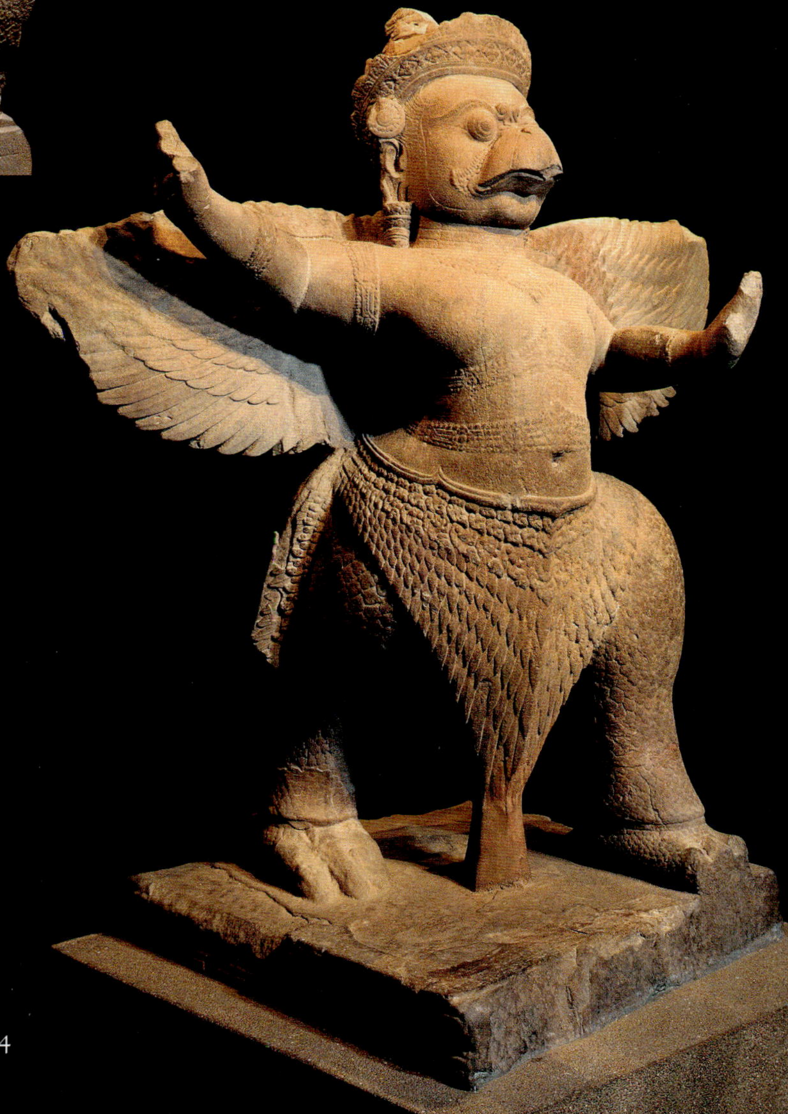

34

35. Varuna. Prasat Kuk Don, Siem Reap, 3rd quarter 10th C. Sandstone, 0.77 m. Ka 1579.

Varuna, whose origins date back to the sacred *Veda* scripts, is one of the dikpalaka, guardians of the cardinal and sub-cardinal directions and the zenith and nadir. Guardian of the west, and also of the waters, particularly the western ocean, Varuna is perceived as a wielder of magic powers. His mount is often the goose (hamsa, also the vehicle of Brahma), here shown in quadruple form. His attributes include the noose (pasha), probably once carried in his broken right hand. The perfection of the carving of feathers and jewels, the naturalism and grace of the torso and the iconic expressiveness of the face are typical of Pre Rup style.

35. Varuna. Prasat Kuk Don, Siem Reap, 3ème quart du 10ème s. Grès, 0,77 m. Ka 1579.

Varuna, dont les origines remontent aux textes sacrés du *Veda*, est l'un des dikpalaka, les protecteurs des points cardinaux et inter cardinaux, du zénith et du nadir. Gardien de l'Ouest, mais aussi des eaux et plus particulièrement de l'Océan d'Occident, Varuna est perçu comme un dispensateur de pouvoirs magiques. Sa monture est souvent l'oie (hamsa, également le véhicule de Brahma), représentée ici sous une quadruple forme. Son attribut principal est le lien (pasha), qui devait être tenu dans la main droite à l'origine. La perfection du traitement des plumes et des bijoux ainsi que la sensibilité du modelé du torse et du visage à l'expression douce sont caractéristiques du style de Pre Rup.

៣៥_ ព្រះពិរុណ (វរុណ) គុកដូន, សៀមរាប, ក្រោយពាក់កណ្តាលស.វ. ទី១០, ថ្មភក់, ០,៧៧ម, ក ១៥៧៩

ព្រះពិរុណដែលមានតាំងពីជំនាន់គម្ពីរវេទមកនោះ ជាទេពមួយអង្គក្នុងចំណោមទេពប្រចាំទិសទាំង១០។ ទេពនេះគង់ប្រចាំទិសខាងលិច ហើយដោយសារមានទំនាក់ទំនងនឹងទឹកផងនោះ ក៏ត្រូវគេចាត់ទុកថានៅប្រចាំមហាសមុទ្រខាងលិច។ គេយល់ថាទេពនេះពូកែខាងមន្តអាគម ហើយមានហង្សជាយានជំនិះដូចព្រះព្រហ្មដែរ។ នៅទីនេះ ហង្សបង្ហាញជា៤បែរទៅគ្រប់ទិស។ ព្រះហស្តស្តាំដែលបាត់ទៅប្រហែលជាកាន់ព្រ័ត្រ ព្រោះធម្មតាជាកេតនភណ្ឌនៃទេពនេះ។ ចម្លាក់នេះសម្អាងឡើងដោយឥតខ្ចោះ។ ស្លាបតូចៗ, អលង្ការ, ចម្លាក់ដងខ្លួន ព្រមទាំងទឹកមុខរស់រវើកដូចក្នុងធម្មជាតិ សុទ្ធសឹងជាលក្ខណៈនៃរចនាបថប្រែរូប។

35. ヴァルナ. シエムリエップ州、プラサート・クック・ドーン、10世紀第３四半期、砂岩、0.77m、Ka 1579

ヴァルナは『リグ・ヴェーダ』を起源とし、四方四維の守護神の1人、天空神である。西方を守護する水神、特に西海の神である。ヴァルナはブラフマの乗り物でもあるハムザ（鵞鳥）を乗り物としており、この像では４羽の鵞鳥に支えられている。破損した右手には絹索を持っていたはずである。羽と胸飾りの彫刻の完璧さ、自然で優雅な胴、表情の豊かさは典型的なプレ・ループ様式といえる。

36. Umamaheshvara. Banteay Srei, gopura I West, Siem Reap, c. 967. Sandstone, 0.65 m. Ka 1797.

The small temple of Banteay Srei, founded by a Brahman called Yajñavaraha, the guru of Jayavarman V, is considered one of the most perfect of Khmer temples for the quality of the relief carving that distinguishes its sanctuaries as well as the free-standing sculptures that were installed there. This image of Shiva with Uma, his spouse, or shakti, on his lap, her right arm tenderly placed on his back, was installed in gopura I West that offered a sanctuary behind the principal temple group. In style it closely resembles the Varuna in Pre Rup style (#35). Uma's head was stolen from the sculpture in the 1970s.

36. Umamaheshvara. Banteay Srei, gopura I ouest, Siem Reap, c. 967. Grès, 0,65m. Ka 1797.

Le petit temple de Banteay Srei, fondé par le brahmane Yajñavaraha, guru de Jayavarman V, est tenu pour l'une des plus belles réalisations de l'architecture khmère en raison de la qualité de son décor architectural et de l'excellence des sculptures qui y ont été découvertes. Cette image de Shiva, accompagné de son épouse Uma qui l'enlace tendrement de son bras dans le dos, était abritée dans le gopura I ouest faisant office de sanctuaire à l'arrière des temples principaux. Le style de cette œuvre est très proche de celui du Varuna du Prasat Kuk Don (#35). La tête d'Uma a été dérobée dans les années 1970.

៣៦_ ព្រះឥសូរនិងនាងឧមា បន្ទាយស្រី, ក្លោងទ្វារខាងលិចទី១, សៀមរាប, រវាងគ.ស.៩៦៧, ថ្មភក់, ០,៦៥ម, ក ១៧៩៧

ប្រាសាទតូចច្រឡឹងសាងដោយព្រាហ្មណ៍ម្នាក់ឈ្មោះ យជ្ញវរាហ ហើយដែលជាព្រះគ្រូព្រះបាទជ័យវរ្ម័នទី៥នេះ គេចាត់ទុកថាជាស្នាដៃល្អឥតខ្ចោះ បើពោលពីចម្លាក់ក្បូរក្បាច់រចនា ព្រមទាំងបដិមាដែលនៅក្នុងប៉មផ្សេងៗនៅទីនោះ។ នេះជារូបព្រះឥសូរដែលមាននាងឧមាជាព្រះជាយា (ឬ "សក្តិ") នៅលើភ្លៅ ហើយដែលគេប្រទះឃើញនៅក្នុងពពួកតួប៉មកណ្តាល។ ដៃស្តាំដ៏ស្រទន់នៃនាងឧមាឱបថង្កេះព្រះឥសូរ។ បើគិតពីរចនាបថវិញ គឺរូបនេះដូចទៅនឹងរូបព្រះពិរុណ (លេខ៣៥) ក្នុងរចនាបថប្រែរូបណាស់។ ព្រះកេសនៃនាងឧមាត្រូវគេលួចនៅដើមទសវត្ស ១៩៧០។

36. シヴァとウマー. シエムリエップ州、バンテアイ・スレイ第１周壁の西楼門、967年頃、砂岩、0.65m、Ka 1797

ジャヤヴァルマン５世が尊師ヤジュニャヴラハーハに建設させたバンテアイ・スレイ寺院は、主祠堂のレリーフの彫刻、およびそこに安置されていた像の完成度から、最も完璧なクメール寺院の１つだといえる。このシヴァとウマーの像は寺院の基壇に安置されていた。シヴァは神妃ウマーを膝に乗せ、ウマーはシヴァの背中に優しく右腕をまわしている。様式的にはNo.35のヴァルナのプレ・ループ様式に似ている。ウマーの頭は1970年代に盗難にあった。

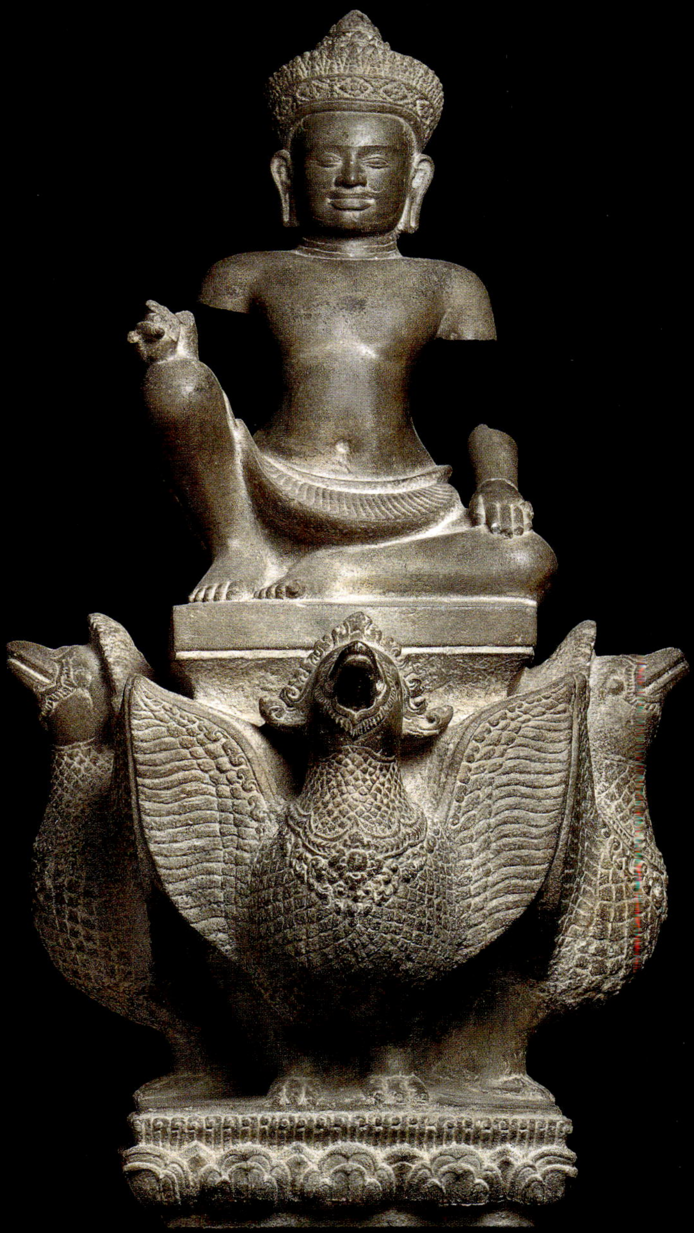

35

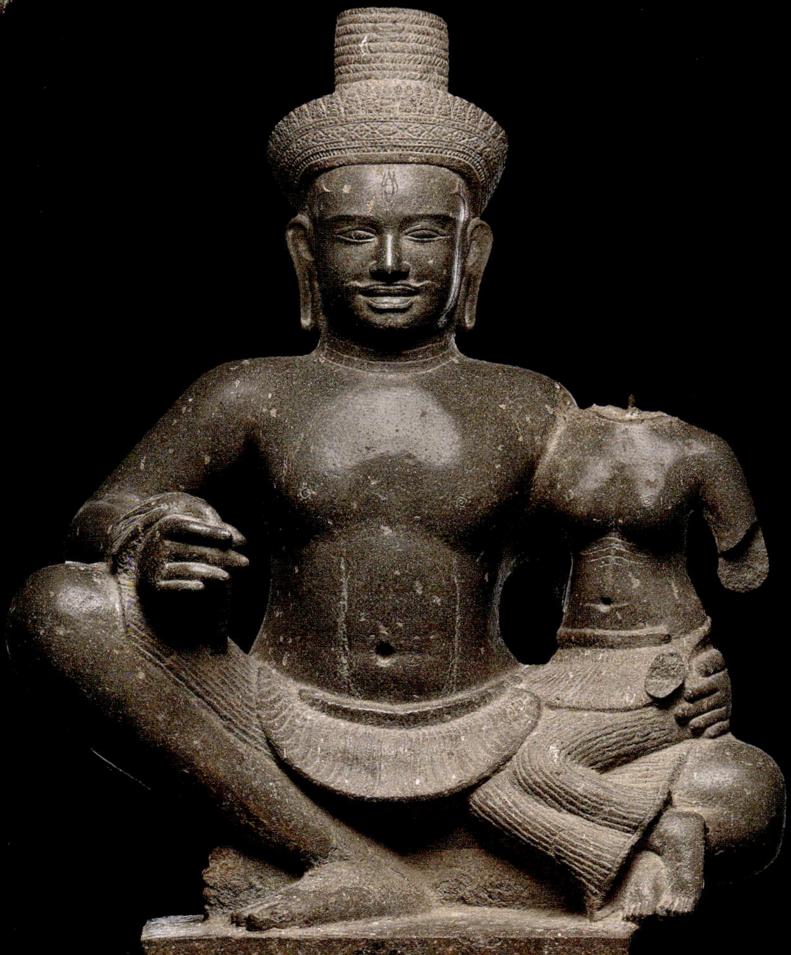

36

37. Guardian figure with lion head. Banteay Srei, Siem Reap, c. 967. Sandstone, 0.83 m. Ka 786.

The central sanctuary of Banteay Srei is protected by four kinds of guardian creatures: fierce genies called yakshas and three kinds of anthropomorphic beast (monkey, raptor and lion). They sit with left leg folded underneath and right knee raised. Where the right hand is intact the creatures hold a vajra, symbol of the thunderbolt. The lion is perhaps the most compelling of the guardians, his fangs bared in a wide grimace. The realism of the anatomy signals a return to naturalism that was heralded in Pre Rup style, while the intricacy of the carving of the mane, the bulging eyes, and the muzzle are characteristic of the style whose name derives from the temple this lion guards.

37. Gardien d'échiffre à tête de lion. Banteay Srei, Siem Reap, c. 967. Grès, 0,83 m. Ka 786.

Les sanctuaires centraux de Banteay Srei étaient protégés par divers gardiens: personnages d'apparence farouche (yaksha) et génies anthropomorphes à tête d'animaux - singes, garuda et lions - (gana). Ils sont assis la jambe gauche repliée sous le corps et le genou droit relevé. Lorsque la main droite est conservée, ces créatures tiennent un vajra symbolisant la foudre. Ce lion est peut-être le plus étonnant de ces gardiens, avec ses crocs découverts par un rictus agressif. L'anatomie vivante des corps participe d'un retour au naturalisme déjà annoncé dans le style de Pre Rup, cependant que la ciselure exubérante de la crinière, des yeux protubérants et de la gueule est caractéristique du style auquel le temple que gardait ce lion a donné son nom.

៣៧_ អ្នកយាមមានក្បាលជាសិង្ហ បន្ទាយស្រី, សៀមរាប, រវាងគ.ស.៩៦៧, ថ្មភក់, ០,៨៣ម, ក ៧៨៦

ក្រុមប៉មកណ្តាលមានអ្នកយាម៤យ៉ាងដែលនៅការពារ គឺយក្សនិងសត្វមានខ្លួនជាមនុស្សបីយ៉ាងទៀត (ស្វា, គ្រុឌ, សិង្ហ) ទាំងអស់នេះអង្គុយលើជើងឆ្វេងដែលបត់មកក្រោយ ហើយបញ្ឈរជង្គង់ស្តាំ។ បើដៃស្តាំមិនទាន់ខូចខាត គេឃើញមានកាន់ដុំពេជ្រ (វជ្រ) ដែលជាតំណាងរន្ទះ។ រូបអ្នកយាមដែលមានក្បាលជាសិង្ហនេះ សក្តិសមជាងគេទាំងអស់ ហើយបញ្ចេញចង្កូមគួរឱ្យស្ញែង។ ចម្លាក់ដងខ្លួនបង្ហាញថាមានការត្រឡប់ទៅរកលំនាំធម្មជាតិវិញ ដូចជានៅរចនាបថប្រែរូបដែរ។ រីឯចម្លាក់សក់និងក្បូរក្បាច់នៃភ្នែកដែលលៀនចេញមក សុទ្ធសឹងជាទីសម្គាល់ថាជារចនាបថបន្ទាយស្រី។

37. 守護神（ナラシンハ）. シエムリエップ州、バンテアイ・スレイ、967年頃、砂岩、0.83m、Ka 786

バンテアイ・スレイ寺院の主祠堂は４種類の守護神に守られていた。ヤクシャと呼ばれる獰猛な鬼神、人間化した猿、鳥、獅子である。これらの像は片膝をつき、右手には金剛杵を持っている。守護神の中でも牙をむき出した人獅子像は迫力がある。肉体のリアリズムはプレ・ループ様式が先駆者の自然主義に回帰したことを意味する。髪房や飛び出た目、鼻面の装飾化された彫刻はバンテアイ・スレイ様式である。

38. Pediment. Banteay Srei, west gopura, 2nd enclosure, Siem Reap, c. 967. Sandstone, 1.96 x 2.42 m. Ka 1660.

The relief carving of Banteay Srei has a richness and complexity never surpassed in Khmer art. While most of the lintels and pediments could be placed in situ after the temple's restoration in 1931-36, a few gopuras (gates), like the one where this pediment belonged, could not be reconstructed. The undulating arch, surrounded by flame-like projections, terminates in kala heads spitting nagas and encloses a dynamic scene from the epic *Mahabharata*. While Balarama and Krishna (avatars of Vishnu) watch, the warrior Bhima, one of the five Pandava brothers seeking to regain their kingdom, fights with Duryodhana, one of the Kaurava brothers who have usurped it.

38. Fronton. Banteay Srei, gopura II ouest, Siem Reap, c. 967. Grès, 1,96 x 2,42 m. Ka 1660.

La sculpture en relief du temple de Banteay Srei présente une richesse et une complexité jamais égalées tout au long de l'évolution de l'art khmer ancien. Alors que la plupart des frontons et des linteaux ont pu être remis en place lors de la restauration du monument entre 1931 et 1936, quelques gopura (porte d'enceinte), dont celui auquel ce fronton appartenait, n'ont pu être entièrement reconstruits. Le rampant ondulant, surmonté de feuillages dressés et terminé par une tête léonine crachant un naga, renferme une scène narrative dynamique dont le thème s'inspire d'un épisode du *Mahabharata*. Sous le regard de Balarama et Krishna (avatars de Vishnu), le guerrier Bhima, l'un des cinq frères Pandava qui cherchent à reconquérir leur royaume dont ils ont été dépossédés par leurs cousins Kaurava, combat contre Duryodhana, l'un de leurs ennemis.

៣៨_ ហោជាង បន្ទាយស្រី, ក្លោងទ្វារខាងលិចកំពែងទី២, សៀមរាប, រវាងគ.ស.៩៦៧, ថ្មភក់, ១,៩៦ម × ២,៤២, ក ១៦៦០

នៅក្នុងសិល្បៈខ្មែរ គ្មានចម្លាក់ណាដែលល្អិតញឹកពាសពេញដូចនៅបន្ទាយស្រីឡើយ។ កាលដែលគេជួសជុលប្រាសាទនេះពីឆ្នាំ១៩៣១ដល់១៩៣៦ ផ្តែរនិងហោជាង ភាគច្រើនគេរៀបចំនៅកន្លែងដើមវិញបានតែមួយចំនួនតូចប៉ុណ្ណោះ ដូចជាហោជាងនេះជាដើមដែលគេយកចេញដោយសារក្លោងទ្វារបាក់បែកអស់ស្តារវិញមិនបាន។ ដងក្តារហោជាងនេះពត់ពេនដូចរលក, មានទ្រនុងនាគមួយជាន់ពីលើ, ឯក្បាលនាគនៅចុងសងខាងក្រោមនោះ ខ្ជាក់ចេញមកដោយរាហូ។ ឈុតរឿងស្រង់ចេញពីរឿងមហាភារត។ ព្រះពលរាមនិងព្រះក្រឹស្នាដែលជាអវតារព្រះនារាយណ៍ មើលមកភិមដែលជាក្សត្រមួយអង្គនៃពួកបាណ្ឌព៥នាក់ ហើយដែលកំពុងប្រយុទ្ធជាមួយទុរ្យោធននៃពួកកោរព ត្បិតពួកនេះបានដណ្តើមយកនគរពីខ្លួន។

38. ペディメント. シエムリエップ州、バンテアイ・スレイ第２周壁の西楼門、967年頃、砂岩、高1.96m、幅2.42m、Ka 1660

バンテアイ・スレイ寺院のこのレリーフは、クメール美術の中でも、その豊かさと複雑さにおいて最高傑作である。同寺院が1931~36年に修復された際、リンテルとペディメントの大半が元の位置に配置されたが、このペディメントが飾っていた楼門は修復不可能だった。波状の圏帯の周縁には火炎のような唐草が刻まれ、両端は怪魚マカラの口から蛇ナーガが吐き出されている。区画内には叙事詩『マハーバーラタ』の一場面がダイナミックに描かれている。バララーマとヴィシュヌの化身クリシュナが見守る中、パンドゥ一家の５王子の次男ビーマが、クル家の100王子の長子ドゥルヨーダナが奪った王国を奪回しようとしている。

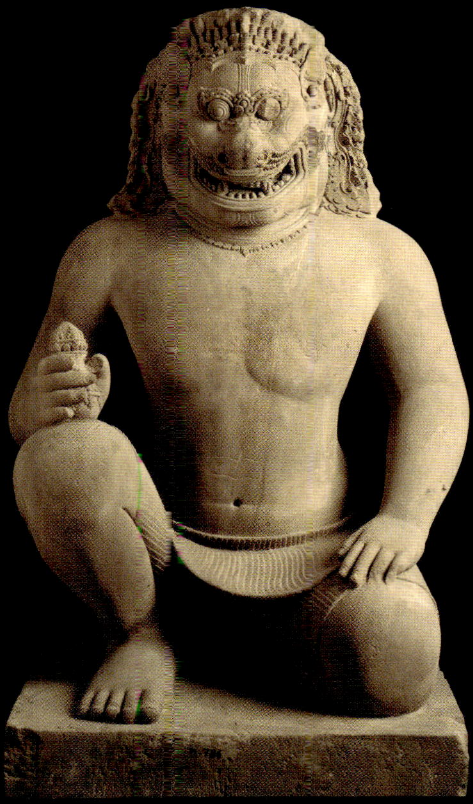

37

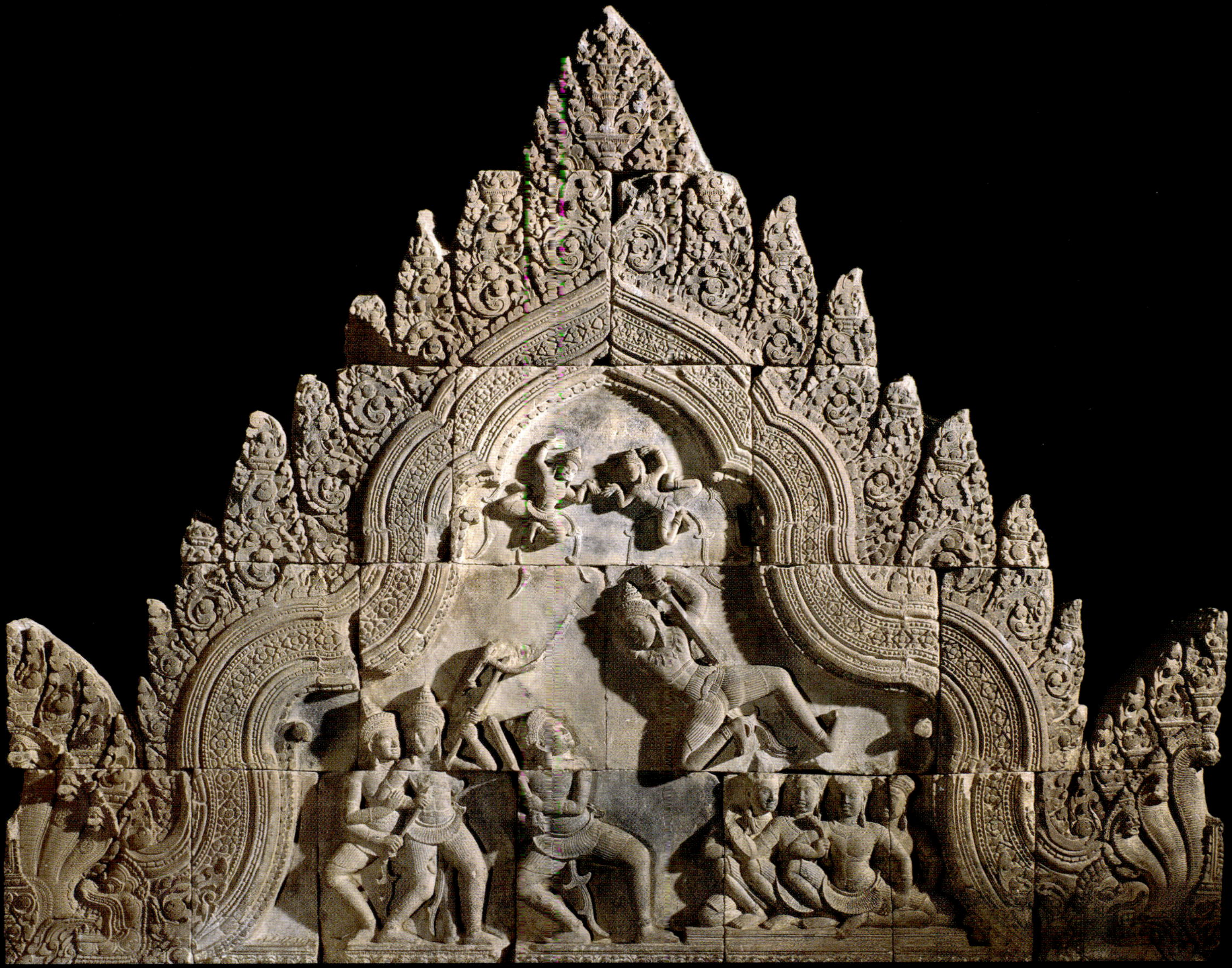

38

39. Lintel. Prasat Sralao, central sanctuary, Siem Reap, 3rd quarter 10th C. Sandstone, 0.82 x 1.86 m. Ka 1819.

The carving style at Prasat Sralao, not far from Banteay Srei, is strongly influenced by that famous contemporary temple. In deep relief, the central figure of Vishnu vigorously brandishes his attributes as he braces himself against his mount, Garuda. Garuda is in flight, his wings outspread, his tail streaming behind and his jewelled belt forming a vertical anchor for the dynamic composition. A thick undulating garland, terminating in the torsos of smaller Garuda figures disgorging rearing naga heads, forms a strong horizontal element that lends clarity to the composition, in which myriad foliate elements adhere to pendant and surging branches. At the top of the lintel in an arcaded frieze, six guardian figures on each side of the composition face centre and draw the eye to Vishnu, whose dominance is further emphasised by an elaborate niche.

39. Linteau. Prasat Sralao, sanctuaire central, Siem Reap, 3ème quart du 10ème s. Grès, 0,82 x 1, 86 m. Ka 1819.

La sculpture du Prasat Sralao se révèle fortement influencée par celle de Banteay Srei, les deux monuments n'étant guère éloignés l'un de l'autre. Au centre de ce linteau, Vishnu, chevauchant sa monture Garuda, brandit vigoureusement ses attributs. Garuda est figuré en attitude de vol, ailes déployées, queue dressée. Sa ceinture orfévrée tombant verticalement au centre du motif offre un ancrage vertical à la composition. L'axe horizontal du linteau est légèrement ondulant et se compose d'une épaisse branche de feuillages d'où s'échappent de multiples folioles dressées et tombantes. Il se termine par de petits garuda crachant des naga dont les tête multiples se redressent vers le haut. Au sommet du linteau, six petits personnages gardiens, placés de chaque côté de Vishnu, attirent l'œil sur le dieu dont l'importance est encore renforcée par l'arcature devant laquelle il se détache.

៣៩_ផ្តែរ ប្រាសាទស្រឡៅ, ប៉មកណ្តាល, សៀមរាប, ក្រោយពាក់កណ្តាល ស.វ.ទី១០, ថ្មភក់, ០,៨២ម × ១,៨៦, ក ១៨១៩

ក្បាច់ចម្លាក់នៅប្រាសាទស្រឡៅដូចក្បាច់បន្ទាយស្រីខ្លាំងណាស់ ដោយសារទទួលឥទ្ធិពលពីប្រាសាទនេះឯង។ ចម្លាក់នោះជ្រៅទៅក្នុងថ្ម។ នៅកណ្តាលផ្តែរជារូបព្រះនារាយណ៍កាន់កេតនភណ្ឌយ៉ាងសង្ហា ហើយជិះគ្រុឌដែលជាជំនិះព្រះអង្គ។ គ្រុឌនោះហោះត្រដាងស្លាប, កន្ទុយវាត់ទៅក្រោយ, ក្រវាត់ចង្កេះមានអលង្ការពាសពេញធ្លាក់ចុះមកដល់ក្រោមជាលំអ។ តួអង្គទាំងពីរនេះ គេឆ្លាក់ក្នុងស៊ុមទ្រវែងមួយ។ អង្កត់រាងដងផ្កាដែលចេញពីកណ្តាលនោះបញ្ចប់សងខាងទៅដោយដងខ្លួនគ្រុឌកំពុងខ្ជាក់ក្បាលនាគចេញពីមាត់។ អង្កត់នោះចែកផ្តែរតាមបណ្តោយជាពីរផ្នែក។ ខាងលើជាសន្លឹកដែលផុសចេញឡើង រីឯខាងក្រោមជាសន្លឹកដែលធ្លាក់រយោង។ នៅខាងលើបង្អស់មានរូបគ្រុឌមួយជួរដែលម្ខាងៗមាន៦បែរមករកគ្នា។

39. リンテル. シエムリエップ州、プラサート・スララウ主祠堂、10世紀第3四半期、砂岩、高0.82m、幅1.86m、Ka 1819

プラサート・スララウ寺院の彫刻様式は、同時期に建立されたバンテアイ・スレイ寺院に強く影響されている。このレリーフでは中央でヴィシュヌがガルーダに乗り、持物を振りかざしてる。飛行中のガルーダは羽を伸ばし、尾が背後に流れており、宝飾がある帯をつけ、ダイナミックな構図に垂直の安定感を与えている。太い波打つ花飾りの両端には口からナーガを吐き出す、より小さいガルーダが彫られ、水平の要素として、多数の花弁や葉やつるで覆われた全体の構図を明確にしている。リンテルの上部には両側の6躯ずつの守護神が中心を向けて向かい合い、ヴィシュヌを観ている。ヴィシュヌの存在は豪華な壁がんで強調されている。

40. Brahma. Phnom Prasat Reach, Mongkol Borei, Battambang, late 10th-early 11th C. Sandstone, 1.10 m. Ka 1669.

Despite Brahma's role, with Vishnu and Shiva, as one of the three triumurti gods, freestanding images of the god such as this are rather rare in Khmer statuary. Known as the Creator, Brahma is usually depicted in relief sculpture, particularly in depictions of Vishnu reclining in cosmic sleep, where Brahma in a lotus blossom rises from his navel to create a new cosmic era. Brahma's four heads gaze over the cardinal directions of the universe. This figure typifies Khleang style, a late-10th-century transition from the smooth elegance and refinement of the Pre Rup style (see #35) to the graceful naturalism of the following Baphuon style (see #43 and #44). Khleang sculpture is notable for the meticulous carving of details such as the pleats of the god's short sampot and the intricate coiffure and jewelled diadem.

40. Brahma. Phnom Prasat Reach, Mongkol Borei, fin 10ème - début 11ème s. Grès, 1,10 m. Ka 1669.

En dépit de son rôle important aux côtés de Shiva et Vishnu dans la trimurti, les images indépendantes de Brahma sont plutôt rares dans l'art khmer. Dans son rôle de créateur, Brahma est souvent figuré en bas-relief, plus particulièrement sur le lotus émanant du nombril de Vishnu dans les représentations du sommeil cosmique du dieu, à l'aube d'une nouvelle ère. Les quatre têtes de Brahma s'orientent aux points cardinaux de l'univers. Cette sculpture est représentative du style des Khleang à la fin du 10ème siècle, un style de transition entre l'élégance et le raffinement hautain du style de Pre Rup (#35) et la grâce juvénile et naturelle du style du Baphuon (#43 et 44). Le style des Khleang est remarquable pour la qualité de traitement méticuleuse des drapés, des coiffures et des diadèmes.

៤០_ព្រះព្រហ្ម ភ្នំប្រាសាទរាជ, មង្គលបុរី, បាត់ដំបង, ចុងស.វ.ទី១០_ដើមស.វ.ទី១១, ថ្មភក់, ១,១០ម, ក ១៦៦៩

ព្រះព្រហ្មជាទេពមួយអង្គក្នុងចំណោមទេពទាំងបីនៃត្រីមូតិ ។ រូបឈររបៀបនេះកម្រមានណាស់នៅក្នុងបដិមាខ្មែរ។ ព្រះព្រហ្មដែលជាអ្នកបង្កើតលោកច្រើនតែឆ្លាក់លើផ្ទាំងថ្ម ជាពិសេសក្នុងរឿងព្រះនារាយណ៍ផ្ទំពេលចប់កល្បម្តងៗដែលព្រះព្រហ្មផុសចេញតាមផ្កាឈូកមួយមកពីផ្ចិតព្រះអង្គ ដើម្បីបង្កើតកល្បថ្មីមួយទៀត។ ព្រះភក្រ្តទាំង៤បែរទៅទិសធំៗទាំង៤។ រូបនេះនៅក្នុងរចនាបថឃ្លាំង ដែលចាប់ផ្តើមពីចុងស.វ.ទី១០ ពោលគឺនៅចន្លោះរចនាបថប្រែរូបដែលអ្វីៗតែងមានភាពសក្តិសមនិងវិចិត្ររចនាខ្លាំង (សូមមើលរូបលេខ៣៥) មកដល់រចនាបថបាភួន (រូបលេខ៤៣និង៤៤)។ លក្ខណៈមួយនៃរចនាបថឃ្លាំង គឺផ្នត់សំពត់ឆ្លាក់លម្អិតផ្ចិតផ្ចង់ រីឯសក់និងមកុដក៏ពុំសាមញ្ញធម្មតាដែរ គឺគេឆ្លាក់ឱ្យបានល្អិតល្អន់។

40. ブラフマー. バッタンバーン州、モンコル・ボレイ、プノン・プラサート・レアチ、10世紀後半~11世紀初、砂岩、1.10m、Ka 1669

ブラフマーはヴィシュヌ、シヴァと3神1体（トリムールティ）を成すが、クメール像でブラフマー単独の姿は稀である。創造神ブラフマーはレリーフとして描かれることが多い。特にヴィシュヌが宇宙を創造する際、へそから、蓮の花が伸びて行き、そこに創造神ブラフマーが生まれるレリーフがよく見られる。ブラフマーの4面は宇宙の四方を眺めている。この像には、10世紀後半の優雅で洗練されたプレ・ループ様式（No.35参照）から、後のバプーオン様式（No.43、44参照）の優美な自然さに至る過渡期のクレアン様式の特徴が見られる。すなわち短い裙の折や髪型、冠帯の細部の入念な彫りがその特徴である。

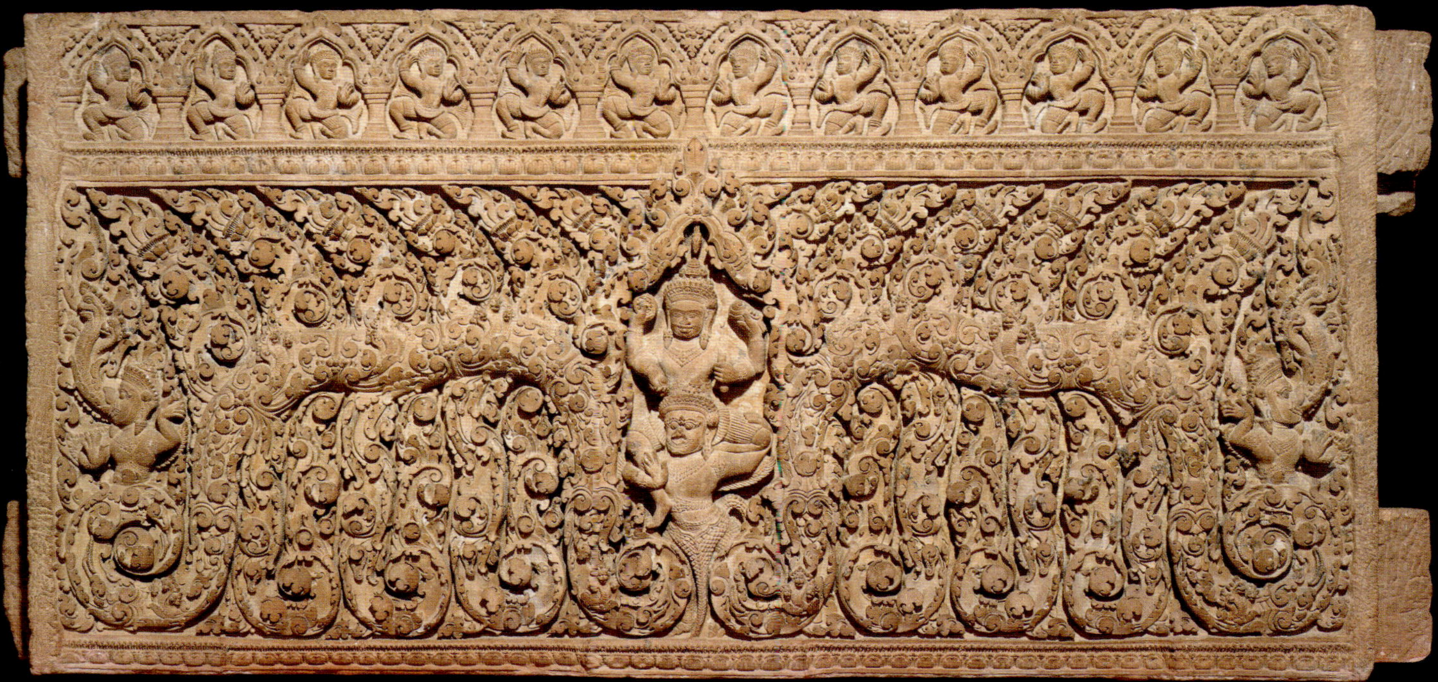

39

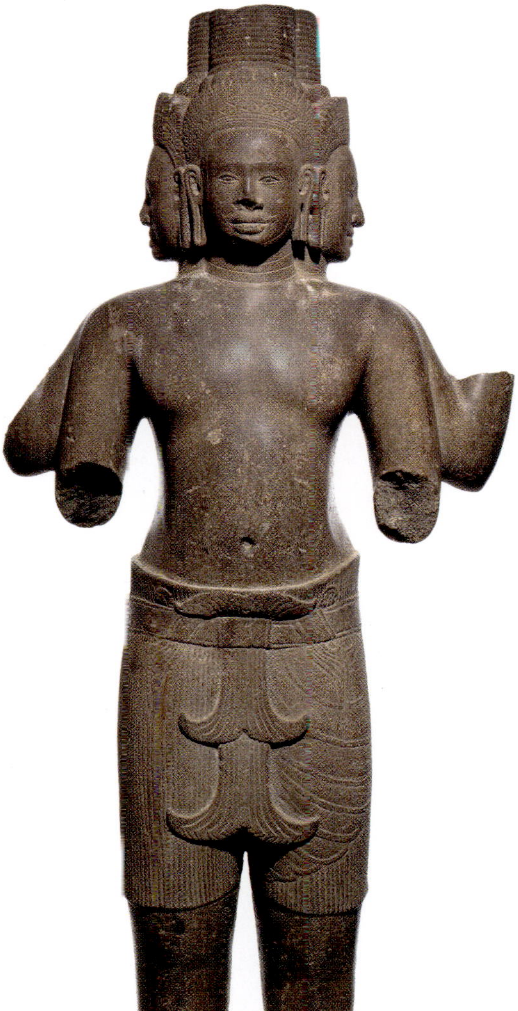

40

41. Lintel. Prasat Pen Chun, Kompong Svay, Kompong Thom, c. mid-11th C. Sandstone, 0.71 x 1.38 m. Ka 1826.

The central figure in this dynamic scene is Krishna, an avatar of Vishnu, whose mount, the mythological eagle-like Garuda, hovers to left and right of the youthful Krishna's head. Krishna braces his arms and legs against four of the heads of the evil serpent Kaliya, who has poisoned the river Yamuna. The god's triumphant expression prefigures the tearing apart of the serpent. This feat is one of several achieved by Krishna in challenges by demons in animal form sent by his jealous uncle Kamsa. The naturalistic modelling of the body and the details of the costume and jewellery are typical of the Baphuon style.

៤១_ផ្តែរ ប្រាសាទប៉ែនជុន, កំពង់ស្វាយ, កំពង់ធំ, ពាក់កណ្តាលស.វ.ទី១១, ថ្មភក់, ០,៧១ម × ១,៣៨, ក ១៨២៦

តួអង្គនៅចំកណ្តាលផ្តែរនេះគឺព្រះក្រឹស្នា ដែលជាអវតារនៃព្រះនារាយណ៍ រីឯគ្រុឌជាជំនិះត្រដាងស្លាបហោះនៅសងខាងព្រះអង្គ។ ជើងនិងដៃនៃព្រះក្រឹស្នាសន្ទឹងហែកក្បាល៤ក្នុងចំណោមក្បាលទាំងអស់នៃនាគកលិយ ដែលបានបំពុលទន្លេយមុនា។ ទេពនេះមានទឹកមុខញញឹមបង្ហាញថានឹងមានជ័យជំនះដោយហែកនាគនោះជាពីរ។ ជ័យជំនះរបៀបនេះមានច្រើននៅក្នុងជីវិតព្រះអង្គ ដែលសុទ្ធសឹងជាជោគជ័យលើពួកអសោរផ្សេងៗ ដែលព្រះបិតុលាព្រះអង្គបញ្ជូនមកឱ្យបង្ករចលាចល ដោយសារច្រណែន។ របៀបច្លាក់ដងខ្លួនតាមលំនាំធម្មជាតិ, ក្បាច់លម្អិតនៃសំពត់ ព្រមទាំងអលង្ការផ្សេងៗជាលក្ខណៈសម្គាល់នៃរចនាបថបាភួន។

41. Linteau. Prasat Pen Chun, Kompang Svay, Kompong Thom, c. milieu du 11ème s. Grès, 0,71 x 1,38 m. Ka 1826.

Le personnage central de cette composition dynamique est Krishna, l'un des avatars de Vishnu, de part et d'autre duquel s'envolent deux garuda. Krishna entoure de ses bras et de ses jambes le féroce serpent Kaliya qui avait empoisonné les eaux de la Yamuna. L'expression de triomphe joyeux du dieu préfigure la mise à mort du serpent. Cette scène illustre l'un des nombreux combats auxquels le jeune Krishna dut se livrer pour vaincre les démons animaux envoyés contre lui par son méchant oncle Kamsa. Le modelé naturaliste du corps et les détails de traitement du costume et des bijoux sont caractéristiques du style du Baphuon.

41. リンテル. コンポントム州、コンポン・スヴァイ、プラサート・ペン・チュン、11世紀中頃、砂岩、高0.71m、幅1.38m、Ka 1826

このダイナミックな場面の中央にはヴィシュヌの化身クリシュナが描かれ、その乗り物ガルーダが頭上左右を舞っている。クリシュナの手足はヤムナー河に毒を流した毒蛇カーリヤの鎌首４つを抑えている。クリシュナの勝ち誇った表情は、カーリヤの身体を引き裂く前兆である。クリシュナは嫉妬したおじが送った動物の姿の悪神に次々と打ち勝つ。身体の自然さと裙と宝飾の細かい彫りは典型的なバプーオン様式である。

42. Linga. Battambang, 10th-13th C. Bronze, rock crystal, silver, 0.115 x 0.145 m. Ga 3557.

The linga is the pre-anthropomorphic representation of Shiva, associated with destruction but also fertility, of which the linga is the symbol (see also #7). Sometimes natural outcrops of stone are perceived as lingas, and sometimes the linga can reach great heights, like the four-metre linga at Phnom Bok. The small size of this example suggests that it was probably for private devotions. The bronze base is monolithic and in a style that gives no precise dating clues. The use of silver for the ring that encircles the base of the linga and of the semi-precious rock crystal for the linga itself indicates its prestigious status.

៤២_លិង្គ បាត់ដំបង, ស.វ.ទី១០_១៣, សំរិត ប្រាក់និងត្បូងថ្ម, ០,១១៥ម × ០,១៤៥, គ ៣៥៥៧

លិង្គជាព្រះឥសូរដែលមិនទាន់មានភិនភាគជាមនុស្ស ហើយជានិមិត្តរូបនៃការបំផ្លាញលោកផង និងការបង្កើតភោគផលផង (ចូរប្រៀបធៀបនឹងរូបលេខ៧)។ ជួនកាលថ្មធម្មជាតិដែលលេចចេញពីដីក៏អាចចាត់ទុកថាជាលិង្គដែរ ហើយម្យ៉ាងទៀតអាចមានទំហំធំធេងដូចជានៅភ្នំបូកជាដើម ដែលលិង្គមួយនោះមានកម្ពស់ដល់ទៅ៤ម។ ឯហេតុដែលលិង្គនេះមានទំហំតូចដូច្នេះ ប្រហែលមកពីជាគ្រឿងសក្ការៈផ្ទាល់ខ្លួននៃនរណាម្នាក់។ បល្ល័ង្កទាំងមូលជាសំរិតតែមួយ ហើយគ្មានចំណុចអ្វីអាចឱ្យសម្គាល់ថាជាសិល្បៈនៅជំនាន់ណាទេ។ គួរសង្កេតថា ថាសទ្រនាប់ធ្វើអំពីប្រាក់ ឯតួលិង្គតែម្តងជាត្បូងថ្ម បង្ហាញថាជាវត្ថុដែលមានតម្លៃ។

42. Linga. Provenance inconnue, 10ème - 13ème s. Bronze, cristal de roche et argent, 0,115 x 0,145 m. Ga 3557.

Le linga est une représentation symbolique de Shiva, associée à la notion de fertilité (voir aussi #7). En raison de leur forme, certains affleurements rocheux peuvent parfois être tenus pour des linga naturels. Divers linga sculptés par l'homme ont pu atteindre des dimensions considérables, tel le linga de quatre mètres au sommet du Phnom Bok. Les petites dimensions de celui-ci semblent indiquer qu'il était votif ou destiné à un usage privé. Le piédestal en bronze est d'une seule pièce et n'apporte guère de renseignement quant à la datation de l'objet. L'utilisation d'argent pour le cerclage du linga à sa base et le cristal de roche lui-même participent du statut précieux de ce petit ensemble.

42. リンガ. バッタンバーン州、10~13世紀、ブロンズ、乳白色の水晶、銀、高0.115m、幅0.145m、Ga 3557

リンガは破壊と生殖の神シヴァの象徴である（No.7参照）。時には自然に突出した岩をリンガと見立てることがあり、中にはプノン・ボクの４mのリンガのような巨大なものも存在する。この小さいリンガは私的な祭壇用であろう。ブロンズの台座の形式はどの時代のものか不明である。リンガには準宝石の水晶が使われ、そのベースに銀の座金がはめこまれていることから貴重なものであったことがわかる。

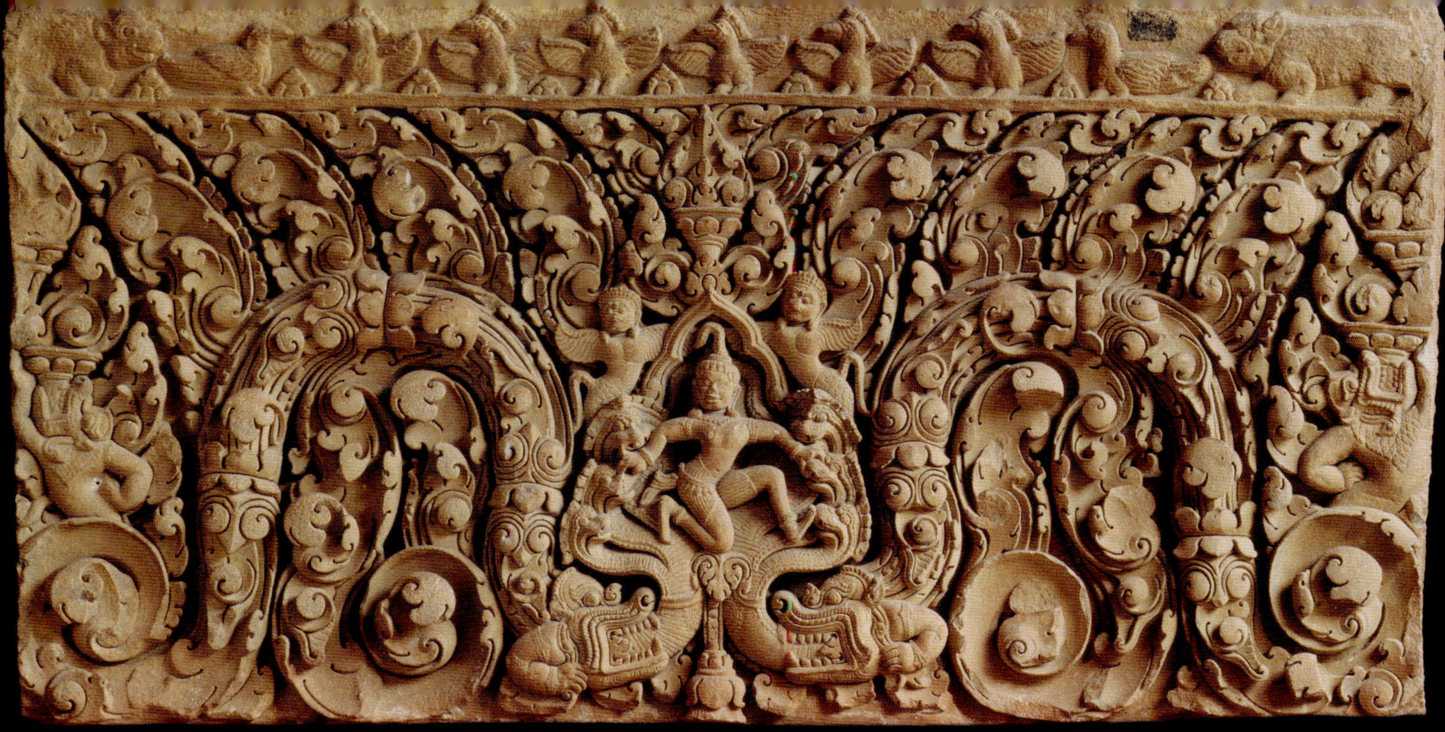

41

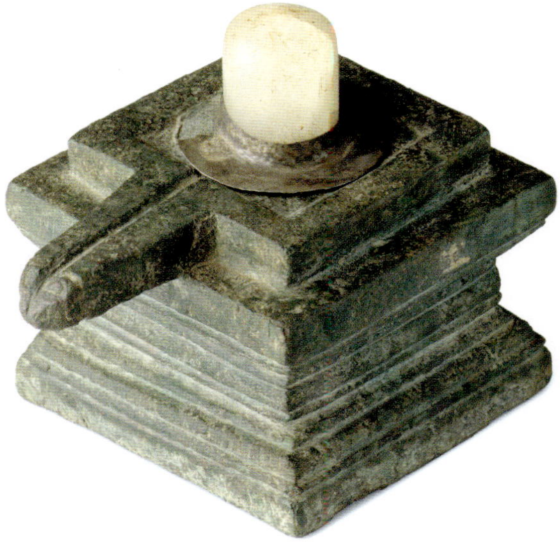

42

43. Male divinity. Unknown provenance (?Battambang), Baphuon style, 11th C. Sandstone, 0.60 m. Ka 2930.

This youthful figure may represent Vishnu, on the evidence of the residual elements of four arms. The conical crown, or mukuta, and the flaring jewelled diadem are typical of Baphuon style, as are the scooped line of the draped cloth forming a sampot that plunges below the umbilicus, and the ends of the cloth tied into an elaborate bow at the rear. Baphuon style, which was predominant for most of the 11th century, is notable for the slenderness of its figures and the naturalism of limbs and musculature, as well as for the delicate moulding of facial features that often include a cleft chin. The face is here so particularized that it suggests a portrait.

43. Divinité masculine. Provenance inconnue (Battambang?), 11ème s. Grès, 0,60 m. Ka 2930.

Bien qu'ils soient incomplets, les quatre bras de ce personnage juvénile peuvent peut-être permettre de reconnaître Vishnu. La couronne conique (mukuta) et le diadème orfévré complexe sont typiques du style du Baphuon, de même que les plis fins et réguliers du sampot dont la ligne s'échancre profondément sous le nombril et dont le nœud d'attache postérieur affecte une découpe en forme d'ailes de papillon. Le style du Baphuon, qui couvre presque tout le 11ème siècle, est remarquable par l'allongement des proportions générales des statues, le naturalisme doux du modelé des corps et des visages, souvent marqués d'un menton bifide. Dans cette délicate sculpture, les traits apparaissent particulièrement individualisés.

៤៣_ទេពភេទប្រុស មិនស្គាល់ប្រភព (បាត់ដំបង?), រចនាបថបាភួន, ស.វ.ទី១១, ថ្មភក់, ០,៦០ម, ក ២៩៣០

រូបទេពដែលស្ថិតនៅក្នុងវ័យក្មេងនេះប្រហែលជាព្រះនារាយណ៍ ដោយសារមានដៃ៤។ មកុដទាំងមូល ទាំងក្បាំងទាំងកំពូល បញ្ជាក់ថានៅក្នុងរចនាបថបាភួន មិនខុសអ្វីពីសំពត់ដែលគេធ្វូតឱ្យឃើញជាផ្នត់ ហើយដែលមានជាយចុះពីលើចង្កេះវៀលមកនៅក្រោមផ្ចិត ហើយដែលនៅខាងក្រោយភ្ជាប់គ្នាដោយមុខចំណងមួយយ៉ាងប្រិតប្រៀង។ រចនាបថបាភួន គេនិយមខ្លាំងស្ទើរតែពេញស.វ.ទី១១។ ចំណុចពិសេសខ្លះ គឺដងខ្លួនមានរាងស្ដើងស្រឡូន ដែលគេឆ្លាក់ឱ្យឃើញសាច់ដុំតាមលំនាំធម្មជាតិ ដូចជានៅលើអវៈយវៈដែរ។ ចម្លាក់ផ្ទៃមុខក៏មានការប្រិតប្រៀង ហើយជាញឹកញាប់គេឃើញមានចង្កាព្រែក។ រូបនៅទីនេះ បើពិនិត្យទៅតាមផ្ទៃមុខប្រហែលជាឆ្លាក់ចម្លងតាមមនុស្សណាម្នាក់ដែលមានពិត។

43. 男神. 出土地不明（バッタンバーン州？）、11世紀、砂岩、高0.60m、Ka 2930

この若々しい姿の石像には４臂あることから、ヴィシュヌだと思われる。円錐形のムクタ、冠帯、カーブを描いた裙の上端、後部で豪華に結ばれている裙の両端など典型的なバプーオン様式である。11世紀に栄えたバプーオン様式では体の細さ、手足や筋肉の自然さ、あごの窪みや繊細な容貌などが顕著である。この像の顔は特定の人物を描いたものであろう。

44. Female divinity. Prasat Trapeang Totung Thngay, Siem Reap, 2nd half 11th C. Sandstone, 1.25m. Ka 1830.

The slender grace of this standing female divinity is typical of Baphuon style, as is the relatively large head with coiffure of locks braided with pearls, broad forehead, and hollow eye sockets where stones were once fixed. The pleated garment clinging to the goddess's legs and the naturalistic musculature of arms and torso is also characteristic of the style. The attributes, judging from the form of the fingers in the remaining hand, were probably detachable and possibly made of precious metal. Since both attributes are now missing, it is not possible to determine the identity of the deity, but the position of her fingers is not inconsistent with holding a lotus blossom (see also #50 and #73). This would suggest the goddess Lakshmi, one of the shakti, or spouses, of Vishnu.

44. Divinité féminine. Prasat Trapeang Totung Thngay, Siem Reap, 2nde moitié du 11ème s. Grès, 1,25 m. Ka 1830.

L'élégance gracile de cette divinité féminine est caractéristique du style du Baphuon, tout comme le sont la tête, proportionnellement grosse pour le corps, les mèches de cheveux, auxquelles se mêlent des perles, le front large et les yeux creux, jadis incrustés. De même, le costume finement plissé et épousant étroitement les jambes ainsi que le modelé naturel du buste et des bras sont spécifiques de l'art du 11ème siècle. À en juger par la position de la main subsistante, les attributs étaient rapportés et vraisemblablement en métal précieux. En raison de leur absence, il est impossible de déterminer l'identité de cette déesse, mais la position des doigts n'est pas incompatible avec le maintien d'une fleur de lotus (voir #50 et #73) qui permettrait peut-être de reconnaître Lakshmi, l'une des shakti ou épouses de Vishnu.

៤៤_ទេវី ប្រាសាទត្រពាំងទទឹងថ្ងៃ, សៀមរាប, ផ្នែកទី២នៃស.វ.ទី១១, ថ្មភក់, ១,២៥ម, ក ១៨៣០

ដងខ្លួនដ៏ស្រឡូនសក្តិសមនេះ ជាលក្ខណៈមួយនៃរចនាបថបាភួន។ ម្យ៉ាងទៀតក៏ជាចំណុចសម្គាល់ទូទៅដែរ គឺក្បាលរាងធំបន្តិច, សក់ក្រងក្លួច, ថ្ងាសទូលាយ, ភ្នែករូងក្រហូង ដោយសារដើមឡើយមានបញ្ចុះត្បូង។ សំពត់ផ្នត់ដែលធ្លាក់ចុះមកដល់កជើង ព្រមទាំងរបៀបឆ្លាក់ដងខ្លួននិងអវៈយវៈតាមលំនាំធម្មជាតិ ក៏ជាទីសម្គាល់នៃរចនាបថនេះដែរ។ គេគនភណ្ឌប្រហែលជាធ្វើអំពីលោហធាតុមានតម្លៃ ដើម្បីឱ្យដោះបានផង បើយោងទៅតាមទម្រង់ម្រាមដៃដែលនៅសល់។ ដោយសារគេគនភណ្ឌបាត់បង់ហើយនោះ យើងមិនដឹងច្បាស់ថារូបនេះជាទេវីណាមួយឡើយ។ ប្រសិនបើដៃស្ដាំដែលនៅសល់នោះកាន់ផ្កាឈូក (ចូរប្រៀបនឹងរូបលេខ៥០និង៧៣) នោះប្រហែលជានាងលក្ស្មីដែលជាព្រះជាយាព្រះនារាយណ៍ហើយ។

44. 女神. シエムリエップ州、プラサート・トラペアン・トトゥン・トゥンガイ、11世紀後半、砂岩、1.25m、Ka 1830

この優雅でほっそりとした女神の立像は、比較的大きな頭、真珠をつけ編んだ髪、広い額、貴石を象嵌してあった眼など、典型的なバプーオン様式である。女神の足にまつわる襞付きの裙、腕と胴の自然な肉付などもその特徴である。残っている指の形状から判断すると、持物は取り外し可能で、貴金属製だったと思われる。両手の持物が紛失しているため、女神が誰か判断するのは困難だが、指の位置から考えると蓮華を持っていたようだ（No.50、73参照）。従ってビシュヌの神妃ラクシュミーと考えられる。

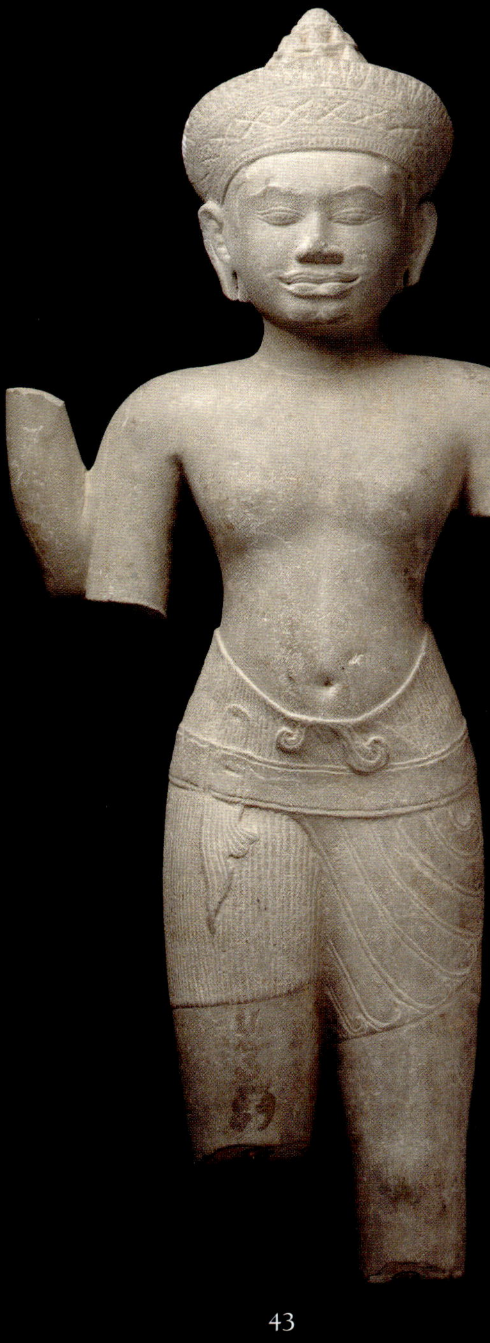

43

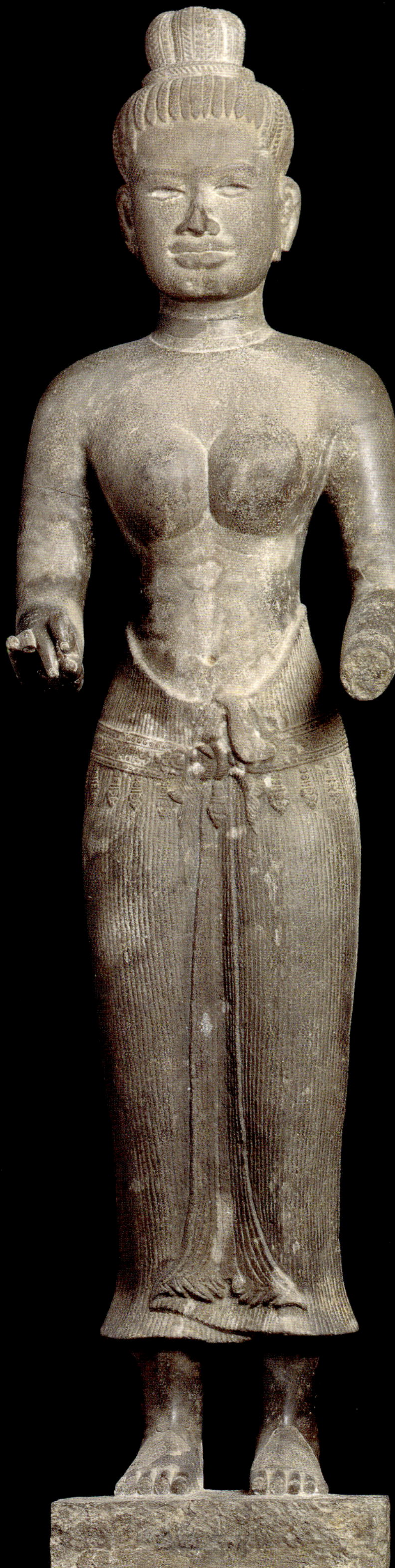

44

45. Vishnu Anantashayin. West Mebon, Angkor, Siem Reap, 2nd half 11th C. Bronze, 1 .22 x 2.22 m. Ga 5387.

This magnificent image of Vishnu is a fragment of a bronze figure that would have measured at least six metres, one of the largest Southeast Asian bronzes ever made. It was cast in several parts and inlaid at brows, eyes and moustache with precious stones or metals, now missing. This representation of Vishnu, frequently seen in Khmer art, shows the god in cosmic sleep between cosmic eras. He reclines on the serpent of eternity, Ananta, who floats on the cosmic ocean. The scene usually also comprises Vishnu's spouse, Lakshmi, who cradles the god's limbs, and a lotus arising from his navel containing the figure of Brahma, poised to create the next cosmic era. According to the Chinese traveller Zhou Daguan, who visited Angkor in 1296, a sculpture like this (that he mistakenly interpreted as a Buddha image) had water flowing from its navel. As this fragment and a few smaller pieces were found on the West Mebon island in the middle of the West Baray, it is possible that the sculpture was related in some way to hydraulic mechanisms with sacred as well as practical implications.

45. Vishnu Anantashayin. Mebon occidental, Angkor, Siem Reap, 2nde moitié du 11ème s. Bronze, 1,22 x 2,22 m. Ga 5387.

Ce magnifique bronze représentant Vishnu n'est qu'un fragment d'une sculpture mesurant environ six mètres de long à l'origine, l'un des plus grands bronzes jamais réalisés en Asie du Sud-Est. Fondue en plusieurs parties, l'œuvre était rehaussée d'incrustations de pierres précieuses et de métal (sourcils, yeux, moustache et barbe). Comme on le voit souvent dans l'art khmer, Vishnu est ici représenté au moment où il s'éveille de son sommeil régénérateur entre deux ères cosmiques. Il est étendu sur le serpent Ananta, symbole de l'océan primordial. La scène inclut généralement Lakshmi, l'épouse du dieu, qui lui masse les chevilles pour l'éveiller, et Brahma, sur le lotus sortant du nombril de Vishnu, prêt à mettre en place la nouvelle création. Selon Zhou Daguan, le voyageur chinois qui visita la capitale khmère en 1296, une sculpture identique à celle-ci (qu'il prit par erreur pour une image du Buddha couché) laissait s'écouler de l'eau de son nombril. Il est possible que cette œuvre, découverte dans l'île du Mebon occidental, au centre du plus grand baray d'Angkor, ait été reliée à un mécanisme hydraulique de nature pratique aussi bien que religieuse.

៤៥_ ព្រះនារាយណ៍ផ្ទំលើពស់អនន្ត មេបុណ្យ, អង្គរ, សៀមរាប, ផ្នែកទី២នៃស.វ.ទី១១, សំរិត, ១,២២ម × ២,២២ម, គ ៥៣៨៧

ព្រះនារាយណ៍សំរិតដ៏វិចិត្រនេះ ដើមឡើយប្រវែងយ៉ាងតិច៦ម ហើយនៅក្នុងចំណោមវត្ថុស្ថាន់នៃអាស៊ីភាគអាគ្នេយ៍ដែលមានទំហំធំ។ គេសិតជាកំណាត់ដាច់ៗពីគ្នា។ កាលមុនមានបញ្ចុះលោហៈ និងត្បូងនៅត្រង់ចិញ្ចើម, ភ្នែកនិងពុកមាត់។ រូបព្រះនារាយណ៍ផ្ទំ គេប្រទះញឹកញាប់នៅក្នុងសិល្បៈខ្មែរ។ នៅចន្លោះកល្បពីរ ព្រះអង្គផ្ទំលើពស់អនន្តដែលមិនចេះស្លាប់ ហើយដែលអណ្តែតលើផ្ទៃសមុទ្រ។ បើរូបពេញលេញ គេតែងឃើញនាងលក្ស្មីច្របាច់ព្រះបាទាព្រះអង្គ ហើយមានឈូកមួយទងចេញពីផ្ចិតព្រះអង្គ មានព្រះព្រហ្មគង់លើដើម្បីនឹងបង្កើតកល្បថ្មីមួយទៀត។ អ្នកការទូតចិន ជីវតាក្វាន់ ដែលមកអង្គរនៅឆ្នាំ១២៩៦ ឃើញរូបរបៀបនេះមានទឹកបាញ់ចេញអំពីផ្ចិត (ប៉ុន្តែគាត់ច្រឡំថាជាព្រះពុទ្ធរូប)។

45. 横たわるヴィシュヌ. シエムリエップ州、アンコール、西メボン、11世紀後半、ブロンズ、高1.22m、幅2.22m、Ga 5387

この素晴らしいヴィシュヌ像は最低6m以上あった大像で、東南アジアのブロンズ彫刻としては最大級である。部分別に鋳造され、眉、眼、口ひげは貴金属で象嵌されていた。このヴィシュヌはクメール美術によくある宇宙創造の眠りについている姿で、宇宙の海に漂う竜王アナンタの上に横たわっている。ヴィシュヌの神妃ラクシュミがヴィシュヌの手足をさすり、臍からはえた蓮花にブラフマーが次の宇宙を創造する姿が一緒に描かれることが多い。1296年にアンコールを訪れた中国人、周達観はこのような像をブッダと勘違いしたが、臍からは水が流れていたと記述している。このヴィシュヌの頭部やそのほかの断片は西バライ中央の西メボン寺院から発見されたが、この像が聖像としてだけでなく、実質的に水圧のメカニズムに関係していた可能性もある。

46. Stele with Shiva and Uma. Pal Hal, Battambang, 1069 CE. Sandstone, 1.06 m. Ka 1823, K.449.

Inscriptions on temples and on stele like this, carved in the reign of Harshavarman III (1066-1080), offer most of the available hard evidence about Khmer dates and genealogy. The front face has two lines of Khmer and thirty-six of Sanskrit, the back has seven and twenty-five respectively. The most important passage relates the erection of a linga in 1069 CE. To the usual homage to the gods and warnings to those who disrespect the religious foundation to which the stele is connected is added a detailed list of the donor's ancestors (who include Shivakaivalya, the priest officiating at the consecration of Jayavarman II in 802), and gifts granted to them in preceding reigns. The presence of carved figures on stele is relatively rare. The naturalistic representation of the torsos of Shiva and his shakti Parvati, Shiva's broad, full-lipped face, and his coiffure plaited and encircled by beads, are all characteristic of the Baphuon style.

46. Stèle avec Shiva et Uma. Pal Hal, Battambang, 1069 A.D. Grès, 1,06 m. Ka 1823, K. 449.

Les stèles inscrites, comme celle-ci, ou les textes gravés aux piédroits des portes des temples fournissent les seuls renseignements de première main sur l'histoire et la chronologie khmères. Gravée sous le règne de Harshavarman III (1066-1080), cette stèle biface comporte, à l'avant, deux lignes en khmer et trente-six lignes en sanskrit, à l'arrière, vingt-cinq lignes en sanskrit et sept en khmer. Le passage le plus important se rapporte à l'érection d'un linga en 1069. À l'hommage habituel aux dieux et aux imprécations contre ceux qui ne respecteraient pas la fondation s'ajoutent une liste détaillée des ancêtres du donateur (comprenant Shivakaivalya, l'un des brahmanes qui officia lors de la consécration de Jayavarman II, en 802) et la liste des dons reçus par la famille sous les différents règnes. La présence d'images sur les stèles est relativement rare. Le modelé naturaliste de Shiva et de sa shakti, Uma (également Parvati), le traitement doux des visages et les coiffures comportant des perles sont autant de caractéristiques du style du Baphuon.

៤៦_ ផ្ទាំងសិលាចារឹកមានរូបព្រះឥសូរនិងនាងឧមា ចាំលហាល, បាត់ដំបង, គ.ស.១០៦៩, ថ្មភក់, ១,០៦ម, ក ១៨២៣, K. 449

អក្សរថ្មនេះចារក្រោមរាជ្យព្រះបាទហសិវរ្ម័ន។ ខាងមុខជាភាសាខ្មែរ២បន្ទាត់និងជាសំស្ក្រឹត៣៦បន្ទាត់ ខាងក្រោយគឺខ្មែរ៧បន្ទាត់ និងសំស្ក្រឹត២៥បន្ទាត់ ។ កន្លែងមួយនោះសំខាន់ ហើយពោលពីលិង្គមួយសាងនៅឆ្នាំ១០៦៩។ ក្រៅពីពាក្យកោតសរសើរអទិទេពនិងពាក្យព្រមានគំរាមដល់ជនណាដែលមិនគោរពទីតម្កល់លិង្គនេះ មានរាយនាមបុព្វការីជននៃអ្នកកសាងលិង្គនោះ (ក្នុងនោះមានឈ្មោះ "សិវកៃវល្យ " ដែលជាអាចារ្យស្មឹងក្នុងរាជាភិសេកព្រះបាទជ័យវរ្ម័នទី២នៅឆ្នាំ៨០២) និងអំណោយដែលអ្នកទាំងនោះបានទទួលក្នុងរាជ្យមុនៗ។ សន្លឹកថ្មដែលមានឆ្លាក់រូបក្រឡោតដូច្នេះពុំសម្បូណ៌ទេ។ លក្ខណៈរចនាបថបាភួនលេចចេញមកច្បាស់ ដូចជាការឆ្លាក់តាមលំនាំធម្មជាតិ, បបូរមាត់ក្រាស, ផ្នួងសក់ក្រងពាត់ដោយអង្កាំ។

46. 石碑. バッタンバーン州、パルハル、1069年、砂岩、1.06m、Ka 1823、K 449

ハルシャヴァルマン3世（1066~1080年）に彫られた寺院や石碑にある碑文は、クメール史や家系を知る貴重な資料となっている。正面にはクメール語が2行、サンスクリット語が36行、裏面にはそれぞれ7行、25行ある。最も重要な記述はリンガが1069年に建立された部分である。その他、神への祈願、信仰を軽視するものへの警告、寄進者の家系（802年のジャヤヴァルマン２世の即位式を司った祭儀官シヴァカイヴァールヤも含まれている）やそれ以前の治世での寄進物などが記述されている。石碑に尊像を浮き彫りで表すのは珍しい。シヴァと神妃パールヴァティーの胴は自然に描かれており、シヴァの四角張った顔とふっくらした唇、小球で飾った編んだ髪など、バプーオン様式の特徴である。

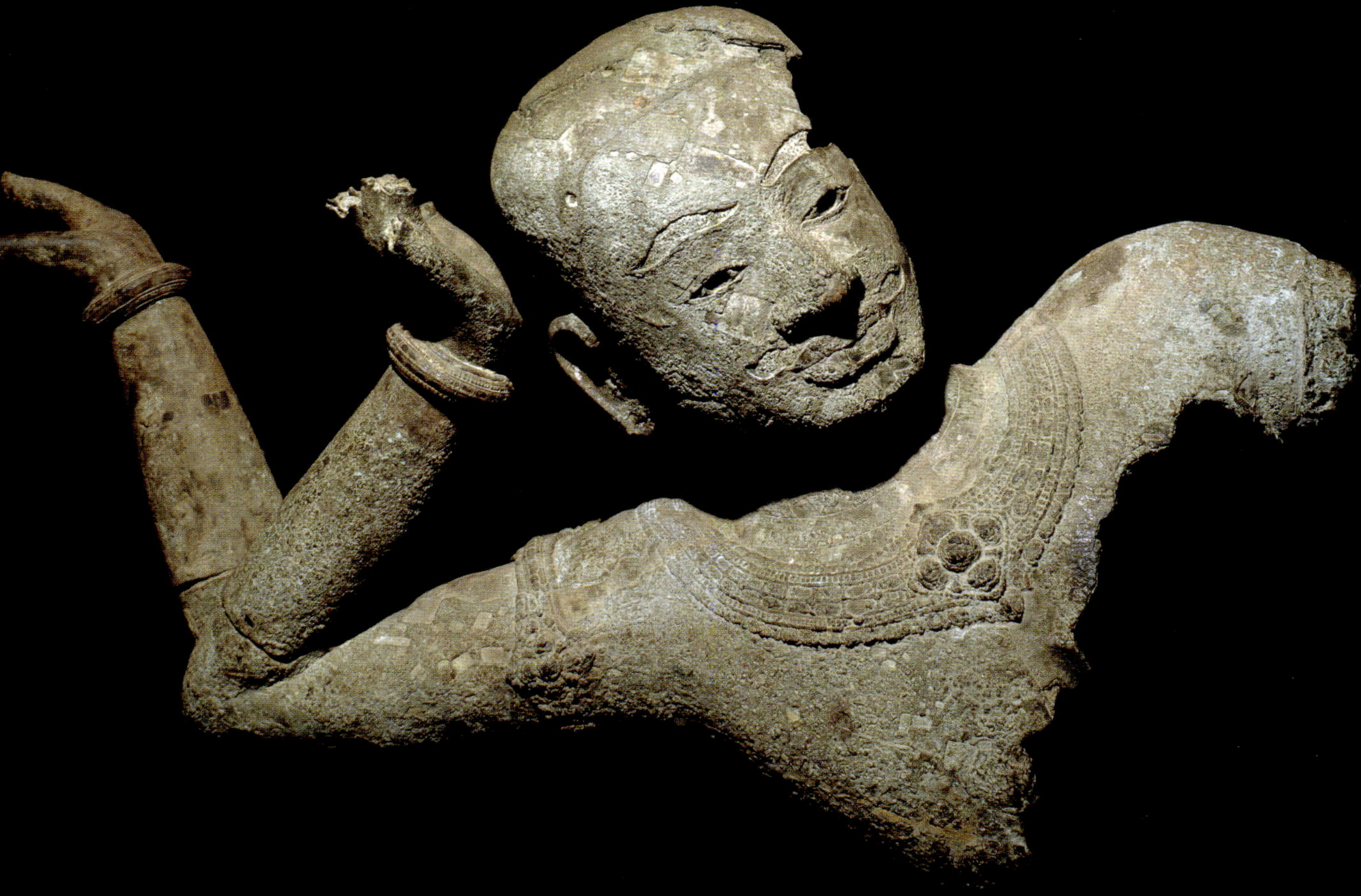

45

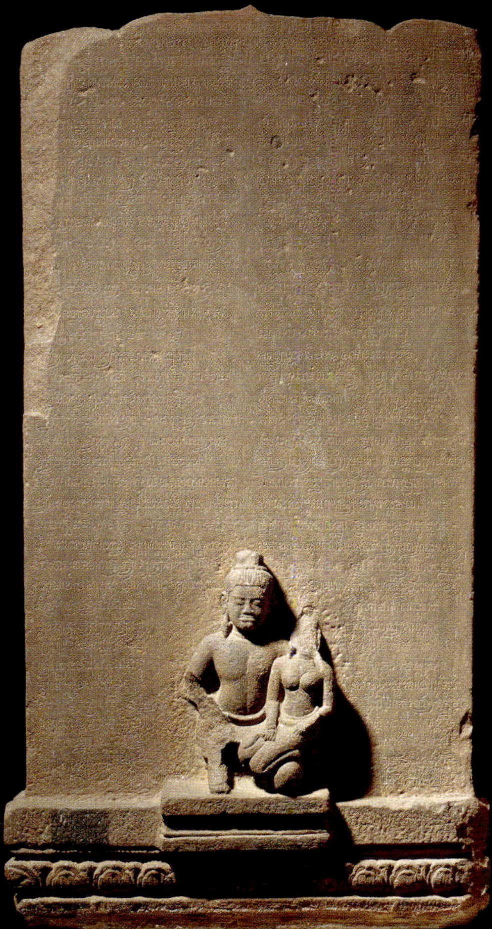

46

47. Buddha on naga. Pheam Cheang plantation, Kompong Cham, 2nd half 11th C. Sandstone, 1.14 m. Ka 1680.

Representations of the Buddha seated on the coils of the naga, with its multi-headed hood protecting him from above, are very common in Khmer art from the eleventh century on. The image relates to the story of the naga Muchilinda who slithered from his lake to raise the sage from the ground, spreading his hood to shelter Buddha's head while he meditated during a heavy rainstorm that lasted seven days. The broad head and finely twisted coiffure with its conical ushnisha cover, as well as the full curved lips, tranquil almond-shaped eyes, cleft chin, and the delicate naturalism of the limbs and torso visible under the transparent outer garment, are characteristic of the Baphuon style. The refinement of the carving and the serenity of expression make this one of the most spiritual sculptures in Khmer Buddhist art.

47. Buddha protégé par le naga. Plantation de Peam Cheang, Kompong Cham, 2nde moitié du 11ème s. Grès, 1,14 m. Ka 1680.

Les représentations du Buddha protégé par un naga polycéphale sont nombreuses dans l'art khmer à partir du 11ème siècle. Cette iconographie se rapporte à l'histoire du naga Muchilinda qui sortit de sa demeure aquatique pour protéger le Bienheureux perdu dans sa méditation au cours d'un terrible orage. Muchilinda fit de son corps un rempart à la fureur des eaux du lac en crue et de ses têtes déployées un parapluie pour abriter le Buddha. Le visage large et la coiffure de tresses délicatement ciselées, avec son couvre ushnisha conique, de même que les lèvres finement ourlées, les yeux en forme d'amande, le menton bifide et le naturalisme sensible des membres et du torse transparaissant sous le vêtement diaphane sont caractéristiques du style du Baphuon. Le raffinement de la sculpture et la sérénité de l'expression du visage font de cette œuvre l'une des plus inspirées de tout l'art bouddhique khmer.

៤៧_ ព្រះពុទ្ធប្រក់នាគ ពាមជាំង, កំពង់ចាម, ផ្នែកទី២នៃស.វ.ទី១១, ថ្មភក់, ១,១៤ម, ក ១៦៨០

ពុទ្ធបដិមាគង់លើភ្នែនពស់ ហើយដែលមានពពារក្បាលច្រើនរបៀបនេះ សម្បូណ៌ណាស់នៅក្នុងសិល្បៈខ្មែរតាំងពីស.វ.ទី១១មក។ រឿងនោះគឺនាគមុចិលិន្ទវារចេញមកពីបឹងមួយ, មកលើកទ្រព្រះពុទ្ធអង្គឱ្យផុតពីដី, បើកពពារបាំងព្រះកេសព្រះអង្គដែលកំពុងធ្វើសមាធិ ដោយសារមានភ្លៀងព្យុះបោកបក់៧ថ្ងៃជាប់គ្នា។ ព្រះកេសាដែលគេឆ្លាក់ដូចក្រងរមូលស្របគ្នាយ៉ាងល្អនោះ បញ្ចប់ទៅដោយមូលីមានរាងដូចសាជី, បបូរមាត់មានរាងជារលកហើយង, ចង្កាព្រែក, ដងខ្លួននិងអវៈយវៈឆ្លាក់តាមលំនាំធម្មជាតិ ហើយមើលឃើញច្បាស់ដោយចីពរដែលគ្រប់ពីលើនោះស្តើង។ ចម្លាក់ល្អិតច្នារផ្ចិតផ្ចង់ដែលជាលក្ខណៈនៃរចនាបថបាពួន និងទឹកជមដែលចេញមកពីព្រះភក្ត្រ បង្ហាញថានេះជាបដិមាមួយដ៏ប្រពៃក្នុងសិល្បៈពុទ្ធសាសនាខ្មែរ។

47. ナーガの上のブッダ. コンポンチャム州、ペアン・チェンの農園、11世紀後半、砂岩、1.14m、Ka 1680

複数の頭を広げてブッダを守るとぐろを巻いたナーガの上に座るブッダの像は、11世紀以後のクメール美術でよくみられる。これは地中の池から現れた蛇神ムチリンダが身体を傘にして、悟りを開いた後も瞑想を続けるブッダを7日間降り続いた大雨から守ったという仏伝の一場面を表している。

編み上げた頭髪、円錐形の肉髻、ふっくらした唇、穏やかな杏仁形の眼、あごの窪み、薄い大衣、手足や体躯の自然さなどバプーオン様式の特徴である。洗練された彫りと穏やかな表情をしたこの像は、クメール仏教美術の中でも最もスピリチュアルな作例である。

48. Hevajra. Banteay Kdei, Angkor, Siem Reap, 2nd half 11th C. Bronze, 0.30 m. Ga 5331.

Tantric Buddhism, also known as Vajrayana and the Diamond Way, of which Hevajra is the most important deity, was very important in Cambodia from the eleventh century onwards. The god is shown in dancing pose reminiscent of images of Shiva Nataraja, his foot trampling the four Mara (the chief evils impeding the path to enlightenment), who are delineated here by the fine lines incised on the recumbent shape. Similar grooves on the legs indicate that the apparent two are in fact four. His sixteen arms hold human and animal attributes representing Hevajra's supernatural powers that can be invoked by a yoga master for acolytes seeking enlightenment. The three heads in the lowest tier may represent the Buddha with the bodhisattva Lokesvara and Vajrapani, while the middle row of four and the single upper head may suggest the five supreme Buddhas, or Jina. Although the sculpture was found in the 12th-century temple of Banteay Kdei, the slender torso, the plunging line of the god's sampot, and the dynamic grace of the image suggest an 11th-century date.

48. Hevajra. Banteay Kdei, Angkor, Siem Reap, 2nde moitié du 11ème s. Bronze, 0,30 m. Ga 5331.

Le bouddhisme tantrique, également connu sous le nom de Vajrayana ou véhicule de Diamant, fut très important au Cambodge dès le 11ème siècle. Hevajra en est l'une des divinités principales. Le dieu est représenté en train de danser, dans une posture qui n'est pas sans évoquer celle de Shiva Nataraja; il terrasse les quatre Mara (démons entravant l'acquisition de l'Éveil) représentés par le corps prostré marqué d'incisions horizontales figurant sous son pied. Une incision verticale le long des jambes indique que le dieu est doté de quatre jambes et non pas deux comme on pourrait le croire au premier regard. Les pouvoirs surnaturels de Hevajra, qu'un maître religieux peut invoquer au cours des cérémonies, sont représentés par ses attributs, figures anthropomorphes ou animalières miniatures tenues dans chacune de ses seize mains. Les trois têtes de la rangée inférieure pourraient représenter le Buddha, et les bodhisattva Lokeshvara et Vajrapani, les quatre têtes du registre médian et la tête supérieure, les cinq Jina, Buddha suprêmes du panthéon du bouddhisme Vajrayana. Bien que cette statuette ait été découverte dans le temple de Banteay Kdei (dernier quart du 12ème siècle), ses proportions élancées, l'échancrure marquant le sampot à la taille, entre autres, plaident pour une datation dans la 2nde moitié du 11ème siècle.

៤៨_ ហេវជ្រ បន្ទាយក្តី, អង្គរ, សៀមរាប, ផ្នែកទី២នៃស.វ.ទី១១, សំរិទ្ធ, ០,៣០ម, គ ៥៣៣១

ក្នុងពុទ្ធសាសនាផ្នែកតន្ត្រ ហៅម្យ៉ាងទៀតថា វជ្រយាន ព្រះហេវជ្រជាទេពសំខាន់ជាងគេ។ នៅស្រុកខ្មែរទេពនេះគេស្គាល់ខ្លាំងចាប់ពីស.វ.ទី១១មក។ រូបនេះ គឺព្រះអង្គរាំ ដែលអាចប្រៀបទៅព្រះឥសូររាំដែរ. ព្រះបាទាជាន់មារទាំង៤ (សត្រូវរារាំងការត្រាស់ដឹង) ដែលគេឆ្លាក់សើៗត្រួតសណ្តូកលើគ្នា។ ដៃទាំង១៦កាន់កេតនភណ្ឌដែលជាសត្វផង ជាមនុស្សផង ហើយដែលតំណាងមហិទ្ធិឫទ្ធិនៃហេវជ្រ។ មហិទ្ធិឫទ្ធិនោះ គ្រូដែលពូកែខាងសមាធិអាចដាស់ឡើងដើម្បីជួយសាវ័កកំពុងស្វែងស្មាធិឱ្យសម្រេចធម៌ឡើង។ ព្រះភ័ក្ត្រ៣នៅក្រោម ប្រហែលជាតំណាងព្រះពុទ្ធព្រមដោយព្រះលោកេស្វរ និងព្រះវជ្របាណី រីឯជួរកណ្តាលដែលមានព្រះភ័ក្ត្រ៤ និងលើបង្អស់ដែលមានតែមួយអាចជាតំណាងព្រះពុទ្ធអង្គដ៏ឧត្តមឬព្រះជិនទាំង៥អង្គ។

48. ヘーヴァジュラ. シエムリエップ州、アンコール・トム、バンテアイ・クデイ、11世紀後半、ブロンズ、0.30m、Ga 5331

ヘーヴァジュラ（喜金剛）は密教仏教、金剛乗仏教の尊格で、カンボジアでは11世紀以後、大変重要になった。ヘーヴァジュラは踊るシヴァと似たポーズで、足はマーラ（4魔、悟りを妨害する魔）を踏みつけている。横たわったマーラは陰刻線で表されている。ヘーヴァジュラの足にも両脚に1条の線があり、４本足を表している。16本の手の人間と動物は、悟りを求める行者のためにヨーガの指導者が呼び出せるヘーヴァジュラの超能力を象徴している。最下段の３面はブッダ、ロケシュヴァラ（観音菩薩）、ヴァジュラパニ（金剛力士）、中央の４面と上段の1面は五仏（五智如来）を表していると思われる。この像は12世紀建立のバンテアイ・クデイ寺院で発見されたが、ほっそりした胴、切れ込んだ裙、ダイナミックな優雅さなどから11世紀制作と思われる。

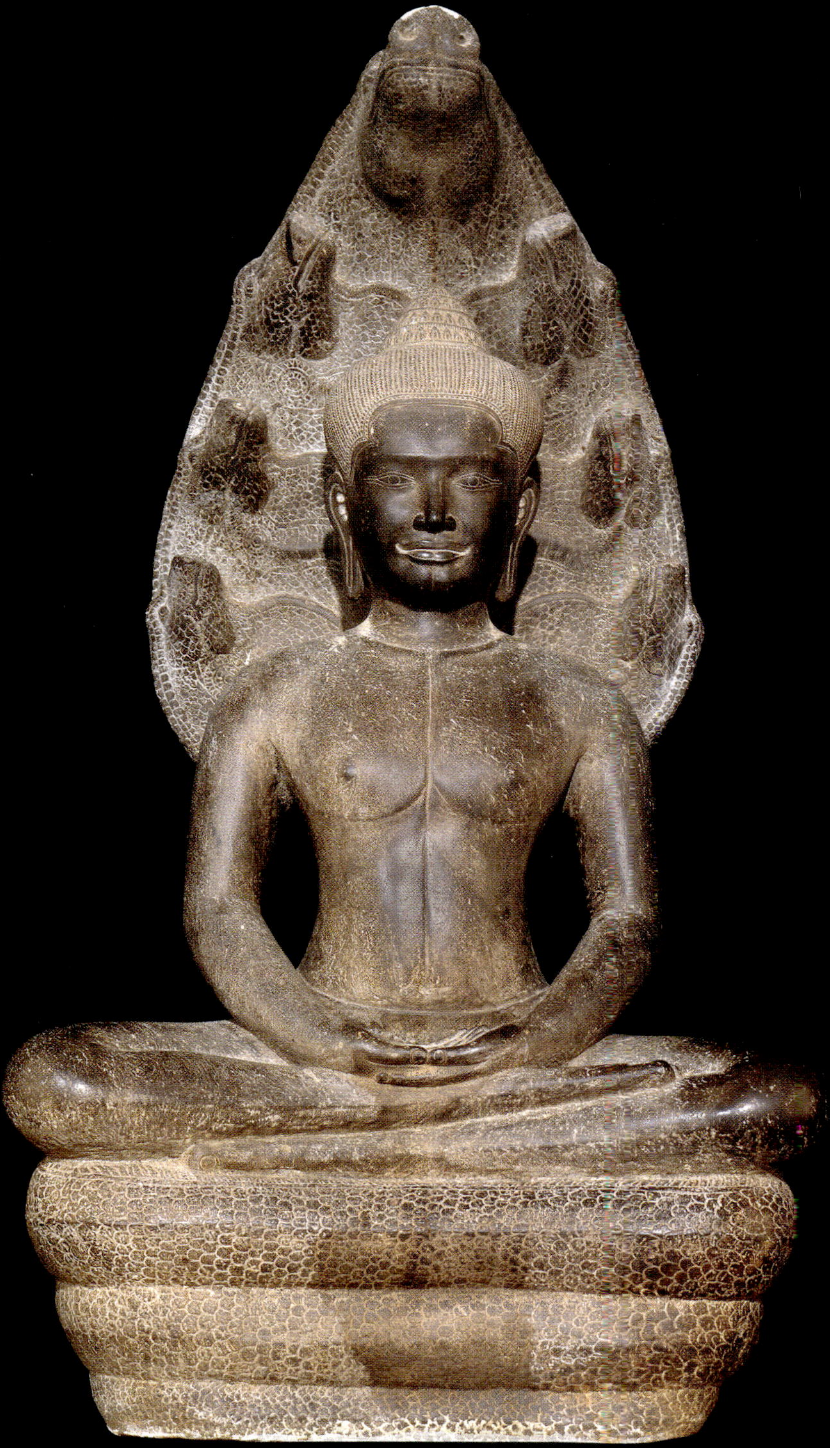

47

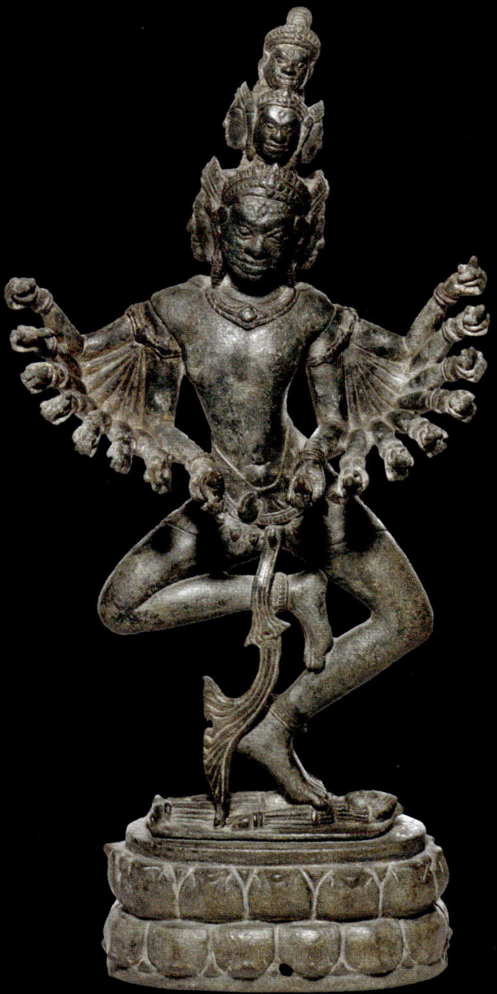

48

49. Buddha on naga. Cave in Serei Saphaon, Banteay Meanchey, 1st half 12th C. Sandstone, 1.04 m. Ka 985.

This image of the Buddha on a seven-headed naga throne is one of the outstanding examples of the Angkor Wat style. The precise representation of the serpent's scales, the sage's facial features, hands, and elaborately incised crown epitomize the perfection of early 12th-century carving without the rigidity that often characterizes the art of this period (see #50). Although the expression is more iconic than that of the Buddha from Peam Cheang (#47), it still suggests a calm spirituality appropriate to the meditating figure. The presence of a crown is indicative of the growing importance in this period of representations of the Buddha adorned with jewels and crown (see #57), suggesting a modification to the simplicity of early conceptions to accord with the increasing emphasis on imperial power.

49. Buddha protégé par le naga. Une grotte de la région de Serei Saphaon, Banteay Meanchey, 1ère moitié du 12ème s. Grès, 1,04 m. Ka 985.

Cette sculpture représentant le Buddha protégé par le naga Muchilinda est l'une des plus belles œuvres du style d'Angkor Vat. La figuration minutieuse des écailles recouvrant le corps du serpent, les traits du visage du Bienheureux, ses mains et le diadème élaboré attestent la perfection de la statuaire du début du 12ème siècle sans présenter la rigidité qui caractérise souvent l'art de cette période (voir par exemple la divinité féminine #50). Bien que l'expression soit plus distante que dans le cas du Buddha de Peam Cheang (#47), elle transcrit pourtant la spiritualité apaisée propre aux représentations du Saint Homme. La présence du diadème participe de l'importance croissante accordée à l'image du Buddha paré à partir de l'époque d'Angkor Vat (voir le Buddha en bronze #57).

៤៩_ព្រះពុទ្ធរូបប្រក់នាគ ល្អាងមួយនៅស្រីសោភ័ណ, បន្ទាយមានជ័យ, ផ្នែកទី១នៃស.វ.ទី១២, ថ្មភក់, ១,០៤ម, ក៩៨៥

ព្រះពុទ្ធរូបគង់លើនាគក្បាល៧ដែលប្រក់ពីលើព្រះអង្គនេះ ជាស្នាដៃសិល្បៈដ៏ត្រចះត្រចង់មួយក្នុងរចនាបថអង្គរវត្ត។ អ្វីៗនៅលើរូបនេះសុទ្ធតែច្លាក់ដោយផ្ចិតផ្ចង់ជាទីបំផុត តាំងពីស្រកាពស់, ទម្រង់ព្រះភ័ក្ត្រ, ព្រះហស្ត, ក្បាំងម្កុដ ដែលគេដឹងថាជាលក្ខណៈសិល្បៈដើមស.វ.ទី១២ (សូមមើលរូបលេខ៥០)។ ព្រះភក្ត្រនៅទីនេះមិនរស់រវើកស្មើនឹងព្រះពុទ្ធរូបបានមកពីពាមជាំង (រូបលេខ៤៧) ក៏ពិតមែន ប៉ុន្តែនៅតែបង្ហាញភាពស្ងប់នឹងនសមនឹងការស្មឹងស្មាធិ៍មែន។ ម្កុដនៅលើរូបនេះជាផ្នែកមួយនៃអលង្ការផ្សេងៗដែលកាន់តែសម្បូណ៌ ហើយស្រោចស្រពលើព្រះពុទ្ធអង្គម្តងបន្តិចៗពីពេលនេះទៅ (សូមមើលរូបលេខ៥៧)។ ភាពសាមញ្ញដែលធ្លាប់មានពីមុនមកក៏ប្តូរទៅរកភាពស្ងប់ស្ងៃង និងការបង្ហាញអនុភាពនៃព្រះពុទ្ធអង្គវិញ។

49. ナーガの上のブッダ. バンテアイメンチェイ州、セレイ・サファオン、12世紀前半、砂岩、1.04m、Ka 985

この７頭のナーガの上のブッダの像はアンコール・ワット様式の卓越した例である。この時代によくみられる固さ（No.50参照）もなく、ナーガの鱗、ブッダの表情、手、ムクタの細かい細工など12世紀初の彫刻の完璧さを代表している。ペアン・チェンのブッダ（No.47）の表情より、肖像的だが、瞑想中の姿にふさわしい穏やかなピリチュアリティーがみられる。ムクタはこの時代のブッダ像が宝飾やムクタをつけて表されるようになったことを示しており、初期の質素さから、王の権力を反映するようになったことがわかる（No.57参照）。

50. Female divinity. Angkor, Siem Reap, 1st half 12th C. Sandstone, 0.865 m. Ka 1867.

The carving of this female divinity epitomizes the Angkor Wat style. The sculptor's skill in representing the elaborately fashioned crown and coiffure cover, the massive leg bands, rich bracelets on upper and lower arms and the heavy necklace, pectoral chains and ear pendant is remarkable. So, too, is the treatment of the pleated skirt cloth with its upper flap and intricately folded front panel, all of which are characteristic of the style. The somewhat archaistic emphasis on imperial dignity harks back to the rigidity of the late ninth and early tenth century in a reversal of the naturalism of the Banteay Srei and Baphuon periods, and the iconic gaze lacks the grace of those styles. Although the hands are intact, it is impossible to be certain about the goddess's identity. Their opposed position since a recent restoration does not offer even a hypothetical identification (see #73).

50. Divinité féminine. Angkor, Siem Reap, 1ère moitié du 12ème s. Grès, 0,865 m. Ka 1867.

Cette divinité féminine est caractéristique du style d'Angkor Vat. La technique d'exécution très fine des nombreuses parures - diadème, couvre chignon, anneaux de pieds, bracelets, brassards, pendants d'oreilles et collier pectoral - est remarquable. La jupe plissée, avec son bord supérieur rabattu et son riche pan antérieur, est propre au style du règne de Suryavarman II. Un certain archaïsme renvoyant aux traditions de la fin du 9ème siècle et du début du 10ème prend ici le contre-pied de l'art plus naturel et vivant des styles de Banteay Srei et du Baphuon dont cette déesse ne possède plus la grâce. Bien que les mains soient préservées, il est impossible de préciser l'identité de la divinité. La position contrastée des mains depuis la récente restauration de l'œuvre n'autorise aucune identification, même hypothétique (voir #73).

៥០_ទេវី អង្គរ, សៀមរាប, ផ្នែកទី១នៃស.វ.ទី១២, ថ្មភក់, ០,៨៦៥ម, ក១៨៦៧

ចម្លាក់លម្អិតដែលឃើញនៅលើរូបនេះជាលក្ខណៈសម្គាល់នៃរចនាបថអង្គរវត្ត ជាពិសេសម្កុដ, កងជើង, កងដៃ និងស្នាប់ដើមដៃ, ស្រង់ក, រយ៉ា។ រីឯសំពត់ដែលមានផ្នត់វិញក៏ដូច្នោះដែរ គឺច្លាក់លម្អិត ហើយខាងលើមានជាយបត់ធ្លាក់មកខាងមុខ។ ប៉ុន្តែរូបទាំងមូលហាក់ដូចជាត្រឡប់ទៅរកភាពទ្រឹងនឹងថ្កល់នៃបដិមាជំនាន់ចុងស.វ.ទី៩ និងដើមស.វ.ទី១០ទៅវិញ, រាប់បញ្ចូលទាំងទឹកមុខនិងក្រសែភ្នែកផង, ពោលគឺមិនបង្ហាញភាពរស់រវើកនៃបដិមាដូចនៅជំនាន់បន្ទាយស្រីនិងបាភួនឡើយ។ ថ្វីត្បិតតែដៃទាំងពីរដែលង្ហាញកាយវិការខុសគ្នានោះនៅល្អនៅឡើយ ក៏យើងពុំអាចអះអាងថានេះជាទេវីណាប្រាកដបាន (សូមមើលរូបលេខ៧៣)។

50. 女神. シエムリエップ州、アンコール、12世紀前半、砂岩、0.865m、Ka 1867

この女神像はアンコール・ワット様式の典型である。冠、足釧、腕釧、臂釧、胸釧、耳輪の装飾性は制作者の高度な技術を示している。裙の襞や上部の折り返し、前面の装飾なども同様である。王家の尊厳を反映して、バンテアイ・スレイやバプーオン様式の自然主義から、9世紀後半や10世紀前半に遡った硬い印象を与えている。手は残っているが、女神が誰か確定できない。最近の修復作業でラクシュミーとするこれまでの仮説も成り立たなくなった（No.73参照）。

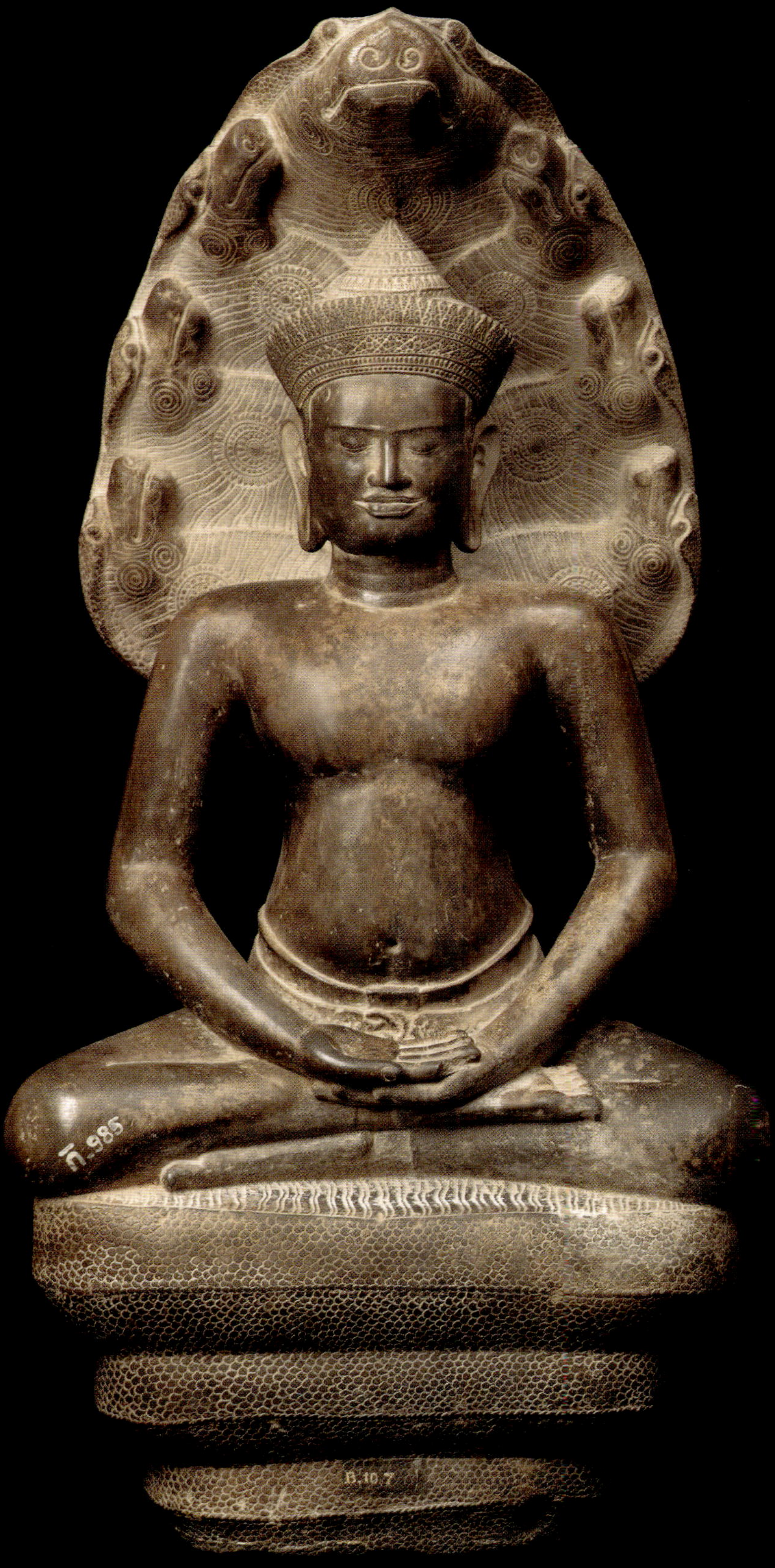

49

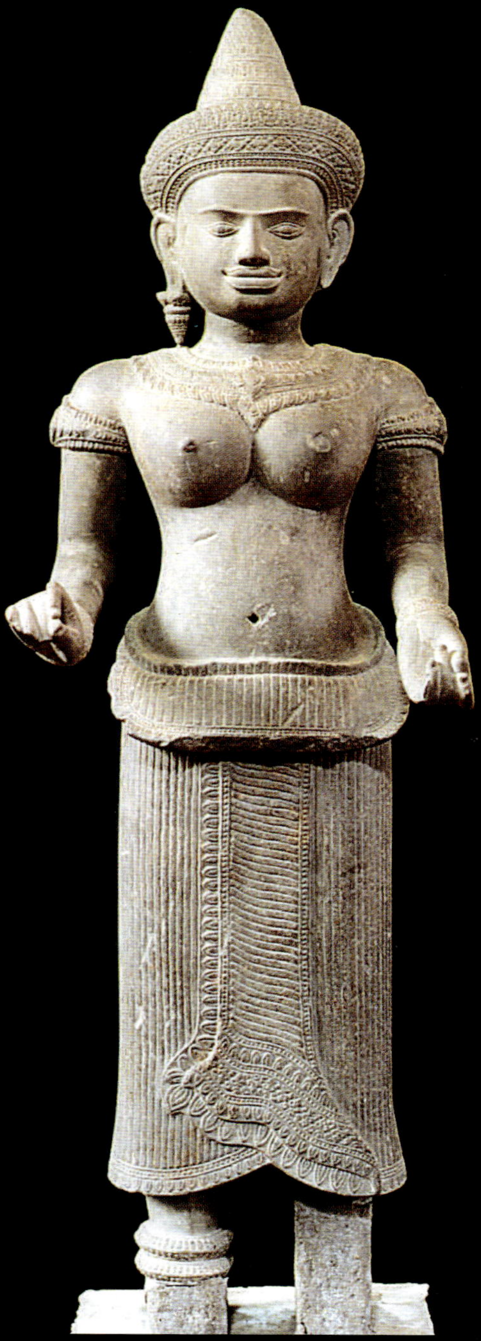

50

51. Vishnu-Vasudeva-Narayana. Kapilapura, Angkor, Siem Reap, 1st half 12th C. Bronze, 0.435 m. Ga 5291.

This version of Vishnu is the supreme form of that god. Many scholars have considered this a statue of Harihara, the god who is half-Shiva, half-Vishnu, because although the attributes the god bears in his hands (an orb - or globe - a disk, a conch, and a mace) all pertain to Vishnu, there is a third eye, the Sanskrit syllable 'Om' and a crown of plaited and piled hair on the god's head. These are usually associated with Shiva. But in an important Vishnuite text of the 10th century these features are associated with yoga masters, indicating that they are present in Shiva not intrinsically but rather as an indication of his status as a yoga master. The supreme form of Vishnu also partakes of these qualities, which explains the unusual iconography of this highly refined and expressive bronze.

51. Vishnu-Vasudeva-Narayana. Kapilapura, Angkor, Siem Reap, 1ère moitié du 12ème s. Bronze, 0,435 m. Ga 5291.

En tant que Vasudeva-Narayana, Vishnu est ici représenté sous son aspect suprême. Nombreux sont les spécialistes qui ont considéré cette statuette comme une image de Harihara, le dieu moitié Vishnu, moitié Shiva. Les attributs, en effet, se rapportent à Vishnu (une sphère, un disque, une conque et une massue), tandis que d'autres caractéristiques renvoient à Shiva (le troisième œil frontal, le chignon d'ascète portant la syllabe OM). Dans un texte vishnuite important du 10ème siècle, ces caractéristiques sont associées aux maîtres du yoga et présentes tout aussi bien en Shiva qu'en Vishnu. Ainsi s'explique l'iconographie inhabituelle de ce bronze raffiné et expressif.

៥១_ ព្រះនារាយណ៍ កបិលបុរ, អង្គរ, សៀមរាប, ផ្នែកទី១នៃស.វ.ទី១២, សំរឹទ្ធ, ០,៤៣៥ម, គ ៥២៩១

នេះជាព្រះនារាយណ៍ក្នុងទិដ្ឋភាពជាទេពកំពូលលើលោក។ អ្នកស្រាវជ្រាវជាច្រើនធ្លាប់យល់ថា នេះជារូបព្រះហរិហរ ដោយសារ ថ្វីត្បិតតែកេតនភណ្ឌនៅក្នុងព្រះហស្តទាំងអស់ជារបស់ព្រះនារាយណ៍ (ផែនដី, ចក្រ, ស័ង្ខ និងដំបង) ប៉ុន្តែមានព្រះនេត្រទី៣ ព្រមទាំងតួអក្សរ "ឱម" និងមកុដដែលកើតឡើងដោយសក់ក្រង ដែលធម្មតាជាទីសម្គាល់នៃព្រះឥសូរ។ ប៉ុន្តែបើយោងតាមសិលាចារឹកសំខាន់មួយនៅស.វ.ទី១០ ហើយដែលទាក់ទងនឹងនិកាយព្រះនារាយណ៍វិញ គឺលក្ខណៈប៉ុន្មានខាងក្រោយនេះទាក់ទងទៅនឹងគ្រូសមាធិធំៗជាទូទៅ មិនចំពោះតែព្រះឥសូរប៉ុណ្ណោះទេ។ ព្រះនារាយណ៍ក្នុងទិដ្ឋភាពជាទេពកំពូលលើលោកក៏ជាគ្រូធំមួយខាងស្ទើងស្មាធិដែរ ដូច្នេះហើយបានជាលក្ខណៈសម្គាល់ខ្លះហាក់ដូចជាពុំធម្មតា។

51. ヴィシュヌ. シエムリエップ州、アンコール、カピラプラ、12世紀前半、ブロンズ、0.435m、Ga 5291

これはヴィシュヌの最高神としての姿を描いている。法螺貝、棍棒、円輪、宝珠というヴィシュヌの持物を手にしながら、シヴァの象徴である第三眼、サンスクリット語オウムの標識、編んだ髪の髪束から、ヴィシュヌとシヴァが合体したハリハラではないかと考えられていた。しかし、10世紀の重要なヴィシュヌ派の記述によると、これらはヨーガの指導者と関係しており、これらの象徴はシヴァ本来のものではなく、ヨーガ指導者としての地位を示すものである。ヴィシュヌの最高神としての姿も同様のシンボルを示すため、この洗練され表情豊かなブロンズ像の稀な姿が説明できる。

52. Vishnu. Wat Khnat, Angkor, Siem Reap, 1st half 12th C. Sandstone, 1.01 m. Ka 1810.

The hieratic expression of this deity is consistent with the somewhat rigid and arrogant expression of statuary of the Angkor Wat period (see #50). Also typical for the style is the meticulous detailing of the carving of the god's elaborate crown and the stylised treatment of his pleated sampot with its narrow anchor-shaped panels in front surmounted by the overhanging flap of the ruffled end of the cloth. The pattern on the belt of two rows of oval motifs bordered by rows of beads is an innovation of this period. Although the figure's hands holding the attributes that would confirm identity have been broken from its arms, four-armed figures such as this, crowned with tiara and conical coiffure cover, can confidently be interpreted as images of Vishnu.

52. Vishnu. Vat Khnat, Angkor, Siem Reap, 1ère moitié du 12ème s. Grès, 1,01 m. Ka 1810.

L'apparence hiératique de cette sculpture participe du style quelque peu rigide et hautain de la première moitié du 12ème siècle. Le costume, avec son plissé stylisé, son pan antérieur en ancre étroite et son nœud d'attache caractéristique, est représentatif du style d'Angkor Vat. La double rangée d'ovales de la ceinture bordée par de petites perles semble se généraliser à cette époque. Bien que les mains soient perdues, et par voie de conséquence les attributs qu'elles tenaient, on identifie traditionnellement les images à quatre bras coiffées d'un diadème et d'un couvre chignon conique comme des représentations de Vishnu.

៥២_ ព្រះនារាយណ៍ វត្តខ្នាត, អង្គរ, សៀមរាប, ផ្នែកទី១នៃស.វ.ទី១២, ថ្មភក់, ១,០១ម, ក ១៨១០

ដំហរាងទ្រឹងនៃរូបនេះត្រូវនឹងបដិមាសម័យអង្គរវត្តនោះឯងហើយ ដែលពុំសូវបត់បែនទៅតាមធម្មជាតិ (សូមមើលរូបលេខ៥០)។ ចំណុចសម្គាល់ខ្លះទៀតក៏ឃើញមាននៅទីនេះ ពោលគឺមកុដដែលមានចម្លាក់ល្អិតល្អិតផូរផង់, ផ្នត់សំពត់ត្រង់ៗហើយស្មើគ្នា ប្រកបដោយបន្ទះមួយរាងយុថ្កាធ្លាក់មកដល់ពាក់កណ្តាលសំពត់ខាងមុខ ឯមួយទៀតធ្លាក់មកដល់ជាយសំពត់ខាងក្រោមតែម្តង។ ការបង្កើតថ្មី គឺខ្សែក្រវាត់មានក្បាច់រាងមូលទ្រវែងតៗគ្នាជាពីរជួរ ឯជាយសងខាងមានក្បាច់ពងត្រី។ ថ្វីត្បិតតែដៃទាំងអស់បាក់បែកអស់ទៅហើយជាមួយកេតនភណ្ឌផង ក៏យើងអាចនៅស្មានបានថានេះជាព្រះនារាយណ៍ ដោយសារមានដៃ៤, ក្បាំងមកុដ ព្រមទាំងដួងរាងសាជី។

52. ヴィシュヌ. シエムリエップ州、アンコール、ワット・クニャット、12世紀前半、砂岩、1.01m、Ka 1810

この神像の聖美術的な表情はアンコール・ワット時代の特徴である硬い、傲慢な表情である（No.50参照）。ムクタの細かい装飾やたくしこまれた裙が前面で細い錨形となって垂れ、その上部はラッフルとなっている様子などもこの時代の特徴である。上下の丸い小球の間に二段の楕円がある帯模様はこの時代に誕生した。腕が破損した為、持物は不明だが、４臂、冠帯と円錐形ムクタからヴィシュヌ像であると確定できる。

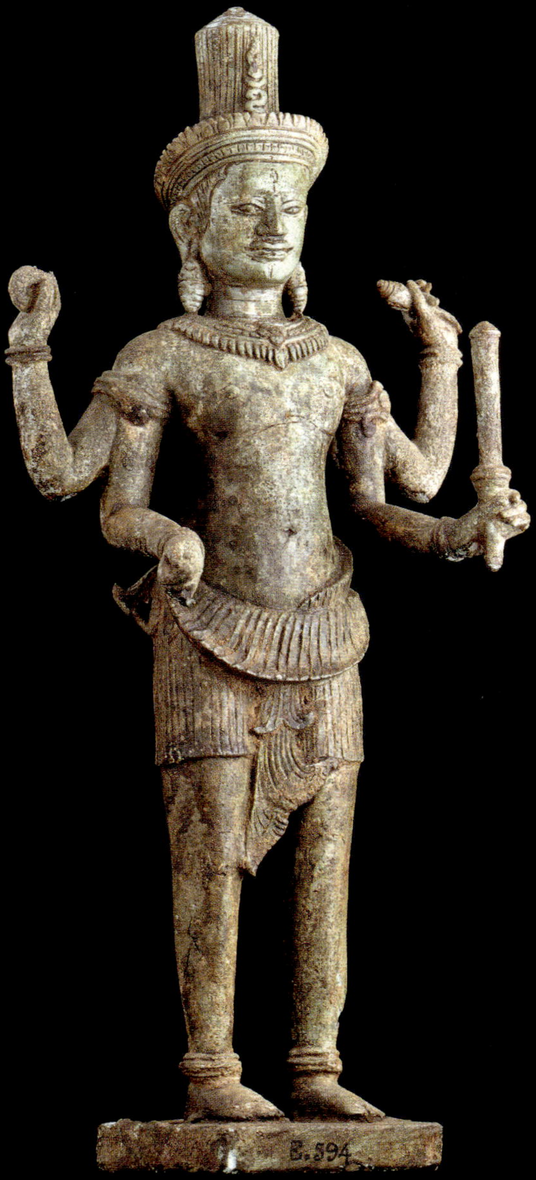

51

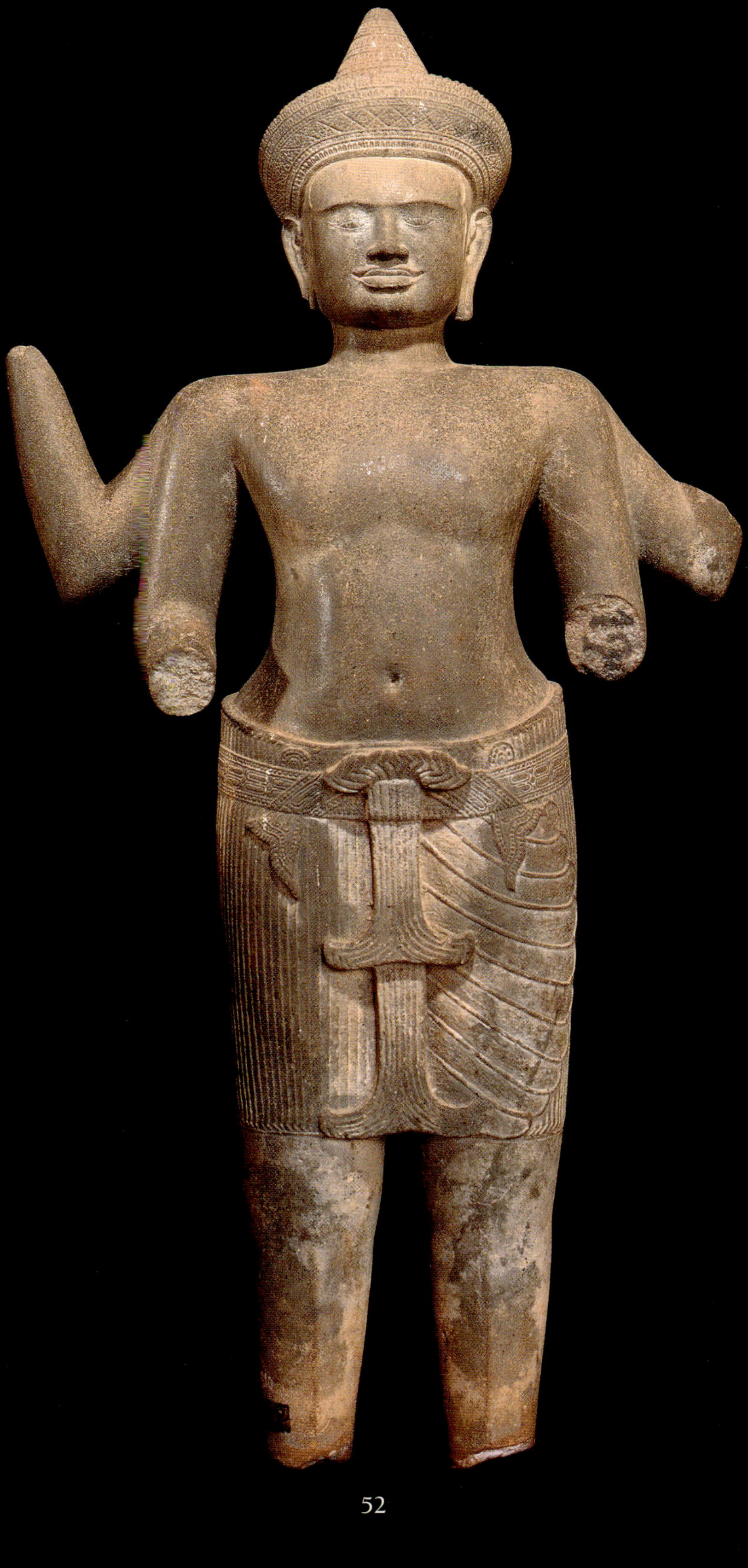

52

53. Kneeling female figure (support for mirror?). Bayon, Angkor Thom, Siem Reap, 1st half 12th C. Bronze, 0.34 m. Ga 5476.

This dynamic image of a woman with one knee raised and one bent to the ground, a pose often depicted in both relief and freestanding carving, is one of the most striking bronze figures in the National Museum's collection. Although she is clearly not a deity, the beauty of her rich jewellery indicates a possible court or temple retainer. Her upraised arms once bore an object that must have been thin and flat, possibly a screen or mirror, as the space between the back and front edges of her crown and the receiving grooves on her hands is narrow. Although the details of pleated garment and jewellery conform to the characteristics of the Angkor Wat morphology, the figure has a suppleness and grace that transcend the style of stone sculptures such as #50 and #52.

53. Personnage féminin agenouillé (support de miroir?). Bayon, Angkor Thom, Siem Reap, 1ère moitié du 12ème s. Bronze, 0,34 m. Ga 5476.

Cette jeune femme figurée un genou en terre, l'autre relevé, dans une position souvent représentée en bas-relief ou en ronde-bosse, est l'un des plus remarquables bronzes des collections du musée national. Bien qu'il ne s'agisse pas d'une divinité, ses riches parures indiquent son rang important. Les bras levés ont dû maintenir un objet mince et plat, peut-être un miroir ou quelque écran, ainsi que le montrent la fente apparaissant au sommet du diadème et la position des doigts. Les détails du costume plissé et des bijoux sont caractéristiques de l'art d'Angkor Vat. Par sa souplesse et sa grâce, cette statuette se démarque toutefois de la production en pierre de cette époque (cf. #50 et #52).

៥៣_ មនុស្សស្រីបញ្ចូចជង្គង់ (ទម្រកញ្ចក់ឆ្លុះមុខ?) បាយ័ន្ត, អង្គរធំ, សៀមរាប, ផ្នែកទី១នៃស.វ.ទី១២, សំរិទ្ធ, ០,៣៤ម, គ ៥៤៧៦

នេះជារូបសំរឹតមួយគួរឱ្យចាប់អារម្មណ៍បំផុតក្នុងសមុច្ច័យសារមន្ទីជាតិ។ ស្រីនេះបញ្ឈរជង្គង់ម្ខាង ឯម្ខាងទៀតបញ្ចូចទៅក្រោម មើលទៅហាក់ដូចជារស់រវើកណាស់។ ឥរិយាបថនេះបញ្ជាក់ថាពុំមែនជាទេពពិតមែនហើយ ប៉ុន្តែអលង្ការស្រោចស្រពលើខ្លួនទាំងអម្បាលម៉ានធ្វើឱ្យយើងគិតថា ប្រហែលជាស្រីស្នំនៅវាំងឬនៅតាមប្រាសាទ។ ដៃទាំងពីរដែលលើកទៅលើនោះ ដើមឡើយប្រហែលជាទ្រវត្ថុអ្វីមួយមានរាងស្តើងហើយសំប៉ែត។ តាមស្មាន ប្រហែលជាកញ្ចក់ ត្បិតរង្វះចង្អូរនៃមកុដព្រមទាំងស្នាមចូតនៅលើបាតដៃសងខាង មានទំហំតូចចង្អៀត។ ផ្នត់សំពត់និងអលង្ការទូទៅអាចឱ្យយើងសម្គាល់ថាជាសិល្បៈអង្គរវត្តហើយ រីឯភាពស្រទន់និងទឹកដមនៃមុខនេះកាន់តែលេចធ្លោរឡើង ខុសពីរូបលេខ៥០និង៥២។

53. ひざまずく女性（鏡台？）. シエムリエップ州、アンコール・トム、バイヨン、12世紀前半、ブロンズ、0.34m、Ga 5476

この片膝をついた女性像は国立美術館の所蔵品の中でも最高傑作である。片膝をつく姿はレリーフや石像でもよくみられる。神ではないが　美しい宝飾を多数、身につけていることから、宮廷か寺院に仕えていた女性を描いたものであろう。支えの髻の前後と両手の溝は狭いので、かかげた両手には薄く平らな物、恐らく鏡がおかれていたとみられる。ひだのある裙や装身具はアンコール・ワット様式の特徴だが、この像はしなやかで優雅で、No.50や52の石像を超越している。

54. Rajendradevi as Gauri. Lolei, Southwest sanctuary tower, Roluos, Siem Reap, first three-quarters 12th C. Sandstone, 1.74 m. Ka 1645.

This imposing figure of the goddess Gauri, one of the shakti of Shiva, was found in the late-9th-century temple of Lolei, where an inscription identifies her and dedicates the figure to Rajendradevi, the maternal ancestor of King Yashovarman who erected the temple in 893. Although in general the statue conforms to the morphology of Preah Ko, which determined the style of the eponymous temple of 879 as well as that of Bakong of 881 and of Lolei, comparison with Bakong images (#28, 29) reveals some important differences. The sensuousness of those torsos is much more naturalistic than the rather rigid stance of this figure, while the treatment of pleats in Gauri's sarong is much more summary and not consistent with 9th-century details. The possibility is strong, based on this evidence, that the sculpture was carved to replace a lost original at the time, in the first half of the 12th century, when additions and restorations were made at Bakong, the temple mountain of Indravarman.

54. Rajendradevi sous les traits de Gauri. Lolei, tour-sanctuaire sud-ouest, Roluos, Siem Reap, trois premiers quarts du 12ème s. Grès, 1,74 m. Ka 1645.

Cette imposante représentation de la déesse Gauri, l'une des épouses du dieu Shiva, fut retrouvée dans le temple de Lolei, un monument remontant à la fin du 9ème siècle. La statue est identifiée par une inscription précisant qu'elle a été consacrée au bénéfice spirituel d'une ancêtre maternelle de Yashovarman, roi fondateur du monument en 893. Bien que cette œuvre se rapproche des sculptures provenant des temples de Preah Ko, consacré en 879, et de Bakong, consacré en 881 (#28, 29), elle s'en distingue pourtant par d'importants détails: la sensualité qui se dégage des œuvres du style de Preah Ko est absente de cette pièce relativement rigide et le traitement des plis du costume ne correspond nullement avec celui des œuvres du 9ème siècle. Il semble très probable que cette sculpture a été réalisée à date tardive pour remplacer un original perdu; peut-être dans la première moitié du 12ème siècle, lorsque des modifications et des restaurations ont été apportées à Bakong, le temple-montagne d'Indravarman.

៥៤_ ព្រះនាងរាជេន្ទ្រទេវី (ក្រោមរូបភាពជាព្រះជាយាព្រះឥសូរ) លលៃ, ប៉មនិរតី, រលួស, សៀមរាប, ស.វ.ទី១២, ថ្មភក់, ១,៧៤ម, ក ១៦៤៥

រូប "គោរី" ជាសក្តិនៃព្រះឥសូរនេះ គេឃើញនៅប្រាសាទលលៃ (សាងឆ្នាំ៨៩៣) ជាមួយសិលាចារឹកមួយដែលបង្ហាញថាជាព្រះនាងរាជេន្ទ្រទេវី ដែលជាព្រះអយ្យកានៃព្រះបាទយសោវរ្ម័ន។ ជាទូទៅឃើញថាចម្លាក់នេះស្របនឹងលំនាំរាងកាយរចនាបថព្រះគោ ក្នុងនោះមានប្រាសាទព្រះគោ (ឆ្នាំ៨៧៩), បាគង (ឆ្នាំ៨៨១) និងលលៃមែន ប៉ុន្តែបើប្រៀបនឹងបដិមាលេខ២៨និង២៩នៅបាគង ឃើញថាមានចំណុចខ្លះខុសគ្នា។ ដងខ្លួននៅបាគងឆ្លាក់តាមលំនាំធម្មជាតិច្រើនជាង មិនដូចរូបនេះមានរាងទ្រឹង ហើយផ្នត់សំពត់ឆ្លាក់ឡើងគ្មានភាពលម្អិតអ្វីទាំងអស់ ពុំស៊ីគ្នានឹងរចនាបថទូទៅនៃស.វ.ទី៩ឡើយ។ ប្រហែលជារូបនេះឆ្លាក់ឡើងដើម្បីយកទៅជំនួសបដិមាចាស់ កាលគេជួសជុលប្រាសាទបាគងឡើងវិញនៅស.វ.ទី១២។

54. ガウリ姿のラージェーンドラデーヴィ. シエムリエップ州、ロルオス、ロレイ南西祠堂、12世紀第1~3四半期、砂岩、1.74m、Ka 1645

このシヴァの神妃ガウリの堂々とした女神像は９世紀末に建立されたロレイ寺院で発見された。碑文によると、このガウリ像は寺院を893年に建立したヤショヴァルマン1世が母方の祖母ラージェーンドラデーヴィに捧げたものである。879年建立のプレア・コー寺院、および881年建立のバコン寺院とロレイ寺院にみられるプレア・コー様式を反映しているが、バコン様式の石像（No.28、29）と比較するとその違いがわかる。No.28、29の石像が体躯がより自然で肉感的であるのに比べ、この像はより硬い。一方、ガウリの衣褶の襞の描き方など簡素化されており、９世紀の特徴と異なる。従って、バコンの増築・修復時に失われた原作の代替品として12世紀前半の彫られたものである可能性が高い。

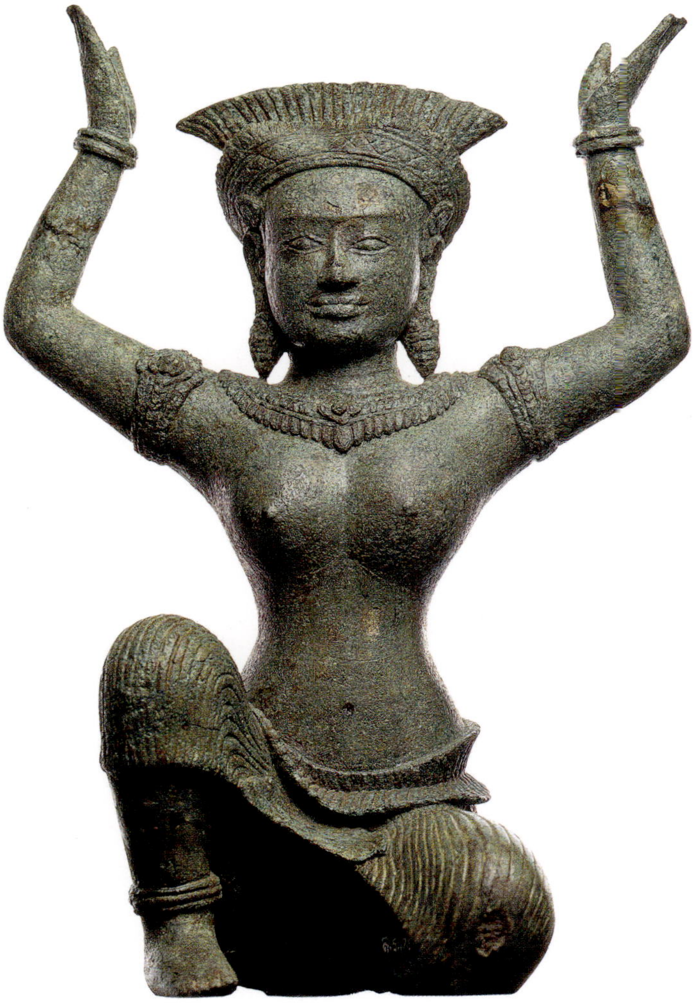

53

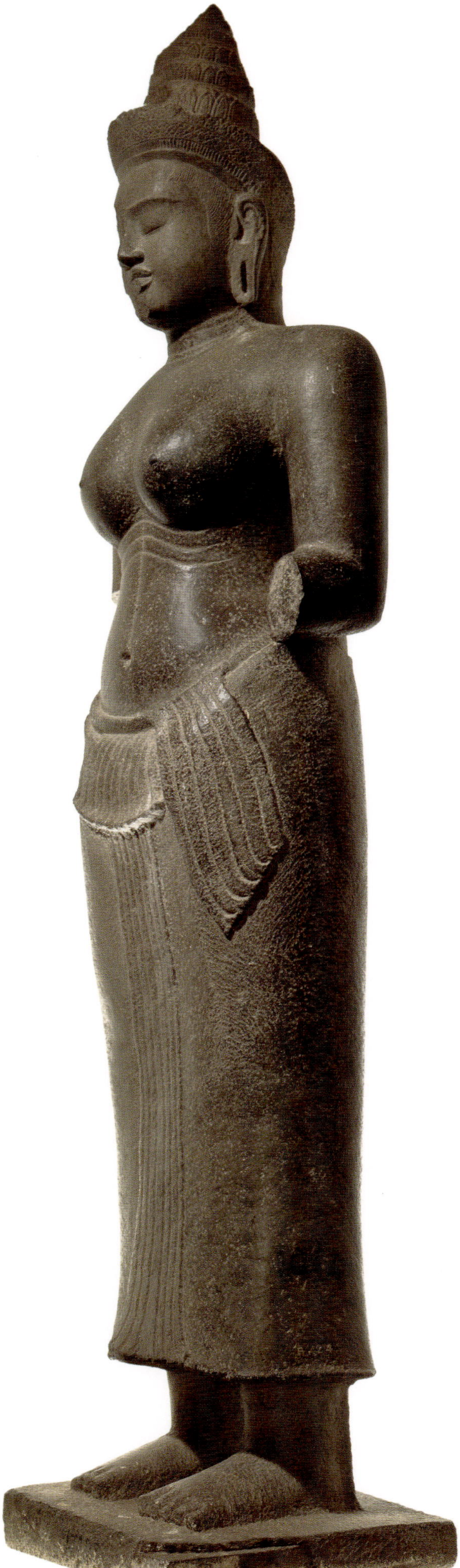

54

55. Shiva and two consorts. Unknown provenance, 12th C. Sandstone, 1.01 m. Ka 705.

Although very worn, traces of a crescent moon in the headdress and of a third eye in the forehead identify the central deity as Shiva. The flanking goddesses are possibly Uma and Ganga, two of his spouses, or shakti, often seen in triads like this, though the absence of attributes makes certainty impossible. Their pleated skirt cloths, conical coiffure covers and richly incised flaring tiaras are typical of Angkor Wat style, but the form of the god's jata, the crown of twisted and piled locks characteristic of Shiva, offers a puzzle, as its cylindrical form harks back to earlier models such as the Umamaheshvara group from Banteay Srei (#36). The treatment of the torsos and the touching placement of the goddesses' inner hands on Shiva's arm is quite naturalistic, but the detachment of the facial expressions and the clumsy modelling of the foreshortened feet display the rigidity typical of Angkor Wat statuary.

55. Shiva et ses deux épouses. Provenance inconnue, 12ème s. Grès, 1,01 m. Ka 705.

Bien que très érodées, les traces d'un croissant de lune, dans le chevelure, et d'un troisième œil, sur le front, permettent de reconnaître Shiva dans le personnage central de cette triade. Malgré l'absence de leurs attributs, les deux déesses pourraient être Uma et Ganga, les épouses ou shakti du dieu, souvent représentées à ses côtés. Si les costumes plissés, le couvre-chignon conique des déesses et les diadèmes au riche décor incisé sont caractéristiques du style d'Angkor Vat, le chignon d'ascète (jata) propre à Shiva dérive de modèles plus anciens, tel le groupe d'Umamaheshvara de Banteay Srei (#36). Le traitement des bustes et la manière touchante dont les déesses placent leur mains sur les avants bras de Shiva participent du réalisme propre à cette œuvre, par ailleurs typique du style d'Angkor Vat dans l'expression impersonnelle des visages et le traitement quelque peu grossier des pieds.

៥៥_ ព្រះឥសូរនិងព្រះជាយាពីរអង្គ មិនស្គាល់ប្រភព, ស.វ.ទី១២, ថ្មភក់, ១,០១ម, ក៧០៥

ថ្វីត្បិតតែរិចរិលច្រើន គេអាចឃើញស្នាមចំណិតព្រះច័ន្ទនៅលើផ្នួងសក់និងព្រះនេត្រទី៣នៃរូបកណ្តាលដែលជាព្រះឥសូរដែរ។ ទេវីនៅសងខាងអាចជានាងឧមានិងនាងគង្គាដែលជាព្រះជាយាឬសក្តិ។ ប៉ុន្តែដោយកេតនភណ្ឌបាត់បង់ទៅហើយនេះគ្រាន់តែជាការស្មានប៉ុណ្ណោះ។ ផ្នត់សំពត់យ៉ាងល្អិត, ផ្នួងសក់រាងសាជី, ក្បាំងម្កុដឆ្លាក់ស្អេកស្កះជាលក្ខណៈរចនាបថអង្គរវត្ត។ ប៉ុន្តែសក់ព្រះឥសូរក្រងត្រួតគ្នាជាថ្នាក់បង្កើតបានជាបំពង់នោះ ធ្លាប់ឃើញមានតែនៅរចនាបថជំនាន់មុន ដូចជាព្រះឥសូរនិងនាងឧមានៅបន្ទាយស្រីជាដើម (រូបលេខ៣៦)។ ដងខ្លួនទេពទាំងអស់ព្រមទាំងដៃទេវីធ្លាក់តាមលំនាំធម្មជាតិ។ ប៉ុន្តែទឹកមុខដែលស្ងួក ព្រមទាំងជើងដែលខ្លី ហើយដែលត្រង់ក្លឹងផងនោះ បញ្ជាក់ថាជាបដិមានៃសិល្បៈអង្គរវត្ត។

55. シヴァと神妃. 出土地不明、12世紀、砂岩、1.01m、Ka 705

微かに冠に三日月、額に第３眼が残っていることからシヴァ像であることがわかる。両側の女神はしばしばシヴァと一緒に3体で描かれる神妃ウマーとガンガーだと思われるが、持物なしには確定できない。裙の襞、円錐形の宝冠、細かく装飾が施された冠帯などアンコール・ワット様式の特徴だが、シヴァの円柱形の髪髻冠は早期のバンテアイ・スレイ寺院のシヴァとウマー（No.36）の形と類似している。体躯と女神たちの手がシヴァの腕におかれている模様は自然に描かれているが、表情や短縮された足のぎこちななどアンコール・ワット様式に典型的な硬さがみられる。

56. Male divinity. Pursat, 12th C. Bronze, 0.29 m. Ga 5328.

It has been suggested that the combination of the four arms usually associated with Vishnu Chaturbhuja, and the third eye in the forehead that usually implies Shiva, suggests that this deity is the god Harihara. But it is more likely, especially given the fact that all the known depictions of that dual god date from pre-Angkorian times, that this represents Vishnu-Vasudeva-Narayana (see #51), whose third eye indicates his status as a yogin, or yoga master. As in that image, the coiled motif studding the coiffure may be the syllable 'Om'. The identical form of the conical chignon cover surmounting a waisted vertical coiffure can be seen in the Vishnu image in the Angkor Wat relief of the Churning of the Ocean of Milk (South wing, East gallery), where he bestrides Mount Mandara, which forms the fulcrum of the churning process. Jewellery and pleated sampot are cast in remarkably refined fashion, while the sensitivity of face and torso are reminiscent of the delicacy of the preceding Baphuon style rather than the stiffness typical of Angkor Wat facture.

56. Divinité masculine. Pursat, 12ème s. Bronze, 0,29 m. Ga 5328.

L'association de quatre bras, caractérisant souvent Vishnu, et d'un troisième œil frontal, normalement réservé à Shiva, a conduit à identifier cette œuvre comme représentant le dieu Harihara. Selon des études récentes, toutefois, il semble plus vraisemblable - particulièrement parce que presque toutes les représentations connues de Harihara datent de l'époque préangkorienne - que l'on ait ici affaire à Vishnu-Vasudeva-Narayana, dont le troisième œil indiquerait le statut de yogin. Le motif ornant la partie antérieure de la coiffure, quant à lui, pourrait représenter la syllabe sacrée "OM". La forme générale de la coiffure de cette statuette est identique à celle de la représentation de Vishnu enlaçant le mont Mandara au centre du célèbre bas-relief du barattage de la mer de lait à Angkor Vat (galerie est, aile sud). Les bijoux et le costume plissé sont réalisés avec une remarquable finesse; la sensibilité du torse et du visage se laisse plus volontiers comparer au style délicat du Baphuon qu'à l'austère grandeur de celui d'Angkor Vat.

៥៦_ ទេពប្រុស ពោធិ៍សាត់, ស.វ.ទី១២, សំរិត, ០,២៩ម, គ៥៣២៨

គេតែងយល់ថារូបមានដៃ៤ ដែលធម្មតាជាព្រះហស្តព្រះនារាយណ៍ កាលណាមានព្រះនេត្រទី៣នៅលើថ្ងាសដែលជាទីសម្គាល់ព្រះឥសូរនោះ គឺបានជាព្រះហរិហរ។ ប៉ុន្តែរូបនេះគួរយកទៅប្រៀបនឹងរូបលេខ៥១ ដែលបង្ហាញពីព្រះនារាយណ៍ផងមានភ្នែកទី៣ផង (ទំនៀមនេះមានតាំងពីមុនសម័យអង្គរម្ល៉េះ) ដែលឱ្យយើងយល់ថាជាគ្រូសមាធិ។ ចំណុចមួយទៀតដែលដូចគ្នា គឺលើផ្នួងសក់មានសញ្ញា ដែលអាចជាសញ្ញា "ឱម"។ ចំណុចដូចគ្នាមួយទៀត ពោលគឺចុងផ្នួងសក់រាងសាជី គេអាចឃើញនៅរូបព្រះនារាយណ៍មុខភ្នំមន្ទរ លើជញ្ជាំងចម្លាក់អង្គរវត្តត្រង់កន្លែងកូរសមុទ្រទឹកដោះ ។ គ្រឿងអលង្ការនិងផ្នត់សំពត់ធ្វើឡើងយ៉ាងលម្អិតនិងជំនិតជួងក្រៃលែង រីឯទឹកមុខនិងចម្លាក់ដងខ្លួនក៏បែរទៅរកភាពរស់រវើកដូចជំនាន់បាពួនវិញ ពុំដូចមកខាងបដិមាជំនាន់អង្គរវត្ត ដែលច្រើនតែមានភាពទ្រឹង។

56. 男神. ポーサット州、12世紀、ブロンズ、0.29m、Ga 5328

この像はヴィシュヌの特徴である４臂があり、額にシヴァの特徴である第３眼があることからハリハラだと言われてきたが、前アンコール時代からのハリハラ像から判断すると、この像は最高神としてのヴィシュヌ（No.51参照）を表したものだろう。第３眼はヨーガの指導者であることを示しており、編んだ髪の飾りはサンスクリット語オウムの標識だと思われる。円錐形に束ねた髪と垂れ下がっている髪はアンコール・ワットの乳海攪拌のレリーフ（第１回廊東面南より）にみられるヴィシュヌと同じである。宝飾や裙の襞は大変に洗練された形に鋳造されており、また顔や体つきの繊細さはアンコール・ワット様式の硬さより、その前のバプーオン様式の特徴といえる。

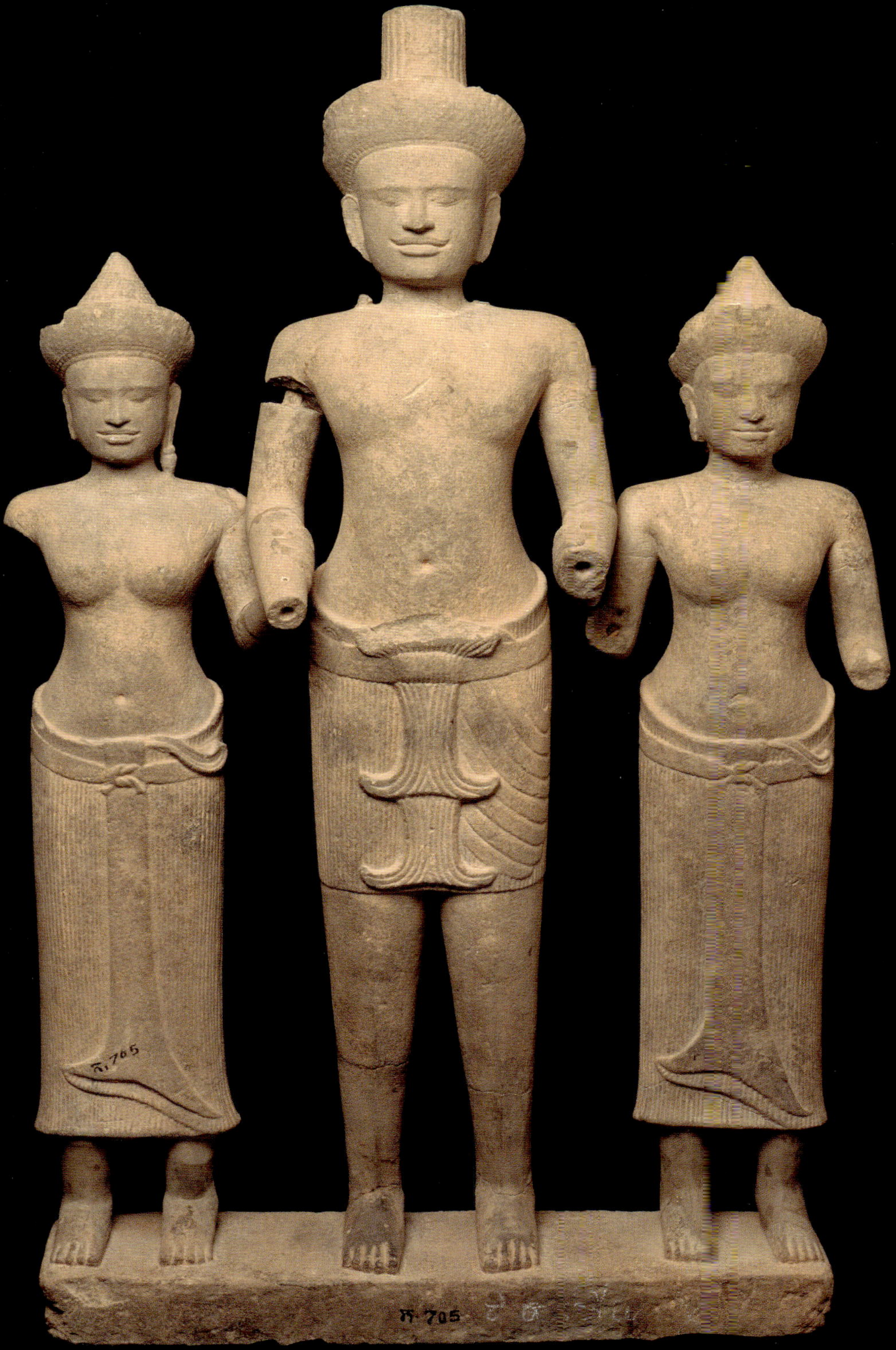

55

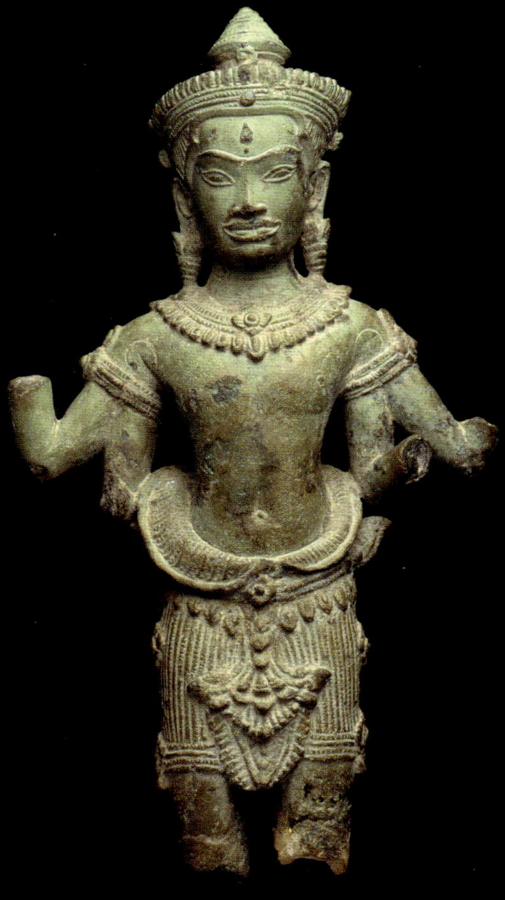

56

57. Adorned Buddha. Angkor Wat, North library, 3rd enclosure, Angkor, Siem Reap, 2nd half 12th C. Bronze, 0.79 m. Ga 2081.

This unusually tall image is an exceptionally fine example of 12th-century bronze casting. Details of the finely moulded face and the intricacy of jewels and belt are matched by the delicacy of the transparent overgarment below which the naturalistic modelling of the slender body is visible. Although earlier representations of the Buddha showed him stripped of jewels and elaborate garments, in the 12th century the tendency developed to present standing versions of the sage in royal guise complete with crown, an association of spiritual with earthly power. The style of the tiara, pectoral ornaments and belt, with its elaborate pendants, conform to Angkor Wat morphology, but the sweetness of the face and the grace of the form are imbued with the spirituality that characterized the art of the Bayon.

៥៧- ព្រះពុទ្ធទ្រង់គ្រឿង អង្គរវត្ត, ហោត្រៃខាងជើង, ផ្លាទី៣, អង្គរវត្ត, សៀមរាប, ផ្នែកទី២នៃស.វ.ទី១២, សំរិត, ០,៧៩ម, គ ២០៨១

នេះជាឧទាហរណ៍រូបសំរិតនៅស.វ.ទី១២ ដែលមានទំហំធំប្លែកជម្មតា ធ្វើឡើងដោយសម្អិតសម្អាងខ្លាំង។ ទាំងព្រះភក្ត្រទាំងគ្រឿងអលង្ការ មានខ្សែក្រវាត់ជាដើម គឺសុទ្ធសឹងធ្វើឡើងយ៉ាងសម្រាំង សមគ្នានឹងស្បង់ចីពរស្តើងគ្របដណ្តប់លើកាយរាងស្រឡូន ដែលលេចច្បាស់ចេញពីក្នុង។ ពីមុនមកព្រះពុទ្ធទ្រង់គ្រឿង ប្រកបដោយអលង្ការនិងស្បង់ចីពរក៏មានដែរ។ តែនៅស.វ.ទី១២ ទំនោរទូទៅ គឺព្រះអង្គទ្រង់ឈរ, ព្រះពស្ត្ររបៀបស្តេច, ទ្រង់មកុដ, ដែលឆ្លុះបញ្ចាំងពីភាពរមួតចូលគ្នានៃពុទ្ធចក្រនិងអាណាចក្រ។ មកុដ, ស្រង់ក, វត្ថពន្ធ, រយ៉ាមានចម្លាក់ល្អិត, សុទ្ធសឹងជាចំណុចសម្គាល់សិល្បៈអង្គរវត្ត។ ប៉ុន្តែទីនេះ ព្រះភក្ត្រដែលមានទឹកដម និងរាងកាយស្រឡូន បង្ហាញពីភាពស្រគត់ស្រគំ ដែលជាលក្ខណៈសិល្បៈបាយ័ន្ត។

57. Buddha paré. Angkor Vat, bibliothèque nord, 3ème enceinte, Angkor, Siem Reap, 2ème moitié du 12ème s. Bronze, 0,79 m. Ga 2081.

Cette sculpture de grande dimension est un des exemples les plus exceptionnels de l'art du bronze au 12ème siècle. Les détails du visage et la finesse des bijoux et de la ceinture le disputent à la délicatesse du vêtement monastique diaphane sous lequel transparaît le modelé naturel du corps. Si l'on rencontre des représentations du Buddha paré avant le 12ème siècle, c'est à cette époque que ce type d'iconographie se développe plus particulièrement. Le Bienheureux est représenté debout, revêtu des insignes de la royauté - parmi lesquels une couronne -, symboles de l'association du pouvoir spirituel et du pouvoir temporel. Le diadème, le pectoral et la ceinture, avec ses riches pendeloques, sont conformes à la typologie des parures du style d'Angkor Vat. La douceur du visage et l'élégance des formes relèvent de la spiritualité propre à l'art du Bayon (fin du 12ème - début du 13ème siècle).

57. 荘厳されたブッダ. シエムリエップ州、アンコール、アンコール・ワット第１回廊内の北経蔵、12世紀後半、ブロンズ、0.79m、Ga 2081

この像は珍しく大きいが、12世紀ブロンズ鋳造の大変に優れた作例である。細かい表情や装身具の細工、透き通った大衣の下にはほっそりした体躯が自然に描かれている。それ以前のブッダは一切装身具を身につけない姿で表されたが、12世紀には王としてのブッダを表すようになり、冠は地上での権力を示している。にぎやかな冠帯、頸飾、帯飾りはアンコール・ワット様式の特徴だが、優しい顔や全体の優雅さはバイヨン様式の特徴であるスピリチュアリティーに溢れている。

58. Adorned Buddha on naga. Thap Banh It ("Silver Towers"), Binh Dinh, Vietnam, 3rd quarter 12th C. Bronze, 0.46 m. Ga 3296.

The richness of the depiction of jewels, crown and garment in this elegant though damaged image of the meditating Buddha seated on the coils of the naga Muchilinda is remarkable, as are the minutely detailed scales and the seven expressive heads that project from the serpent's raised hood. As in #47 and #49, the iconography alludes to the legend of the naga's protection of the sage as he meditated during a seven-day rainstorm. This presentation of the Buddha is one of the most frequently encountered in Khmer art, particularly in the 12th and 13th centuries. The sculpture's provenance from Binh Dinh, formerly Vijaya, the capital of the Cham kingdom (in what is now Central Vietnam), the long-term enemy of the Khmer empire, gives an insight into the region's history. During the reign of Jayavarman VII (1181-?1218) the Khmer dominated Champa between 1190 and 1203, and this image of the Buddha was probably taken there during that time. The small box in the Buddha's lap suggests that this is Bhaishajyaguru, or the Medicine Buddha, who is associated with Jayavarman's stated compassion for the health of his people.

៥៨- ព្រះពុទ្ធទ្រង់គ្រឿងប្រក់នាគ "តួប៉មប្រាក់" ប៊ិញឌិញ, វៀតណាម, ផ្នែកខាងក្រោយនៃស.វ.ទី១២, សំរិត, ០,៤៦ម, គ ៣២៩៦

រូបនេះខូចខាតខ្លះ ប៉ុន្តែនៅឃើញក្បាច់អលង្ការ, មកុដ, ស្បង់ចីពរយ៉ាងល្អិត។ នេះគឺព្រះពុទ្ធទ្រង់គ្រឿង សមាធិនៅលើរង្វេលនាគមុចិលិន្ទ ដែលក្បាលទាំង៧មានភាពរស់រវើក ហើយពោរពេញទៅដោយក្បូរក្បាច់។ រឿងពាក់ព័ន្ធនោះបានរៀបរាប់សម្រាប់រូបលេខ៤៧និង៤៩រួចហើយ។ រូបប្រភេទនេះសម្បូណ៌ណាស់នៅក្នុងសិល្បៈខ្មែរ ជាពិសេសនៅស.វ.ទី១២និង១៣។ ប្រភពដែលបានមកគឺប៊ិញឌិញ, ពីមុនហៅ "វិជ័យ", ជារាជធានីនគរចាម្ប (វៀតណាមភាគកណ្តាល) ដែលធ្លាប់មានសង្គ្រាមញឹកញាប់ជាមួយខ្មែរ។ ជំនាន់ព្រះបាទជ័យវរ្ម័នទី៧ ខ្មែរត្រួតត្រាចាម្បពីឆ្នាំ១១៩០ដល់១២០៣។ បដិមានេះប្រហែលនាំយកទៅស្រុកចាម្បសម័យនោះ។ វត្ថុតូចក្នុងព្រះហស្តនេះ ប្រហែលបញ្ជាក់ថាជាព្រះពុទ្ធអង្គដែលជា "គ្រូថ្នាំ"។

58. Buddha paré protégé par le naga. Thap Banh It ("Tours d'argent"), Binh Dinh, Vietnam, 3ème quart du 12ème s. Bronze, 0,46 m. Ga 3296.

La richesse de traitement des bijoux, de la couronne et du vêtement de cet élégant Buddha assis en méditation sur le corps enroulé du naga Muchilinda est remarquable, tout comme sont exceptionnellement expressives les sept têtes dressées du serpent. À l'instar des #47 et 49, cette image fait allusion à l'épisode de la vie du Buddha au cours duquel le naga Muchilinda offrit sa protection au Saint Homme, au cours d'un terrible orage qui devait durer sept jours. Cette iconographie est particulièrement fréquente aux 12ème et 13ème siècles au Cambodge. Le lieu de provenance de cette sculpture - la province du Binh Dinh, où se trouvait l'une des anciennes capitales du Champa, Vijaya, - apporte d'intéressantes informations sur l'histoire de la région. En effet, le royaume cham, ennemi de longue date de son grand voisin khmer, fut un temps soumis à la tutelle du Cambodge sous le règne de Jayavarman VII (1181 - 1218?). Les Khmers, en effet, ont occupé le pays de 1190 à 1203, et il est probable que cette sculpture est arrivée au Champa à cette époque. Le petit récipient tenu dans le giron permet d'identifier cette image comme une représentation de Bhaishajyaguru, le Buddha de médecine, associé au souci que le roi prenait de la santé de son peuple.

58. ナーガの上のブッダ. ヴェトナム、ビン・ディン省、銀塔、12世紀第３四半期、ブロンズ、0.46m、Ga 3296

損傷しているが、とぐろを巻いたナーガの上で瞑想するブッダの宝飾、冠、衣の描き方、ナーガの７頭の豊かな表情や細かく描かれた鱗など素晴らしい出来である。No.47、49同様、これはナーガがブッダを7日間の大雨から守った伝説を描いたものだ。クメール美術では好んでこの姿が描かれるが、特に12、13世紀に好まれた。この像はクメール王国の宿敵であるチャンパ王国（現在のヴェトナム中部）の首都ヴィジャヤ（現在のビン・ディン）からのものであり、地域の歴史の洞察に役立つ。ジャヤヴァルマン７世時代（1181~1218年？）、1190~1203年にかけてクメール王国がチャンパを支配した。このブッダ像は当時、チャンパから持ち込まれたのだろう。ブッダの膝上の小さい箱から、この像は人民の健康を思いやるジャヤヴァルマン７世に結びつけた薬師如来を表していると思われる。

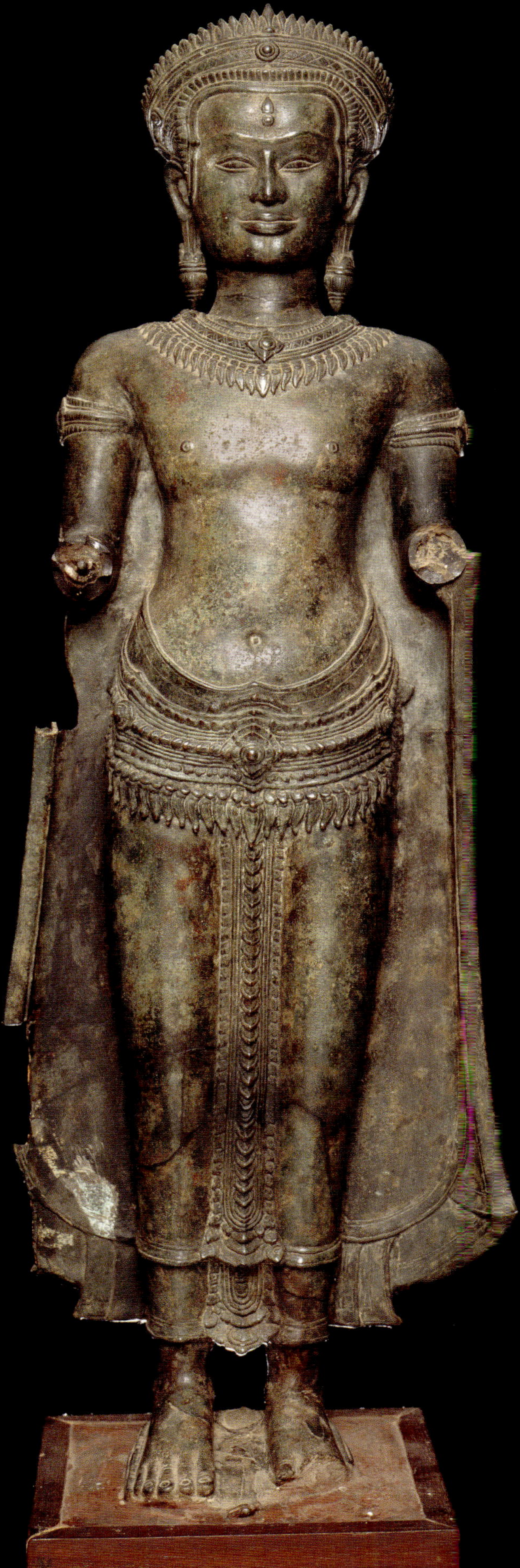

57

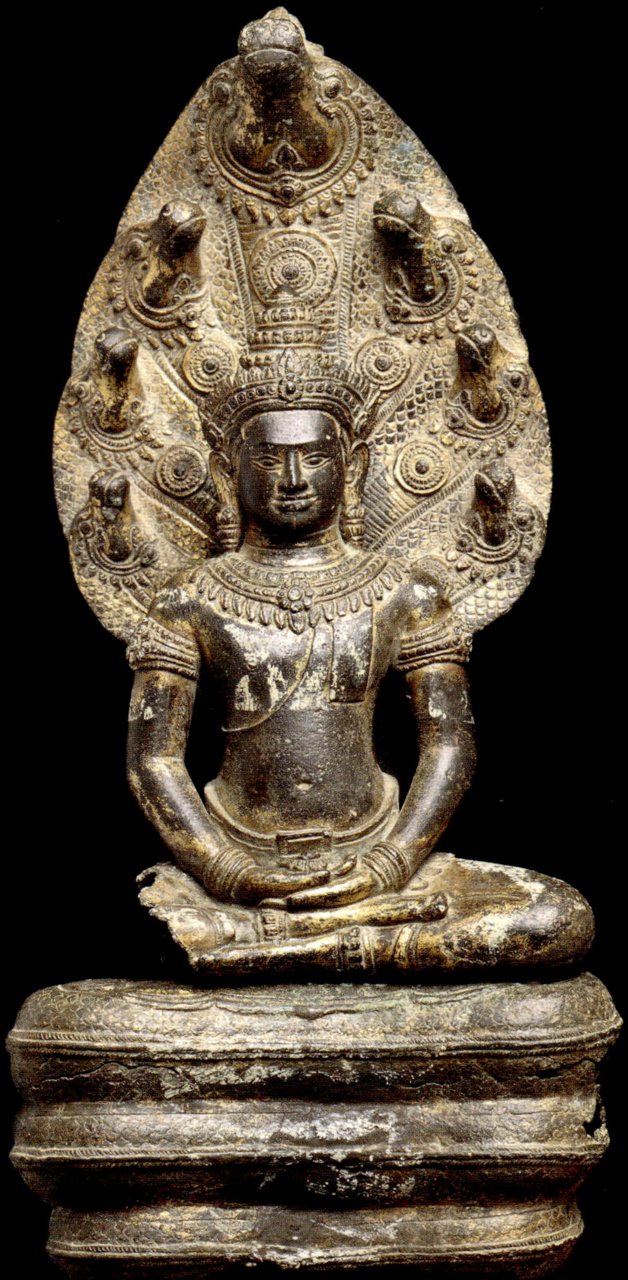

58

59. Incense burner in lotus form. Danrun, Mongkol Borei, Battambang, 12th C. Bronze, 0.24 x 0.32 m. Ga 5730.

Khmer bronze artists produced a great variety of models for the incense burners that were ubiquitous in religious ceremonies (see #72). The absence of sacred figures with prescribed attributes left the creator free to experiment with form and imagery. This graceful lotus, symbol of purity, with undulating stem, is among the most original versions of ritual objects in Khmer art. Abstracted makara heads encircle the stalks as they rise from the two lotus-pad bases of the vessel, while a five-headed naga springs from the same node as the open blossom, reinforcing connections with the realm of water and its associations with fertility

59. Brûle-parfum en forme de lotus. Danrun, Mongkol Borei, Battambang, 12ème s. Bronze, 0,24 x 0,32 m. Ga 5730.

Les brûle-parfum, objets omniprésents dans les cérémonies religieuses, ont souvent été traités de manière originale par les bronziers khmers. Dans le cas d'œuvres ne présentant pas une iconographie spécifique, comme ici, les artistes pouvaient donner libre cours à leur fantaisie. Cet élégant lotus, symbole de pureté, avec sa tige ondulante ornée de têtes de monstres et le petit naga qui semble s'échapper de la corolle, est l'une des pieces métalliques les plus originales de tout l'art khmer. Il souligne l'étroite symbiose entre certains animaux du bestiaire ancien – le naga, un symbole des eaux – et la fertilité – représentée ici par le lotus lui-même.

៥៩_ ភាជន៍ដុតគ្រឿងក្រអូប (?) រាងផ្ការំចង់ ដានរុន, មង្គលបុរី, បាត់ដំបង, ស.វ.ទី១២, សំរិត, ០,២៤ម × ០,៣២, គ ៥៧៣០

សិល្បៈសំរឹតបុរាណមានផលិតវត្ថុច្រើនបែបច្រើនយ៉ាងសម្រាប់ការបូជា ដូចជាភាជន៍ដុតគ្រឿងក្រអូបជាដើម (សូមមើលរូបលេខ៧២)។ វត្ថុនេះគ្មានរូបទេពអ្វីមួយឡើយ ដូច្នេះជាងស្មិតអាចរចនាក្បូរក្បាច់តាមចិត្តខ្លួនច្រើន។ ផ្ការំចង់ដ៏ពិចិត្រដែលបង្ហាញពីភាពឥតមន្ទិលនេះ មានដើមពត់ពែនល្អប្លែក។ នៅគល់ដើមទាំងពីរមានរូបម្ករដែលហាក់ដូចជាខ្ទាក់ដើមនោះចេញមក រីឯនៅគល់ទងផ្កាមានរូបនាគក្បាល៥ពត់ពែនចេញមកដែរ។ នាគនេះមានន័យខ្លាំងណាស់ ត្បិតជានិមិត្តរូបនៃទឹកនិងភោគផល។

59. 蓮の香炉. バッタンバーン州、モンコル・ボレイ、ダンルン、12世紀、ブロンズ、高0.24m、長0.32m、Ga 5730

クメールのブロンズ作家たちは、宗教儀式には欠かせない香炉をさまざまな形で制作した（No.72参照）。決められた特徴がある聖像から解放され、形態やイメージを自由に表現したのである。清らかさの象徴であるこの蓮には波上の花柄がついており、クメール美術の宗教儀式用具の中でも、もっともオリジナルな作例である。抽象化された怪魚マカラの頭部が茎を囲み、５頭の蛇ナーガが開花した蓮華と同じ節から出ており、水と肥沃さの関係を強調している。

60. Finial with Buddha on naga. River near Kas Prag, Banteay Cha, Kompong Cham, late 12th-early 13th C. Bronze, 0.495 m. Ga 5593.

Bronze fitments like this were made to decorate the ends of poles on chariots or palanquins, lending a religious identity to objects not intrinsically sacred. Examples can be seen on chariots in the reliefs of Angkor Wat and other temples, where gods, kings, and generals are depicted in procession or battle. This example is typical of such accoutrements in being cast in several parts. Its morphology conforms to the style of the Bayon, though somewhat formalized in the treatment of the naga's coils, which are reduced to a wedge shape tapering to the socket of the finial's attachment to the pole, and of the radiating hood, where details of the serpent's seven heads are subsumed into a leaf or fan shape that suggests an aureole.

60. Extrémité de palanquin représentant le Buddha protégé par le naga. Rivière près de Kas Prag, Banteay Cha, Kompong Cham, fin 12ème - début 13ème s. Bronze, 0,495 m. Ga 5593.

Des pièces comme celle-ci servaient à décorer les extrémités de hampe ou de palanquin. Elles conféraient un caractère religieux à des objets dont la nature n'était pas intrinsèquement sacrée. Divers exemples de ce type figurent dans les scènes de procession ou de bataille des bas-reliefs d'Angkor Vat ou d'autres temples. Ces objets sont généralement composés de plusieurs éléments. Celui-ci appartient au style du Bayon en dépit du traitement un peu sec du corps enroulé du naga et de ses têtes inscrites dans une ogive en forme d'éventail ou de feuille évoquant une auréole.

៦០_ គ្រឿងបំពាក់មានព្រះពុទ្ធរូបប្រក់នាគ តំបន់កោះប្រាក់, បន្ទាយចា, កំពង់ចាម, ចុងស.វ.ទី១២_ដើមស.វ.ទី១៣, សំរិត, ០,៤៩៥ម, គ ៥៥៩៣

វត្ថុអំពីសំរិតបៀបនេះ គេធ្វើឡើងដើម្បីតុបតែងលំអចុងជន្ទោលរទេះឬគ្រែស្នែងហាក់ដូចជាបំពាក់របស់ប្រើប្រាស់ជាធម្មតាឱ្យមានលក្ខណៈជាសាសនា។ គេអាចឃើញឧបករណ៍ខ្លះៗនៅលើរូបរទេះ លើជញ្ជាំងចម្លាក់អង្គរវត្ត ឬប្រាសាទដទៃទៀតដែលគេតែងឃើញមានទេពនានា, ព្រះរាជាឬមេទ័ពនៅក្នុងក្បួនដង្ហែអ្វីមួយ។ ឧទាហរណ៍ដែលយើងមាននេះគឺជាផ្នែកមួយនៃវត្ថុដែលគេសិតជាច្រើនផ្នែក។ បើមើលតាមរូបរាងគឺនៅក្នុងរចនាបថបាយ័ន្ត ប៉ុន្តែអ្វីៗក៏បង្ហាញឡើងដោយសង្ខេប គឺរង្វេលពស់ក៏មិនច្រើនជាន់ ហើយមកជាប់នឹងរង្វេលបំពង់ រីឯពពារនាគដែលបញ្ចេញក្បាល៧ក៏សង្ខេបមកជាទម្រង់ស្លឹកឈើ ឬផ្លិតអ្វីមួយ។

60. ナーガの上のブッダ（飾り金具）. コンポンチャム州、バンテアイ・チャー、コッ・プラッ村の川岸、12世紀末~13世紀初頭、ブロンズ、0.495m、Ga 5593

この様なブロンズの金具は輿などの棒の装飾用であり、宗教的なイメージは神聖さを失っている。アンコール・ワットやその他の寺院の神、王、将軍が行進している様子や戦闘場面のレリーフにその例が見られる。この飾り金具は典型的で部分別に鋳造された。バイヨン様式だが、ナーガのとぐろは形式化されており、ソケット部分に向けて細くなっている。一方、７頭は扇形になり、後光となっている。

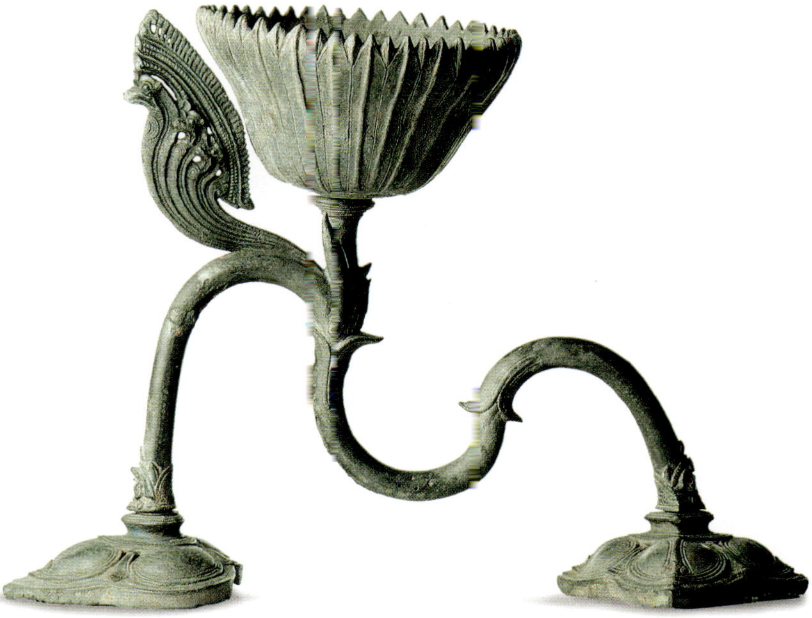

59

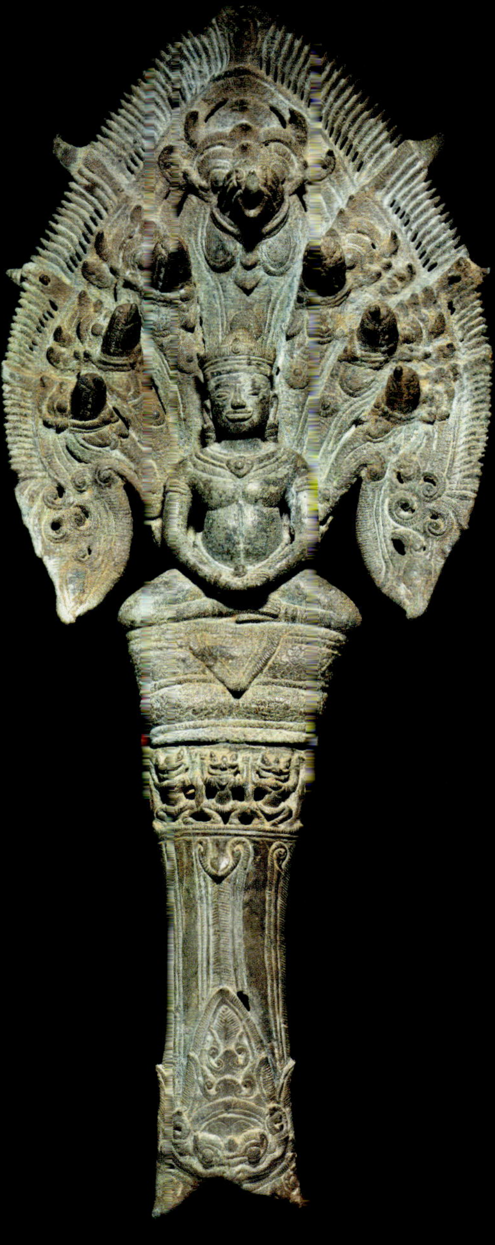

60

61. Head of Jayavarman VII. Bakan (formerly Preah Khan), Kompong Svay, Kompong Thom, late 12th-early 13th C. Sandstone, 0.415 m. Ka 989.

This head of King Jayavarman VII is possibly the most famous Khmer image in existence. It is the most beautiful of many such sculptures that were distributed throughout the Khmer realm in the late 12th and early 13th centuries; several were found in present-day Thailand. Their unmistakable features make it certain that this is genuinely a portrait. The representation is of a deeply reflective and spiritual being. All traces of kingly glory have been stripped from the monarch and he is shown with a simple coiffure knotted in ascetic fashion and eyes downcast. Like the Buddha, he wears no crown or ear pendants, projecting simplicity and compassion that accord well with Jayavarman's stated intention to empathize with the sufferings of his people. The gentle expression, naturalistic and deeply humanistic yet exuding quiet strength, expresses the epitome of the Bayon style.

61. Tête de Jayavarman VII. Bakan (Preah Khan), Kompong Svay, Kompong Thom, fin 12ème - début 13ème s. Grès, 0,415 m. Ka 989.

Cette tête du roi Jayavarman VII est sans doute la plus célèbre de toutes les sculptures khmères. Il s'agit de la plus belle pièce d'une série d'images identiques représentant le souverain et retrouvées dans toutes les régions couvertes par l'empire khmer, y compris l'actuelle Thaïlande, à la fin du 12ème siècle et au début du 13ème. Les traits fortement individualisés du visage permettent d'affirmer qu'il s'agissait bien là de portraits. Le roi apparaît comme un personnage de grande intériorité et de haute spiritualité. Toute marque de gloire temporelle est effacée ici: le petit chignon est celui d'un ascète et les yeux sont mi-clos. Tel le Buddha, le souverain ne porte aucun bijou; la simplicité et la compassion qui émanent de ce visage s'accordent bien à l'idée selon laquelle le roi participait des souffrances de son peuple. L'expression douce, naturelle et humaniste, marquée aussi par une sorte de force calme, exprime à merveille l'idéal esthétique qui sous-tend tout le style du Bayon.

៦១_ ព្រះកេសព្រះបាទជ័យវរ្ម័នទី៧ បាកាណ (ហៅប្រឡំថាព្រះខ័ន), កំពង់ស្វាយ, កំពង់ធំ, ចុងស.វ.ទី១២_ដើមស.វ.ទី១៣, ថ្មភក់, ០,៤១៥ម, ក ៩៨៩

នេះជាចម្លាក់ល្អជាងគេក្នុងចំណោមរូបព្រះបាទជ័យវរ្ម័នទី៧ ដែលសាងនៅចុង ស.វ.ទី១២ និងដើមស.វ.ទី១៣។ ចម្លាក់ទាំងនេះមួយភាគឃើញនៅថៃឡង់ដ៍បច្ចុប្បន្ន។ ដោយសារដូចៗគ្នាគ្មានថ្គាំថ្គងកន្លែងណាសោះនោះ យើងយល់ថានេះជារូបឆ្លាក់ចម្លងតាមព្រះរាជាពិត។ ព្រះរាជាដែលគេដឹងថាជាអ្នកចម្បាំងខ្លាំងក្លានៅទីនេះពុំឃើញដូច្នោះឡើយ គឺគេឃើញជាមនុស្សសាមញ្ញ, ព្រះកេសាក្ងួចជាកំប៉ោយ, ឥរិយាបថសមាធិ, ព្រះនេត្រសម្លឹងចុះមកក្រោម។ ដូចព្រះពុទ្ធអង្គដែរ ព្រះរាជាឥតមានមកុដឬរយ៉ាអ្វីឡើយ ជាការបង្ហាញភាពសាមញ្ញនិងក្ដីករុណាស្របតាមការប្រកាសទឹកព្រះទ័យថា ទុក្ខសោកប្រជារាស្ត្រជាកង្វល់ធំជាងទុក្ខព្រះអង្គផ្ទាល់។ ការបង្ហាញកម្លាំងក្នុងភាពស្ងប់ស្ងាត់នេះជាលក្ខណៈពិសេសនៃសិល្បៈបាយ័ន្ត។

61. ジャヤヴァルマン７世頭部. コンポン・トム州、コンポン・スヴァイ、バカン、12世紀末~13世紀初頭、砂岩、0.415m、Ka 989

ジャヤヴァルマン７世の頭部はクメール美術のイメージの中でも、最も有名である。12世紀末から13世紀初頭にかけてクメール王国中に配置された多くのこの様な石像の中でも最も美しい。一部は現在のタイで発見されている。独特の表情から肖像であることが明らかだ。深く瞑想したスピリチュアルな姿である。王としての装飾は排除し、髪は行者のように頭頂に小さくまとめ、眼は閉じている。ブッダのように、冠や耳飾はつけず、簡素さと思いやりを示している。これはジャヤヴァルマン7世が人民の苦しみに共感する意図を反映している。表情は優しく、自然で人間的で、静かな力強さは典型的バイヨン様式である。

62. Jayavarman VII in meditation. Angkor Thom (head) & Krol Romeas (torso), Siem Reap, late 12th-early 13th C. Sandstone, 1.35 m. Ka 1703.

Like the head of Jayavarman (#61), this representation of the king was distributed throughout his realm and several fragmentary examples survive. This, however, is the great masterpiece. Even more than the king's head, the image has come to symbolize the Khmer kingdom and is deeply revered by the Khmer people, who leave offerings at its base. Its paramount simplicity and the slightly inclined posture and downcast eyes indicate the monarch's detachment from worldly concerns. The naturalistic rendering of musculature, the skeleton visible beneath the skin, and a body somewhat thickened in maturity add to the humanism of the subject. Yet for all its apparent humility, the figure radiates power, an impression augmented by the marked swelling of the abdomen that indicates prana, or the inner breath of spiritual strength.

62. Jayavarman VII. Angkor Thom (tête) & Krol Romeas (torse), Siem Reap, fin 12ème - début 13ème s. Grès, 1,35 m. Ka 1703.

Comme l'œuvre précédente (#61), cette sculpture fait partie d'un groupe dont des exemples, souvent fragmentaires, ont été retrouvés sur l'ensemble du territoire khmer. Il s'agit de la plus belle de toutes. Plus encore que la tête de Preah Khan, cette statue est un symbole pour le peuple cambodgien. Elle est l'objet d'une véritable vénération et les visiteurs n'hésitent pas à déposer diverses offrandes devant son socle. L'extrême simplicité de l'œuvre, mais aussi la posture légèrement penchée vers l'avant et les yeux mi-clos soulignent le détachement des choses de ce monde auquel avait atteint le monarque. Le rendu naturaliste de la musculature d'un corps quelque peu alourdi dans sa maturité ajoute à l'humanisme du sujet. Cependant, en dépit de son apparente humilité, le personnage dégage une forte impression de puissance, d'autant plus sensible que le relâchement de l'abdomen traduit avec beaucoup d'acuité la notion de prana, le souffle vital, vecteur de force spirituelle.

៦២_ ព្រះបាទជ័យវរ្ម័នទី៧សមាធិ អង្គរធំ (ព្រះកេស), ក្រោលរមាស (ខ្លួន), សៀមរាប, ចុងស.វ.ទី១២_ដើមស.វ.ទី១៣, ថ្មភក់, ១,៣៥ម, ក ១៧០៣

ដូចជាបដិមាលេខ៦១ដែរ រូបព្រះរាជានេះតម្កល់នៅគ្រប់ទិសទី ថ្វីបើសំណល់នៅតែបន្តិចបន្តួចក៏ដោយ។ នេះជាស្នាដៃយ៉ាងធំមួយពិត។ សព្វថ្ងៃប្រជាជនខ្មែរតែងគោរពបូជា ជូនកាលមានទាំងដង្វាយផង។ ព្រះរូបនេះមានភាពសាមញ្ញបំផុត។ ព្រះកាយឈ្ងោកមកមុខបន្តិច, ព្រះនេត្រសម្លឹងមកក្រោម បញ្ជាក់ថាព្រះរាជាលែងវិលវល់ជំពាក់ព្រះទ័យនឹងលោកិយទៀតហើយ។ ចម្លាក់សាច់ដុំមានលំនាំតាមធម្មជាតិ, ឆ្អឹងលេចចេញពីក្រោមស្បែកនៅកន្លែងខ្លះ, ដងខ្លួនដែលរីកឡើងទៅតាមវ័យ... សុទ្ធសឹងបង្ហាញពីព្រះរាជាតាមរូបពិត។ ប៉ុន្តែទោះមើលទៅឃើញថាមានភាពទន់ភ្លន់ក្ដី ក៏បដិមានេះហាក់បង្ហាញអនុភាពដែលជះសាយឡើង ពិសេសពោះរាងធំនោះជាសញ្ញានៃ "ប្រាណ" ពោលគឺដង្ហើមចូលដែលភ្ជាប់នឹងពលំផ្លូវចិត្ត។

62. 瞑想するジャヤヴァルマン７世. シエムリエップ州、頭部：アンコール・トム、トルソ：クロル・ロメアス、12世紀末~13世紀初頭、砂岩、1.35m、Ka 1703

ジャヤヴァルマン７世の頭部（No.61 ）同様、この王が瞑想する姿を描いた石像は王国中に設置され、その断片が残っているが、偉大な傑作である。この坐像彫刻は頭部以上にクメール王国を象徴するイメージで、現在でも崇敬されており、奉献物が捧げられている。質素さ、少し上体を曲げた姿勢、閉じた眼は世俗の煩わしさから超然とした態度を表している。自然な筋肉、肌下の骨、成熟していくらかふっくりした体躯など人間らしさが溢れている。謙遜した姿でありながら、権力を感じさせる。胸の厚みは精神的力を象徴する内なる力（プラナ）を示している。

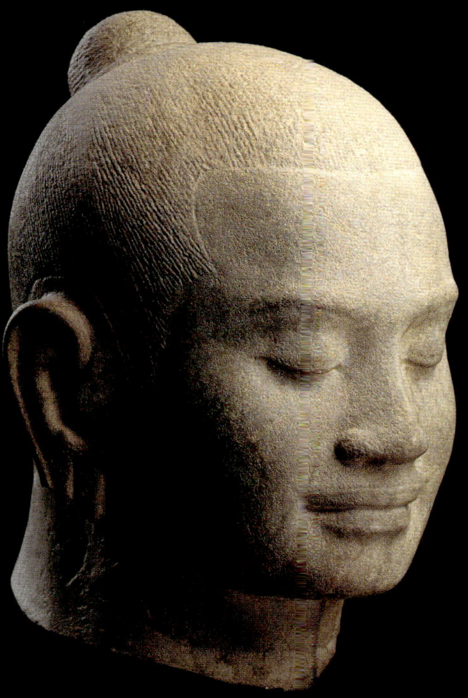

61

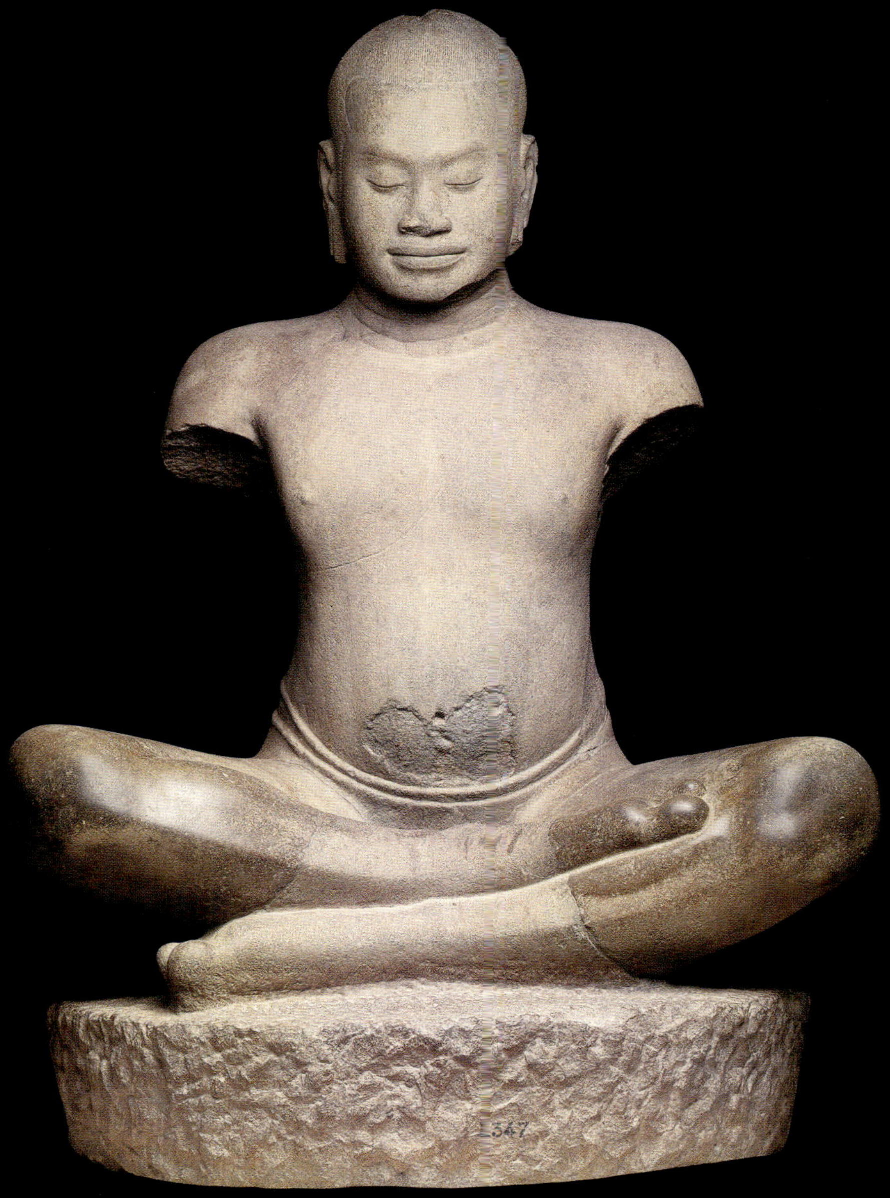

62

63. Prajñaparamita (?) as a child. A bush, north of Angkor Thom, Siem Reap, late 12th-early 13th C. Sandstone, 0.945 m. Ka 1691.

The strong resemblance of the face of this child to the faces in portrait heads of Jayavarman VII suggest that it could be a portrait of a relative, perhaps a daughter. Her possible representation as the bodhisattva Prajñaparamita, the Buddhistic representation of transcendental wisdom, accords with the increasing importance of this deity, along with the bodhisattva of compassion, Lokeshvara, and the Buddha himself, as Mahayana Buddhism predominated as the state religion during the reign of Jayavarman VII. Identifying royal personages with divine beings was known in Brahmanistic times, but images like this child, and of Jayavarman's first consort, Jayarajadevi, possibly in the guise of the bodhisattva Tara, demonstrate that the practice was also known in Buddhist kingdoms.

63. Prajñaparamita (?) sous les traits d'une enfant. Un buisson au nord d'Angkor Thom, Siem Reap, fin 12ème-début 13ème s. Grès, 0,945 m. Ka 1691.

La grande ressemblance du visage de cette petite fille avec celui de Jayavarman VII suggère qu'il pourrait s'agir d'une parente du roi ou même d'un de ses enfants. Sa figuration en tant que Prajñaparamita, divinité bouddhique incarnant la connaissance suprême, souligne l'importance de cette déesse dans le bouddhisme mahayanique d'État de Jayavarman VII. Elle y occupe une place majeure, aux côtés du bodhisattva de la compassion, Lokeshvara, et du Buddha lui-même. L'usage d'identifier des personnages royaux avec des divinités était bien connu à l'époque où prédominait le brahmanisme; des œuvres comme celle-ci ou encore les représentation de la première épouse du souverain, la reine Jayarajadevi, vraisemblablement figurée sous les traits de la déesse Tara, attestent le même usage dans le bouddhisme.

៦៣_ ប្រាជ្ញាបារមី (?) ក្នុងវ័យក្មេង គុម្ពោតមួយខាងជើងអង្គរធំ, សៀមរាប, ចុងស.វ.ទី១២_ដើមស.វ.ទី១៣, ថ្មភក់, ០,៩៤៥ម, ក ១៦៩១

ព្រះភក្ត្រនៃបដិមានេះដូចគ្នានឹងព្រះបាទជ័យវរ្ម័នទី៧ខ្លាំងណាស់ ជាហេតុឱ្យយើងគិតថាអាចជាសមាជិកណាមួយនៃព្រះញាតិវង្ស ឬជាបុត្រីព្រះរាជាផងក៏មិនដឹង។ ម្យ៉ាងទៀតរូបនេះអាចបង្ហាញឡើងក្រោមរូបភាពព្រះពោធិសត្វប្រាជ្ញាបារមី ដែលជំនាន់នោះគេនិយមកាន់តែខ្លាំងទៅៗ ព្រមជាមួយគ្នានឹងព្រះលោកេស្វរដែលជាព្រះពោធិសត្វមានករុណា និងព្រះពុទ្ធអង្គតែម្តង។ ការភ្ជាប់ខ្លួននៃព្រះញាតិវង្សទៅនឹងទេពនានា ជាទំនៀមដែលមានមកតាំងពីព្រហ្មញ្ញសាសនាមកម្ល៉េះ ប៉ុន្តែរូបដូចជាក្មេងស្រីនេះ ព្រមទាំងរូបព្រះនាងជ័យរាជទេវី ដែលជាព្រះអគ្គមហេសី ហើយដែលបង្ហាញឡើងក្រោមរូបភាពព្រះពោធិសត្វ "តារា" បង្ហាញថាទំនៀមនេះគេនិយមដែរនៅនគរផ្សេងៗដែលកាន់ព្រះពុទ្ធសាសនា។

63. 女尊. シエムリエップ州、アンコール・トム北の森、12世紀末~13世紀初頭、砂岩、0.945m、Ka 1691

この子供の顔はジャヤヴァルマン７世の頭部の表情と大変に似ており、ジャヤヴァルマン７世の親族、恐らく娘の肖像と思われる。像は諸仏の母で知恵を象徴する菩薩プラジュニャーパーラミター（般若波羅蜜多）を表しているようだ。この菩薩はローケーシュヴァラ（観世音菩薩）とブッダとともに、ジャヤヴァルマン７世時代に大乗仏教が国教になると、その重要性を増した。国教がヒンズー教の時代から王族を神になぞらえることはあったし、子供やジャヤヴァルマン７世の第一王妃ジャヤラージャデーヴィーをターラー（菩薩）として描くような王族の神格化は他の仏教王国にもみられた。

64. Prajñaparamita with eleven heads. Koh Kong, 2nd half 12th C. Bronze, 0.134 m. Ga 5333.

Stylistically this dynamic figure is consistent with the meticulously cast bronzes of the Bayon style, with strongly individualized facial features, elaborate jewellery and pleated skirt cloth. Images of Prajñaparamita, who is identified by the meditating figure of the Buddha Amitabha seated in her headdress, were common in Tantric Buddhist practices of the late twelfth century, where the enlightenment of the bodhisattva of transcendental wisdom was invoked to assist the meditator in the search for perfection. The attributes in her radiating twenty-two arms cannot be deciphered but they would have been aids in concentration. The representation of her eleven heads, with seven in the lower row (six of them uniquely in profile) and four, gazing in the four cardinal directions, on the upper, is unusual. Numbers are significant in Buddhist iconography, and the eleven heads are perhaps symbolic of certain practices in the search for enlightenment.

64. Prajñaparamita à onze têtes. Koh Kong, 2ème moitié du 12ème s. Bronze, 0,134 m. Ga 5333.

Cette statuette complexe est caractéristique des œuvres en bronze du style du Bayon, avec leurs visages fortement individualisés, leurs bijoux somptueux et leurs vêtements plissés. Les représentations de Prajñaparamita - que l'on reconnaît ici grâce à l'image du Buddha Amitabha assis en méditation dans sa coiffure - sont fréquentes dans l'art du bouddhisme tantrique à la fin du 12ème siècle, où la déesse de la connaissance suprême était invoquée par l'officiant dans la recherche de la perfection. Les attributs tenus par les vingt-deux mains ne sont pas identifiables; la symbolique qu'ils incarnaient devait aider sur la voie de la concentration. La disposition des onze têtes - sept au registre inférieur (six étant de profil) et quatre, orientées selon les points cardinaux, au registre supérieur - est inhabituelle. Les nombres étant chargés de signification dans les iconographies religieuses, les onze têtes de cette statuette jouaient peut-être un rôle dans certains rituels devant conduire le pratiquant à l'Éveil.

៦៤_ ប្រាជ្ញាបារមីដែលមានព្រះកេស១១ កោះកុង, ផ្នែកទី២នៃស.វ.ទី១២, សំរិត, ០,១៣៤ម, គ ៥៣៣៣

បើគិតតាមរចនាបថ រូបដែលមានចលនារស់រវើកនេះនៅក្នុងសម័យបាយ័ន្ត។ ព្រះភក្ត្រខុសគ្នាពីមួយទៅមួយ, អលង្ការមានក្បូរក្បាច់លម្អិតខ្លាំង, ឯសំពត់ក៏ មានផ្នត់ល្អិតញឹក។ គេដឹងថាជាប្រាជ្ញាបារមីដោយសារមានព្រះពុទ្ធអមិតភទ្រង់ភ្នែននៅផ្នួងសក់។ រូបរបៀបនេះមានជាទូទៅនៅចុងស.វ.ទី១២ ដោយសារពុទ្ធសាសនាប្រភេទ "តន្ត្រ" លើកតម្កើងព្រះពោធិសត្វដែលបានត្រាស់ដឹង ពិសេសពីសំណាក់អ្នកធ្វើសមាធិដែលប៉ងទៅដល់ "បារមី "។ ដៃទាំង២២សុទ្ធសឹងកាន់វត្ថុអ្វីមួយ ដែលកំណត់ថាអ្វីច្បាស់ពុំបាន តែយើងយល់ថាជាឧបករណ៍ជំនួយក្នុងការធ្វើសមាធិ។ ព្រះកេសទាំង១១នេះ គឺ៧នៅជួរក្រោម (ក្នុងនោះ៦ មើលពីចំហៀង, ៤នៅជួរលើសម្លឹងទៅគ្រប់ទិស)។ យើងពុំទាន់យល់ន័យដៃចំនួន១១នោះនៅឡើយទេ។

64. 女尊. ココン州、12世紀後半、ブロンズ、0.134m、Ga 5333

このダイナミックな像は、個別化された表情、細かく細工された宝飾、裙の襞などバイヨン様式のブロンズ鋳造技術で作られた。プラジュニャーパーラミター（般若波羅蜜多）の姿であることは、阿弥陀の化仏を頭部に抱いていることから明らかである。12世紀末の密教仏教でよくみられる知恵の完成を求める瞑想者を助ける菩薩である。22臂の意味は不明だが、瞑想の集中を助ける意味があるのかも知れない。11面は下の７面の6面は左右で3面ずつ半面で、上の４面は四方を見つめているのが珍しい。数字は仏教上意味があり、11面は悟りを開くための修行を象徴しているのであろう。

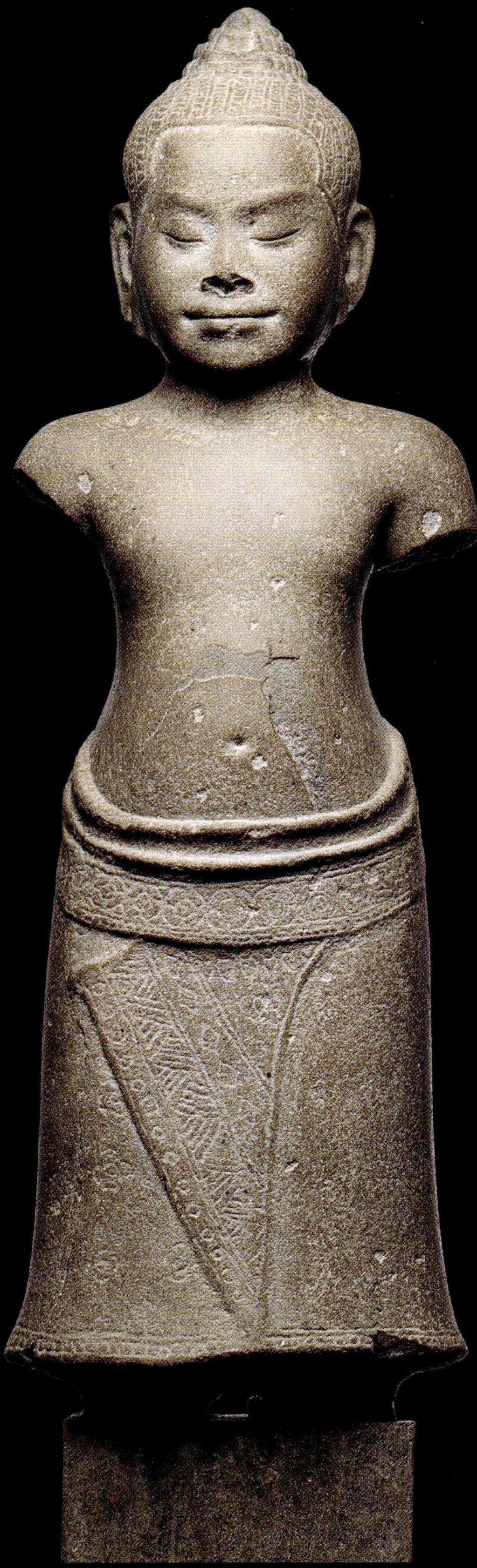

63

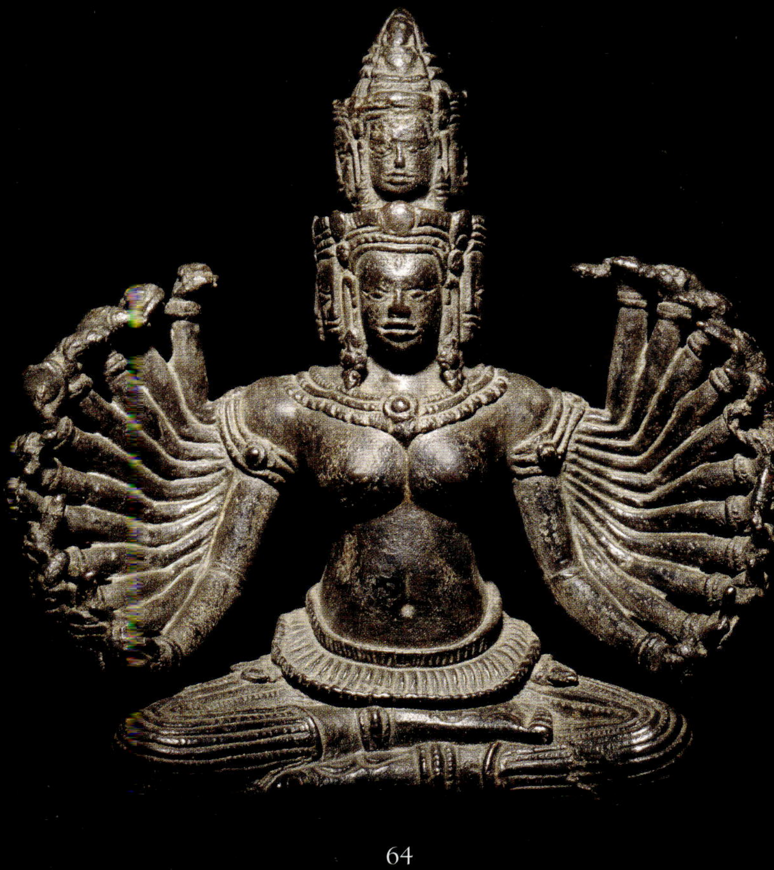

64

65. Adorned Buddha on naga. Anlong Sar, Touk Chor, Battambang, 12th C. Bronze, 0.41 m. Ga 5357.

The iconic perfection of this figure of the Buddha seated in meditation on the coils of the naga is typical of the refinement of bronze casting in the first half of the 12th century. The almond-shaped eyes, broad cheekbones and forehead, as well as the elaborate jewellery, the naturalism of the body and limbs and the benign expression of the face are, however, more characteristic of Bayon style, suggesting a transitional date in mid-century. This representation of the Buddha, its iconography alluding to the protection offered by the naga Muchilinda - whose expressive heads enhance the vitality of the sculpture - when the sage was meditating during a rainstorm, is one of the most frequently created during the 12th century in Cambodia (see also #47, 58),

65. Buddha paré protégé par le naga. Anlong Sar, Touk Chor, Battambang, 12ème s. Bronze, 0,41 m. Ga 5357.

La perfection de cette représentation du Buddha assis en méditation sur le corps enroulé du naga est propre aux bronzes réalisés au cours de la première moitié du 12ème siècle. Les yeux en amande, la largeur du visage, ainsi que les bijoux, le modelé naturel du corps et l'expression bienveillante du visage, en revanche, semblent plus caractéristiques de l'époque de Jayavarman VII, permettant d'envisager pour cette pièce une datation vers le milieu du 12ème siècle, à la transition de l'art d'Angkor Vat et de l'art du Bayon. Comme les #47 et 58, cette image se rapporte à l'épisode de la vie du Buddha au cours duquel il fut protégé par le naga Muchilinda - dont les sept têtes expressives renforcent ici la vitalité de l'œuvre - alors qu'il méditait pendant un terrible orage. Il s'agit de l'un des types iconographiques les plus fréquents dans l'art khmer au 12ème siècle.

៦៥_ ព្រះពុទ្ធទ្រង់គ្រឿងប្រក់នាគ អន្លង់ស, ទឹកជោរ, បាត់ដំបង, ស.វ.ទី១២, សំរិត, ០,៤១ម, គ ៥៣៥៧

ព្រះពុទ្ធទ្រង់សមាធិនៅលើរង្វេលនាគនេះ គេសិតឡើងដោយសម្អិតសម្អាងជាទីបំផុត ដូចជារូបសំរិតទូទៅនៅផ្នែកទី១នៃស.វ.ទី១២ដូច្នោះដែរ។ ភ្នែករាងទ្រវែងបញ្ចូចនៅខាងចុងមុខ, ថ្ពាសទូលាយ, អលង្ការក្បូរក្បាច់ស្អែកស្កះ, ទឹកមុខ, រាងកាយបង្ហាញឡើងតាមលំនាំធម្មជាតិ, ទាំងនេះសុទ្ធសឹងមានទំនោរទៅរចនាបថបាយ័ន្ត ធ្វើឱ្យយើងគិតថាប្រហែលជាសាងឡើងនៅរវាងពាក់កណ្តាលស.វ.ទី១២។ បដិមាដែលជាព្រះពុទ្ធប្រក់ដោយនាគមុចិលិន្ទ (នៅទីនេះនាគហាក់ដូចជារស់រវើក) នៅពេលដែលព្រះអង្គធ្វើសមាធិក្រោមព្យុះភ្លៀងរបៀបនេះ គេនិយមណាស់នៅស.វ.ទី១២ (ចូរមើលរូបលេខ ៤៧និង៥៨)។

65. ナーガの上のブッダ. バッタンバーン州、トゥク・チョル、アンロン・サル、12世紀、ブロンズ、0.41m、Ga 5357

このとぐろを巻いたナーガの上で瞑想する完璧なブッダは12世紀前半のブロンズの優れた鋳造技術の典型である。しかし、杏仁形の眼、幅広い頬と額、にぎやかな宝飾、体躯と手足の自然さ、温和な表情はバイヨン様式の特徴であり、12世紀半ばの変遷期に作られたと考えられる。ナーガの表情豊かな頭によって、この像は生き生きとしている。ナーガに守られた瞑想中のブッダ像は、12世紀に最も頻繁に作られた像の1つである（No.47、58参照）

66. Buddhistic triad. Prei Monti, Roluos, Siem Reap, late 12th-early 13th C. Bronze, 0.545 m. Ga 2424, Ga 5470.

Buddhistic triads proliferated in Cambodia in the 12th century when Mahayana Buddhism began to dominate Khmer society. The meditating Buddha, seated on an open lotus on the naga's coiled body, holds what is probably a small medicine box in his hands, indicating that he represents Bhaishajyaguru, the Healing Buddha. He is flanked on his right by Lokeshvara, the bodhisattva of compassion, whose four arms hold a flask possibly containing the liquid of immortality, a lotus bud, a rosary, and a book. On the sage's left stands Prajñaparamita, embodying infinite wisdom and holding a book and a lotus bud. Both bodhisattvas, with the Amitabha Buddha in their headdresses, have a third eye, perhaps signifying perfection, in the forehead; Prajñaparamita has incised beauty lines at throat, breast and abdomen. The fusion of compassion and wisdom lead to healing and the path to enlightenment that is embodied in the Buddha himself, a state recognized in the word "uru", Sanskrit for "great", incised into the base at his feet. This triad is one of the finest examples in existence, with meticulous detailing of typically Bayon style facial features - curving brow line, slanted eyes, and generous expressive lips – and of rich jewels and textiles.

66. Triade bouddhique. Prei Monti, Roluos, Siem Reap, fin 12ème - début 13ème s. Bronze, 0,545 m. Ga 2424 et Ga 5470.

Les triades bouddhiques se rencontrent en grand nombre au Cambodge au 12ème siècle, lorsque le bouddhisme du Mahayana commence à dominer la pensée religieuse dans la société khmère. Le Buddha, figuré sur un lotus épanoui lui servant de trône, est assis en méditation sur le corps enroulé du naga. Il tient probablement un coffret à médicaments, indiquant qu'il s'agit ici de Bhaishajyaguru, le Buddha de médecine. Il est flanqué de Lokeshvara, à sa droite, et de Prajñaparamita. à sa gauche. Le bodhisattva de la compassion tient le vase, contenant la liqueur d'immortalité (?), le lotus, le rosaire et le livre. La déesse de la sagesse suprême tient, pour sa part, le livre et le lotus. Tous deux se caractérisent, en outre, par le Buddha Amitabha figuré dans leur coiffure et le troisième œil frontal, symbole de perfection (?). On notera la présence de plis de beauté incisés sur la gorge, sous la poitrine et sur l'abdomen de la déesse. L'union de la compassion et de la sagesse conduit le dévot sur la voie de la guérison et de l'Éveil, incarné ici par le Buddha lui-même. Cette triade est l'une des plus parfaites en son genre, avec de nombreux détails caractéristiques du style du Bayon: ligne courbe des sourcils, yeux allongés, lèvres généreuses, pour les visages, mais aussi riches bijoux ou encore tissus sophistiqués, pour les costumes.

៦៦_ ត្រៃរូបពុទ្ធសាសនា ព្រៃមន្ទី, រលួស, សៀមរាប, ចុងស.វ.ទី១២_ដើមស.វ.ទី១៣, សំរិត, ០,៥៤៥ម, គ ២៤២៤_គ ៥៤៧០

ត្រៃរូបបែបនេះសម្បូណ៌ណាស់នៅស.វ.ទី១២ ពេលដែលមហាយានចាប់ផ្តើមវាតឥទ្ធិពលមកលើសង្គមខ្មែរ។ រូបនេះគឺព្រះពុទ្ធអង្គសមាធិនៅលើផ្កាឈូកមួយ ដែលទ្រដោយរង្វេលនាគ។ លើព្រហស្តនោះ ប្រហែលជាខ្ចបថ្នាំ បង្ហាញថានេះជាព្រះពុទ្ធ “គ្រូថ្នាំ”។ ខាងស្តាំគឺព្រះលោកេស្វរ ដែលជាពោធិសត្វនៃករុណាធម៌ ហើយដែលព្រះហស្តទាំង៤ មានកាន់ថូទឹកអម្រឹត, ក្រពុំឈូក, ផ្គាំ, គម្ពីរ។ ខាងឆ្វេងគឺប្រាជ្ញាបារមី ជានិមិត្តរូបនៃចំណេះ ដែលដៃម្ខាងកាន់ក្រពុំឈូកនិងម្ខាងទៀតកាន់គម្ពីរ។ ទាំងពីរអង្គសុទ្ធសឹងមានព្រះពុទ្ធអមិតភនៅផ្នួងសក់រៀងៗខ្លួន និងព្រះនេត្រទី៣នៅលើថ្ងាស។ ប្រាជ្ញាបារមីមានផ្នត់នៅក, ចុងដង្ហើម, និងក្រោមផ្ចិត។ ករុណានិងប្រាជ្ញា លុះបូកបញ្ចូលគ្នាទៅគឺនាំទៅរកផ្លូវស្ងប់និងពន្លឺត្រាស់ដឹង។

66. 仏教の三尊像. シエムリエップ州、ロルオス、プレイ・モンティ、12世紀末~13世紀初頭、ブロンズ、0.545m、Ga 2424、Ga 5470

大乗仏教が中心となり始めた12世紀、仏教の三尊像が普及した。瞑想中のブッダはとぐろを巻いたナーガの上の蓮華に座り、小箱を手にしていることから、薬師如来であると思われる。ブッダの右はローケーシュヴァラ（観音菩薩）が立ち、４臂は不死の水を貯えた水瓶、蓮華の蕾、数珠、経冊を執っている。左に立つプラジュニャーパーラミター（般若波羅蜜多菩薩）は無限の知恵を象徴し、経冊と蓮華の蕾を執っている。両菩薩とも頭部に阿弥陀の化仏を抱き、額には完璧さを意味する第３眼がある。プラジュニャーパーラミターの首、胸、腹部には陰刻線がある。ブッダの台座にはサンスクリット語で「偉大」と刻まれており、慈悲と知恵がブッダに象徴される悟りにいたることを象徴している。この三尊像は現存のブロンズ像の中でも優れた作例で、弓形の眉、つりあがった眼、表現豊かな唇、宝飾と布の模様などバイヨン様式の典型である。

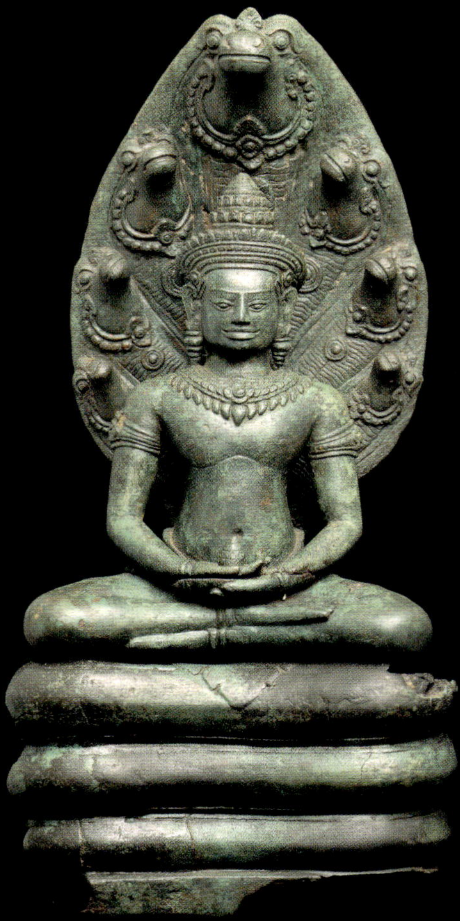

65

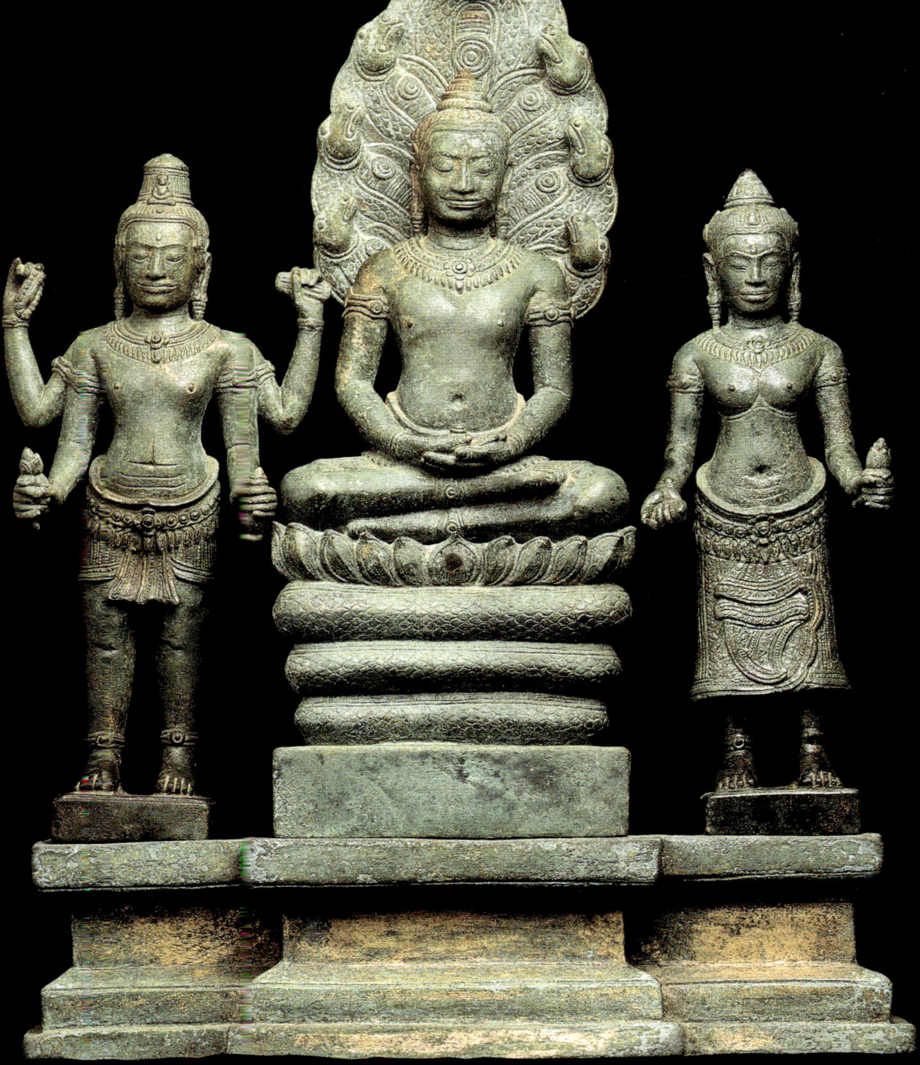

66

67. Lokeshvara. North Khleang, Angkor Thom, Siem Reap, late 12th-early 13th C. Bronze, 0.44 m. Ga 5340.

Lokeshvara's name means "Lord of the World", and he was an important cult figure in the reign of Jayavarman VII, who identified this bodhisattva with the posthumous form of his late father. He was the central focus of the temple of Preah Khan, built in 1191 to commemorate Jayavarman's father, and it has been suggested that the compassion embodied in Lokeshvara symbolized healing after the loss and violence of the Cham invasion of 1177. This magnificently crafted bronze figure, of whose four attributes only the lotus bud is still present, has facial features and elaborate jewellery typical of Bayon style. Also characteristic of this style are the very solid legs and clearly delineated kneecaps. The lotus flower on his head and the cylindrical piling up of his hair, perhaps recarved, demonstrate the ecumenical nature of iconography in the Bayon period, the former associated with the supreme form of Vishnu, the latter with Shiva.

67. Lokeshvara. Khleang nord, Angkor Thom, Siem Reap, fin 12ème - début 13ème s. Bronze, 0,44 m. Ga 5340.

Le nom Lokeshvara signifie, "Seigneur du monde". Il s'agissait de l'une des divinités les plus importantes sous le règne de Jayavarman VII qui identifiait le bodhisattva à la forme posthume de son père défunt. Une statue de Lokeshvara trônait au centre du temple de Preah Khan, consacré en 1191 au bénéfice spirituel dans l'au-delà du père du monarque. Certains spécialistes considèrent que la compassion incarnée par Lokeshvara symbolise la guérison après les souffrances et la violence engendrées par l'attaque cham de 1177. Ce magnifique bronze présente les traits du visage et le traitement du corps caractéristiques du style du Bayon, avec ces jambes solides et l'indication précise de la rotule, par exemple. On notera le traitement particulier de la coiffure, apparemment retaillée.

៦៧_ ព្រះលោកេស្វរ ឃ្លាំងខាងជើង, អង្គរធំ, សៀមរាប, ចុងស.វ.ទី១២_ដើមស.វ.ទី១៣, សំរិត, ០,៤៤ម, គ ៥៣៤០

ពាក្យសំស្ក្រឹតថា "លោកេស្វរ" ប្រែថា "ម្ចាស់នៃលោក" ដែលគេបូជាខ្លាំងនៅរាជ្យព្រះបាទជ័យវរ្ម័នទី៧។ គឺជាព្រះពោធិសត្វដែលព្រះរាជានេះភ្ជាប់ទៅនឹងមរណនាមនៃព្រះបិតាព្រះអង្គផង។ ឯព្រះរូបនោះតម្កល់នៅកណ្តាលប្រាសាទព្រះខ័នដែលសាងឡើងនៅឆ្នាំ១១៩១។ គេយល់ថាធម៌ករុណានៃព្រះលោកេស្វរជាធម៌រំងាប់ការឈឺចាប់ផ្សេងៗ ដែលបណ្តាលមកពីការលុកលុយរបស់ចាម្ប នាឆ្នាំ១១៧៧។ សំរិតនេះធ្វើឡើងផ្ចិតផ្ចង់ក្រៃលែង។ គេឥតភណ្ឌនៅក្នុងព្រះហស្តទាំង៤នៅសល់តែមួយទេ គឺក្រពុំឈូក។ ទម្រង់ព្រះភក្រ្តនិងអលង្ការស្របទៅតាមរចនាបថបាយ័ន្តទាំងស្រុង។ ជើងរាងគ្រមាំង ដោយមានឆ្អឹងពីរបង្ហាញថាជាជង្គង់, ឯផ្កាឈូកនៅលើព្រះកេស និងផ្នួងសក់រាងបំពង់កើតឡើងពីចង្វាយសក់ក្រង។

67. ローケーシュヴァラ（観音菩薩）．シエムリエップ州、アンコール・トム、北クレアン、12世紀末~13世紀初頭、ブロンズ、0.44m、Ga 5340

ローケーシュヴァラはジャヤヴァルマン７世の統治期間、重要なカルトの対象だった。ジャヤヴァルマン７世は父親の死後、ローケーシュヴァラを父とした彫像を作り、父を奉って1191年、建立したプリア・カーン寺院に安置した。ローケーシュヴァラが象徴する慈悲は、チャンパーの1177年の侵攻による損害後の癒しを意味するとも言われている。この素晴らしいブロンズ像には蓮華の蕾しか持物が残っていないが、表情と精巧な装身具はバイヨン様式の典型である。太めの足としっかり描かれた膝頭も同様式の特徴である。頭上の蓮華と円柱形の髪はそれぞれヴィシュヌとシヴァの象徴だが、バイヨン時代のイコノグラフィーの普遍化を示している。

68. Shrine with Hevajra and yoginis. Unknown provenance, late 12th-early 13th C. Bronze, 0.205 m. Ga 2494.

Hevajra is the chief deity in Tantric Buddhism, which was very important in Cambodia from as early as the eleventh century (see #48). With his eight heads and radiating sixteen arms, all of which would have held attributes, he is usually presented in a dynamic dance pose as in this image. The upper rows of heads represent the five Jinas, or supreme Buddhas, while the lower row of three probably embody the Buddha flanked by Lokeshvara and Vajrapani. Hevajra dances on the four Mara, or chief evils of the world, shown here as one image with incised lines indicating the other three. The god is surrounded by eight yoginis (two are missing), emanations of Hevajra himself who also dance to subdue evil and aid in the meditation and ritual practices that lead to enlightenment. The superstructure of the intricately cast shrine, with its meditating figures over the portals and its protective naga heads rearing at the corners, is unfortunately missing.

68. Sanctuaire miniature avec Hevajra et les yogini. Provenance inconnue, fin 12ème - début 13ème s. Bronze, 0,205 m. Ga 2494.

Hevajra est une divinité majeure du tantrisme bouddhique dont l'importance se manifeste au Cambodge dès le 11ème siècle (voir #48). Avec ses huit têtes et ses seize bras disposés de manière rayonnante, le dieu est généralement représenté dans l'attitude dynamique de la danse. Les cinq têtes supérieures figurent les cinq Jina ou Buddha suprêmes, les trois têtes inférieures représentent le Buddha flanqué de Lokeshvara et Vajrapani. Hevajra danse généralement sur les quatre Mara incarnant les passions qui entravent la progression spirituelle. Le dieu est ici entouré par les yogini; seules six des huit déesses subsistent aujourd'hui. Ces divinités dansent elles-mêmes pour subjuguer le mal et aident le pratiquant dans sa méditation devant le conduire à l'Éveil. La toiture du sanctuaire, dont les frontons sont occupés par des personnages en attitude de méditation sous un rampant en forme de naga, n'a malheureusement pas été retrouvée.

៦៨_ ប្រាសាទដែលមានហេវជ្រនិងយោគិនី មិនស្គាល់ប្រភព, ចុងស.វ.ទី១២_ដើមស.វ.ទី១៣, សំរិត, ០,២០៥ម, គ ២៤៩៤

ហេវជ្រជាមេនៃទេពទាំងឡាយក្នុងពុទ្ធសាសនាផ្នែក "តន្ត្រ" ហើយដែលខ្មែរនិយមខ្លាំងតាំងពីស.វ.ទី១១ (សូមមើលរូបលេខ៤៨)។ នៅទីនេះព្រះអង្គកំពុងរាំ។ ព្រះកេសមាន៨, ព្រះហស្តមាន១៦ដែលដើមឡើយ ប្រហែលសុទ្ធតែកាន់គេតនភណ្ឌផ្សេងៗ។ ព្រះកេសពីរជួរខាងលើតំណាងឱ្យព្រះជិនស្រីទាំង៥អង្គ, ឯព្រះកេស៣ជួរក្រោមប្រហែលជាព្រះពុទ្ធនៅកណ្តាល អមសងខាងដោយលោកេស្វរនិងវជ្របាណិ។ ហេវជ្ររាំលើមារទាំង៤ដែលតំណាងភាពអាក្រក់នៃលោក។ មារទាំងនោះ គេបញ្ចូលមកក្នុងរូបតែមួយដោយមានចម្លាក់ខ្សែឆ្នូត បញ្ជាក់ថាមានមារ៣ទៀត។ ធម្មតាមានយោគិនី៨រាំជុំវិញ (ពីរបាត់ទៅហើយ) ដែលជានិមិត្តរូបព្រះហេវជ្រខ្លួនឯងនោះតែម្តង ហើយដែលរាំដូចគ្នាដើម្បីបង្ក្រាបភាពអាក្រក់នោះ។

68. ヘージュヴァラと祠堂形台座．出土地不明、12世紀末~13世紀初頭、ブロンズ、0.205m、Ga 2494

ヘージュヴァラは密教仏教の尊格で、カンボジアでは11世紀頃から重要になった（No.48 参照）。８面と持物を手にした16臂を持ち、通常このようにダイナミックに踊る姿で表される。上２段の頭は五仏（五智如来）、下段の３面はブッダとローケーシュヴァラ（観音菩薩）とヴァジュラパニ（金剛力士）を表していると思われる。ヘージュヴァラはマーラ（４魔、悟りを妨害する魔）の上で踊っている。横たわったマーラは３陰刻線で表されている。ヘージュヴァラは８体のヨーギニー（八瑜伽女、２体喪失）に囲まれているが、ヘージュヴァラが踊って魔を抑止し、悟りを開く瞑想を助けることを意味する。祠堂上部には禅定印を結んだ趺坐像をナーガが縁取っているが、その上部構造は喪失している。

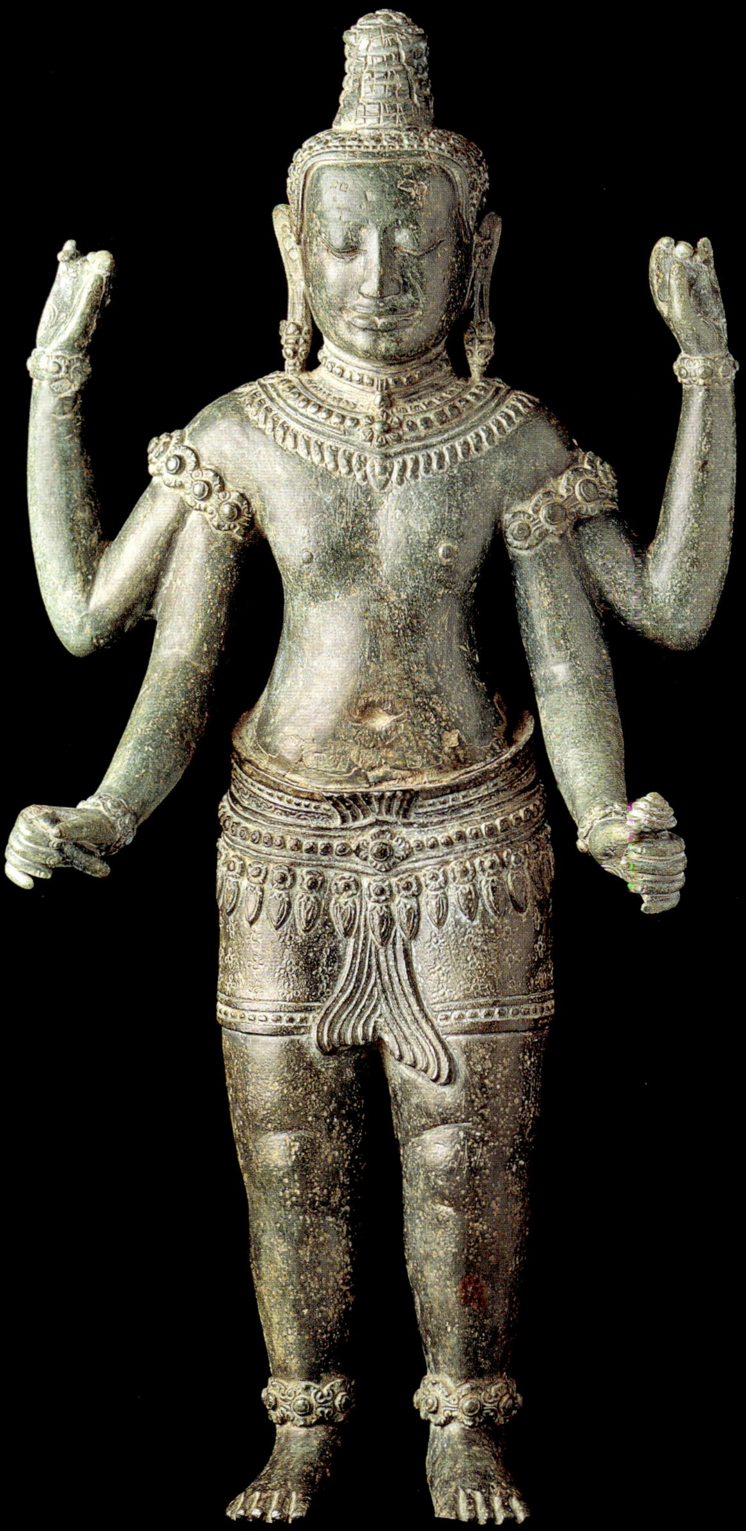

67

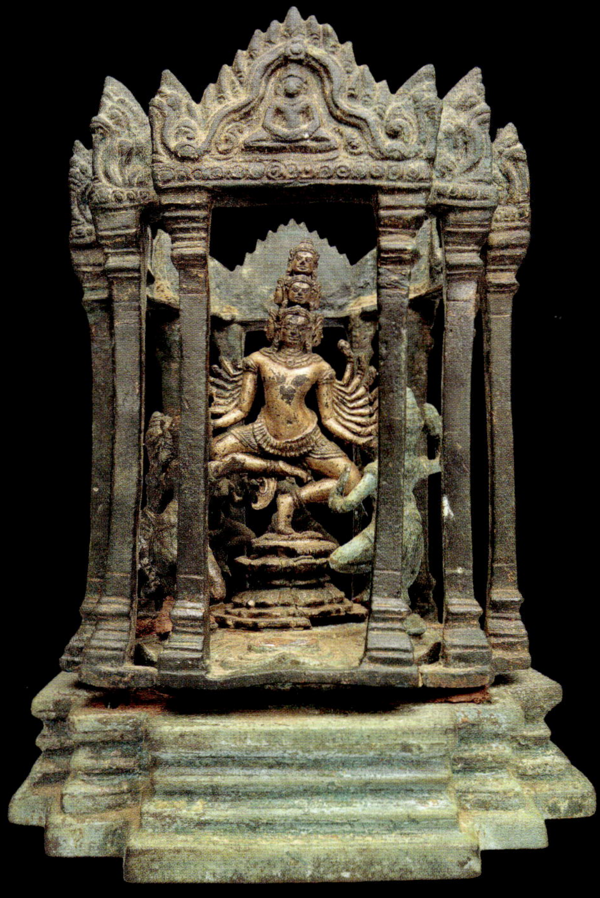

68

69. Ritual conch. Shore of Tonle Sap, Angkor, Siem Reap, 12th-13th C. Bronze, 0.28 m. (conch), 0.10 (tripod). Ga 5484, Ga 5485.

Conches modelled on the natural shell were common in religious rituals and were made of ceramic material as well as metal. Sometimes they served as containers of holy water, sometimes as musical instruments to be blown. This example has an elaborately fashioned end that was probably a mouthpiece. The fan-shaped flap over the hollow body is decorated with a figure of Hevajra and six yoginis, indicating that it was used in ceremonies invoking enlightenment. The elaborate tripod that supports the conch, which may not be part of the original ensemble, depicts worshippers on the pointed petals at the top and kala, or monster, masks spitting garuda figures on its three feet. The perfection of casting epitomizes the bronze skills of the Bayon style.

69. Conque rituelle. Berge du Tonle Sap, Angkor, Siem Reap, 12ème - 13ème s. Bronze, 0,28 m. (conque), 0,10 m. (trépied). Ga 5484 et Ga 5485.

Des répliques de conques en céramique ou en métal étaient fréquemment utilisées dans les rituels religieux. Elles servaient parfois de récipient pour l'eau consacrée ou encore d'instrument de musique. Cet exemple appartient à la deuxième catégorie en raison de son extrémité complexe. La partie centrale, en forme d'éventail, est décorée d'une image d'Hevajra entouré de six yogini, indiquant que l'objet a dû servir dans des rituels d'Éveil. Le trépied sur lequel est présentée cette conque n'est pas celui qui l'accompagnait à l'origine. Les pétales qui bordent sa partie supérieure sont ornés de figures d'orants et les trois pieds sont rehaussés par une tête de monstre crachant de petits garuda. L'œuvre est caractéristique du style du Bayon.

៦៩_ ស័ង្ខ មាត់ទន្លេសាប, អង្គរ, សៀមរាប, ស.វ.ទី១២_១៣, សរិត, ០,២៨ម (ស័ង្ខ), ០,១០ម (ជើងទម្រ), គ ៥៤៨៤, គ ៥៤៨៥

គេធ្វើរូបនេះដោយធ្វើពុម្ពលើខ្យងស័ង្ខធម្មជាតិផ្ទាល់។ ស័ង្ខរបៀបនេះជួនកាលជាកុលាលភាជន៍ផង។ គេតែងដាក់ទឹកសម្រាប់បង្ហូរប្រសិទ្ធិ ឬមួយប្រើជាឧបករណ៍សំឡេងសម្រាប់ផ្លុំ។ រូបនេះមានក្បាច់សម្អិតសម្អាងខ្លាំងណាស់, ចុងគូថចប់ទៅដោយអ្វីមួយដែលជាអណ្ដាតសម្រាប់ផ្លុំ។ ផ្នែកគ្រលោមខាងក្រោមចេញជាសន្លឹកមួយដែលបត់ឡើងមកលើ។ លើនោះមានរូបហេវជ្រព្រមទាំងយោគិនី៦ បញ្ជាក់ថាគេប្រើនៅក្នុងពិធីដែលរំលឹកការត្រាស់ដឹង។ ជើងទម្រក៏សិតឡើងដោយផ្ចិតផ្ចង់ណាស់ដែរ ប៉ុន្តែមិនទៀងថាជាគូដើមនៃស័ង្ខនេះឡើយ។ មាត់ទម្រមានត្របកឈូកពាត់ជុំវិញ ដែលនីមួយៗមានរូបទេពប្រណម្យ។ ជើងទាំង៣សាយឡើងលើជារូបរាហូខ្ជាក់គ្រុឌ។ ភាពឥតខ្ចោះនៃរូបសរិតនេះស្របនឹងសិល្បៈជំនាន់បាយ័ន្ត។

69. 法螺貝. シエムリエップ州、アンコール、トンレサープ湖岸、12~13世紀、ブロンズ、法螺貝0.28m、三脚台0.10m、Ga 5484、Ga 5485

儀礼用の法螺貝は陶器や金属で作られ、浄水の容器や楽器として使われた。この法螺貝は吹き口が装飾されている。扇形の殻口はヘージュヴァラは６体のヨーギニーの鋳出があり、悟りを開くための儀式に使われたことがわかる。三脚台は本来一具のものではないが、三脚の花弁には崇拝者、下部はガルーダを吐き出すカーラが描かれている。鋳造の完成度はバイヨン様式の代表傑作である。

70. Vajra. Preah Theat, Chikreng, Siem Reap, 12th-13th C. Bronze, 0.125 m. Ga 5483.

The vajra, ('hard, powerful' in Sanskrit) is an important symbol in both Brahmanism and Buddhism. In the former it is an attribute of Indra, king of the gods and of thunder and lightning, and represents these forces of nature. This example is Buddhistic and would be held in the right hand of a priest during sacred Buddhist rituals; a bell (ghanta) would be held in his left hand. Rather than being associated with lightning as in Brahmanism, the vajra in Buddhistic symbolism emphasises the hardness of the object and is equated with the diamond and its qualities of purity and strength. The image is particularly important in the Tantric sect, which is sometimes called the Diamond Way or Vajrayana. Originally there were five prongs at each end of this vajra; these represented the four cardinal directions plus the zenith as well as the five Jina, or Tathagata, the transcendental Buddhas.

70. Vajra. Preah Theat, Chikreng, Siem Reap, 12ème - 13ème s. Bronze, 0,125 m. Ga 5483.

Le vajra ("foudre", "diamant" en sanskrit) est un symbole important tant dans l'hindouisme que dans le bouddhisme. Dans la première de ces religions, le vajra est l'attribut d'Indra, dieu de l'orage et rois des dieux. Il représente alors la foudre. Cet exemple, toutefois, est bouddhique. Il s'agit d'un instrument rituel que l'officiant tenait dans la main droite pendant certaines cérémonies, alors que de la main gauche il manipulait une cloche (ghanta). Plutôt qu'avec l'éclair, comme il en est dans l'hindouisme, le vajra est comparé avec le diamant dans le tantrisme bouddhique, en raison de ses qualités de dureté et de pureté. Son importance est telle qu'on parle volontiers de Vajrayana, Véhicule de diamant, à propos de cette forme évoluée et complexe du bouddhisme. Il y avait à l'origine cinq pointes à chacune des extrémités; elles représentaient les directions cardinales et le zénith aussi bien que les cinq Jina ou Tathagata: les Buddha suprêmes.

៧០_ វជ្រ ព្រះធាតុ, ជីក្រែង, សៀមរាប, ស.វ.ទី១២_១៣, សរិត, ០,១២៥ម, គ ៥៤៨៣

វជ្រជាសំស្ក្រឹតមានន័យថា "ខ្លាំងពូកែ" ជាវត្ថុដែលប្រើនៅក្នុងព្រហ្មញ្ញសាសនាផងពុទ្ធសាសនាផង។ ក្នុងព្រហ្មញ្ញសាសនា វជ្រជាកេតនភណ្ឌនៃព្រះឥន្ទ្រដែលជាទេពនៃផ្គរនិងរន្ទះ។ វជ្រនៅទីនេះប្រើក្នុងព្រះពុទ្ធសាសនា ហើយត្រូវកាន់នៅដៃស្ដាំក្នុងកិច្ចផ្សេងៗ។ ជាមួយគ្នានេះគេតែងកាន់កណ្ដឹង (ហៅថា "ឃណ្ដា") នៅដៃឆ្វេង។ ក្នុងពុទ្ធសាសនា វជ្រមិនសំដៅទៅរន្ទះទេ តែមានន័យថាជាពេជ្រ ព្រោះជានិមិត្តរូបនៃភាពបរិសុទ្ធនិងភាពរឹងមាំ។ នៅក្នុងនិកាយតន្ត្រ វត្ថុនេះសំខាន់ខ្លាំងណាស់ នាំឱ្យគេហៅនិកាយនោះថា "វជ្រយាន" ពោលគឺយានពេជ្រ។ កាលនៅពេញលេញ វត្ថុនេះមានមុខស្រួច៥ តំណាងទិសទាំង៤បូកនិងទិសខាងលើដែលជាស្នូលកណ្ដាលផង តំណាងព្រះជិនស្រីឬព្រះតថាគតទាំង៥អង្គផង។

70. 金剛杵. シエムレアップ州、チクレン、プレア・テアト、12~13世紀、ブロンズ、0.125m、Ga 5483

金剛杵はヒンズー教と仏教両方で重要な象徴である。ヒンズー教では雷と稲妻の神インドラの持物で、自然界の力を象徴する。この金剛杵は仏教のものであり、仏僧は儀礼中、右手に金剛杵、左手には金剛鈴を持った。仏教の金剛杵は硬さを意味し、金剛の純粋さと力を象徴する。密教仏教では重要なシンボルである。元来、両端は五鈷杵の形で、四方および絶頂と同時に五仏（五智如来）を象徴している。

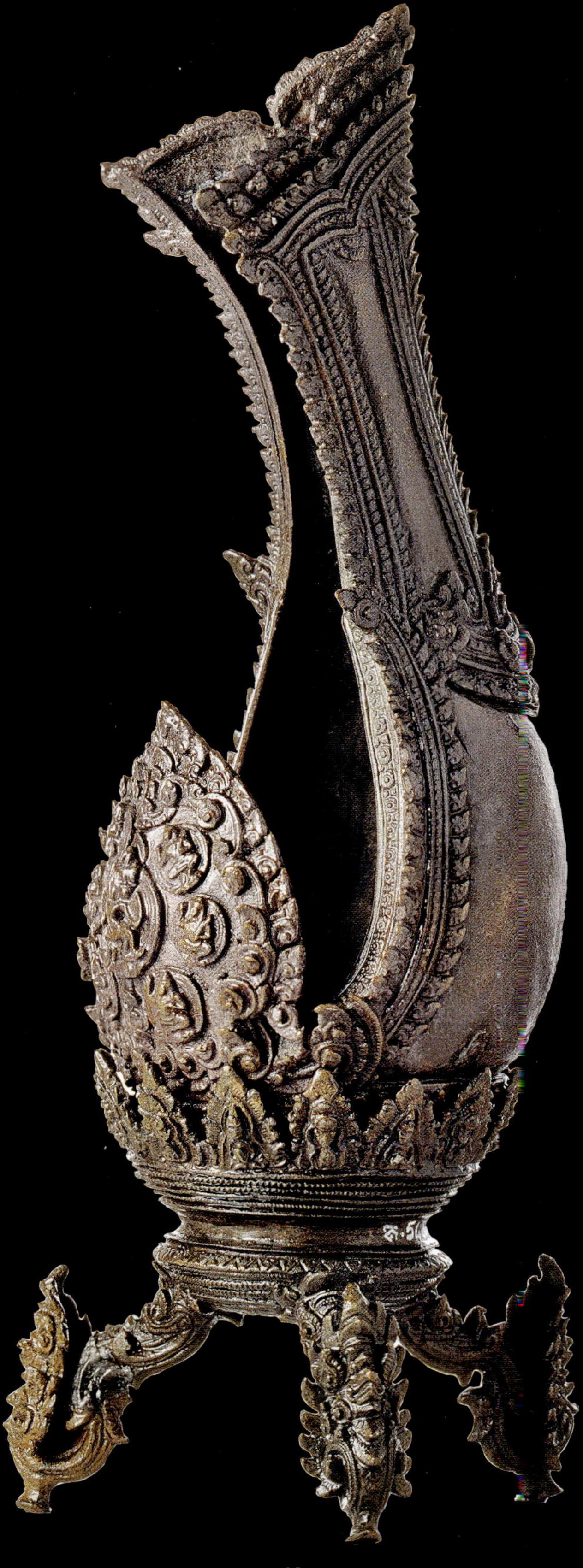

69

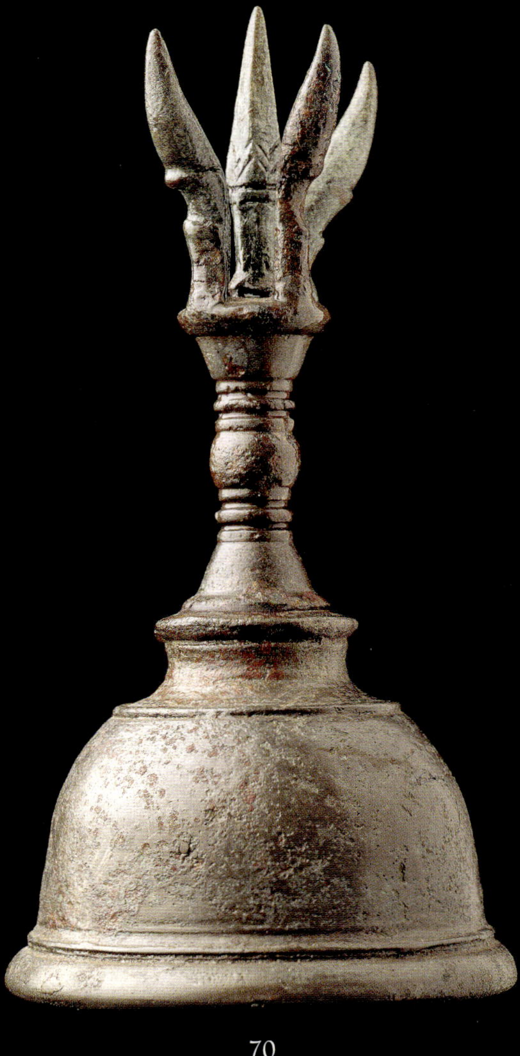

70

71. Military standard in monkey form (Hanuman?). Prasat Phnom Bayang, Takeo, late 12th-early 13th C. Bronze, 0.177 m. Ga 5472.

This dynamic figure, recognizable as a senior officer from the heavy chain of office that crosses his chest, was originally the finial of a military standard born into the field in combat. Similar images can be seen in reliefs on the Bayon temple that illustrate battle scenes during the 12th century. The conception of a military commander in monkey form derives from the Hindu epic of the *Ramayana*, where Prince Rama's forces were aided by the monkey army led by the white monkey general Hanuman.

៧១_ ចុងដងទង់រូបស្វា (ហនុមាន?) ប្រាសាទភ្នំបាយ៉ង់, តាកែវ, ចុងស.វ.ទី១២_ដើមស.វ.ទី១៣, សំរិត, ០,១៧៧ម, គ ៥៤៧២

ស្វាដ៏រស់រវើកនេះជាមេទ័ព សម្គាល់បានដោយសង្វារមានក្បូរក្បាច់ស្អែកស្ពះពាក់នៅលើទ្រូង។ នេះគឺជាចុងដងទង់ដែលគេតែងកាន់ទៅសមរភូមិ។ គេអាចឃើញរូបរបៀបនេះនៅលើចម្លាក់ប្រាសាទបាយ័ន្ត ដែលរៀបរាប់ពីសង្គ្រាមនៅស.វ.ទី១២។ គេទុកស្វាជាមេទ័ពរបៀបនេះ ដោយចម្លងតាមរឿងរាមកេរ្តិ៍ ត្បិតក្នុងរឿងនោះព្រះរាមមានជំនួយការជួវទ័ពដោយមានមេទ័ពធំជាស្វាសមួយមាននាមថាហនុមាន។

71. Enseigne militaire en forme de singe (Hanuman?). Phnom Bayang, Takeo, fin 12ème - début 13ème s. Bronze, 0,177 m. Ga 5472.

Cette statuette dynamique, dans laquelle on reconnaît un personnage ayant rang de chef militaire en raison de la lourde chaîne qui lui barre le torse, était la partie supérieure d'une enseigne portée au combat. De tels objets sont souvent représentés dans les bas-reliefs d'Angkor Vat et du Bayon. L'iconographie procède de l'épopée indienne du *Ramayana*, où les singes, particulièrement le grand singe blanc Hanuman, apparaissent en tant qu'alliés de Rama dans ses combats.

71. 軍旗装飾金具. タケオ州、プラサート・プノン・バヤン、12世紀末~13世紀初頭、ブロンズ、0.177m、Ga 5472

胸飾りから上官とわかるこのダイナミックな姿は戦場に運ばれた軍旗の装飾金具である。同様の姿がバイヨン寺院の12世紀の戦闘場面を描いたレリーフにもみられる。猿の姿の将軍は、白猿の軍隊長ハヌマーンがラーマ王子の軍を助けるインド大叙事詩『ラマヤーナ』に由来している。

72. Censer or lamp in the form of a kneeling woman. Danrun, Mongkol Borei, late 12th-early 13th C. Bronze, 0.165 m. Ga 5467.

Figures like this, with only corollary connections to sacred images, impose fewer restrictions on the artist than do the depictions of divine beings. Such creations, like the finial in #71, embody a dynamism that is mostly seen in Khmer art in narrative reliefs and small bronzes like this. The hollow in the four-petalled lotus flower calyx that forms the vessel on the head of the kneeling woman shows evidence of burning, leading to the possibility that the figure contained oil or perfume. It may have been placed on an altar during religious rituals, which is consistent with the reverent position and hands held in anjali, or worshipping mode, and with the purity symbolized by the lotus. The facial features, with slanted eyes, undulating brows and broad mouth are consistent with Bayon style, while the costume details and jewels accord with that of Angkor Wat.

៧២_ ភាជន៍អុចគ្រឿងក្រអូប ឬចង្កៀងជារូបស្រីលុតជង្គង់ ដានរុន, មង្គលបុរី, ចុងស.វ.ទី១២_ដើមស.វ.ទី១៣, សំរិត, ០,១៦៥ម, គ ៥៤៦៧

រូបដែលមិនមែនជាទេពពេញលេញរបៀបនេះពុំបង្ករការលំបាកដល់ជាងស្មិតឡើយ។ ដូចចុងដងទង់លេខ៧១ខាងលើនេះដែរ វត្ថុរបៀបនេះតែងបង្ហាញនូវភាពរស់រវើក ដែលឃើញជាទូទៅលើផ្ទាំងចម្លាក់និទានរឿង។ នៅបាតភាជន៍ដែលមានត្របក៤នេះ គេឃើញមានស្នាមដុត។ ហេតុនេះយើងអាចយល់ថា វត្ថុទាំងមូលនេះធ្លាប់មានផ្ទុកប្រេងឬគ្រឿងក្រអូបនៅខាងលើ។ ប្រហែលពីមុនមកគេតាំងនៅលើអាសនៈអ្វីមួយសម្រាប់ធ្វើកិច្ចបូជា។ ការស្មាននេះសមទៅនឹងឥរិយាបថស្ត្រីព្រមទាំងដៃដែលផ្គុំអញ្ជលី ហើយម្យ៉ាងទៀតក៏ស្របនឹងផ្កាឈូកដែលជានិមិត្តរូបនៃភាពបរិសុទ្ធដែរ។ ទម្រង់មុខ, ភ្នែកតឹងទាញឡើងលើ, ចិញ្ចើមរាងង, រង្វះមាត់ធំ, សំពត់មានផ្នត់... ទាំងនេះសុទ្ធសឹងជាលក្ខណៈនៃរចនាបថបាយ័ន្ត។

72. Brûle-parfum ou lampe en forme de personnage féminin agenouillé. Danrun, Mongkol Borei, fin 12ème - début 13ème s. Bronze, 0,165 m. Ga 5467.

Ce petit personnage féminin agenouillé en attitude de prière pourrait figurer, comme #53, quelque assistant au cours d'un rituel. Le lotus placé sur sa tête comportait des traces de combustion; il s'agissait vraisemblablement d'un brûle-parfum ou d'une lampe à huile. Les petits bronzes, comme celui-ci, étaient faciles à transporter et probablement destinés à un usage rituel privé. Ils sont difficiles à dater car leur évolution a pu ne pas suivre le même rythme que celui des images principales. Les traits du visage, avec ces yeux allongés et la ligne incurvée des sourcils, sont typiques du style du Bayon alors que le costume et les bijoux se rapportent au style d'Angkor Vat.

72. ひざまずく女性（香炉または燭台）. モンコル・ボレイ州、ダンルン、12世紀末~13世紀初頭、ブロンズ、高0.165m、Ga 5467

尊像との関係が強くない像は神の姿を描く場合のような制限がないため、レリーフやNo.71の装飾金具、この小ブロンズ像のようにクメール美術の中でもダイナミックさが感じられる。両膝をついた女性の頭上の４弁の蓮華の中には焦げあとが残っており、香炉か燭台であったことがわかる。合掌する姿や清らかさを象徴する蓮華から、宗教儀式で祭壇に飾られていたと思われる。つりあがった眼、弓形の眉、大きな口などの表情や裙の襞はバイヨン様式の典型である。

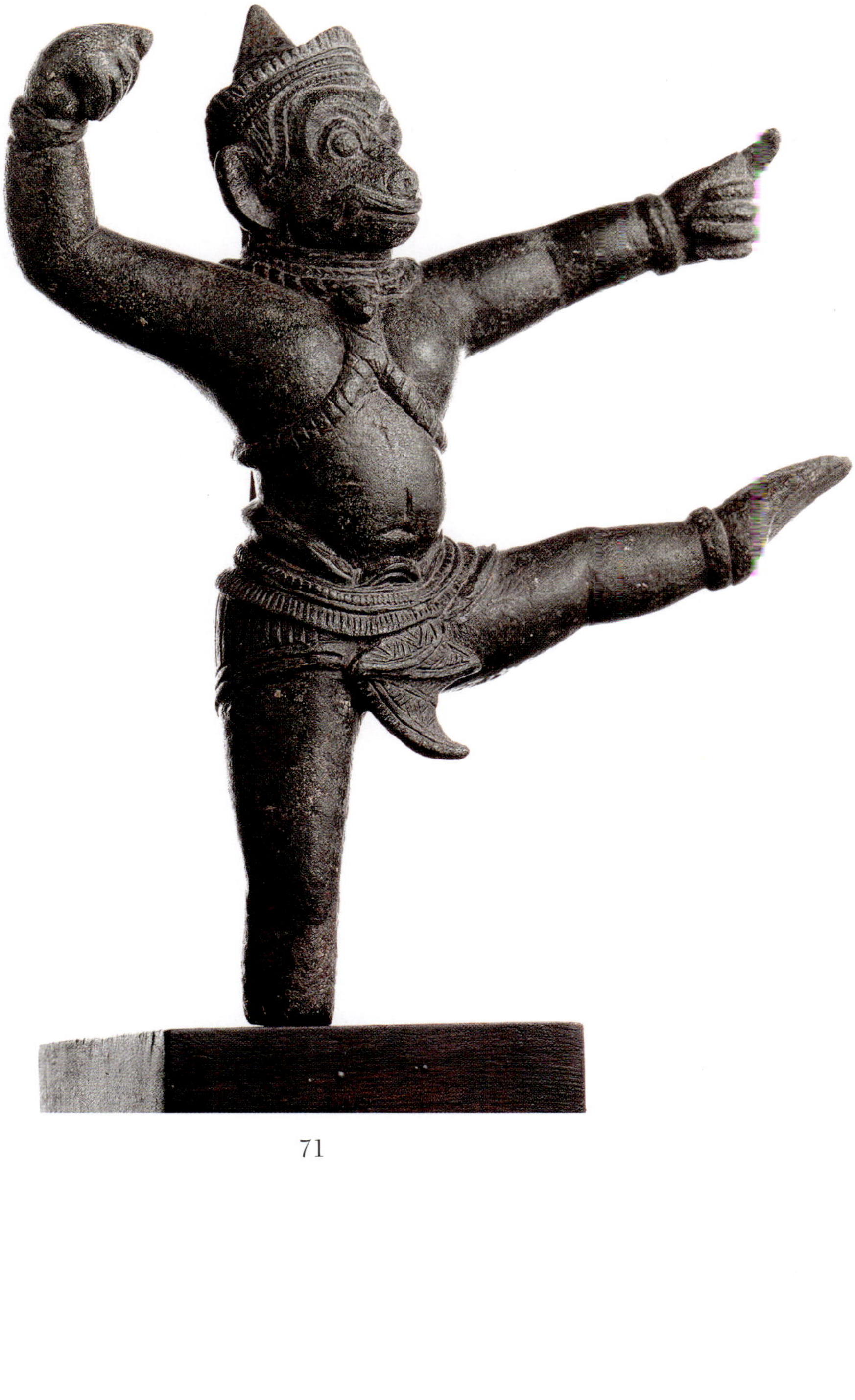

71

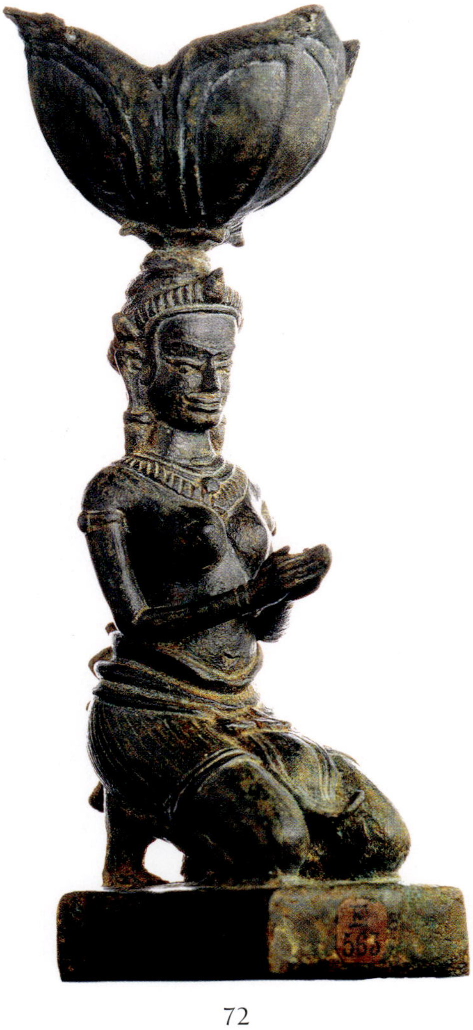

72

73. Lakshmi. Preah Ko, Roluos, Siem Reap, late 12th-early 13th C. Sandstone, 1.88 m. Ka 1698.

This imposing goddess, identifiable as Lakshmi (a shakti, or spouse, of Vishnu) from the lotus bud held in both hands, has the serene expression and naturalistic rendition of torso that exemplify the aesthetic of the Bayon style. The extreme slenderness of her torso, with breasts smaller than usual for Khmer feminine figures, closely resembles that of representations of a kneeling divinity usually identified as the bodhisattva Tara, as do her facial features. This has led to the speculation that this Lakshmi, like the Tara images that were widely distributed in the Khmer empire during Jayavarman VII's reign, may represent the king's first wife, Jayarajadevi, who died young and was succeeded as queen by her sister, Indradevi. Inscriptions tell us that Indradevi had statues of her sister, the king and herself erected in many places. The apparent paradox of her personification in both Brahmanistic and Buddhistic guise may perhaps be explained by the ecumenical nature of religion in the Bayon period.

73. Lakshmi. Preah Ko, Roluos, Siem Reap, fin 12ème - début 13ème s. Grès, 1,88 m. Ka 1698.

Cette imposante déesse peut être reconnue comme Lakshmi, l'épouse de Vishnu, grâce au lotus qu'elle tient dans chacune de ses mains; elle présente l'expression sereine et le modelé vivant et naturel propres au style du Bayon. La sveltesse particulière du torse, avec cette poitrine moins développée que dans la plupart des autres images féminines khmères, mais aussi les traits du visage, évoquent les représentations d'une divinité féminine agenouillée, généralement tenue pour figurer Tara. Cette ressemblance a conduit à l'hypothèse selon laquelle cette Lakshmi, de même que les Tara agenouillées, pourraient avoir été des portraits de la première épouse du roi Jayavarman VII, Jayarajadevi, qui mourut jeune et fut remplacée, en tant que première reine, par sa propre sœur, Indradevi. Les inscriptions nous apprennent qu'Indradevi fit ériger des statues de Jayarajadevi, du roi et d'elle-même en de nombreux lieux. L'apparent paradoxe de voir la même personne représentée en tant que divinité bouddhique et hindoue peut sans doute s'expliquer par le caractère tolérant, voire syncrétique, des religions à l'époque du Bayon.

៧៣_ នាងលក្ស្មី ព្រះគោ, រលួស, សៀមរាប, ចុងស.វ.ទី១២_ដើមស.វ.ទី១៣, ថ្មភក់, ១,៨៨ម, ក ១៦៩៨

ទេវីដែលមានរាងដ៏បងនេះសម្គាល់បានថាជានាងលក្ស្មី ដោយសារមានក្រពុំឈូកនៅដៃទាំងសងខាង។ ទឹកមុខមានភាពស្ងប់ស្រគត់ស្រគំ។ រីឯដងខ្លួនច្លាក់ដូចធម្មជាតិ ប្រកបដោយសោភ័ណភាព ដូចធ្លាប់ឃើញក្នុងរចនាបថបាយ័ន្តជាធម្មតា។ ដងខ្លួននោះស្តើងស្រឡូនខ្លាំងណាស់, ឯទ្រូងក៏ស្តើងជាងស្ត្រីធម្មតា, អាចប្រដូចទៅទេវីលុតជង្គង់នានាដែលគេយល់ថាជាព្រះពោធិសត្វ "តារា"។ ចំណុចនេះធ្វើឱ្យអ្នកខ្លះយល់ថាជាព្រះរូបព្រះនាងជ័យរាជទេវី ដែលជាព្រះជាយាដំបូងនៃព្រះបាទជ័យវរ្ម័នទី៧ ហើយដែលចូលទីវង្គតក្នុងវ័យក្មេងនៅឡើយ មុនព្រះនាងឥន្ទ្រទេវីឡើងជាព្រះមហេសី។ ការជឿដូច្នេះមកពីរូប "តារា" មានច្លាក់តម្កល់ទុកគ្រប់ទិសទីនៅជំនាន់នោះ។

73. ラクシュミー. シエムリエップ州、ロルオス、プレアー・コー、12世紀末~13世紀初頭、砂岩、1.88m、Ka 1698

この像は手に蓮華の蕾を持つことから、ヴィシュヌの神妃ラクシュミーだとわかる。穏やかな表情と体躯の自然さはバイヨン様式の典型である。通常、クメール美術にみられる女性像より小さい胸のほっそりした姿は、表情と同様、膝まずいて描かれるターラー（菩薩）に似ている。ジャヤヴァルマン７世時代、国中に建立されたターラー像同様、このラクシュミー像が王の第１王妃ジャヤラージャデーヴィーである可能性もある。ジャヤラージャデーヴィーは若くして他界し、姉インドラデヴィーが後妻となり、妹、王、自分自身の像を国中に建立した。ヒンドゥー教と仏教の尊像になぞらえて造像しているのは、バイヨン時代、宗教が混在していたためと考えられる。

74. Ganesha. Unknown provenance, late 12th-early 13th C. Bronze, 0.255 m. Ga 2321.

The elephant-headed god Ganesha, son of Shiva and Parvati, has always been a popular deity. As patron of new enterprises he offers success, although as lord of obstacles he can create impediments as well as prevent them. Combining the large size of the elephant with the small form of the human being, Ganesha represents the unity of macrocosm with microcosm. The *Mahabharata* states that Ganesha was the scribe of that epic at the dictation of Vyasa; he is therefore associated with letters and is the protector of knowledge. A snake curves across his chest and over his left shoulder, while another forms a noose in one of his four hands. The upper right hand holds his own broken-off tusk. A beaded object in the lower right hand cannot be identified with certainty; the attribute in the fourth hand is missing. The heavy jewellery, including the elaborate belt visible at the rear, and the short pleated sampot are characteristic of Bayon style.

74. Ganesha. Provenance inconnue, fin 12ème - début 13ème s. Bronze, 0,255 m. Ga 2321.

Le dieu à tête d'éléphant Ganesha, fils de Shiva et Parvati, a toujours été une divinité très vénérée au Cambodge. En tant que protecteur des nouvelles entreprises, il offre le succès; et sous ses traits de Seigneur des obstacles, il peut tout aussi bien susciter des difficultés ou les aplanir. Possédant la taille monumentale de l'éléphant et celle, plus modeste, de l'être humain, Ganesha représente l'identité fondamentale entre macrocosme et microcosme. Ganesha est réputé avoir été le scribe du *Mahabharata* sous la dictée de son auteur, le sage Vyasa; il est ainsi associé au monde des lettres et considéré comme le protecteur de la connaissance. Dans ce très beau bronze, un serpent barre la poitrine du dieu en partant de l'épaule gauche; un autre forme un nœud dans l'une de ses mains. Dans sa main supérieure droite, Ganesha tient sa propre défense cassée. L'attribut tenu dans la main antérieure droite ne peut pas être identifié avec certitude et le quatrième attribut a malheureusement disparu. Les bijoux assez lourds, notamment la ceinture complexe visible dans le dos, ainsi que le costume plissé sont caractéristiques du style du Bayon.

៧៤_ ព្រះគណេស មិនស្គាល់ប្រភព, ចុងស.វ.ទី១២_ដើមស.វ.ទី១៣, សំរិត, 0,២៥៥ម គ ២៣២១

ទេពមានព្រះកេសដំរីនេះ ជាបុត្រនាងបាព៌តីនេះ មានប្រជាប្រិយភាពខ្លាំង។ គឺជាទេពនៃជោគជ័យក្នុងការងារ តែជាមួយគ្នានោះក៏ជាទេពនៃឧបសគ្គដែរ។ ទេពនេះអាចបង្ករឬបញ្ចៀសបញ្ហា។ ក្បាលដំរីបើប្រៀបទៅនឹងទំហំខ្លួនមនុស្សនោះ ឃើញថាធំណាស់។ គេអះអាងថាព្រះគណេសជាអ្នកកត់ត្រារឿងមហាភារត តាមការពោលរបស់ "វ្យាស"។ ដូច្នេះហើយទើបគេទុកព្រះគណេសជាទេពនៃអក្សរសាស្ត្រនិងវិជ្ជាទូទៅ។ អលង្ការស្រោចលើខ្លួន, មានពស់មួយពាក់ជៀងពាត់មកស្មាឆ្វេងនិងខ្សែមួយពាត់ជាចំណងនៅលើដៃម្ខាង។ ដៃស្តាំខាងលើកាន់កំណាត់ភ្លុករបស់ខ្លួនឯង។ វត្ថុមានក្បាច់ដូចផ្កាំនៅដៃស្តាំខាងក្រោម ពុំអាចសន្មតថាជាអ្វីប្រាកដឡើយ។ រីឯកេតនភណ្ឌនៅដៃទី៤គឺបាត់ទៅហើយ។

74. ガネーシャ. 出土地不明、12世紀末~13世紀初頭、ブロンズ、0.255m、Ga 2321

シヴァとパールヴァーティーの息子ガネーシャは人気がある。障害を作ったり、除去する神だが、起業の神として事業の成功をもたらす。大きな象と小さい人間を合わせたガネーシャは大宇宙と小宇宙の融和を象徴している。ガネーシャが聖者ヴィヤーサの大叙事詩『マハーバーラタ』を口述筆記したことから、知恵神でもある。胸から左肩に蛇をかけ、手のひらにも蛇が輪を描いている。右第２手に自分の欠けた牙を持つ。左右第１手の持物は不明である。宝飾や帯の飾り、短い裙は典型的なバイヨン様式である。

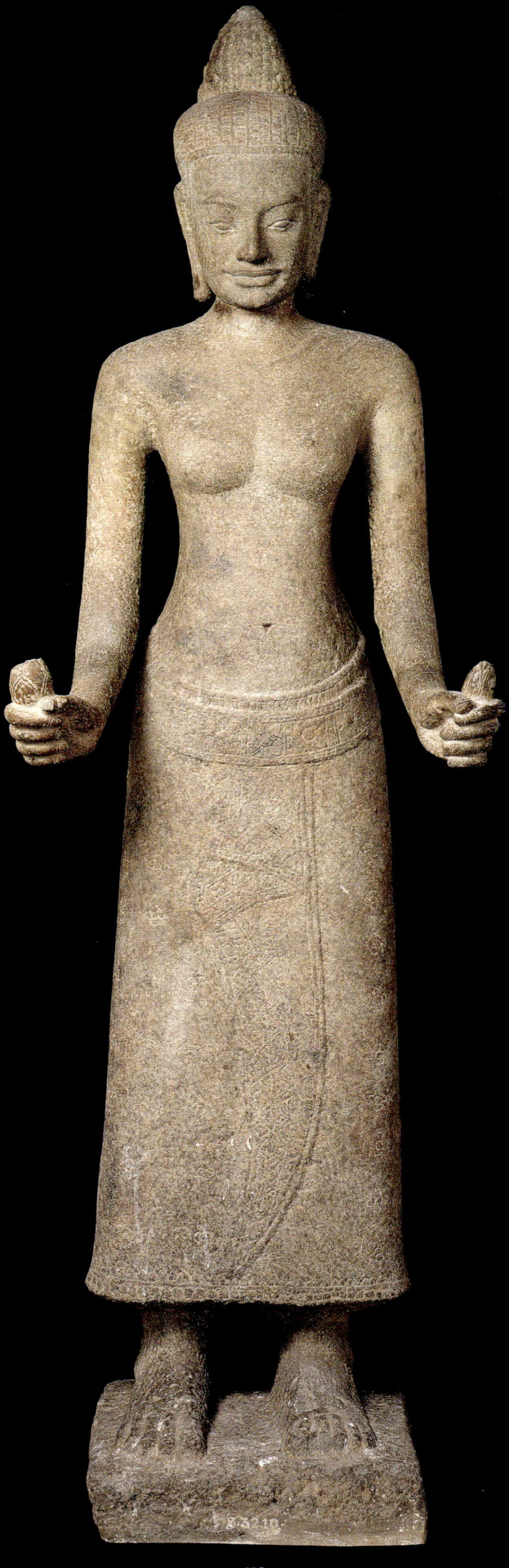

73

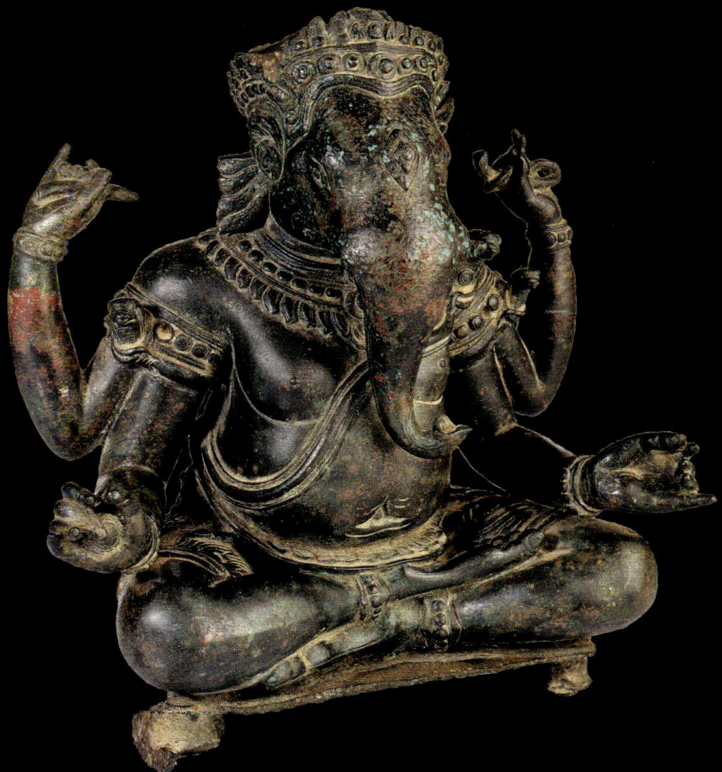

74

75. Narasimha. Angkor Wat, Siem Reap, late 12th-early 13th C. Sandstone, 1.51 m. Ka 1796.

Narasimha (Man-lion) is one of the zoomorphic avatars, or manifestations, of Vishnu, whose other forms include a boar and a turtle as well as anthropomorphic entities such as Krishna and Rama. In Cambodia Narasimha is seen most frequently in relief carving, particularly on temple lintels, often in the dynamic gesture of tearing the heart from the evil demon Hiranyakashipu. This statue is the only known freestanding example. It is rather surprising that most of these Brahmanistic zoomorphic representations were created at the king's behest during the reign of Jayavarman VII. One can speculate that such sculpture was commissioned in the spirit of ecumenical inclusion that characterized that monarch. The refined carving of muzzle, fangs, mane and jewellery of this Narasimha is an outstanding example of the expressive style of the Bayon.

75. Narasimha. Angkor Vat, Siem Reap, fin 12ème - début 13ème s. Grès, 1,51 m. Ka 1796.

Narasimha (l'Homme-lion) est l'un des avatars zoomorphes de Vishnu, au nombre desquels se comptent aussi le Sanglier et la Tortue, aux côtés des aspects anthropomorphes bien connus que sont, par exemple, Krishna et Rama. Au Cambodge, Narasimha est le plus souvent figuré en bas-relief, notamment sur les linteaux, en train d'étriper le démon Hiranyakashipu. Cette statue est le seul exemple connu en ronde bosse. On peut s'étonner que de telles images hindoues zoomorphes aient été réalisées sous le règne du roi bouddhiste Jayavarman VII. Quelle que soit la religion dominante, toutefois, il semble qu'un certain esprit de tolérance ou même de syncrétisme a toujours caractérisé la pensée religieuse et les cultes khmers. Les détails de la gueule, des crocs, de la crinière et des parures de ce Narasimha en font un exceptionnel exemple de l'art expressif du Bayon.

៧៥_ នរសិង្ហ អង្គរវត្ត, សៀមរាប, ចុងស.វ.ទី១២_ដើមស.វ.ទី១៣, ថ្មភក់, ១,៥១ម, ក ១៧៩៦

នរសិង្ហ (មនុស្សមានក្បាលសិង្ហ) ជាអវតារមួយនៃព្រះនារាយណ៍ ដែលអាចជារូបសត្វដទៃដូចជាជ្រូកព្រៃ, អណ្តើក ឬក៏ជារូបមនុស្សដូចជាព្រះក្រឹស្ណា ឬព្រះរាមជាដើម។ នៅប្រទេសកម្ពុជាគេច្រើនតែឃើញនរសិង្ហឆ្លាក់នៅលើផ្តាំងថ្ម ដូចជាផ្តែរប្រាសាទជាដើម កំពុងហែកទ្រូងរូងយកថ្លើមអសោរ។ នរសិង្ហឆ្លាក់ជាបដិមារបៀបនេះ ជាឧទាហរណ៍តែមួយគត់ដែលយើងស្គាល់។ ជាការចម្លែកបន្តិចដែរ ដែលរូបសត្វក្នុងព្រហ្មញ្ញសាសនាសាងឡើងតាមបញ្ជានៃព្រះបាទជ័យវរ្ម័នទី៧។ ចំណុចនេះអាចឱ្យគិតថា ដោយសារព្រះរាជានេះមានគំនិតបង្រួបបង្រួមសាសនាផ្សេងៗ។ ច្រមុះ, ចង្កូម, សក់ ព្រមទាំងអលង្ការបង្ហាញច្បាស់ថានៅក្នុងរចនាបថបាយ័ន្ត។

75. 獅子. シエムリエップ州、アンコール・ワット、12世紀末~13世紀初頭、砂岩、1.51m、Ka 1796

半神半獅子はヴィシュヌの化身の１つである。その他にも猪や亀、クリシュナやラーマのアヴァターラがある。カンボジアでは寺院のリンテルのレリーフとして悪魔の心臓を裂く獅子が描かれることが多い。これは唯一の独立像である。意外なことに、仏教徒のジャヤヴァルマン７世時代にヒンドゥー教関連の半神半獣の像が数多く造像された。これはヒンドゥー教も否定しない王の意図を反映したものと思われる。鼻口、牙、たてがみ、宝飾は表現力豊かなバイヨン様式の素晴らしい例である。

76. Seated figure of Yama (?) (so-called Leper King). **Angkor Thom, Siem Reap, late 12th-early 13th C or earlier?. Sandstone, 1.53 m. Ka 1860.**

This is one of the best-known works in the National Museum because of the legend attached to it. Found near the northeast corner of the ceremonial terraces in front of the Royal Palace in Angkor Thom, on the terrace that is popularly called the Leper King Terrace, the sculpture was said to be the image of a monarch of Angkor, perhaps Jayavarman VII or his son, who erected a temple and possibly this statue in gratitude for being cured of leprosy. There is no evidence for this belief, and it is more likely that the subject is Yama, the god of death, who is referred to under his name "Dharmaraja" in a small inscription on the base. The flowing locks and projecting fangs are consistent with this identity. It is furthermore convincing in that the terrace in question was possibly a cremation platform, which would logically be associated with Yama. Recent research has suggested that the image should be dated to an earlier period, possibly even pre-Angkorian.

76. Le Roi lépreux (Yama?). Angkor Thom, Siem Reap, fin 12ème - début 13ème s. ou plus tôt? Grès, 1,53 m. Ka 1860.

Cette sculpture est l'une des plus célèbres du musée national de Phnom-Penh en raison de la légende qui y est attachée. Découverte à l'angle nord-est des terrasses royales d'Angkor Thom, précisément sur la terrasse qui porte son nom, la statue était censée représenter un souverain d'Angkor, peut-être Jayavarman VII ou son fils, qui érigea un temple et, selon toute probabilité, cette sculpture, en guise de remerciement pour avoir été guéri de la lèpre. Aucune preuve ne vient confirmer la légende et la statue est plus vraisemblablement une représentation de Yama, le juge des morts. Les cheveux bouclés et les crocs semblent confirmer cette identification hypothétique, par ailleurs renforcée par le fait que la terrasse sur laquelle l'œuvre se trouvait est censée être une terrasse de crémation où la présence de Yama se révèlerait logique. Des recherches récentes indiquent que l'œuvre pourrait être plus ancienne que ce que l'on croyait jusqu'ici et peut-être remonter à l'époque préangkorienne.

៧៦_ ព្រះយម (?) ក្នុងឥរិយាបថអង្គុយ (ហៅថាស្តេចគម្លង់) អង្គរធំ, សៀមរាប, ចុងស.វ.ទី១២_ដើមស.វ.ទី១៣ ឬមុននោះទៀត, ថ្មភក់, ១,៣១ម, ក១៨៦០

បដិមានេះនៅក្នុងចំណោមរូបដែលគេស្គាល់ជាងគេនៅក្នុងសារមន្ទីរជាតិ ដោយសារទាក់ទងទៅនឹងរឿងព្រេងមួយ។ គេឃើញរូបនេះដំបូងនៅលើលានមួយនៅក្លៀសានអង្គរធំ ដែលគេនិយមហៅថាលានស្តេចគម្លង់។ អ្នកខ្លះពោលថានេះជាបដិមាព្រះរាជាមួយអង្គនៅអង្គរ, អាចជាព្រះបាទជ័យវរ្ម័នទី៧ ឬបុត្ររបស់ព្រះអង្គ ដែលបានសាងប្រាសាទមួយព្រមទាំងរូបនេះ ដោយសារបានជាសះស្បើយពីរោគឃ្លង់។ ប៉ុន្តែឥតមានអ្វីជាភស្តុតាងសម្រាប់ជំនឿនេះឡើយ។ ប្រហែលជារូបព្រះយមដែលជាទេពនៃសេចក្តីស្លាប់។ ណាមួយសក់ក្រេងជារមូរ ព្រមទាំងចង្កូមដែលចេញពីមាត់បង្ហាញថាសមជាព្រះយមដែរ។ ម្យ៉ាងទៀតលាននោះគួរជឿថាជាទីបូជាសពដូចគេអះអាងមែន។ ក្នុងករណីនេះឃើញថាស្របនឹងទីតាំងនៃព្រះយមពិត។

76. ヤーマ坐像. シエムリエップ州、アンコール・トム、12世紀末~13世紀初頭、砂岩、1.53m、Ka 1860

その伝説から国立博物館の中でも最もよく知られた像である。アンコール・トム都城の「ライ病王のテラス」の北東の角に発見されたこの像は、ハンセン氏病が治ったことを感謝して寺院を建立したジャヤヴァルマン７世かその息子の彫像だといわれている。しかしこの伝説には根拠がなく、垂れ下がる髪と牙があることから、夜魔天（閻魔大王）だと思われる。テラスが王を荼毘に付す場所でもあったことから、夜魔天との関連は理に適う。最近の調査結果によると、より古いものである可能性がある。

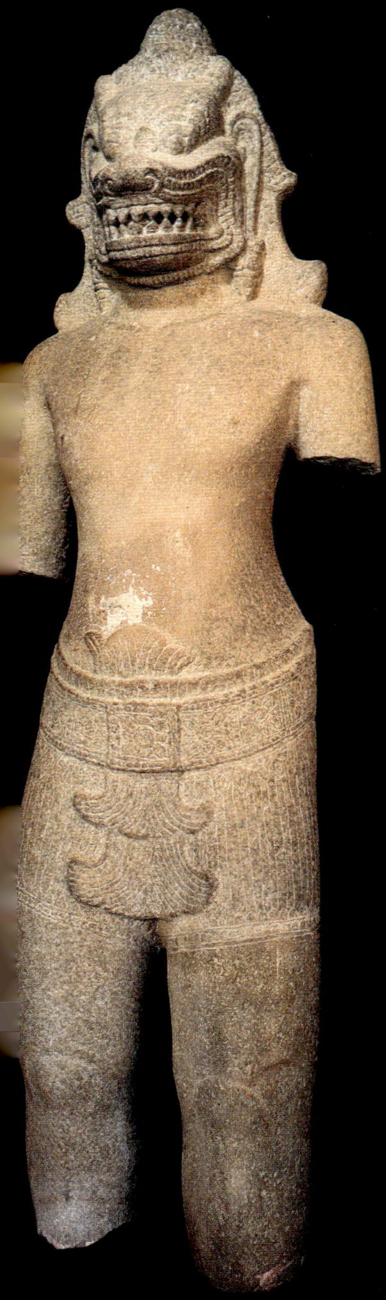

75

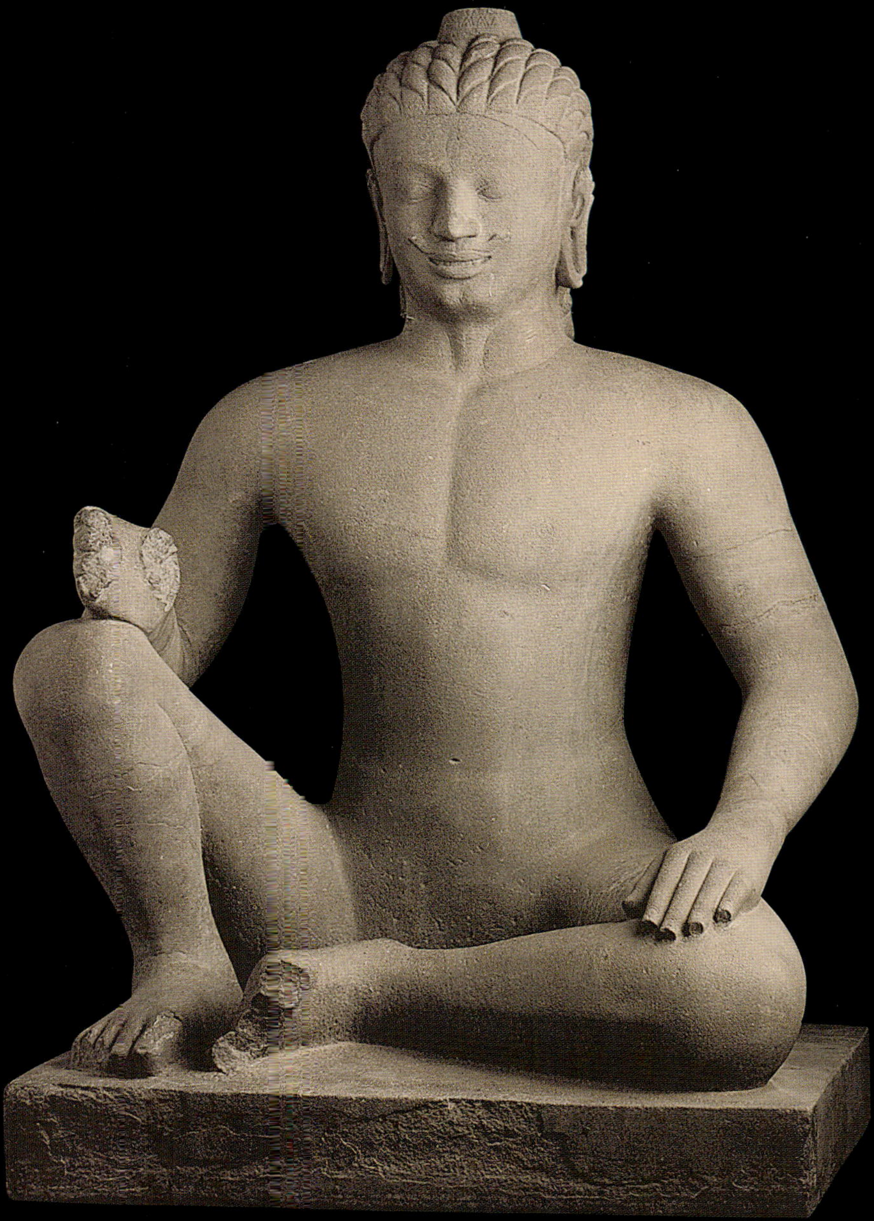

76

77. Buddha. Kong Pisei, Kompong Speu, 14th C. Bronze with lacquer, 0.85 m. Ga 2057.

Although lacking the extreme spirituality of Bayon and immediately post-Bayon statues of the Buddha (so-called Commaille Buddhas named after the first conservator of the Angkor site), this masterfully cast bronze image projects a meditative calm and humanistic realism that demonstrate continuity in Khmer sculptural skills in later periods. The rendering of the outer robe delicately reveals the outlines of both undergarment and the musculature of the body beneath it, while the representation of facial features has an iconic dignity. The schematic treatment of the sage's curls, which show vestiges of a coating of lacquer, and the somewhat stolid legs predict a decline in sculptural subtlety. The complex flame (rashmi) projecting from the ushnisha (the cranial protuberance that is one of the distinguishing features of the Buddha) reveals Sri Lankan influence, a Theravada characteristic that perhaps reached Cambodia via Thai art.

77. Buddha. Kong Pisei, Kompong Speu, 14ème s. Bronze et traces de laque, 0,85 m. Ga 2057.

Bien que dépourvue de la spiritualité qui marquait les œuvres du style du Bayon et de l'époque immédiatement postérieure - avec, par exemple, les Buddha dits de type Commaille, du nom de leur inventeur, Jean Commaille, le premier conservateur du site d'Angkor - cette œuvre magistrale véhicule un calme méditatif et un réalisme humaniste attestant les qualités de l'art khmer aux époques tardives. Le manteau monastique laisse subtilement transparaître le vêtement inférieur et la musculature du corps, cependant que les traits du visage sont empreints de dignité. Le traitement schématique des boucles de cheveux, où apparaissent quelques vestiges de laque, ainsi que des jambes un peu lourdes préfigurent toutefois un certain déclin dans la qualité de la statuaire. La flamme (rashmi) au-dessus de l'ushnisha (la protubérance crânienne qui est l'une des marques distinctives du Buddha) - une caractéristique de l'iconographie du bouddhisme Theravada - trahit une influence cinghalaise, peut-être parvenue au Cambodge via certaines écoles d'art de l'actuelle Thaïlande.

៧៧_ ព្រះពុទ្ធរូប គងពិសី, កំពង់ស្ពឺ, ស.វ.ទី១៤, សំរិតនិងម្រាក់, 0,៨៥ម, គ ២០៥៧

បដិមានេះពុំអាចប្រៀបស្មើទៅនឹងព្រះពុទ្ធរូបសម័យបាយ័ន្ត និងក្រោយបាយ័ន្ត (គេនិយមហៅថា ព្រះពុទ្ធរូប Commaille) ក៏ពិតមែន តែក៏អាចចាត់ទុកថាជាស្នាដៃដ៏វិចិត្រមួយអំពីសំរិតដែរ។ ភាពស្រគត់ស្រគំ, ចិត្តស្ងប់, រូបរាងធ្វើតាមធម្មជាតិ ... បង្ហាញថាជាសិល្បៈដែលតពូជពង្សត្រង់ពីបុរាណមក។ ចីពរស្តើងរហូតដល់ធ្វើឱ្យឃើញស្បង់នៅខាងក្នុងច្បាស់ ព្រមទាំងសាច់ដុំដងខ្លួនខាងលើផង។ ព្រះភក្ត្រមានភាពសក្តិសមថ្លៃថ្នូរ។ ឯរបៀបបង្ហាញសក់ (ដែលមានស្នាមម្រាក់នៅជាប់លើ) និងជើងរាងក្រទាំងនោះ បង្ហាញថាចម្លាក់បដិមាមានភាពចុះអន់ថយ។ អណ្តាតភ្លើងផុសចេញមកពីព្រះមូលីបង្ហាញថាទទួលឥទ្ធិពលពីស្រីលង្កាដោយសារជាលក្ខណៈព្រះពុទ្ធអង្គក្នុងសាសនាថេរវាទ ដែលប្រហែលចូលមកតាមរយៈសិល្បៈសៀម។

77. ブッダ. コンポンスプー州、コン・ピセイ、14世紀、ブロンズ、0.85m、Ga 2057

バイヨン時代およびその直後のブッダ像（コマイユ仏）のようなスピリチュアリティーはないが、このブロンズ像は瞑想の静寂と人間的リアリズムを感じさせ、後期クメールにも継続された高技術を示している。大衣からその下の裙と筋肉が明瞭にわかる。表情には尊像としての威厳がある。塗料の痕跡がみられる螺髪は粒上で、足の描き方とともに巧妙さが欠けている。頂上肉髻の上のラシュミーと呼ばれる火焔状の装飾は、上座仏教における仏像の特長で、タイ経由でカンボジアに伝達されたスリランカの影響を示している。

78. Vishnu-Vasudeva-Narayana. North Khleang, Angkor, Siem Reap, 16th C?. Bronze, 0.67 m. Ga 5457.

The magnificent bronze-casting skills demonstrated in this image of the universal monarch aspect of Vishnu give evidence of the continuing artistry of Khmer sculptors in the centuries after the abandonment of Angkor in the face of the invading forces of the Thai in 1431. Found in the North Khleang building to the east of the Royal Terrace of Angkor Thom, it may be a product of the period when King Ang Chan I (1516-1566) temporarily brought the Khmer capital back to Angkor. It is not certain why such an iconographically perfect representation of Vishnu and his four attributes (see #5, 27), with his massive jewellery, elaborate crown (in the hollow of which were found pieces of gold) and sumptuous clothing, should have been created when Cambodia had been continuously following Theravada Buddhism for more than two centuries. Perhaps it was connected with attempts by Ang Chan to revive the glory of Angkor, for which Vishnu had often been a protective deity in the past.

78. Vishnu-Vasudeva-Narayana. Khleang nord, Angkor, Siem Reap, 16ème s. (?). Bronze, 0,67 m. Ga 5457.

Cette très belle image de Vishnu sous son aspect de monarque universel démontre la remarquable continuité de qualité de l'art du bronzier khmer après l'abandon d'Angkor sous la pression des armées thaï en 1431. Découverte dans le Khleang nord, à l'est des terrasses royales, cette œuvre pourrait avoir été réalisée à l'époque où le roi Ang Chan I (1516-1566) ramena temporairement la capitale à Angkor. On ignore pourquoi une telle image du dieu Vishnu, avec ses quatre attributs traditionnels (voir #5, 27), ses bijoux pesants, sa couronne très élaborée (dans laquelle furent retrouvées quelques fragments d'or) et son vêtement somptueux, a été réalisée en un temps où le pays s'inscrivait, depuis plus de deux siècles déjà, dans l'esprit du bouddhisme Theravada. Peut-être faut-il mettre cette pièce en relation avec le désir d'Ang Chan de raviver les gloires de l'époque angkorienne, au cours de laquelle Vishnu avait eu une grande importance.

៧៨_ ព្រះនារាយណ៍ ឃ្លាំងខាងជើង, អង្គរ, សៀមរាប, ស.វ.ទី១៦(?), សំរិត, 0,៦៧ម, គ ៥៤៥៧

ស្នាដៃសំរិតដ៏ពិចិត្រដែលឃើញនៅឃ្លាំងខាងជើងនេះ បង្ហាញព្រះនារាយណ៍ក្នុងទិដ្ឋភាពជាទេពកំពូលលើលោក។ ទឹកដៃជាងពុំទាន់បាត់បង់នៅឡើយ ថ្វីត្បិតតែអង្គរត្រូវបោះបង់តាំងពីឆ្នាំ១៤៣១មក។ តាមស្មានប្រហែលជាសាងឡើងកាលព្រះបាទអង្គច័ន្ទ (១៥១៦_១៥៦៦) នាំរាជធានីទៅអង្គរវិញមួយរយៈ។ គេពុំដឹងទេថាហេតុអ្វីបានជារូបព្រះនារាយណ៍ដៃ៤ដ៏ពិចិត្រ (មើលរូបលេខ៥, ២៧), អលង្ការស្អេកស្កះ, មកុដប្រកបដោយក្បូរក្បាច់ (លើមកុដឃើញមានបំណែកមាស) ព្រមទាំងសម្លៀកបំពាក់ថើតថាយនេះ សាងឡើងជំនាន់ដែលកម្ពុជាកាន់ពុទ្ធសាសនាថេរវាទជាង២០០ឆ្នាំមកហើយនោះ។ មើលទៅ ប្រហែលជាមកពីព្រះបាទអង្គច័ន្ទចង់ឱ្យអង្គររស់ឡើងវិញដូចអតីតកាល ត្បិតព្រះនារាយណ៍ធ្លាប់ជាទេពរក្សានគរ។

78. ヴィシュヌ. シエムリエップ州、アンコール、北クレアン、16世紀?、砂岩、0.67m、Ga 5457

この宇宙の創造主ヴィシュヌ像にみられる素晴らしい技術から、アユタヤ朝による1431年の攻撃でアンコール王都を放棄した数世紀後も、ブロンズ鋳造技術が維持されたことがわかる。アンコール・トム都城の王のテラス東、北クレアンで発見されたこのヴィシュヌ像は王都を数十年、アンコールに戻したアン・チャン１世（1516~1566年）時代の作だと思われる。カンボジアが上座仏教国になってから２世紀以上経った時代に、なぜ宝飾豊かで豪華な衣をまとったヴィシュヌ像（No.5、27参照）が作られたのか定かでない。恐らくアン・チャン１世がヴィシュヌが守護神だったアンコール王都の栄華を復活させようとしたためだと考えられる。

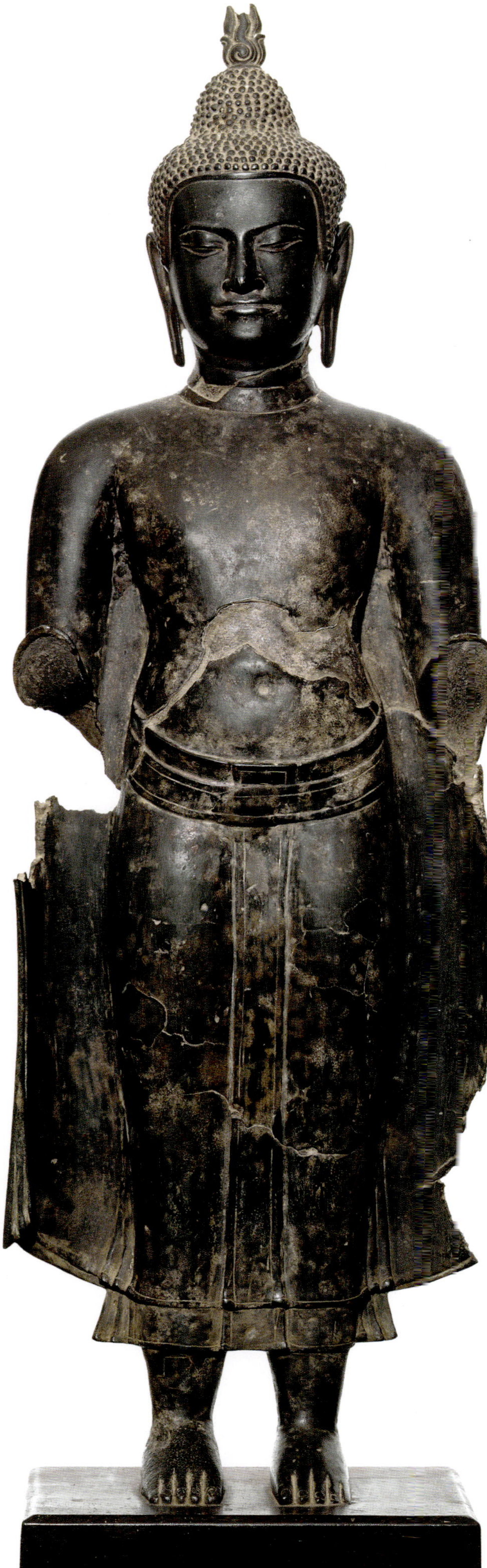

77

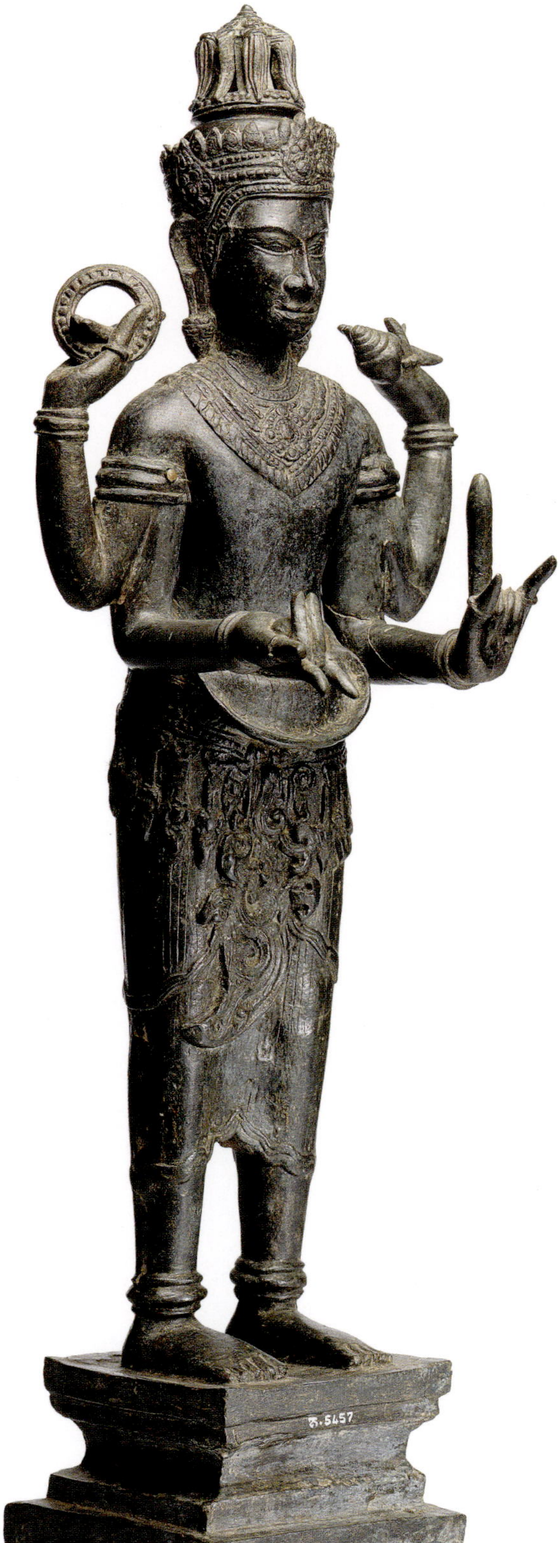

78

79. Adorned Buddha. Angkor Wat, Siem Reap, 16th C?. Wood, 2.45 m. Gha 311.

Despite the existence of some excellent figures in stone and bronze (#77, 78), Khmer sculpture and architecture of the post-Angkor period was predominantly of wood. Since both tropical climate and pests are destructive, many of these have disappeared or are in bad repair. This tall image of the Buddha, his eyes downcast in meditation, adorned in rich jewellery and wearing an intricately carved diadem and coiffure cover, demonstrates the elegance and spirituality intrinsic to Khmer craftsmanship. The smooth surfaces of the termination of the forearms reveal a technique that evolved in the later centuries of hands carved separately from the main figure and later fixed to the arms by armatures. Traces remain of the lacquer that was applied to the figure, a coating of black on which was added a layer of red, with gilding giving the final touch. Such coating helped to preserve the wood.

79. Buddha paré. Angkor Vat, Siem Reap, 16ème s. (?). Bois et traces de laque, 2,45 m. Gha 311.

En dépit de l'existence de belles images en pierre et en bronze (#77, 78), la statuaire postangkorienne était majoritairement en bois, tout comme l'architecture. En raison du climat tropical et des insectes, nombre de ces œuvres ont disparu ou sont en très mauvais état. Cette grande statue du Buddha, pourvue de riches parures et portant un couvre chignon et un diadème délicatement ciselés, atteste l'élégance et la spiritualité de l'art khmer à date tardive. Les mains étaient fixées aux bras selon une technique d'assemblage à tenon et mortaise dont des œuvres postérieures montrent l'évolution. Des traces de laque subsistent en divers endroits. Il s'agissait d'un revêtement de laque noire sur lequel était appliquée une couche de laque rouge, support de la dorure qui recouvrait l'œuvre. Un tel enduit servait aussi à protéger le bois.

៧៩_ ព្រះពុទ្ធទ្រង់គ្រឿង អង្គរវត្ត, សៀមរាប, ស.វ.ទី១៦(?), ឈើ, ២,៤៥ម, ឃ ៣១១

ថ្វីត្បិតតែគេឃើញមានបដិមាល្អត្រចះត្រចង់ជាថ្មឬជាសំរិត (រូបលេខ៧៧, ៧៨) ជាទូទៅស្ថាបត្យកម្មនិងចម្លាក់ខ្មែរក្រោយសម័យអង្គរតែងធ្វើពីឈើ។ តែដោយធាតុអាកាសនិងសត្វល្អិត សំណង់និងវត្ថុទាំងនោះតែងបាត់បង់ទៅ ឬមួយទទួលការជួសជុលដែលពុំសមស្រប។ នេះគឺព្រះពុទ្ធរូបយ៉ាងខ្ពស់, ព្រះនេត្រសម្លឹងមកក្រោម, ពោរពេញទៅដោយអលង្ការព្រមទាំងម្កុដនិងក្បាំង, បង្ហាញថាទឹកដៃជាងនៅខ្ពស់។ ផ្ទៃរាបស្មើពីកែងដៃមកចុង បង្ហាញថាជំនាន់នោះគេធ្វើដៃដាច់ដោយឡែក បន្ទាប់មកទើបយកមកភ្ជាប់នឹងកំភួនដៃដោយពន្លួញ។ គេឃើញសល់ស្នាមលាបលនជាប់នឹងខ្លួន ព្រមទាំងព្រះភក្ត្រ ពោលគឺស្រទាប់ម្រាក់ដែលពីលើនោះគេលាបពណ៌ក្រហម និងទឹក មាសផង។ ស្រទាប់នេះរក្សាឈើឱ្យគង់វង្សបានយូរ។

79. ブッダ. シエムリエップ州、アンコール・ワット、16世紀?、木、2.45m、Gha 311

一部の素晴らしい石像、ブロンズ像（No.77、78）の例外を除き、後アンコール時代の彫刻は大半が木製である。熱帯気候と害虫によって多くは破壊されたり、破損状態にある。このブッダ像は眼を閉じ、宝飾で飾られ、細かく彫られた冠帯と宝冠を身につけ、クメール工芸技術の優雅さとスピリチュアリティーを示している。腕の先端の表面はなめらかで、手は別に彫られ、後に腕に取り付けられていたことがわかる。黒の下塗りの上に赤、そして金メッキが施されていた跡が残っているが、塗料は木像の保護に役立った。

80. Kneeling worshipper. Angkor Wat, Siem Reap, 15th? -16th C. Wood, 0.91 m. Gha 315.

Despite its vulnerability to the ravages of climate and insects, wood is a medium that lends itself very well to expressive carving. The sensitive rendition of the innocence and piety embodied in this image of a youthful worshipper in an attitude of reverent prayer makes it one of the most memorable examples of Khmer Theravadin art. The richness of the diadem and the headdress with its tiered petals and upper tall bud, as well as the jewelled belt with elaborate pendant of brocaded cloth or metal, do not detract from the impression of spiritual simplicity that infuses this figure to such an extent that offerings are made to it by visitors. The small opening in the torso reveals a container that may have held sacred texts or offerings.

80. Orant agenouillé. Angkor Vat, Siem Reap, 15ème (?) - 16ème s. Bois et traces de laque, 0,91 m. Gha 315.

Malgré sa vulnérabilité aux ravages causés par les insectes et le climat, le bois fut un matériau très prisé par les sculpteurs khmers. Le sentiment d'innocence et de piété émanant de cette représentation d'un jeune dévot en attitude de prière en font l'un des exemples les plus remarquables de l'art du bouddhisme Theravada. La richesse du diadème et de la coiffure, avec son étagement de pétales et son sommet en forme de bouton, de même que la ceinture orfévrée à long pan antérieur de tissu ou de métal, ne déparent pas l'impression de simplicité spirituelle véhiculée par cette statue qui, aujourd'hui encore, est l'objet de témoignages de dévotion attentionnés de la part des visiteurs. La petite cavité dans le torse était destinée à contenir quelque texte sacré ou quelque offrande.

៨០_ ទេពប្រណម្យ អង្គរវត្ត, សៀមរាប, ស.វ.ទី១៥(?)_១៦, ឈើ, ០,៩១ម, ឃ ៣១៥

ថ្វីត្បិតតែធន់ពុំបានយូរជាមួយអាកាសធាតុនិងសត្វល្អិត ឈើមានអំណោយផលដល់ការឆ្លាក់។ រូបនេះ ទឹកមុខបង្ហាញអំពីយុវវ័យ, ភាពបរិសុទ្ធ និងចិត្តសាទ្ធា។ ឯឥរិយាបថក៏ប្រណម្យយ៉ាងសុភាពរាបសារផង ធ្វើឱ្យគេចាត់ទុកថាបដិមានេះនៅក្នុងចំណោមស្នាដៃសិល្បៈថេរវាទដែលត្រចះត្រចង់ជាងគេ។ ក្បាំងរចនាយ៉ាងប្រណីតបន្ទាប់មកម្កុដចាប់ផ្ដើមមានថ្នាក់ៗដែលមានក្បាច់ត្របកឈូកបញ្ចប់ទៅដោយក្រពុំ ឬពន្លករុក្ខជាតិអ្វីមួយ។ ខ្សែក្រវាត់មានក្បាច់ពាសពេញ ដូចជាផ្នត់ខាងមុខដែលធ្លាក់ចុះមកដែរ ហើយដែលអាចជាក្រណាត់ប៉ាក់ឌិនឬជាលោហធាតុ... ទាំងនេះសឹងបង្ហាញពីសាទ្ធាមោះមុត តែនៅក្នុងភាពសាមញ្ញ។ ខាងលើផ្ចិតឃើញសន្ទុះមួយរាងបួនជ្រុងទ្រវែង បង្ហាញថាកាលមុនគេដាក់វត្ថុសក្ការៈ មានគម្ពីរជាដើម។

80. 祈る人. シエムリエップ州、アンコール・ワット、15世紀?~16世紀、木、0.91m、Gha 315

木材は熱帯気候と害虫に弱いが、彫刻しやすい素材である。両手を胸前に合わせ祈る若者の姿は、クメールの上座仏教美術の中でも印象に残る作例である。冠帯や花弁と蕾形の宝冠の装飾、刺繍された布か金属の飾りがついた宝飾付き帯はこの像の素朴なスピリチュアリティーを損なっておらず、今日でも捧げ物を残す訪問者がみられる。胴部の穴から小箱が見えるが、経冊や奉納品の容器だったと思われる。

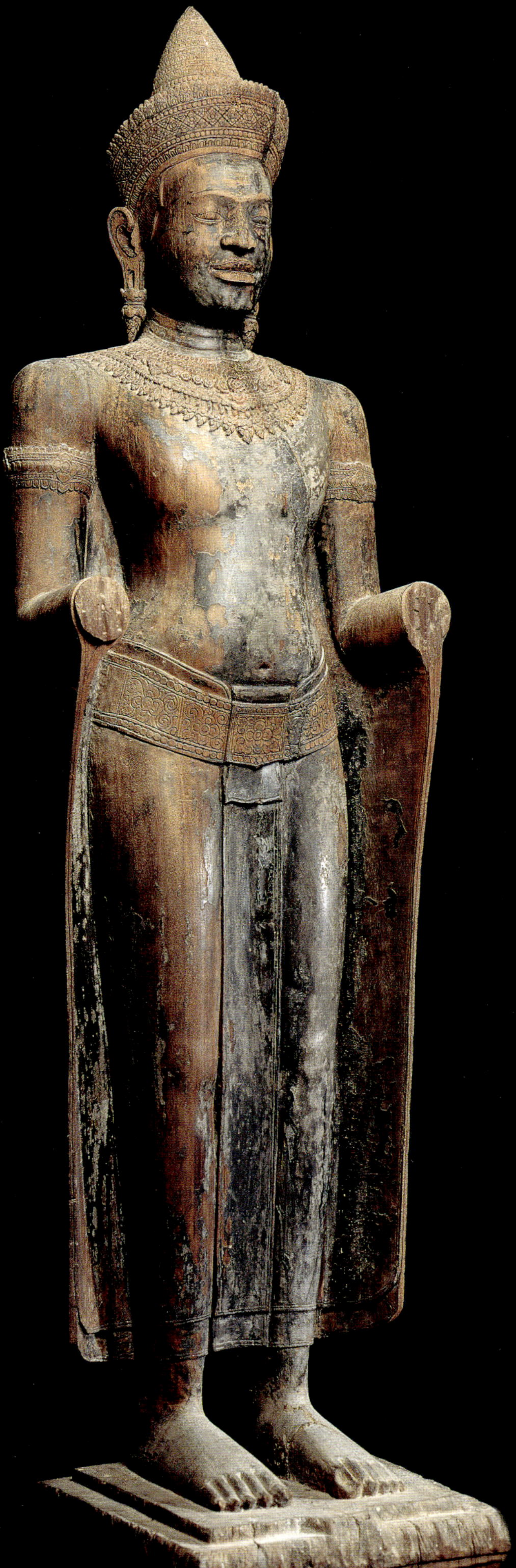

79

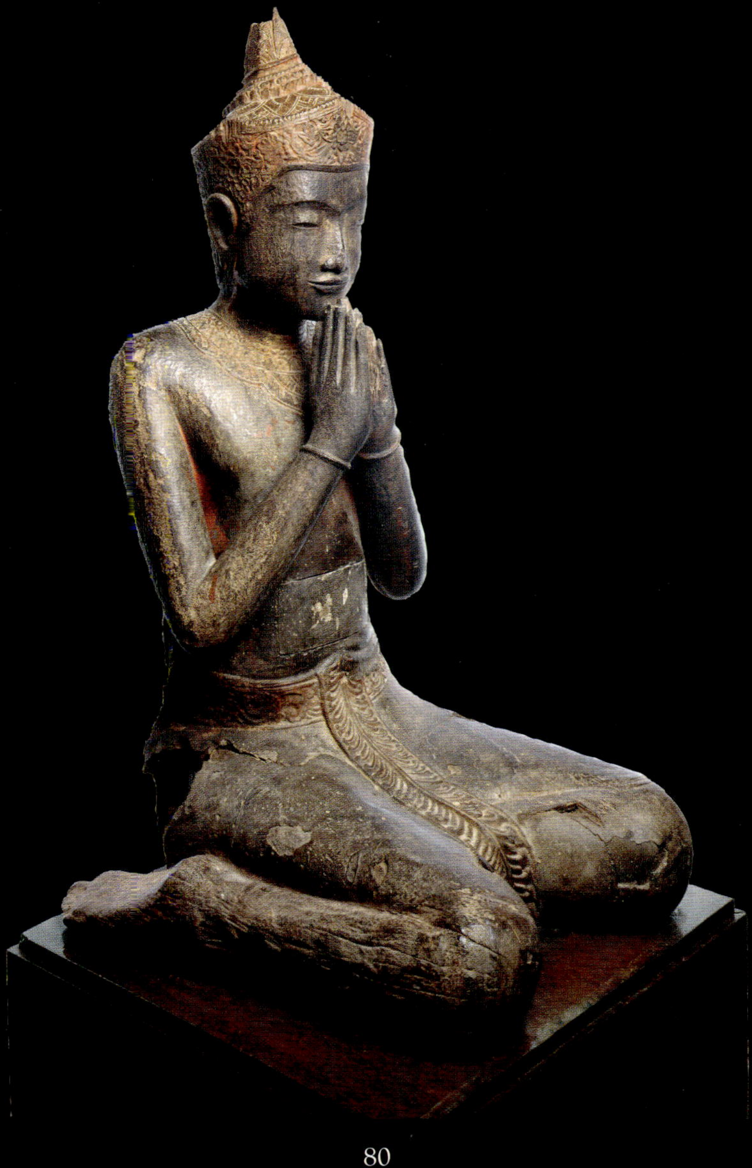

80

Glossary

amrita	nectar of immortality obtained through the churning of the Ocean of Milk by the gods (deva) and the giants (asura) using Mount Mandara as paddle, Vishnu's turtle avatar Kurma as base, and the serpent Vasuki as cable
Avalokiteshvara	bodhisattva of compassion (also Lokeshvara); bears the figure of seated Amitabha Buddha in his headdress (see also Prajñaparamita and Tara)
avatar	manifestation of a Brahmanic god
baray	man-made reservoir, developed by the Khmer as part of their sophisticated hydraulic works from early in the first millennium CE
bodhisattva	being having achieved Enlightenment who has postponed entering nirvana to help others attain that state
Brahma	Brahmanic god of creation, associated with Shiva and Vishnu in the trinity, or trimurti
Brahmanism	religion of India, also known as Hinduism, brought by the Aryans; it has a large pantheon of deities representing manifold aspects of the supreme deity
Buddha	Indian prince (c. 500 BCE) of the Shakya clan who abandoned worldly concerns to seek Enlightenment and release from the endless cycle of existence
Champa	country in central Vietnam occupied by the Cham people, first mentioned in Chinese records of the 3rd century CE; long-term foes of the Khmer
devaraja	lit. "god-king"; symbol of kingly authority and the king's association with a god
Devi	shakti or spouse of Shiva; also takes the form of Uma, Parvati, Durga and Kali
Durga	known as Durga Mahishasuramardini, slayer of the previously invincible buffalo demon, Mahisha, through powers expressly granted by many gods; shakti of Shiva
Ganesha	elephant-headed god, son of Shiva and Uma, overcomer of obstacles and protector of new enterprises
Garuda	eagle-like mythological bird; the vahana (mount, or vehicle) of Vishnu
Hanuman	white monkey general, leader of Rama's simian army
Harihara	god who is half Shiva (on his right), half Vishnu (on his left)
Hevajra	chief deity in Vajrayana Buddhism
jatamukuta	crown of matted, braided locks associated with Shiva
kala	monster, often depicted as a head over entrances
Kaurava	family of 100 brothers, the enemies of the Pandava in the *Mahabharata*
Krishna	one of the manifestations (avatars) of Vishnu
lakshana	the distinguishing physical traits of the Buddha (e.g., his ushnisha, or cranial protrusion)
Lakshmi	shakti of Vishnu
linga	phallic non-material symbol of Shiva
Lokeshvara	see Avalokiteshvara
Mahabharata	Indian epic relating the war between the Kaurava and the Pandava
Mahayana	school of Buddhism, also called the Greater Vehicle, where the Buddha is aided by a pantheon of bodhisattvas in seeking the path that leads to Enlightenment
Maitreya	bodhisattva who is also the Buddha of the future
Mount Meru	sacred cosmic mountain, home of the Brahmanic gods, the *axis mundi*
Mount Mandara	mountain used as a fulcrum in the churning of the Ocean of Milk; one of the sacred peaks in the Brahmanic heaven in the Himalayas
mudra	positions of the hands of the Buddha that impart specific meanings
mukuta	crown
naga	serpent, usually in the form of a cobra with extended hood, symbol of water and the underworld; often shown protecting the Buddha seated on its coils
Nandin	the bull mount, or vahana, of Shiva
nirvana	the absence of being, attained after meditation and Enlightenment, the ultimate goal of Buddhism
Pandava	five sons of Pandu (Yudhisthira, Bhima, Arjuna, Nakula and Sadewa) opposed to the Kaurava family in the *Mahabharata*
Parvati	one of the shakti of Shiva
phnom	mountain (Khmer)
Prajñaparamita	Buddhist spirit of transcendental wisdom; female counterpart to Avalokiteshvara in the balance of wisdom and compassion that comprises the whole in Mahayana Buddhism; has Amitabha Buddha in her headdress; see also Tara
Rama	one of the avatars of Vishnu; hero of the *Ramayana*
Ramayana	Indian epic relating the story of Rama and the struggle to defeat the demon Ravana, who has stolen Rama's wife Sita and taken her to his kingdom, Lanka
rishi	Shivite ascetic
sampot	traditional Khmer garment formed by winding a long strip of cloth around the waist and between the legs
shakti	female spouse of a god, the expression of his female aspect
Shiva	Brahmanic god of destruction and fertility; with Brahma and Vishnu, one of the three deities of the trimurti
stupa	Buddhist funerary monument, often containing relics of the Buddha
Tara	spirit in Mahayana Buddhism, recognizable by the figure of the Amitabha Buddha in her headdress, as in that of Avalokiteshvara and Prajñaparamita (which see)
Theravada	so-called Way of the Masters, an early and ascetic school of Buddhism; also known as Hinayana, or the Lesser Vehicle
trimurti	trinity of Brahmanic gods comprising Brahma, Shiva, and Vishnu
Uma	shakti of Shiva
ushnisha	cranial protrusion that is one of the lakshana of the Buddha
vahana	mount of a god, such as Garuda for Vishnu, Nandin for Shiva
Vajimukha	lit. "horse-faced"; one of two such avatars of Vishnu
vajra	Sanskrit: hard, powerful; compared to the diamond, so has overtones of purity and brightness, hence its connection with Vajrayana (Tantric) Buddhism (see below); in Brahmanism, symbol of the thunderbolt, the attribute of Indra, king of the gods and god of storms
Vajrayana	school of Buddhism, also known as Tantrism and the Diamond Way, where enlightenment can be gained more rapidly through the intervention of a guru and by initiation into rituals; its symbol is the vajra
Varuna	Brahmanic deity; guardian of the West
Vishnu	Brahmanic god of preservation; with Brahma and Shiva, a member of the trimurti
Yama	god of the underworld and hell, judge of the dead
Zhou Daguan	Chinese envoy who visited Angkor in 1296-97 and wrote an informative account of life in the Khmer capital, *Cambodia, the Land and its People*

Glossaire

amrita	liqueur d'immortalité obtenue au terme du barattage de l'Océan de lait par les dieux (deva) et les démons (asura) à l'aide du mont Mandara, qui servit de baraton, du serpent Vasuki, qui fit office de corde, et avec le concours de Vishnu, dans son avatar de la tortue, qui soutint le Mandara afin qu'il ne s'enfonce pas dans les profondeurs de l'Océan de lait.
Avalokiteshvara	bodhisattva de la compassion (également Lokeshvara); il porte l'image du buddha Amitabha dans sa coiffure (voir également Prajñaparamita et Tara).
avatara	"descente"; manifestation d'un dieu brahmanique
baray	"réservoir" entouré de digues, l'un des éléments essentiel du système hydraulique développé par les Khmers dès l'époque préangkorienne.
bodhisattva	être ayant atteint le stade de l'Éveil mais refusant d'entrer dans le nirvana pour aider les autres à atteindre cet état.
Brahma	dieu hindou de la création, il est associé à Shiva et Vishnu dans la trimurti ou triade brahmanique.
brahmanisme	religion indienne, également connue sous le nom d'hindouisme, dont l'origine remonte aux Aryens; elle possède un important panthéon de dieux et de déesses représentant les multiples aspects d'une divinité suprême.
Buddha	prince indien (c. 500 av. J.-C.) du clan des Shakya qui se détourna des contingences mondaines pour chercher l'Éveil et la délivrance du cycle éternel des existences.
Champa	royaume indianisé du Vietnam central mentionné dès le 3ème siècle dans les sources chinoises; au long de leur histoire, les Cham se sont souvent opposés aux Khmers.
devaraja	"dieu-roi"; symbole de l'autorité royale, divinité protectrice du royaume khmer
Devi	shakti ou épouse de Shiva; également désignée sous les noms de Uma, Parvati, Durga et Kali.
Durga	shakti de Shiva; sous le nom de Mahishasuramardini, elle détruit l'invincible démon buffle, Mahisha, grâce aux pouvoirs que lui ont donnés de nombreux dieux.
Ganesha	dieu à tête d'éléphant, fils de Shiva et Uma; il est invoqué pour surmonter les obstacles et protège les nouvelles entreprises.
Garuda	être mythologique moitié homme, moitié oiseau rapace; vahana ("véhicule" ou "monture") de Vishnu.
Hanuman	singe blanc, général en chef de l'armée simiesque alliée de Rama.
Harihara	dieu moitié Shiva (sa partie droite), moitié Vishnu (sa partie gauche).
Hevajra	divinité importante du bouddhisme Vajrayana.
jatamukuta	chignon de tresses porté notamment par Shiva.
Kala	tête de monstre figurant le plus souvent au-dessus des portes.
Kaurava	nom de famille des 100 frères ennemis des Pandava dans le *Mahabharata*.
Krishna	un des avatars de Vishnu.
lakshana	traits physiques distinctifs du Buddha (e.g. l'ushnisha ou protubérance crânienne).
Lakshmi	shakti de Vishnu.
linga	symbole phallique de Shiva.
Lokeshvara	voir Avalokiteshvara.
Mahabharata	épopée indienne relatant la guerre entre les Kaurava et les Pandava.
Mahayana	"Grand véhicule", forme du bouddhisme dans laquelle les bodhisattva aident les fidèles dans leur progression spirituelle.
Maitreya	un bodhisattva, également le Buddha du futur.
mont Meru	montagne cosmique sacrée, demeure des dieux brahmaniques; axis mundi.
mont Mandara	montagne utilisée comme baraton lors du barattage de l'Océan de lait; l'un des sommets sacrés de la cosmographie hindoue.
mudra	désigne les différentes positions des mains ayant une signification particulière.
mukuta	couronne.
naga	serpent cobra à têtes multiples, symbole des eaux et du monde souterrain; souvent représenté protégeant le Buddha assis sur son corps enroulé.
Nandin	le taureau, monture (vahana) de Shiva.
nirvana	état de non renaissance représentant le salut, but ultime recherché par les bouddhistes.
Pandava	les cinq fils de Pandu (Yudhishthira, Bhima, Arjuna, Nakula et Sahadeva) opposés aux Kaurava dans le *Mahabharata*.
Parvati	l'un des noms de la shakti de Shiva.
phnom	mot khmer désignant une colline ou une montagne.
Prajñaparamita	divinité bouddhique de la sagesse suprême; contrepartie féminine d'Avalokiteshvara dans le binôme sagesse/compassion exprimant l'un des idéaux du bouddhisme Mahayana; elle porte l'image du buddha Amitabha dans sa coiffure; voir aussi Tara.
Rama	l'un des avatars de Vishnu; héros du *Ramayana*.
Ramayana	épopée indienne contant l'histoire de Rama et sa lutte contre le démon Ravana qui avait enlevé sa femme Sita pour s'en faire une épouse dans son royaume de Lanka.
rishi	ascète shivaïte.
sampot	vêtement traditionnel au Cambodge, composé d'une longue pièce d'étoffe drapée autour des hanches et passée entre les jambes.
shakti	épouse d'un dieu, manifestation de son aspect féminin.
Shiva	dieu hindou de la fertilité et de la destruction; avec Brahma et Vishnu, il est l'un des membres de la trimurti.
stupa	monument funéraire bouddhique censé contenir des reliques; à l'origine, celles du Buddha lui-même.
Tara	divinité du bouddhisme Mahayana; elle porte le buddha Amitabha dans sa coiffure tout comme Avalokiteshvara et Prajñaparamita.
Theravada	"Voie des anciens", la forme la plus ancienne du bouddhisme, également Hinayana ("Petit véhicule").
trimurti	triade hindoue comprenant Shiva, Vishnu et Brahma.
Uma	l'un des noms de la shakti de Shiva.
ushnisha	protubérance crânienne, l'un des lakshana du Buddha.
vahana	monture d'un dieu, comme Nandin pour Shiva ou Garuda pour Vishnu.
Vajimukha	"face de cheval", l'une des deux manifestations équines de Vishnu.
vajra	"foudre", "diamant" en sanskrit; par extension ce qui a la pureté et la limpidité du diamant, d'où l'association du mot avec le tantrisme bouddhique ou Vajrayana (voir ci-dessous); dans l'hindouisme, symbole de la foudre, l'attribut d'Indra, roi des dieux et dieu de l'orage.
Vajrayana	"Véhicule de diamant", forme du bouddhisme également désignée sous le nom de bouddhisme tantrique; le salut peut être atteint plus rapidement que dans les autres formes de la religion grâce à l'enseignement d'un guru et à une initiation.
Varuna	divinité hindoue, dieu gardien de l'Ouest.
Vishnu	dieu hindou de la préservation; avec Shiva et Brahma, l'un des membres de la trimurti.
Yama	juge des morts, dieu des mondes souterrains et des enfers.
Zhou Daguan	voyageur chinois à la cours d'Angkor en 12[illegible]6-97; il laissa une description vivante d'Angkor et de la vie quotidienne dans la capitale khmère à cette époque: *Mémoires sur les coutumes du Cambodge*.

សទ្ទានុក្រម

កាល ជាអាសោរដែលគេតែងឃើញតែក្បាលជាញឹកញាប់នៅតាមទ្វារ។

កោរព គឺជាគ្រួសារដែលមានបងប្អូនប្រុស១០០នាក់។ អ្នកទាំងនេះសុទ្ធសឹងជាសត្រូវនៃពួកបាណ្ឌពក្នុងរឿងមហាភារត។

គ្រិស្ណ សក្តិនៃព្រះនារាយណ៍។

គណេស ទេពនេះជាបុត្រព្រះឥសូរនិងនាងឧមា មានក្បាលជាដំរី ហើយជាទេពដែលឈ្នះឧបសគ្គគ្រប់បែបយ៉ាង ព្រមទាំងជាអ្នកជួយជំរុញការងារផ្សេងៗឱ្យបានសម្រេចឡើង។

ជីវតាក្វាន់ អ្នកការទូតចិនម្នាក់ដែលមកអង្គរនៅឆ្នាំ១២៩៦_៩៧ ហើយដែលបានទុកកំណត់ហេតុយ៉ាងសំខាន់មួយ អំពីជីវិតនៅរាជធានីខ្មែរ។

តារា ទេពនៅក្នុងពុទ្ធសាសនាមហាយាន ដែលមានព្រះពុទ្ធរូបអមិតភនៅក្នុងផ្នួងសក់ដូចជាព្រះលោកេស្វរ ឬប្រាជ្ញាបារមីដែរ។

ត្រីមូរ្តិ ក្រុមទេពទាំង៣ក្នុងព្រហ្មញ្ញសាសនាដែលមានព្រះព្រហ្ម, ព្រះឥសូរ និងព្រះនារាយណ៍។

ទុគ៌ា ជួនកាលគេហៅទេពនេះថា “នាងទុគ៌ាសម្លាប់ស្តេចក្របី“ ព្រោះអាសោរស្តេចក្របីដែលពុំធ្លាប់ចាញ់នរណាម្តងនោះក៏ត្រូវនាងសម្លាប់បានដោយសារនាងបានទទួលអាវុធពីគ្រប់អាទិទេពមកប្រយុទ្ធ។ នាងទុគ៌ាជា “សក្តិ”នៃព្រះឥសូរ។

នន្ទី ព្រះគោ ជាជំនិះនៃព្រះឥសូរ។

បព៌តី សក្តិមួយក្នុងចំណោមសក្តិផ្សេងៗនៃព្រះឥសូរ។

បាណ្ឌព បុត្រទាំង៥នៃបាណ្ឌុ ពោលគឺ យុធិស្ថិរ, ភិម, អជុិន, នកុល និង សទេវ។ អ្នកទាំងនេះជាសត្រូវនឹងគ្រួសារកោរពនៅក្នុងរឿងមហាភារត។

ប្រាជ្ញាបារមី នៅក្នុងពុទ្ធសាសនាមហាយាន ទេពស្រីនេះជានិមិត្តរូបនៃចំណេះដ៏ខ្ពង់ខ្ពស់បំផុត បីដូចជាថាសជញ្ជីងមួយមានទម្ងន់ស្មើគ្នានឹងថាសមួយទៀតដែលជាករុណាធម៌នៃព្រះលោកេស្វរ។

ពាជីមុខ មានន័យថាមុខសេះ ដែលជាអវតារមួយនៃព្រះនារាយណ៍។

មន្ទរ គឺជាឈ្មោះភ្នំមួយដែលក្រុមអាសោរនិងក្រុមទេពប្រើជាខ្នុរក្នុងការកូរសមុទ្រទឹកដោះ។ គេជឿថានេះជាភ្នំមួយក្នុងចំណោមភ្នំខ្ពស់ៗនៃហិមល័យ ដែលជាលំនៅនៃទេពក្នុងព្រហ្មញ្ញសាសនា។

មហាភារត រឿងឥណ្ឌាយ៉ាងវែងមួយនិយាយពីចម្បាំងរវាងពួកកោរពនិងពួកបាណ្ឌព។

មុទ្រា កាយវិការផ្សេងៗនៃព្រះពុទ្ធ ដែលនីមួយៗសុទ្ធតែមានន័យជាក់ច្បាស់។

មេត្រីយ៍ ទេពនេះជាពោធិសត្វផង និងជាព្រះពុទ្ធដែលនឹងត្រាស់នៅអនាគតផង។

មេរុ ភ្នំជាលំនៅនៃទេពនេះ គឺជាស្នូលលោកទាំងមូល។

លក្ស្មី សក្តិនៃព្រះនារាយណ៍។

លោកេស្វរ ព្រះពោធិសត្វដែលយកករុណាធម៌ជាធំ។ លើផ្នួងសក់ព្រះអង្គមានព្រះពុទ្ធអង្គតូចមួយហៅថា អមិតភ(សូមមើល“ប្រាជ្ញាបារមី”និង“តារា”)

វជ្រ មានន័យថា “រឹង”, “ខ្លាំងក្លា” ហើយដែលគេប្រដូចទៅនឹងត្បូងពេជ្រ ដែលភ្លឺថែងចាំងផង និងបរិសុទ្ធផង។ គំនិតនេះហើយដែលឱ្យឈ្មោះទៅ “វជ្រយាន” ដែលជាព្រះពុទ្ធសាសនាប្រភេទ តន្ត្រ (សូមមើលពាក្យនេះ)។ នៅក្នុងព្រហ្មញ្ញសាសនា វជ្រជានិមិត្តរូបនៃរន្ទះ ហើយជាកេតនភណ្ឌនៃព្រះឥន្ទ្រ ដែលជាស្តេចលើទេពទាំងឡាយ ហើយដែលជាទេពនៃព្យុះសង្ឃរាជផង។

សក្តិ ព្រះជាយានៃទេព ឬក៏ជាធាតុស្រីដែលនៅក្នុងខ្លួនទេពប្រុសនីមួយៗ។

ហរិហរ មួយចំហៀងខ្លួនខាងស្តាំនៃទេពនេះជាព្រះឥសូរ ឯមួយចំហៀងខ្លួនខាងឆ្វេងជាព្រះនារាយណ៍។

ហេវជ្រ នេះជាអាទិទេពនៃពុទ្ធសាសនាវជ្រយាន។

用語解説

A

アムリタ：デーヴァ（善神）とアスラ（阿修羅＝悪魔）が曼荼羅山に大蛇ヴァスキを巻きつけ、ヴィシュヌの亀クールマの上に乗せ、引っ張り合い、乳海撹拌して得た不老不死の妙薬

アヴァローキテーシュヴァラ：観世菩薩；別名ローケーシュヴァラ；頭部には座位の化仏が描かれている（プラジュニャーパーラミター、ターラーを参照のこと）

アーヴァターラ：ヒンドゥー教神の化身

B

バライ：１世紀初期以後、洗練された水力学で作られた巨大貯水池

ボディサットヴァ：菩薩；悟りを開いても涅槃に入らず、衆生が悟りを開くのを助けた

ブラフマー：創造神。シーヴァとヴィシュヌとで３神１体（トリムールティ）を成す

バラモン教：アーリア人がもたらしたインドの宗教；ヒンドゥー教。最高神の多様な側面を多数の神々が象徴している

ブッダ：紀元前500年頃に存在した釈迦族の王子；悟りと輪廻転生からの解放を求めて出家した

C

チャンパ：ヴェトナム中部のチャム族の王国；3世紀の中国の史料に初めて登場する。アンコール朝の長年の敵

D

デヴァラージャ：神王；王の権限と神との関係の象徴

デヴィ：シャクティー；シヴァの神妃；ウマー、パールヴァティー、ドゥルガー、カーリーなどとも呼ばれる

ドゥルガー：ドゥルガー・マヒシャスラマルディーニーとも呼ばれる；多くの神々から携わった力によって不敵だった水牛の悪魔マヒシャを殺した；シヴァの神妃

G

ガネーシャ：シヴァとパールヴァティーの間に生まれた頭部が象の神；障害を取り除き、新起業を守る神

ガルダ：ヴィシュヌの乗り物とされる聖鳥で鷲の形をしている

H

ハヌマーン：猿の王国の軍隊長の白い猿でラーマ王子を助ける

ハリハラ：シヴァ（右半分）とヴィシュヌ（左半分）の合体神

ヘーヴァジュラ：ヴァジュラヤナ仏教（金剛乗仏教）の主神

J

ジャタムクタ：シヴァの髪束を花弁のように重ねた髪冠

K

カーラ：楣（まぐさ）の装飾に描かれることが多い魔よけ

カウラヴァ：マハーバーラタでパンダヴァ王家と敵対関係にある100人の王子を擁する王家

クリシュナ：ヴィシュヌの化身

L

ラクシャナ：ブッダのウシュニシャ（頂上肉髻）などの特相

ラクシュミー：ヴィシュヌの神妃

リンガ：男根型のシヴァの象徴

ロケシュヴァラ：アヴァローキテーシュヴァラを参照のこと

M

マハーバーラタ：カウラヴァ王家とパンダヴァ王家の戦いを描いたインドの大叙事詩

マハヤナ：大乗仏教；菩薩に助けられてブッダは悟りを開く

マイトレーヤ：弥勒；将来現れるブッダ（未来仏）になる菩薩

メール山：須弥山（しゅみせん）；ヒンドゥー教の神々が宿る宇宙の中心をなす神聖な山

曼荼羅山：乳海撹拌の支柱となった山；ヒマラヤ山脈のヒンドゥー教の聖なる山頂の１つ

ムードラ：特定の意味をもつブッダの手の組み合わせ

ムクタ：宝冠

N

ナーガ：コブラの頭を持つ水と地底界を象徴する蛇；とぐろを巻いた蛇身に鎮座するブッダを守る姿がしばしば描かれる

ナンディン：シヴァのヴァーハナ（乗り物）とされる牡牛

ナーヴァナ：涅槃；仏教の究極的目的である、瞑想で達した悟りの世界

P

パンダヴァ：マハーバーラタでカウラヴァ王家と戦うパーンドゥ王の5人の王子（ユディスティラ、ビーマ、アルジュナ、ナクラ、サハデワ）

パールヴァティー：シヴァの神妃の一人

プノン：クメール語で山

プラジュニャーパーラミター：般若波羅蜜多菩薩；般若仏母；大乗仏教でアヴァローキテーシュヴァラ（観音菩薩）の知恵と慈悲のペアとなる女性菩薩；髪飾りには阿弥陀仏がある；ターラを参照のこと

R

ラーマ：ヴィシュヌの化身；ラーマーヤナの主人公

ラーマーヤナ：ラーマとラーマの妻シーターを自分の王国ランカに誘拐したラーヴァナとの戦いを描いたインド大叙事詩

リーシー：シヴァ派の行者

S

サンポット：裙（くん）；長布を腰に巻き付け、その前面の布を股に通して後ろに回し、尻に巻き付ける伝統的衣装

シャクティー：神妃；神の女性面を表す

シヴァ：破壊と繁殖の神；ブラフマーとヴィシュヌとで３神１体（トリムールティ）を成す

ストゥーパ：ブッダの遺骨を納めた塔婆（とうば）、卒塔婆（そとうば）

T

ターラー：菩薩；大乗仏教の女神；アヴァローキテーシュヴァラ、プラジュニャーパーラミター同様、髪飾りに阿弥陀仏がある

トリムルティ：ブラフマー、シヴァ、ヴィシュヌが成す３神１体

U

ウマー：シヴァの神妃

ウシュニシャ：ブッダの特相の１つである頂上肉髻

V

ヴァハーナ：ヴィシュヌのガルーダやシヴァのナンディンなど神の乗り物

ヴァジムカ：馬面のヴィシュヌの化身

ヴァジュラ：金剛杵；サンスクリット語で堅固という意味；ダイアモンドのように純粋で輝いているという意味合いもあり、密教仏教に関係；ヒンドゥー教では神王で嵐の神であるインドラの雷の象徴

ヴァジュラヤナ：密教仏教；タントラ教、金剛乗仏教としても知られ、導師の仲介と儀式の伝授によってより早く悟りが開ける；ヴァジュラがシンボル

ヴァルナ：ヒンドゥー教の西方の守護神

ヴィシュヌ：宇宙の維持を司る神；ブラフマーとシヴァとで３神１体を成す

Y

ヤーマ：地底界と地獄の神

Z

周達観：1296～97年、アンコール朝を訪れた元の使節の一員で「真臘風土記」を記した

Bibliography

Abbreviations

BEFEO: *Bulletin de l'École française d'Extrême-Orient*. EFEO: L'École française d'Extrême-Orient.

Ang, C., E. Prenowitz and A. Thompson. *Angkor, Past, Present, and Future*. APSARA & UNESCO, 1996.

Ang, Choulean. *Brah Ling*. Phnom Penh, 2004.

Barth, A. and A. Bergaigne. *Inscriptions sanskrites de Campa et du Cambodge*. Paris, 1885-1893,

Bellwood, P. S. *Prehistory of Southeast Asia. The Cambridge History of Southeast Asia*, 1, 1985.

Bénisti, M. *Rapports entre le premier art khmer et l'art indien*. 2 vols. *Mémoires archéologiques* V, EFEO. Paris, 1970.

Bhattacharya, K. *Les Religions brahmaniques dans l'ancien Cambodge, d'après l'épigraphie et l'iconographie*. EFEO 49, Paris, 1961.

Boisselier, J. *La Statuaire khmère et son évolution*. EFEO 37. Saigon, 1955.

Boisselier, J. *Trends in Khmer Art*. . Edited by Natasha Eilenberg, translated by Natasha Eilenberg and Melvin Elliott. Ithaca 1989.

Boisselier, J. *Manuel d'archéologie d'Extrême-Orient*. Part I: *Asie du Sud-Est*. Vol I: *Le Cambodge*. Paris, 1966.

Boulbet, J., et B. Dagens. *Les sites archéologiques de la région du Bhnam Gulen (Phnom Kulen. Arts Asiatiques* 27 (1973).

Brand, Michael and Chuch Poeurn. *The Age of Angkor. Treasures from the National Museum of Cambodia* , exhib. cat. The Australian National Gallery, Canberra 1992.

Briggs, Lawrence Palmer. *The Ancient Khmer Empire*. Philadelphia, 1951.

Brown, R. *The Ceramics of South-East Asia. Their Dating and Identification*. Singapore and Oxford, 1988.

Bunker, Emma C. and Douglas Latchford. *Adoration and Glory. The Golden Age of Khmer Art*. Chicago, 2004.

Cent objets disparus. International Council of Museums (ICOM-ÉFEO). Paris, 1993.

Chan Vitharin and Preap Chanmara. *Kbach, A Study of Khmer Ornament*. Drawings and photographs by Chan Vitharin. Ly Daravuth and Ingrid Muan, Eds. Translation by Ingrid Muan. Phnom Penh, 2005.

Chandler, D. P. *A History of Cambodia*. Boulder, Colorado, 1983 and Sydney, 1992.

Chandler, D. P., and I. Mabbett. *The Khmers*. Oxford, 1995.

Cœdès, G. *Inscriptions du Cambodge*, 8 vols. Hanoi, then Paris, 1937-1966.

Cœdès, G. *The Indianized States of Southeast Asia*. Ed. W.F. Vella. Trans. S. Cowing. Hawaii, 1968.

Cœdès, G. *Articles sur le pays khmer*. 1. Paris, 1989. 2. Paris, 1992.

de Coral-Rémusat, G. *L'Art khmer. Les grandes étapes de son évolution. Études d'art et d'ethnologie asiatiques* 1. Paris, 1951 (2nd edition).

Dagens, B. *Angkor - la forêt de pierre*. Coll. Découvertes 64. Paris, 1989.

Dalsheimer, Nadine. *Les Collections du musée national de Phnom Penh; L'art du Cambodge ancien*. Paris, 2001.

Delaporte, L. *Voyage au Cambodge. L'architecture khmère*. Paris, 1880.

Dupont, P. *La Statuaire préangkorienne*. Ascona, 1955.

Finot, L. "Arts et archéologies khmers. 2". *BEFEO* 17 (1917), 360-372.

Freeman, M. and C. Jacques. *Ancient Angkor*. Bangkok, 1999.

Giteau, M. *Guide du Musée national de Phnom-Penh 1, Sculpture*. Phnom Penh, 1960.

Giteau, M. *Les Khmers. Sculptures khmères-Reflets de la civilisation d'Angkor*. Fribourg, 1965.

Giteau, M. *Guide du Musée national de Phnom-Penh II. Mobilier en pierre, éléments d'architecture, inscriptions*. Phnom-Penh, 1966 (1).

Giteau, M. *Iconographie du Cambodge postangkorien*. EFEO 100. Paris, 1975.

Giteau, M. *Chefs-d'œuvre de la Peinture cambodgienne dans les monastères bouddhiques post-angkoriens*. Torino, 2003

Glaize, M. *Les monuments du groupe d'Angkor*. Paris, 1963 (reprinted 1994) (Saigon 1944).

Green, Gillian. *Traditional Textiles of Cambodia*. Bangkok, 2003.

Groslier, B. Ph. *Angkor. Hommes et pierres*. Paris, 1968.

Groslier, B. Ph. "La cité hydraulique angkorienne: exploitation ou surexploitation du sol?". *BEFEO* 66 (1979).

Groslier, G. *Arts et archéologie khmers* 1/3. Paris, 1921-1923.

Groslier, G. *Les Collections khmères du musée Albert-Sarraut à Phnom-Penh*. *Ars Asiatica* 16. Paris, 1931.

Hall, K. R. and J. K. Whitmore (Eds.). *Explorations in Early South-East Asian History: the origins of South-East Asian Statecraft*. Ann Arbor, 1976.

Higham, C. *The Archaeology of Mainland Southeast Asia: From 10,000 BC to the Fall of Angkor*. Cambridge, 1989.

Izu, Kenro. *Passage to Angkor*. Introduction and poems by Helen Ibbitson Jessup. Santa Fe, 2003.

Jacques, Claude and Michael Freeman. *Angkor: Cities and Temples*. Bangkok, 1997.

Jessup, Helen Ibbitson and Thierry Zéphir, Eds. *Sculpture of Angkor and Ancient Cambodia: Millennium of Glory*. Washington, DC and Paris, 1997.

Jessup, Helen Ibbitson. *Art & Architecture of Cambodia*. London, 2004.

Khun, Samen. *The New Guide to the National Museum*. Phnom Penh, 2002.

Khun, Samen. *Preah Neang Tevi*. Phnom Penh, 2005.

Kulke, H. *The Devaraja Cult*. Data Paper 108, Southeast Asia Program, Cornell University. Ithaca, 1978.

Laur, Jean. *Angkor, an Illustrated Guide to the Monuments*. Paris, 2002.

Le Bonheur, A. *Art khmer*. 2nd ed. Paris, 1986.

Le Bonheur, A. and Jaroslav Poncar. *Des Dieux, des Rois, des Hommes. Les bas-reliefs d'Angkor Vat et du Bayon*. Geneva, 1995.

Lobo, W. "Reflections on the Tantric Buddhist God Hevajra in Cambodia". *Southeast Asian Archeology 1994. Proceedings of the 5th International Conference of the European Association of Southeast Asian Archaeologists*. Hull, 1997.

Lunet de Lajonquière, E. *Inventaire descriptif des Monuments du Cambodge*, 3 vols. EFEO 4, 8, 9. Paris, 1902-1911.

Mabbett, I. W. "Devaraja". *Journal of Southeast Asian History* 10/2 (Sept 1969), 202-223.

Mabbett, I. W. "Divine Kingship in Angkor". *Acarya-Vandana, D.R. Bhandarkar Birth Centenary Volume*, Ed. Samaresh Bandyopadhyay. Calcutta, n.d., 277-285.

Malleret, L. L'Archéologie du Delta du Mékong, 4 vols. 1: *L'Exploration archéologique et les fouilles d'Oc-Eo*; 2: *La Civilisation matérielle d'Oc-Eo*; 3: *La Culture de Fou-nan*; 4: *Le Cisbassac* EFEO 43. Paris, 1959-1963.

Mannikka, Eleanor. *Angkor Wat. Time, Space, and Kingship*. Hawaii, 1996.

Marchal, H. *Le Décor et la Sculpture khmers*. Paris, 1951.

Marr, D. G. and A. C. Milner (Eds.). *Southeast Asia in the 9th to 14th Centuries*. Singapore, 1986.

Mus, P. "Le sourire d'Angkor. Art, foi et politique bouddhiques sous Jayavarman VII". *Artibus Asiae* 24 (1961), 363-381.

Parmentier, H. "L'inventaire descriptif des monuments du Cambodge". *BEFEO* 11 (1911).

Parmentier, H. "Complément à l'Inventaire descriptif des monuments du Cambodge". *BEFEO* 13/1 (1913), 1-61.

Parmentier, H. *L'Art khmer primitif*, 2 vols. EFEO 21 and 22. Paris, 1927.

Parmentier, H. "Complément à l'art khmer primitif". *BEFEO* 35 (1935).

Parmentier, H. *L'Art khmer classique. Monuments du quadrant nord-est*, 2 vols. EFEO 29 b. Paris, 1939.

Pelliot, P. *Mémoires sur les coutumes du Cambodge de Tcheou Ta-Kouan, version nouvelle suivie d'un commentaire inachevé*. Paris, 1951.

Pou, Saveros. *Rœmakerti (xvie-xviie siècles)*, translation and commentary. Paris, 1977.

Rooney, D. F. *Khmer Ceramics*. Kuala Lumpur, 1984.

Rooney, D. F. *Angkor Observed. A Travel Anthology of 'Those There Before'*. Bangkok, 2001.

Roveda, V. *Khmer Mythology*. Bangkok, 1997.

Roveda, V. and Jaro Poncar. *Sacred Angkor. The Carved Reliefs of Angkor Wat*. Bangkok, 2003.

Smith, R. B., and W. Watson (Eds.). *Early South East Asia, essays in Archaeology, History, and Historical Geography*. New York, Kuala Lumpur, 1979.

Stern, Ph. *Le Bàyon d'Angkor et l'évolution de l'art khmer*. (*Annales du musée Guimet, Bibliothèque de vulgarisation*, 47). Paris, 1927.

Stern, Ph. "Le temple-montagne khmer, le culte du *linga* et le *devaraja*". *BEFEO* 34 (1934), 611-616.

Udaya. Journal of Khmer Studies. Ang Choulean and Ashley Thompson (Eds.). Phnom Penh, Vol. 1 2000, Vol. 2 2001, Vol. 3 2002, Vol. 4 2003, Vol. 5 2005, Vol. 6 pending.

Thompson, Ashley. *Le rappel des âmes. Calling the Souls*. Phnom Penh, 2005.

Vann Molyvann. *Les Cités khmères anciennes*. Phnom Penh, 1999.

Vickery, Michael. "Some remarks on Early State Formation in Cambodia". *Southeast Asia in the 9th to 11th Centuries*, 95-115. Eds. D. G. Marr and A. Milner. Singapore, 1986.

Vickery, Michael. "What and where was Chenla?". *BEFEO* 80/2 (1993), 197-212. Paris, 1994.

Vickery, Michael. *Society, Economics, and Politics in Pre-Angkor Cambodia. The 7th-8th Centuries*. Tokyo, 1998.

Woodward, Hiram W., Jr. "Tantric Buddhism at Angkor Thom". *Ars Orientalis*, 12 (1981), 57-67.

Zéphir, Thierry. "L'Art Khmer" in *L'art de l'Asie du Sud-Est*, 151-249, Paris, 1994. Translated as *Art of Southeast Asia*. New York, 1998.

Zéphir, Thierry. *L'Empire des Rois Khmers*. Paris, 1997. Translated as *Khmer: Lost Empire of Cambodia*. London, 1998.

Zéphir, Thierry, photographs by Luca Tettoni, translation by Milton Osborne. *Angkor, A Tour of the Monuments*. Singapore, 2004.

Zhou Daguan. *The Customs of Cambodia*. Ed. Michael Smithies. Bangkok, 2001.

Friends of Khmer Culture

Friends of Khmer Culture supports the expression, conservation, and stimulation of all forms of Khmer cultural creativity, and promotes Khmer scholarship and education. We work with Cambodian and international scholars and institutions in our mission to assist in the rebuilding of civil society and to encourage understanding of Khmer culture both within Cambodia and worldwide. Aiding the National Museum of Cambodia has always been one of our most important aims, and we hope that the proceeds from our publication, and the interest in the museum the book may generate, will encourage support for the many needs of this national treasure.

Friends of Khmer Culture (FOKCI) is a 501(c)(3) organization, and funds donated are fully deductible under the law of the U.S.A. If you would like to know more about us, please visit our web site (where you may make a contribution online), or write to us:

Friends of Khmer Culture, Inc.
P.O. Box 164
Norfolk, CT 06058-0164, U.S.A.
Email info@khmerculture.net
Website www.khmerculture.net

Friends of Khmer Culture

Friends of Khmer Culture a pour vocation de soutenir toute forme de créativité culturelle au Cambodge, mais aussi de promouvoir l'éducation et la science.
Nous travaillons avec des chercheurs cambodgiens, des spécialistes étrangers et diverses institutions internationales en vue de participer à la reconstruction de la société civile et à une meilleure compréhension de la culture khmère, tant au Cambodge que partout ailleurs dans le monde.
Apporter une aide au Musée National du Cambodge a toujours été pour nous une préoccupation majeure et nous espérons que nos publications, par le biais de l'intérêt qu'elles pourront susciter après du grand public, contribueront à répondre aux multiples besoins de cette institution.

Friends of Khmer Culture (FOKCI) est une organisation de type 501(c)(3). Les fonds offerts sont totalement déductibles dans le cadre de la loi américaine. Pour en savoir plus, veuillez consulter notre site web, sur lequel il vous sera possible de laisser un avis. Vous pouvez aussi nous écrire :

Friends of Khmer Culture, Inc.
P.O. Box 164
Norfolk, CT 06058-0164, U.S.A.
Email info@khmerculture.net
Site web www.khmerculture.net

អំពី Friends of Khmer Culture

Friends of Khmer Culture គាំទ្រការបញ្ចេញ, ការសិក្សា និងជំរុញឱ្យមានការបង្កបង្កើតថ្មីគ្រប់បែបយ៉ាងក្នុងវិស័យវប្បធម៌ខ្មែរ ព្រមទាំងលើកស្ទួយការសិក្សានិងបណ្តុះបណ្តាល។ យើងប្រាស្រ័យការងារជាមួយអ្នកស្រាវជ្រាវ ព្រមទាំងស្ថាប័នជាតិនិងអន្តរជាតិ ដើម្បីជួយស្តារឡើងវិញនូវសង្គមស៊ីវិល និងជំរុញឱ្យមានការយល់ដឹងវប្បធម៌ ទាំងនៅក្នុង ទាំងនៅក្រៅប្រទេសកម្ពុជា។ ជារៀងមក យើងតែងតែចាត់ទុកការជួយសារមន្ទីរជាតិថាជាបេសកកម្មសំខាន់។ យើងសង្ឃឹមថាការជួយផ្សព្វផ្សាយសារមន្ទីរជាតិតាមរយៈការបោះពុម្ពសៀវភៅនឹងបានជាគុណប្រយោជន៍ដល់សម្បត្តិវប្បធម៌ជាតិ។

Friends of Khmer Culture (FOKCI) ជាអង្គការដែលរដ្ឋទទួលស្គាល់ថាមិនមែនរកស៊ីធ្វើជំនួញ ដូច្នេះអំណោយទាំងអម្បាលម៉ានអាចកាត់រួចពន្ធបានតាមច្បាប់នៅសហរដ្ឋអាមេរិក។ បើលោកអ្នកត្រូវការ ពត៌មានបន្ថែមទៀត សូមមើលវែបសាយខាងក្រោម ឬសរសេរមកយើង៖

Friends of Khmer Culture, Inc.
P.O. Box 164
Norfolk, CT 06058-0164, U.S.A.
Email : info@khmerculture.net
Website : www.khmerculture.net

Friends of Khmer Culture（フレンズ・オブ・クメール・カルチャー）はクメール文明のあらゆる形の創造性の表現や保存、活性化を支援し、クメール文化の研究と教育を推進する団体です。カンボジアおよび世界中の学者や組織と協力し、市民社会の再構築を支援し、カンボジア国内と世界のクメール文明の理解を推進しています。カンボジア国立博物館支援は当団体の最優先課題の１つであり、この図録の売り上げ、および図録がもたらす博物館に対する興味により、国宝の数多くのニーズを支援できることを期待しています。

Friends of Khmer Culture (FOKCI)は米国の非営利団体（501(c)(3)）であり、寄付は米税法上、免税扱いとなります。FOKCIにご関心がある方は、ホームページをご覧になるか、下記まで連絡ください。

Friends of Khmer Culture, Inc.
P.O. Box 164
Norfolk, CT 06058-0164, U.S.A.
Eメール info@khmerculture.net
ホームページ www.khmerculture.net